Data Envelopment Analysis and Effective Performance Assessment

Farhad Hossein Zadeh Lotfi
Islamic Azad University, Iran

Seyed Esmaeil Najafi
Islamic Azad University, Iran

Hamed Nozari
Islamic Azad University, Iran

A volume in the Advances in
Business Information Systems
and Analytics (ABISA) Book
Series

www.igi-global.com

Published in the United States of America by
    IGI Global
    Business Science Reference (an imprint of IGI Global)
    701 E. Chocolate Avenue
    Hershey PA 17033
    Tel: 717-533-8845
    Fax: 717-533-8661
    E-mail: cust@igi-global.com
    Web site: http://www.igi-global.com

Library of Congress Cataloging-in-Publication Data

Names: Lotfi, Farhad Hossein Zadeh, 1967- editor. | Najafi, Seyed Esmaeil, 1975- editor. | Noazari, Hamed, 1984- editor.
Title: Data envelopment analysis and effective performance assessment / Farhad Hossein Zadeh Lotfi, Seyed Esmaeil Najafi, Hamed Noazari, editors.
Description: Hershey, PA : Business Science Reference, [2017] | Includes bibliographical references and index.
Identifiers: LCCN 2016017595| ISBN 9781522505969 (hardcover) | ISBN 9781522505976 (ebook)
Subjects: LCSH: Data envelopment analysis.
Classification: LCC HA31.38 .D3835 2017 | DDC 519.7/2--dc23 LC record available at https://lccn.loc.gov/2016017595

This book is published in the IGI Global book series Advances in Business Information Systems and Analytics (ABISA) (ISSN: 2327-3275; eISSN: 2327-3283)

British Cataloguing in Publication Data
A Cataloguing in Publication record for this book is available from the British Library.

Advances in Business Information Systems and Analytics (ABISA) Book Series

ISSN: 2327-3275
EISSN: 2327-3283

MISSION

The successful development and management of information systems and business analytics is crucial to the success of an organization. New technological developments and methods for data analysis have allowed organizations to not only improve their processes and allow for greater productivity, but have also provided businesses with a venue through which to cut costs, plan for the future, and maintain competitive advantage in the information age.

The **Advances in Business Information Systems and Analytics (ABISA) Book Series** aims to present diverse and timely research in the development, deployment, and management of business information systems and business analytics for continued organizational development and improved business value.

COVERAGE

- Management information systems
- Data Management
- Geo-BIS
- Big Data
- Business Information Security
- Business Systems Engineering
- Forecasting
- Data Analytics
- Performance Metrics
- Information Logistics

IGI Global is currently accepting manuscripts for publication within this series. To submit a proposal for a volume in this series, please contact our Acquisition Editors at Acquisitions@igi-global.com or visit: http://www.igi-global.com/publish/.

Titles in this Series

For a list of additional titles in this series, please visit: www.igi-global.com

www.igi-global.com

701 E. Chocolate Ave., Hershey, PA 17033
Order online at www.igi-global.com or call 717-533-8845 x100
To place a standing order for titles released in this series,
contact: cust@igi-global.com
Mon-Fri 8:00 am - 5:00 pm (est) or fax 24 hours a day 717-533-8661

Table of Contents

Detailed Table of Contents

Chapter 1

A. Ghazi, Islamic Azad University, Iran
F. Hosseinzadeh Lotfi, Islamic Azad University, Iran
G. H. Jahanshahloo, Kharazmi University, Iran
M. Sanei, Islamic Azad University, Iran

There exist a wide range of research studies that apply the Multiple Criteria Decision Making (MCDM) techniques in Data Envelopment Analysis (DEA) methodology and vice versa. Also, MCDM is divided into two subsets, Multiobjective Decision Making (MODM) and Multiattribute Decision Making (MADM). Early studies of DEA methodology utilized the MODM concepts and consequently, most studies in the relationships between MCDM and DEA have involved the usage of MODM techniques in DEA. There remains a large volume of papers in this field; yet, none of them classifies this relationship. Hence, in this research the authors focused on classification of this field that is divided into six groups. Then, some papers in each group are selected for consideration.

Chapter 2

Ali Ebrahimnejad, Islamic Azad University, Iran
Farhad Hosseinzadeh Lotfi, Islamic Azad University, Iran

A key issue in the preferential voting framework is how voters express their preferences on a set of candidates. In the existing voting systems, each voter selects a subset of candidates and ranks them from most to least preferred. The obtained preference score of each candidate is the weighted sum of votes receives in different places. Thus, one of the most important issues for aggregating preferences rankings is the determination of the weights associated with the different ranking places. To avoid the subjectivity in determining the weights, various models based on Data Envelopment Analysis (DEA) have been appeared in the literature to determine the most favorable weights for each candidate. This work presents a survey on models and methods to assess the weights in voting systems. The existing voting systems are divided into two areas. In the first area it is assumed that the votes of all the voters to have equal importance and in the second area voters are classifies into different groups and assumed that each group is assigned a different voting power. In this contribution, some of the most common models and procedures for determining the most favorable weights for each candidate are analyzed.

The Malmquist Productivity Index (MPI) evaluates the productivity change of a Decision Making Unit (DMU) between two time periods. DEA considers performance analysis at a given point of time. Classic Malmquist Productivity Index shows regress and progress of a DMU in different periods with efficiency and technology variations without considering the present value of money. In this chapter Application of Malmquist productivity index in integrated units of power plant is discussed. Four units of one of the power plants are assessed & the data of its five successive years are supplied. Also application of Malmquist productivity index (precise data) in Safa Rolling and pipe plants for the time period of 2007 – 2012 is studied.

One of the fundamental issues facing universities, research centers and institutes of higher education is the absence of an integrated system for performance evaluation. Data Envelopment Analysis (DEA) is a mathematical and management technique for evaluation of Decision Making Units (DMUs) with multiple input and output. The original DEA does not perform full-ranking; instead, it merely provides classification into two groups: efficient and inefficient. Among the available multi-attribute decision-making methods only Analytic Network Process (ANP) can be used to evaluate performance systematically due to the dependencies and feedbacks caused by the mutual effects of the criteria. The DEA-ANP hybrid algorithm, is designed to eliminate the disadvantage of full-ranking in the DEA method, as well as the disadvantage of subjective evaluation in the ANP method. The goal of this chapter is measuring educational and research performance of seventeen faculties, for the academic year 2009-2010, by using the DEA-ANP hybrid algorithm.

Chapter 5

Chandra Sekhar Patro, GVP College of Engineering (Autonomous),
India

In the present competitive business environment, it is essential for the management of any organisation to take wise decisions regarding supplier evaluation. It plays a vital role in establishing an effective supply chain for any organisation. Most of the experts agreed that there is no one best way to evaluate the suppliers and different organizations use different approaches for evaluating supplier efficiency. The overall objective of any approach is to reduce purchase risk and maximize overall value to the purchaser. In this paper Data Envelopment Analysis (DEA) technique is developed to evaluate the supplier efficiency for an organisation. DEA is a multifactor productivity technique to measure the relative efficiency of the decision making units. The super efficiency method of DEA provides a way, which indicates the extent to which the efficient suppliers exceed the efficient frontier formed by other efficient suppliers. A case study is undertaken to evaluate the supplier performance and efficiency using DEA approach.

Chapter 6

M. Vaez-Ghasemi, Islamic Azad University, Rasht Branch, Iran
Z. Moghaddas, Islamic Azad University, Qazvin Branch, Iran

Malmquist Productivity Index (MPI) is taken into consideration by different researchers in different theoretical and scientific fields after S. Malmquist presented it. This index has a profound meaning and is used in a number of applications for performance evaluation. In literature, there exist variety of subjects consider this index, each of which tries to develop it from different points of view. Here, the aim, in accordance to the importance of this index, is to try gathering most of the issues, related to this subject, from the oldest one to the newest one, in a framework of a review chapter.

Chapter 7

Z. Moghaddas, Islamic Azad University, Qazvin Branch, Iran
M. Vaez-Ghasemi, Islamic Azad University, Rasht Branch, Iran

Data envelopment analysis as a mathematical technique formulated based on linear programming problems which enables decision makers to evaluate Decision-Making Units (DMUs) with multiple inputs and outputs. One of the important issue in DEA technique which is widely discussed by researchers is ranking efficient units. Since these units are not comparable among each other. Ranking DMUs is an important issue in theory and practice and many applications in this field are performed. Considering the ranking order senior managers try to better guiding the system. In literature there exist different ranking models each of which tries to make improvements in this subject. Many researchers try to make advances in theory of ranking units and overcome the difficulties exist in presented methods. Each of the existing ranking method has its own specialties and advantages. As each of the existing method can be viewed from different aspects, it is possible that somewhat these groups have overlapping with the others.

Chapter 8

Alireza Shayan Arani, Islamic Azad University, Iran
Hamed Nozari, Islamic Azad University, Iran
Meisam Jafari-Eskandari, Payam Noor University of Shemiranat, Iran

Performance evaluation and selection and ranking of suppliers is very important due to the competitiveness of companies in the present age. The nature of this kind of decision is usually complex and lacks clear structure and many qualitative and quantitative performance criteria such as quality, price, flexibility, and delivery times must be considered to determine the most suitable supplier. Given that in the supplier evaluation may offer undesirable outputs and random limitations, providing a model for evaluating the performance of suppliers is of utmost importance. With regard to the issue of multi-criteria selection of suppliers, one of the most efficient models to choose suppliers is DEA.in this paper to measure the strong performance and development of undesirable output and random limitations concept the SBM model is used.

Preface

Performance evaluation is essential in making future decisions. In this context effectiveness and organizational productivity must be taken into account so that economic growth can be monitored in future decision. Productivity Promoting is achieved with efficient use of production factors and plays an important role in sustained economic growth and sustainable production. In an organization, if we measure optimal use of inputs to produce outputs, in fact, the performance is assessed. If we measure the achieving the goals of the generated output, in fact, the effectiveness is assessed and from combination of the two, productivity could be extracted. One of the convenient and efficient tools in this context is DEA that as a non-parametric method used to calculate the efficiency of decision-making. Today the use of data envelopment analysis is rapidly expanding and in the evaluation of different organizations and industries such as banking, postal, hospital, schools, power plants, refineries, etc. are used. A lot of theoretical and practical developments in DEA models have happened that understanding of various aspects of it is inevitable. Using data envelopment analysis models addition to determine the relative performance, determine weak points in various indices and specifies the organization's policy to promote efficiency and productivity by offering them favorable rate. For this reason, in this book we try to have some practical uses of data envelopment analysis. Although efforts have been made to appear good book, but experts help is always helpful in increasing the richness of the book.

Hamed Nozari
Islamic Azad University, Iran

Chapter 1

Classifying the Usage of Multiple Objective Decision Making Techniques in Data Envelopment Analysis

A. Ghazi
Islamic Azad University, Iran

G. H. Jahanshahloo
Kharazmi University, Iran

F. Hosseinzadeh Lotfi
Islamic Azad University, Iran

M. Sanei
Islamic Azad University, Iran

ABSTRACT

There exist a wide range of research studies that apply the Multiple Criteria Decision Making (MCDM) techniques in Data Envelopment Analysis (DEA) methodology and vice versa. Also, MCDM is divided into two subsets, Multiobjective Decision Making (MODM) and Multiattribute Decision Making (MADM). Early studies of DEA methodology utilized the MODM concepts and consequently, most studies in the relationships between MCDM and DEA have involved the usage of MODM techniques in DEA. There remains a large volume of papers in this field; yet, none of them classifies this relationship. Hence, in this research the authors focused on classification of this field that is divided into six groups. Then, some papers in each group are selected for consideration.

DOI: 10.4018/978-1-5225-0596-9.ch001

INTRODUCTION

Decision making is the study of identifying and choosing alternatives based on the values and preferences of the decision maker. In the mathematical science, optimization is an appropriate tool for making a good choice when confronted with alternative decisions. Decisions often involve several conflicting objectives. Consequently, this has led to optimization under multiple objectives. Multiple criteria decision making (MCDM) and data envelopment analysis (DEA) are two powerful tools in decision making and the management science.

MCDM is associated with structuring and solving decision and planning problems involving multiple criteria (objectives). The problems of MCDM can be classified into two categories, multiobjective decision making (MODM) and multiattribute decision making (MADM). The difference between them is that the former concentrates on decision space, MODM on mathematical programming with several objective functions with continuous decision space, whereas MADM focuses on problems with discrete decision space. Current research is focused on the problems that have an infinite number of alternatives, i.e., MODM. A MODM problem includes a vector of decision variables, objective functions and constraints where decision makers make efforts to optimize the objective functions with respect to the constraints. Multiobjective linear programming (MOLP) is one of the most important forms used to describe MODM problems, which are specified by linear objective functions that are to be optimized under to a set of linear constraints. In multiobjective programming (MOP) problems, the notion 'efficient' and 'Pareto optimal' is utilized instead of the optimal solution, because there is not a feasible solution to optimize all objective functions at the same times. The most preferred solution (MPS) is an efficient solution that best satisfies the decision maker's utility function (Hwang & Masud, 1979; Stuere, 1986).

DEA was originally developed within the operations research and management science frameworks. DEA is a nonparametric methodology for performance assessment of decision making units (DMUs) with multiple inputs and multiple outputs. Preliminary, Charnes et al. (1978) offered efficient frontier of production possibility set (PPS) based on the work of Farrell (1957) in the constructing nonparametric productivity function. They assigned an efficiency score to each DMU respect to the distance of it with the constructed efficient frontier. For obtaining the efficiency scores they introduced the mathematical linear programming problems. Now days, the traditional models are improved to satisfy the needs of the decision makers. Traditional DEA models make efforts to make the DMU under evaluation as efficient as possible by assigning favorable weights to inputs and outputs. Therefore, this leads to the varying weights for variables from one DMU to another, which is not realistic. Moreover, traditional DEA models are restrictive in benchmarking of DMUs on efficient frontier.

Charnes et al. (1978) were worked on MODM before DEA was offered. Consequently, in the first presented paper in the DEA context they used the MODM concepts. Since MODM has a robust theory, it is a powerful tool in solving DEA problems. Therefore, by implementation of the MODM techniques the robust DEA models are constructed. To date, there exists a body of research into the link between MODM and DEA; however, none of them classifies the relationships between these two methodologies. Current research classifies the usage of the MODM techniques in DEA methodology into six groups. These six groups are as follows; first, the standard DEA models obtained from MOLP problems are discussed. Generally, there exist two purposes in incorporating the performance information of the decision maker in DEA models. The first one of the performance information is used to derive more effective targets that can be referred to benchmarking models which will be discussed in the second group. The next objective is to incorporate the performance information to derive more effective efficiency scores that can be referred to as value efficiency which will be discussed in the third group. Also, an existing alternative solution is a major problem of the cross efficiency method. To remove the mentioned problem, the secondary goal DEA models based on the lexicographic method was proposed that is discussed in the fourth group. One of the approaches to solving the optimistic problem of traditional DEA models is the use of a common set of weights model. There are two types of the common set of weights models, based on multiobjective problems and based on single objective problems. In this research the author focused on the common set of weights models obtained from MOP problems. Therefore, the fifth group contains the common set of weights models used to obtain the efficiency scores, the most efficient DMU and the discriminant analysis (DA) based on DEA problem. At last, in the sixth group obtaining efficient hyperplanes of PPS using MOP problems is discussed.

This research is organized as follows; Section 2, provides a brief introduction to MODM and DEA methodologies. Section 3, classifies the usage of the MODM techniques in DEA, also, some papers related to these groups are reviewed. Conclusions and idea for future works is presented in the last section.

BACKGROUND

Multiple Objective Decision Making

Generally, a MODM problem is formulated as follows (Hwang & Masud 1979; Sueyoshi & Kirihara 1998):

$$Max \quad \left\{ f_1\left(x\right),....,f_k\left(x\right) \right\}$$
$$s.t. \quad x \in S \tag{1}$$

where $S = \left\{ x \in \Re^n \,\middle|\, Ax = b, x \geq 0, b \in \Re^m \right\}$. A MODM problem considers a vector of decision variables, objective functions and constraints, in which the decision maker attempts to find solution on the decision space to maximize (minimize) all objective functions. However, in these problems there does not remain a point in S that maximizes all objectives, simultaneously. Therefore, instead of optimal solution concept of 'efficient solution' and 'Pareto optimal solution' is adopted (Hwang & Masud 1979; Stuere 1986).

Definition 1: $x^* \in S$ is called an efficient solution (strong efficient solution) if there is no $x \in S$ such that $C^T x \geq C^T x^*$ and $C^T x \neq C^T x^*$.

Definition 2: $x^* \in S$ is called a weak efficient solution if there is no $x \in S$ such that $C^T x > C^T x^*$.

In MODM problem (1), if all objective functions and all constraints are in linear form, it is called MOLP problem. There are several methods to obtain efficient solutions of the MOLP problem. Moreover, in solving a MOLP problem some preference information from the decision maker is required. There are four types of methods to give preference information of the decision maker in the MOLP problem, include (Hwang & Masud 1979):

1. Methods for no preference information given, such as; Global criterion methods.
2. Methods for a priori preference information given, such as; Goal programming method and Lexicographic method.
3. Methods for a progressive preference information given, such as; Steuer method and Zionts-Wallenius method.
4. Methods for a posteriori preference information given, such as; Adaptive search method and Parametric methods.

Data Envelopment Analysis

Let (X_j, Y_j) be n homogeneous DMUs ($j=1,\ldots,n$) for evaluation and each of them consume m inputs x_{ij} ($i=1,\ldots,m$) to produce s outputs y_{rj} ($r=1,\ldots,s$). The general PPS is constructed as follows:

$$T = \left\{ (X,Y) \left| \sum_{j=1}^{n} \lambda_j x_{ij} \leq x_i, i = 1,...,m, \sum_{j=1}^{n} \lambda_j y_{rj} \geq y_r, r = 1,...,s, \lambda_j \in \Lambda, j = 1,...,n \right. \right\}$$

$$(2)$$

where Λ is one of the following sets,

$$\Lambda_C = \left\{ \lambda = (\lambda_1,...,\lambda_n) \left| \lambda_j \geq 0, j = 1,...,n \right. \right\},$$

$$\Lambda_V = \left\{ \lambda = (\lambda_1,...,\lambda_n) \left| \sum_{j=1}^{n} \lambda_j = 1, \lambda_j \geq 0, j = 1,...,n \right. \right\}$$

$$(3)$$

T_C and T_V are PPSs with constant returns to scale (CRS) and variables returns to scale (VRS) technologies, respectively. The DEA model used to measure the relative efficiency of DMU_o (under evaluation DMU) based on CRS technology is constructed as follows (Charnes et. al. 1978).

$$Max \quad \phi$$

$$s.t. \quad \sum_{j=1}^{n} \lambda_j x_{ij} + s_i^- = x_{io}, \qquad\qquad i = 1,...,m,$$

$$\sum_{j=1}^{n} \lambda_j y_{rj} - s_r^+ = \phi y_{ro}, \qquad\qquad r = 1,...,s, \qquad (4)$$

$$s_i^-, s_r^+ \geq 0, \qquad i = 1,...,m, \quad r = 1,...,s,$$

$$\lambda_j \geq 0, \qquad j = 1,...,n.$$

Model (4) is called the output oriented CCR model in envelopment form.

Definition 3: If an optimal solution $\left(\phi^*, \lambda^*, S^{-*}, S^{+*} \right)$ of Model (4) where satisfies $\phi^* = 1$ and is zero slacks ($S^{-*}=0$, $S^{+*}=0$), then DMU_o is called CCR efficient.

Otherwise DMU_o is called inefficient. The dual of Model (4) (without considering slacks in the constraints) is constructed as follows (Charnes et. al. 1978):

$$Min \quad \sum_{i=1}^{m} v_i x_{io}$$

$$s.t. \quad \sum_{r=1}^{s} u_r y_{ro} = 1,$$

$$\sum_{r=1}^{s} u_r y_{rj} - \sum_{i=1}^{m} v_i x_{ij} \leq 0, \qquad j = 1,...,n,$$

$$u_r, v_i \geq 0, \quad r = 1,...,s, \; i = 1,...,m.$$

(5)

Model (5) is called the output oriented CCR model in multiplier form.

Definition 4: DMU_o is called CCR efficient if and only if in Model (5), $\sum_{i=1}^{m} v_i^* x_{io} = 1$ and there exists at least one optimal solution (U^*, V^*) with $U^* > 0$ and $V^* > 0$.

Otherwise DMU_o is called inefficient. Two Models (4) and (5) were initially introduced by Charnes et al. (1978). Then, the BCC model that is based on VRS technology was introduced by Banker et al. (1984). Note that, the BCC model is the extension of the CCR model where VRS technology adopted instead of CRS technology. Similarly, the DEA models can be formulated as the input oriented one. Moreover, the input oriented and output oriented CCR (BCC) models are the special cases of the combined oriented CCR (BCC) model as follows (Chambers, Chung, & Fare 1998; Halme et. al 2000):

$$Max \quad \theta$$

$$s.t. \quad \sum_{j=1}^{n} \lambda_j x_{ij} \leq x_{io} - \theta d_{ix}, \qquad i = 1,...,m,$$

$$\sum_{j=1}^{n} \lambda_j y_{rj} \geq y_{ro} + \theta d_{ry}, \qquad r = 1,...,s,$$

$$\lambda_j \in \Lambda_C, \qquad j = 1,...,n,$$

(6)

where the direction vector $d=(d_x, d_y) = (d_{1x},...,d_{mx}, d_{1y},...,d_{ay})$ indicate the direction that DMU_o is moved to lie on the efficient frontier. Hence, DMU_o lies on the efficient frontier by the highest decrease in its inputs and the highest increase in its outputs. If the optimal value of Model (6) is zero then DMU_o lies on the efficient frontier, and vice versa.

RESULTS OF CLASSIFICATION

In this section the classification of the MODM techniques in DEA methodology is carried out. This section includes six subsections. In each subsection one DEA methodology where the MODM techniques are implemented for constructing it is reviewed. Since a large volume of papers are available in this fields, the authors selected some of them in each group to review.

Standard DEA models

The traditional nonradial models constructed by MOLP problems. However, radial models can be reformulated as MOLP problems. In this subsection the standard DEA models were obtained from MOLP problems are reviewed. Since, MCDM methodology has a powerful theory, the standard DEA models are more preferred as MOLP problems. The two phase process model is the first implementation of MODM techniques in construction DEA models (Charnes & Cooper 1985; Charnes et. al 1985; Charnes, Cooper, & Rhodes 1978; Charnes, Cooper & Rhodes 1979).

Let ϕ^* is optimal objective value of Model (4), considering ϕ^*, the following LP using variables $\left(\lambda, S^-, S^+\right)$ is constructed as (Charnes & Cooper 1985; Charnes et. al 1985; Charnes, Cooper, & Rhodes 1978; Charnes, Cooper & Rhodes 1979):

$$
\begin{aligned}
Max \quad & \sum_{i=1}^{m} s_i^- + \sum_{r=1}^{s} s_r^+ \\
s.t. \quad & \sum_{j=1}^{n} \lambda_j x_{ij} + s_i^- = x_{io}, & i = 1,...,m, \\
& \sum_{j=1}^{n} \lambda_j y_{rj} - s_r^+ = \phi^* y_{ro}, & r = 1,...,s, \qquad (7) \\
& s_i^-, s_r^+ \geq 0, \quad i = 1,...,m,\ r = 1,...,s, \\
& \lambda_j \geq 0, \qquad j = 1,...,n.
\end{aligned}
$$

The objective of Model (7) is to find an optimal solution that maximizes the sum of input excess and output shortfalls while keeping $\phi = \phi^*$. This approach is called the two phase process. Models (4) and (7) are phase 1 and phase 2, respectively. Generally, the two phase process model is based on the linear programming as follows:

$$Max \quad \phi + \varepsilon \left(\sum_{i=1}^{m} s_i^- + \sum_{r=1}^{s} s_r^+ \right)$$

$$s.t. \quad \sum_{j=1}^{n} \lambda_j x_{ij} + s_i^- = x_{io}, \qquad\qquad i = 1,...,m,$$

$$\sum_{j=1}^{n} \lambda_j y_{rj} - s_r^+ = \phi y_{ro}, \qquad\qquad r = 1,...,s, \qquad\qquad (8)$$

$$s_i^-, s_r^+ \geq 0, \qquad i = 1,...,m, \ r = 1,...,s,$$

$$\lambda_j \geq 0, \qquad\qquad j = 1,...,n,$$

where ε is a small non-Archimedean number. This model is the first implementation of the sum weighted and the lexicographic methods in DEA. Moreover, Banker and Morey (1986) extended this two phase process model in the presence of discretionary and nondiscretionary inputs as follows:

$$Min \quad \theta - \varepsilon \left(\sum_{i \in D} s_i^- + \sum_{r=1}^{s} s_r^+ \right)$$

$$s.t. \quad \sum_{j=1}^{n} \lambda_j x_{ij} + s_i^- = \theta x_{io}, \qquad\qquad i \in D,$$

$$\sum_{j=1}^{n} \lambda_j x_{ij} + s_i^- = x_{io}, \qquad\qquad i \in ND, \qquad\qquad (9)$$

$$\sum_{j=1}^{n} \lambda_j y_{rj} - s_r^+ = y_{ro}, \qquad\qquad r = 1,...,s,$$

$$s_i^-, s_r^+ \geq 0, \qquad i = 1,...,m, \ r = 1,...,s,$$

$$\lambda_j \geq 0, \qquad\qquad j = 1,...,n,$$

where D and ND refer to discretionary and nondiscretionary inputs, respectively. In most research in DEA, the output (input) oriented CCR model is constructed using two famous viewpoint as envelopment and multiplier forms. The output oriented CCR model with another view as MOLP form is constructed as follows (Cooper, Seiford, & Tone 2007):

$$Max \quad \left\{ \frac{\sum_{j=1}^{n} \lambda_j y_{1j}}{y_{1o}} , ... , \frac{\sum_{j=1}^{n} \lambda_j y_{sj}}{y_{so}} \right\}$$

$$s.t. \quad \sum_{j=1}^{n} \lambda_j x_{ij} \leq x_{io}, \qquad\qquad i = 1, ..., m, \tag{10}$$

$$\lambda_j \geq 0, \qquad j = 1, ..., n.$$

To use this model output vectors must be positive. To solve MOLP (10) the maximin formulation is implemented. Hence, MOLP (10) is converted to the following model:

$$Max \quad \phi$$

$$s.t. \quad \frac{\sum_{j=1}^{n} \lambda_j y_{rj}}{y_{ro}} \geq \phi, \qquad\qquad r = 1, ..., s,$$

$$\sum_{j=1}^{n} \lambda_j x_{ij} \leq x_{io}, \qquad\qquad i = 1, ..., m, \tag{11}$$

$$\lambda_j \geq 0, \qquad j = 1, ..., n.$$

Model (11) is the output oriented CCR model in envelopment form. Similarly, the input oriented CCR model is constructed using a MOLP problem with m objective functions and to solve it the minimax formulation is applied. Also, this method for constructing the input (output) oriented BCC model in envelopment form is implemented. To test the Pareto Koopmans efficiency of the unit (x_o, y_o), Cherens et al. (1985) proposed the additive model as follows:

$$Max \quad \sum_{i=1}^{m} s_i^- + \sum_{r=1}^{s} s_r^+$$

$$s.t. \quad \sum_{j=1}^{n} \lambda_j x_{ij} + s_i^- = x_{io}, \qquad\qquad i = 1, ..., m,$$

$$\sum_{j=1}^{n} \lambda_j y_{rj} - s_r^+ = y_{ro}, \qquad\qquad r = 1, ..., s, \tag{12}$$

$$\lambda_j \geq 0, \qquad j = 1, ..., n.$$

Definition 5: In Model (12), (x_o, y_o) is Pareto Koopmans efficient unit if and only if $\sum_{i=1}^{m} s_i^{-*} + \sum_{r=1}^{s} s_r^{+*} = 0$, in other words, all optimal slacks of Model (12) are zero.

Model (12) is the usage of the sum weighted method in DEA. Also, Ali and Seiford (1990) showed this model is translation invariance. Cooper (2005) compared the linear goal programming model with the additive model. The standard version of the linear goal programming model is as follows:

$$Min \quad \sum_{i=1}^{m} \left(\delta_i^- + \delta_i^+ \right) + \sum_{r=1}^{s} \left(\delta_r^- + \delta_r^+ \right)$$

$$s.t. \quad \sum_{j=1}^{n} x_j a_{ij} + \delta_i^- - \delta_i^+ = g_i, \qquad\qquad i = 1, ..., m,$$

$$\sum_{j=1}^{n} y_j b_{rj} + \delta_r^- - \delta_r^+ = g_r, \qquad\qquad r = 1, ..., s, \qquad (13)$$

$$x_j, y_j \geq 0, \qquad j = 1, ..., n,$$

$$\delta_i^-, \delta_i^+ \geq 0, \qquad i = 1, ..., m,$$

$$\delta_r^-, \delta_r^+ \geq 0, \qquad r = 1, ..., s,$$

where δ_i^-, δ_i^+ represent deviations from each goal $g_i(i=1,...,m)$ on inputs indeed δ_r^-, δ_r^+ represent deviations from each goal $g_r(r=1,...,s)$ on outputs. The above mentioned models are different in planning time, Cooper's model (13) (Cooper 2005) reflect the future planning performance but the additive model evaluates past performance. To obtain the Russell measure attributed to R. R. Russell, the researchers presented several methods to solve the following MOLP problem,

$$Min \quad \left\{ \theta_1, ..., \theta_m, -\phi_1, ..., -\phi_s \right\}$$

$$s.t. \quad \sum_{j=1}^{n} \lambda_j x_{ij} \leq \theta_i x_{io}, \qquad\qquad i = 1, ..., m,$$

$$\sum_{j=1}^{n} \lambda_j y_{rj} \geq \phi_r y_{ro}, \qquad\qquad r = 1, ..., s, \qquad (14)$$

$$\theta_i \leq 1, \qquad i = 1, ..., m,$$

$$\phi_r \geq 1, \qquad r = 1, ..., s,$$

$$\lambda_j \geq 0, \qquad j = 1, ..., n.$$

Pastor et al. (1999) determined the average of the input and the output efficiency and then combine these two efficiency components in a ratio form. As a result, the enhanced Russell model constructed as:

$$Min \quad \frac{1/m \sum_{i=1}^{m} \theta_i}{1/s \sum_{r=1}^{s} \phi_r}$$

$$s.t. \quad \sum_{j=1}^{n} \lambda_j x_{ij} \leq \theta_i x_{io}, \qquad i = 1,...,m,$$

$$\sum_{j=1}^{n} \lambda_j y_{rj} \geq \phi_r y_{ro}, \qquad r = 1,...,s, \qquad (15)$$

$$\theta_i \leq 1, \qquad j = 1,...,m,$$

$$\phi_r \geq 1, \qquad r = 1,...,s,$$

$$\lambda_j \geq 0, \qquad j = 1,...,n.$$

Generalized DEA model using MOLP structure is proposed as follows (Wei & Yu 1993; Wei, Yu & Lu 1993; Yu, Wei, & Brockett 1996):

$$Max \quad \left\{ y_1,...,y_s,-x_1,...,-x_m \right\}$$

$$s.t. \quad \sum_{j=1}^{n} \lambda_j \bar{x}_{ij} - x_i \leq 0, \qquad i = 1,...,m,$$

$$\sum_{j=1}^{n} \lambda_j \bar{y}_{rj} - y_r \geq 0, \qquad r = 1,...,s, \qquad (16)$$

$$\delta_1 \left(\sum_{j=1}^{n} \lambda_j + \delta_1 (-1)^{\delta_3} \lambda_{n+1} \right) = \delta_1,$$

$$\lambda_j \geq 0, \qquad j = 1,...,n,$$

$$x_i, y_r \geq 0, \qquad i = 1,...,m, \ r = 1,...,s.$$

where $\left(\bar{x}_1,..., \bar{x}_m \right)$ and $\left(\bar{y}_1,..., \bar{y}_s \right)$ are vectors of input and output, respectively. Also, $(\delta_1, \delta_2, \delta_3)$ are $\{0,1\}$ binary parameters (* indicates either 0 or 1), different values of parameters and variable changes lead to the different standard DEA models as follows;

1. **Input Oriented BCC Model:** When $(\delta_1, \delta_2, \delta_3) = (1,0,*)$ and $\left(x_i, y_r\right) = \left(\theta \bar{x}_{io}, \bar{y}_{ro}\right)$ for all i,r, then, the values $\bar{x}_{io}, \bar{y}_{ro}$ are constant and also, the maximization of $-\theta \bar{x}_{io}$ and $\bar{y}_{ro}$ are equivalent to minimization of θ.

2. **Output Oriented BCC Model:** When $(\delta_1, \delta_2, \delta_3) = (1,0,*)$ and $\left(x_i, y_r\right) = \left(\bar{x}_{io}, \phi \bar{y}_{ro}\right)$ for all i,r, then, the values $\bar{x}_{io}, \bar{y}_{ro}$ are constant and also, the maximization of $\bar{x}_{io}$ and $\phi \bar{y}_{ro}$ are equivalent to maximization of ϕ.

3. **Additive BCC Model:** When $(\delta_1, \delta_2, \delta_3) = (1,0,*)$ and $\left(x_i, y_r\right) = \left(\bar{x}_{io} - s_i^-, \bar{y}_{ro} + s_r^+\right)$ for all i,r, then, the values $\bar{x}_{io}, \bar{y}_{ro}$ are constant and also, s_i^- and s_r^+ are maximized.

4. **Russell DEA Model:** When $(\delta_1, \delta_2, \delta_3) = (1,0,*)$ and $\left(x_i, y_r\right) = \left(\theta_i \bar{x}_{io}, \phi_r \bar{y}_{ro}\right)$ for all i,r, then the values $\bar{x}_{io}, \bar{y}_{ro}$ are constant and also, $-\theta_i \bar{x}_{io}$ and $\phi_r \bar{y}_{ro}$ are maximized.

Benchmarking

The problem of benchmarking or target setting is one of the objective in DEA. The purpose of the benchmarking approaches is not to measure efficiency, but to determine appropriate projection point on the efficient frontier. If the projection point is closer to the MPS it maximizes the decision maker's implicit utility function. Benchmarking with using the radial projection of an inefficient DMU is too restrictive; therefore, the standard DEA models inappropriately project the inefficient DMUs onto the efficient frontier which is a disadvantage in DEA. Over the past years, in order to remove this problem a large number of studies have suggested MOLP problems in DEA methodology for benchmarking. Moreover, in most cases in order to solve the proposed MOLP problems the interactive MOP techniques are applied. Primarily, Golany (1988) was implemented an interactive MOP technique in the DEA context for benchmarking.

Joro et al. (1998) argued that the output oriented CCR model in envelopment form is often structurally similar to the MOLP problem based on the reference point model proposed by Wierzbicki (1980). The reference point model is used to solve MOLP problems. By changing variables the reference point model is reformulated as follows:

$$Max \quad \sigma + \delta 1^T S^+$$
$$s.t. \quad Y\lambda - \sigma W - S^+ = g,$$
$$X\lambda \qquad + S^- = b, \qquad\qquad (17)$$
$$\lambda, S^-, S^+ \geq 0,$$
$$\delta > 0.$$

By comparing the two above mentioned models, there are some differences between them, such as; in Model (17), W, g and b are replaced by y_o, 0 and x_o in the output oriented CCR model, respectively. Moreover, in the objective function of Model (17) slacks exist only in production outputs. Therefore, if DMU_o is weakly efficient, Model (17) might evaluate it as efficient. Figures 1 and 2 portray the output oriented CCR model where $m=1$, $s=2$ and $X=1^T$ indeed the reference point model where $g=y_o$ and $b=1$, respectively.

Using radial models of DEA (Figure 1.), C^* and E^* are the projected points of C and E, respectively. In MOLP (Figure 2.), the projected point of C and E depend on the weighting vector used in the achievement function (Wierzbicki 1980) that it is one of nondominated points. Based on the Russell's efficiency measure, Lins et al. (2004) proposed a model based on MOLP problem to determine nonradial projections for inefficient DMUs onto the efficient frontier. Their proposed model overcame the drawbacks of nonradial model of both Thanassoulis and Dyson and Zhu to determine the benchmark DMU. As a weakness in DEA models, the problem is the weights of increasing outputs and decreasing inputs are chosen arbitrary before testing the model. Therefore, Lins et al. (2004) to solve mentioned problem proposed the following model in order to obtain an efficient target for the observed DMU_o:

Figure 1. Illustration of DEA

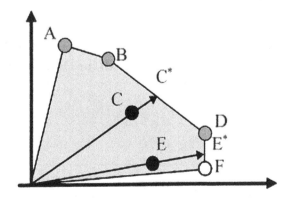

Figure 2. Illustration of MODM

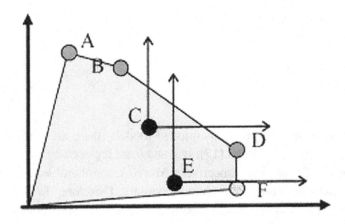

$$Max \quad \left\{ \phi_1, ..., \phi_s \right\}$$
$$Min \quad \left\{ \theta_1, ..., \theta_m \right\}$$

$$s.t. \quad \sum_{j=1}^{n} y_{rj} \lambda_j = \phi_r y_{ro}, \qquad\qquad r = 1, ..., s, \qquad\qquad (18)$$

$$\sum_{j=1}^{n} x_{ij} \lambda_j = \theta_i x_{io}, \qquad\qquad i = 1, ..., m,$$

$$\lambda_j, \phi_r, \theta_i \geq 0, \quad j = 1, ..., n, \ r = 1, ..., s, \ i = 1, ..., m.$$

Suppose ϕ_r^*, θ_i^* ($\forall r, i$) are the optimal solution of MOLP (18), then, the benchmark DMU is constructed as follows:

$$\begin{cases} y_{ro}^* = \phi_r^* y_{ro}, & r = 1, ..., s, \\ x_{io}^* = \theta_i^* x_{io}, & i = 1, ..., m. \end{cases} \qquad\qquad (19)$$

$(x_{io}^*, y_{ro}^*)(\forall i, r)$ lies on the efficient frontier. Can will be added the following restrictions to MOLP (18) for obtaining benchmark DMU that is dominated the observed DMU_o as follows:

$$\begin{cases} \phi_r^* \geq 1, & r = 1, ..., s, \\ \theta_i^* \leq 1, & i = 1, ..., m. \end{cases} \qquad\qquad (20)$$

Moreover, Yang et al. investigated the equivalence between the output oriented CCR model in envelopment form and a MOLP problem using the minimax formulation. In this examination, the implemented MOLP problem is as follows:

$$
Max \quad \left\{ \sum_{j=1}^{n} \lambda_j y_{1j}, \ldots, \sum_{j=1}^{n} \lambda_j y_{sj} \right\}
$$

$$
s.t. \quad \sum_{j=1}^{n} \lambda_j x_{ij} \leq x_{io}, \qquad\qquad i = 1, \ldots, m, \tag{21}
$$

$$
\lambda_j \geq 0, \quad j = 1, \ldots, n.
$$

In other words, based on the minimax formulation, MOLP (21) is converted to the output oriented CCR model in envelopment form. The purpose for establishing this equivalence is to use MOLP problem (21) instead of the output oriented CCR model in envelopment form to conduct efficiency analyses. Then, the interactive MOP techniques can be used to locate the MPS or set target values for DMU_o. Yang et al. used the interactive tradeoff analysis procedure based on the gradient projection and local region search method (Yang 1999; Yang 7 Li 2002; Yang & Sen 1996) to locate a MPS that can maximaize the decision makers local preference information. Indeed, Wong et al. (2009) solved MOLP (21) using five interactive methods to compare and analyze them. These interactive techniques are as follows; G-D-F (Geoffrion, Dyer & Feinberg 1972), Wierzbicki (1980), STEM (Benayoun et al 1971), Tchebychev (Steuer 1977; Steuer & Choo 1983) and STOM (Nykowski & Zolkiewski 1985) As a result, the Tchebychev method is preferred because it is user-friendly and easy-to-understand solution process. However, the number of iterations in this approach is more than others. Yet, they argue that the accuracy of the results is more important than the length of solution process. Later, some researchers have applied Yang et al.'s idea (Yang & Sen 1996) to establish an equivalence between MOLP problems and the standard DEA models, and to set target values for the observed DMU. Also, Hosseinzadeh Lotfi et al. (2010) established an equivalence between the general combined oriented CCR model and a MOP problem. In this examination, the above mentioned MOP problem is as follows:

$$
Max \quad \left\{ \frac{\left(x_{1o} - \sum_{j=1}^{n} \lambda_j x_{1j} \right)}{d_{1x}}, \ldots, \frac{\left(x_{mo} - \sum_{j=1}^{n} \lambda_j x_{mj} \right)}{d_{mx}}, \frac{\left(\sum_{j=1}^{n} \lambda_j y_{1j} - y_{1o} \right)}{d_{1y}}, \ldots, \frac{\left(\sum_{j=1}^{n} \lambda_j y_{sj} - y_{so} \right)}{d_{sy}} \right\}
$$

$$
s.t. \quad \lambda \in \Lambda_C. \tag{22}
$$

In other words, based on the min ordering formulation MOP (22) is converted to the combined oriented CCR model. The interactive MOP methods could be applied to solve MOP (22). They used the Zionts-Wallenius's method (Zionts & Wallenius 1976) to design an interactive procedure to search the MPS and maximaize the decision maker's implicit utility function.

A body of research exists in DEA about problems that make the output increase as high as possible for a given input while the optimal objective value of the DEA model remains unchanged. The researchers called these problems as the inverse DEA. The basic idea of the inverse DEA problem is the extending concepts of the inverse optimization to the DEA context.

Golany (1988) suggested an algorithm based on the interactive MOP method to help the decision makers in setting up their own desired outputs. In each iteration of the proposed algorithm, the new information provided by the decision maker is applied to adjust the procedure, leading to points where have greater effectiveness for the decision maker. This algorithm has five steps. Step 1 and 2 are similar to the first step of the STEM (Benayoun et al 1971) algorithm and using the results of Model (23) the payoff matrix is built,

$$
\begin{aligned}
Max \quad & Y_{ro}, \quad r = 1, ..., s \\
s.t. \quad & Y\lambda - y_o = 0 \\
& X\lambda \le x_o \\
& e^T\lambda = 1 \\
& \lambda \ge 0.
\end{aligned} \tag{23}
$$

Step 3 find an average point using Model (24),

$$
\begin{aligned}
Max \quad & \sum_{r=1}^{s} \left(y_{ro} \Big/ \overline{Y}_r \right), \\
s.t. \quad & Y\lambda - y_o = 0 \\
& X\lambda \le x_o \\
& e^T\lambda = 1 \\
& \lambda \ge 0,
\end{aligned} \tag{24}
$$

where $\bar{Y}_r = \left(\frac{1}{n}\right)\sum_{j=1}^{n} y_{rj}$. In step 4, a sequence of programs one for each y_{ro} is solved to generate a set of efficient points for the given resource vector x_o. Step 5 aids the decision maker to focus on the efficient frontier to make her/his final selection. The new information provided by decision maker in step 5, helped them to correct the objective function. The algorithm uses the empirical production function where it is similar to the production function generated by DEA at the efficiency evaluation stage that is to set the target values for the outputs. Moreover, Wei et al. (2000) offered an inverse DEA model as the MOLP problem with the purpose of determining how many more output/input levels are needed to be produced when some input/output levels of a DMU increase; indeed, the efficiency score not be changed. To formulate the inverse problem, assume the inputs of DMU_o increase from x_o to $\alpha_o = (\alpha_1,\ldots,\alpha_m) = x_o + \Delta x_o$ ($\Delta x_o \geq 0$ and $\Delta x_o \neq 0$), this method estimate the output vector β if the efficiency score DMU_o is still z_o. Here $\beta = (\beta_1,\ldots,\beta_s)^T = y_o + \Delta y_o \in \mathbb{R}^s$, $\Delta y_o \geq 0$. The proposed method is constructed based on Theorem 1 as follows:

Theorem 1: Considering the following linear programming:

$Max \quad z$

$s.t. \quad \displaystyle\sum_{j=1}^{n}\lambda_j x_{ij} \leq x_{io}, \qquad\qquad\qquad i = 1,\ldots,m,$

$\qquad\quad \displaystyle\sum_{j=1}^{n}\lambda_j y_{rj} \geq z\,y_{ro}, \qquad\qquad\qquad r = 1,\ldots,s, \qquad\qquad (25)$

$\qquad\quad \delta_1\left(\displaystyle\sum_{j=1}^{n}\lambda_j + \delta_2\left(-1\right)^{\delta_3}\nu\right) = \delta_1,$

$\qquad\quad \nu \geq 0,$

$\qquad\quad \lambda_j \geq 0, \qquad j = 1,\ldots,n,$

where $\delta_1, \delta_2, \delta_3 \in \{0,1\}$ are parameters for constructing different models. Suppose that the optimal value of Model (25) for DMU_o is z_o, and the inputs for this DMU are going to increase from x_o to $\alpha_o = (\alpha_1,\ldots,\alpha_m) = x_o + \Delta x_o$ ($\Delta x_o \geq 0$ and $\Delta x_o \neq 0$).

Let $\left(\bar{\beta},\bar{\lambda},\bar{\nu}\right)$ be a weak Pareto solution of the MOLP problem as follows:

$$V - Max \quad (\beta_1, ..., \beta_s)$$

$$s.t. \quad \sum_{j=1}^{n} \lambda_j x_{ij} \leq \alpha_{io}, \qquad\qquad i = 1, ..., m,$$

$$\sum_{j=1}^{n} \lambda_j y_{rj} \geq \beta_r z_o, \qquad\qquad r = 1, ..., s,$$

$$\beta_r \geq y_{ro}, \qquad\qquad r = 1, ..., s, \qquad\qquad (26)$$

$$\delta_1 \left(\sum_{j=1}^{n} \lambda_j + \delta_2 (-1)^{\delta_3} \nu \right) = \delta_1,$$

$$\nu \geq 0,$$

$$\lambda_j \geq 0, \qquad j = 1, ..., n,$$

where z_o is the optimal solution of Model (25) and $(\alpha_1, ..., \alpha_m)$ is defined before. Then, when the outputs of DMU_o increase to $\bar{\beta}$, the optimal value of the new DEA problem i.e., Model (27), is still z_o,

$$Max \quad z$$

$$s.t. \quad \sum_{j=1}^{n} \lambda_j x_{ij} + \alpha_{io} \lambda_{n+1} \leq \alpha_{io}, \qquad\qquad i = 1, ..., m,$$

$$\sum_{j=1}^{n} \lambda_j y_{rj} + \beta_r \lambda_{n+1} \geq \beta_r z, \qquad\qquad r = 1, ..., s,$$

$$\delta_1 \left(\sum_{j=1}^{n} \lambda_j + \delta_2 (-1)^{\delta_3} \nu \right) = \delta_1, \qquad\qquad (27)$$

$$\nu \geq 0,$$

$$\lambda_j \geq 0, \qquad j = 1, ..., n,$$

That is, the efficiency score of DMU_o under this pair of new inputs-outputs remain unchanged.

Conversely, let $(\bar{\beta}, \bar{\lambda}, \bar{\nu})$ be a feasible solution of Model (26). If the optimal value of Model (27) is z_o, then, $(\bar{\beta}, \bar{\lambda}, \bar{\nu})$ must be a weak Pareto solution of Model (26).

Proof: See Wei, Zhang & Zhang (2000).

The basic idea of Theorem 1 was based on the work of Zhang and Cui (1996). However, in some cases the proposed model may be converted to the single object LP problem.

Value Efficiency

The value efficiency is an approach to incorporate decision maker's preference information in DEA models that preliminary presented by Halme et al. (1999). As value function has not explicit form, it is approximated by indifference curve at the MPS. Thus, researchers proposed different approaches to approximate the value function. The value efficiency scores are calculated based on value function for each DMU in comparison with DMUs which have the same value as the MPS.

Halme et al. (1999) proposed a method to measure the value efficiency analysis. They approximated the contour using the possible tangents of a value function at the MPS. This method is based on the assumptions; the value function must be pseudoconcave, strictly increasing in outputs, strictly decreasing in inputs, and reaching its maximum at the MPS on the efficient frontier. Because the value function is pseudoconcave, the value of units is less or equally preferred than the MPS, in other words, the value efficiency scores are optimistic estimates of the true ones. They provided the following theorem in order to determinate the value efficiency score of an unit:

Theorem 2: Let $u^* = \left(y^*, -x^*\right) \in PPS$ be the decision maker's MPS. Then, $u = (y, -x)$, is an arbitrary unit in the PPS, value inefficient with respect to any strictly increasing pseudoconcave value function $v(u)$ with a maximum at point u^*, if the optimum value Z^* of the following problem is strictly positive:

$$
\begin{aligned}
Max \quad & Z = \sigma + \varepsilon\left(1^T S^+ + 1^T S^-\right) \\
s.t. \quad & Y\lambda - \sigma\omega^y - S^+ = y, \\
& X\lambda + \sigma\omega^x + S^- = x, \\
& A\lambda + \delta = b, \\
& \lambda, s^-, s^+ \geq 0, \\
& \varepsilon > 0, \left(Non - Archimedean\right) \\
& s^+, s^- \geq 0, \\
& \lambda_j \geq 0 \ if \ \lambda^*_j = 0, \qquad j = 1,...,n, \\
& \delta_j \geq 0 \ if \ \delta^*_j = 0, \qquad j = 1,...,k,
\end{aligned}
\tag{28}
$$

where $\lambda^* \in \Lambda$, μ^* corresponds to the MPS: $y^* = Y\lambda^*$, $x^* = X\lambda^*$.

Proof: See Halme et al (1999).

Model (28) indicates the simple modification in the standard DEA model which takes into account the value judgment according to the MPS. Moreover, Halme and Korhonen (2000) proposed the problem of incorporating additional preference information into the value efficiency analysis to improve the resolution of the estimating of the value efficiency scores. They imposed the weight restrictions as $-\mu^T B^y + \nu^T B^x \geq c$, $B^y \in \mathbb{R}^{p \times r}$, $B^x \in \mathbb{R}^{m \times r}$ to the dual of Model (28). Then, the above mentioned model is converted to:

$$
\begin{aligned}
&Min \quad W = \nu^T g^x - \mu^T g^y + \eta^T b \\
&s.t. \quad -\mu^T Y + \nu^T X + \eta^T A - \gamma = 0, \\
&\qquad \mu^T \omega^y + \nu^T \omega^x = 1, \\
&\qquad -\mu^T B^y + \nu^T B^x - \xi = c, \\
&\qquad \mu, \nu \geq 1\varepsilon, \\
&\qquad \gamma_j \begin{cases} \geq 0 & if \ \lambda_j^* = 0 \\ = 0 & if \ \lambda_j^* > 0 \end{cases} \qquad j = 1, ..., n, \\
&\qquad \eta_j = \begin{cases} \geq 0 & if \ \delta_j^* = 0 \\ \geq 0 & if \ \delta_j^* > 0 \end{cases} \qquad j = 1, ..., k, \\
&\qquad \xi \geq 0, \\
&\qquad \varepsilon > 0 \ (Non - Archimedean).
\end{aligned}
\tag{29}
$$

Whenever the restricted value efficiency model (29) is infeasible, the weight constraints are in conflict with the MPS or they are in conflict with constraints of the basic model. Also, Zohrebandian (2011) developed Halme et al.'s method (1999) by applying the general MOLP problem with CRS technology. The considered MOLP problem is as follows:

$$
\begin{aligned}
&Max \quad \{-x_1, ..., -x_m, y_1, ..., y_s\} \\
&s.t. \quad \sum_{j=1}^{n} \lambda_j \bar{x}_{ij} \leq x_i, \qquad i = 1, ..., m, \\
&\qquad \sum_{j=1}^{n} \lambda_j \bar{y}_{rj} \geq y_r, \qquad r = 1, ..., s, \\
&\qquad \lambda_j \geq 0, \quad j = 1, ..., n,
\end{aligned}
\tag{30}
$$

Zohrebandian (2011) proposed the following algorithm in the three steps:

Step 1: To identify the direction $\left(W_x, W_y\right)$ in order to project each DMU on the tangent hyperplane.

Step 2: To solve MOLP (30) by the Zionts-Wallenius' method (Zionts & Wallenius 1976) in order to identify the MPS as $\left(x^*, y^*\right)$ indeed the set of preference input and output weights of decision maker as $\left(u^*, v^*\right)$.

Step 3: These input and output weights approximate the tangent hyperplane of the value function of the decision maker at the MPS which itself approximate the indifference contour of this value function at the MPS.

Step 4: The value efficiency score for each $DMU_j \left(j = 1, ..., n\right)$ is defined as:

$$\theta = \frac{-v^* x_j + u^* y_j}{-v^* W_x + u^* W_y}.$$

In this method the value efficiency scores are calculated for each DMU by comparing the inefficient units to units having the same value as the MPS without solving any LP problem.

Secondary Goal

In the cross efficiency approach (Sexton, Silkman & Hogan 1986), there is a major disadvantage when the CCR model in multiplier form enjoys the alternative optimal weights. Consequently, this approach will give different rank ordering. To solve this problem, Doyle and Green (1994) offered the incorporation of the secondary goal formulation which is the usage of the lexicographic method in the DEA context. Several researchers proposed a large number of the secondary goal DEA models, but none of them guarantee the optimal solution is unique.

Doyle and Green (1994) suggested different ways to formulate the secondary goal DEA models with aggressive minimizing the objective of all other DMUs. The first one is constructed as follows:

$$Min \quad A_o = \sum_{j=1, j \neq o}^{n} \frac{\sum_{r=1}^{s} u_r y_{rj}}{\sum_{i=1}^{m} v_i x_{ij}}$$

$$s.t. \quad \sum_{r=1}^{s} u_r y_{rj} - \sum_{i=1}^{m} v_i x_{ij} \leq 0, \qquad j = 1, ..., n, j \neq o, \tag{31}$$

$$\sum_{r=1}^{s} u_r y_{ro} - E_o^* \sum_{i=1}^{m} v_i x_{io} = 0,$$

$$u_r, v_i \geq 0, \qquad r = 1, ..., s, \ i = 1, ..., m,$$

where E_o^* is the efficiency score of DMU_o using the CCR model. Model (31) leads to the nonlinear fractional programming which is not convert to linear programming, conveniently. Indeed, another secondary goal DEA model is proposed as follows:

$$Min \quad B_o = \frac{\sum_{r=1}^{s}\left(u_r \sum_{j=1,j\neq o}^{n} y_{rj}\right)}{\sum_{i=1}^{m}\left(v_i \sum_{j=1,j\neq o}^{n} x_{ij}\right)}$$

$$s.t. \quad \sum_{r=1}^{s} u_r y_{rj} - \sum_{i=1}^{m} v_i x_{ij} \leq 0, \qquad\qquad j = 1,...,n, j \neq o,$$

$$\sum_{r=1}^{s} u_r y_{ro} - E_o^* \sum_{i=1}^{m} v_i x_{io} = 0,$$

$$u_r, v_i \geq 0, \qquad r = 1,...,s,\ i = 1,...,m.$$

(32)

Note that, Model (32) can be converted to the linear programming using the Charns and Cooper transformation (Charnes, Cooper, & Rhodes 1978). The benevolent formulation for Models (31) and (32) are obtained by maximizing the secondary goals A_o and B_o, respectively. Also, Liang et al. (2008) extended the Doyle and Green's secondary goal DEA models by introducing different objective functions as follows:

1.   Minimizing the total deviation from the ideal point:

For each DMU the ideal point is that $\alpha_j = \sum_{r=1}^{s} u_r y_{rj} - \sum_{i=1}^{m} v_i x_{ij} = 0, \ j = 1,...,n$.

In evaluation of each DMU, considering α_j as goal achievement variables, then, the ideal point model is converted to a goal programming problem. In the proposed model, minimizing the deviation variables $\alpha_j'\left(j = 1,...,n\right)$ in evaluation of DMU_o is calculated using 1 norm as follows:

$$Min \quad \sum_{j=1}^{n} \alpha'_j$$

$$s.t. \quad \sum_{r=1}^{s} u_r y_{rj} - \sum_{i=1}^{m} v_i x_{ij} + \alpha'_j = 0, \qquad\qquad j = 1, ..., n,$$

$$\sum_{i=1}^{m} v_i x_{io} = 1, \qquad\qquad\qquad (33)$$

$$\sum_{r=1}^{s} u_r y_{ro} = 1 - \alpha_o^{*},$$

$$u_r, v_i, \alpha'_j \geq 0, \qquad r = 1, ..., s, \ i = 1, ..., m, \ j = 1, ..., n,$$

where α_o^{*} is the efficiency measure of DMU_o in the CCR model in multiplier form.

Theorem 3: Model (33) is the equivalent form of the Doyle and Green model (1994).
Proof: See Liang, Wu, Cook and Zhu (2008).

2.   Minimizing the maximum efficiency score:

Instead of applying 1 norm in calculating the deviation variables $\alpha'_j, j = 1, ..., n$ the infinity norm is used.

3.   Minimizing the mean absolute deviation:

In this model the average of the absolute deviations of data points from the mean is computed.

At last, using the optimal weights of the above mentioned secondary goal DEA models the cross efficiency scores of all DMUs are calculated. Another drawback of the previous aggressive and benevolent secondary goal DEA models is the achievement of a better ranking is less important than the maximization of the individual score. To overcome this problem, Wu et al. (2009) proposed a mixed integer linear programming DEA model where the principle of rank priority enjoys more preference than the efficiency score. Their proposed method is proceeded in the four steps manner as follows:

Step 1: Determining the efficiency scores all DMUs using the CCR model.
Step 2: Choosing the optimal weights of the secondary goal in ranking ordering formulation by the following mixed integer linear programming,

$$Min \quad I_o = \sum_{j=1}^{n} z_j^o$$

$$s.t. \quad \sum_{r=1}^{s} u_r y_{rj} - \sum_{i=1}^{m} v_i x_{ij} \leq 0, \qquad\qquad j = 1,...,n,$$

$$\sum_{i=1}^{m} v_i x_{io} = 1,$$

$$\sum_{r=1}^{s} u_r y_{ro} = E_o^*,$$

$$\frac{\displaystyle\sum_{r=1}^{s} u_r y_{rj}}{\displaystyle\sum_{i=1}^{m} v_i x_{ij}} - h_j^o = E_o^*, \qquad\qquad j = 1,...,n, \qquad (34)$$

$$0 \leq h_j^o + M z_j^o < M + \varepsilon, \qquad\qquad j = 1,...,n,$$

$$z_j^o \in \{0,1\}, \qquad j = 1,...,n,$$

$$u_r, v_i \geq 0, \qquad r = 1,...,s, \ i = 1,...,m,$$

$$h_j^o \ is \ free, \qquad j = 1,...,n,$$

where M is a big positive number and ε is a non Archimedean element. The first three groups of the constraints in Model (34) grantee all optimal solutions of the CCR model in multiplier form is considered. Fourth groups of constraints indicate the efficiency comparison between DMU_o and other DMUs. Indeed, $h_j^o \geq 0$ implies $z_j^o = 0 \left(j = 1,...,n\right)$. $z_j^o \in \{0,1\}$ and the objective function of Model (34) make an attempt to find the optimal solutions in evaluation DMU_o with as many $z_j^{o*} = 0$ as possible.

Step 3: According to the aggressive formulation (Doyle & Green 1994) of the secondary goal DEA model, the following programming select the optimal solution among the alternative optimal solutions (if any) provided by Model (34),

$$Min \quad \sum_{j=1,j\neq o}^{n} \left(\sum_{r=1}^{s} u_r y_{rj} - \sum_{i=1}^{m} v_i x_{ij} \right)$$

$$s.t. \quad \sum_{r=1}^{s} u_r y_{rj} - \sum_{i=1}^{m} v_i x_{ij} \leq 0, \qquad\qquad j = 1,...,n,$$

$$\sum_{i=1}^{m} v_i x_{io} = 1,$$

$$\sum_{r=1}^{s} u_r y_{ro} = E_o^*,$$

$$\sum_{r=1}^{s} u_r y_{rj} - h_j^o \sum_{i=1}^{m} v_i x_{ij} = E_o^* \sum_{i=1}^{m} v_i x_{ij}, \qquad j = 1,...,n, \qquad (35)$$

$$0 \leq h_j^o + M z_j^o < M + \varepsilon, \qquad\qquad j = 1,...,n,$$

$$z_j^o \in \{0,1\}, \qquad j = 1,...,n,$$

$$u_r, v_i \geq 0, \qquad r = 1,...,s, \ i = 1,...,m,$$

$$h_j^o \ is \ free, \qquad j = 1,...,n,$$

where I_o^* is the optimal value in Model (34).

Step 4: According to the optimal weights of Model (35), the cross efficiency matrix is constructed to obtain the cross efficiency scores all DMUs. Also, the two aggressive and benevolent models may lead to the two different rank priority results; therefore, selecting one of them is a hard task. For removing this problem, Wang and Chin (2010) proposed a neutral secondary goal DEA model for the cross efficiency evaluation where each DMU determines the optimal weights purely from its own point of view. The neutral secondary goal DEA model is formulated as follows:

$$Max \quad Min \quad \frac{u_r y_{ro}}{\sum_{i=1}^{m} v_i x_{io}}, \qquad r \in \{1,...,s\}$$

$$s.t. \quad \frac{\sum_{r=1}^{s} u_r y_{rj}}{\sum_{i=1}^{m} v_i x_{ij}} \leq 1, \qquad\qquad j = 1,...,n, j \neq o, \qquad (36)$$

$$\frac{\sum_{r=1}^{s} u_r y_{ro}}{\sum_{i=1}^{m} v_i x_{io}} = E_o^*,$$

$$u_r, v_i \geq 0, \qquad r = 1,...,s, \ i = 1,...,m,$$

where $\dfrac{u_r^* y_{ro}}{\sum\limits_{i=1}^{m} v_i^* x_{io}}$ is the efficiency of r th output in evalution DMU_o. In Model (36),

DMU_o searches a set of input and output weights to maximize its efficiency and at the same time to make each output being as efficient as possible to produce sufficient efficiency as an individual, which is the biggest advantage of the neutral secondary goal DEA model over the previous metioned secondary goal formulations. Through the Charnes and Cooper transformation (Charnes, Cooper, & Rhodes 1978) and the maximin formulation, Model (36) is converted to the linear programming model. Then, using the optimal weights of the mentioned linear programming the cross efficiency scores of all DMUs are calculated. Moreover, in order to select the symmetric weights (Dimitrov & Sutton 2010) in a secondary goal DEA model, Jahanshahloo et al. (2011) added the symmetric constraints into output weights to reward symmetric output as far as it preserves linearity. The proposed method proceeds in the two following steps:

Step 1: To determine the efficiency scores all DMUs using the CCR model.
Step 2: To construct the cross efficiency matrix, the optimal solutions of the following secondary goal DEA model is used:

$$
\begin{aligned}
Min \quad & e^T Z_o e \\
s.t. \quad & u_o y_o = 1, \\
& u_o x_o = \phi_o^*, \\
& -v_o X + u_o Y \leq 0, \\
& u_{or} y_{or} - u_{ot} y_{ot} \leq z_{ort}, \qquad r = 1,...,s, \quad t = 1,...,s, \\
& -u_{or} y_{or} + u_{ot} y_{ot} \leq z_{ort}, \qquad r = 1,...,s, \quad t = 1,...,s, \\
& u_o, v_o \geq d,
\end{aligned} \tag{37}
$$

where ϕ_o^* is the optimal value of the output oriented CCR model in evaluating DMU_o. The objective function and last two groups of constraints in Model (37) grantee that the optimal weights are symmetric.

Theorem 4: $\left(u_o^*, v_o^*, Z_o^*\right)$ is the optimal solution of Model (37), if and only if $\left(u_o^*, v_o^*\right)$ the optimal solution of the output oriented CCR model in multiplier form.
Proof: See Jahanshahloo et al (2005).

Common Set of Weights

The standard DEA models give each DMUs the maximum flexibility in selecting the weights to include the efficiency score and the benchmark DMU. There are several methods for facing the optimistic problem, the common set of weight methods is one of them preliminary introduced by Charnes et al. (1989) and Kornbluth (1991) by including cone restrictions to the MOP problem. In the common set of weight models only one hyperplane is generated as the efficient frontier to evaluate all DMUs. The advantages of these models include; the common weight concept reduces computational compared with the standards DEA model, almost all common weights models are based on MOP problems that have strong theoretical background; and the common weight models have the higher discrimination power than the standard DEA models.

Charnes et al. (1989) extended the CCR model in multiplier form by introducing additional weight restrictions in the predetermined space $v \in V$ and $u \in U$ to the MOP problem. Then, based on the work of Charnes et al. (1989), Kornbluth (1991) suggested a MOLP problem including cone restrictions to reduce weight flexibility in the MOLP problem. The restricted MOLP problem is constructed as follows:

$$
\begin{aligned}
Max \quad & \left\{ \sum_{r=1}^{s} u_r y_{r1}, ..., \sum_{r=1}^{s} u_r y_{rn}, -\sum_{i=1}^{m} v_i x_{i1}, ..., -\sum_{i=1}^{m} v_i x_{in} \right\} \\
s.t. \quad & \sum_{r=1}^{s} u_r y_{rj} - \sum_{i=1}^{m} v_i x_{ij} \leq 0 && j = 1, ..., n, \\
& \sum_{i=1}^{m} v_i x_{ij} \geq q_{\lim}, && j = 1, ..., n, \quad\quad (38) \\
& u \in \bar{U}, \ v \in \bar{V} \\
& q_{\lim} \ \ some \ arbitary \ positive \ lower \lim it,
\end{aligned}
$$

where $\bar{U}$ and $\bar{V}$ are cone restrictions which are more general than the proposed bound restrictions by Dyson and Thanassoulis (1998). MOLP (38) gives more information than the standard DEA models, because the standard models are optimistic and their objective is to find the maximum efficiency score for the DMU under evaluation but no attention has been paid to the efficiency scores of others. Moreover, Belton and Vickers (1993) proposed another common set of weights model as follows:

$$Min \quad \sum_{j=1}^{n} D_j$$

$$s.t. \quad \sum_{r=1}^{s}\left(y_{ro} - y_{rj}\right)u_r - \sum_{i=1}^{m}\left(x_{io} - x_{ij}\right)v_i + D_j \geq 0, \quad j = 1,...,n, \tag{39}$$

$$\sum_{i=1}^{m} v_i + \sum_{r=1}^{s} u_r = 1,$$

$$u_r, v_i, D_j \geq 0, \quad r = 1,...,s, \ i = 1,...,m, \ j = 1,...,n.$$

Model (39) is the dual of proposed model by Charnes et al. (1985). Model (39) is measured the efficiency DMUs based on the distance form according to the efficient frontier; however, the CCR model is measured the efficiency DMUs based on the ratio form (Charnes, Cooper & Rhodes 1978). If the optimal value of Model (39) is zero then DMU_o is efficient; otherwise it is inefficient. Also, based on the work of Belton and Vickers (1993), Stewart (1996) suggested the following linear programming that uses infinity norm instead of 1 norm in Model (39),

$$Min \quad \Delta$$

$$s.t. \quad \sum_{r=1}^{s}\left(y_{ro} - y_{rj}\right)u_r - \sum_{i=1}^{m}\left(x_{io} - x_{ij}\right)v_i + D_j \geq 0, \quad j = 1,...,n,$$

$$\sum_{i=1}^{m} v_i x_{io} = 1, \tag{40}$$

$$\Delta - D_j \geq 0, \quad j = 1,...,n,$$

$$u_r, v_i, D_j \geq 0, \quad r = 1,...,s, \ i = 1,...,m, \ j = 1,...,n.$$

The dual of Model (40) is equivalent to the input oriented BCC model in envelopment form. As a result, it demonstrates the CCR model based on the ratio form of the efficiency definition and the distance from of the linear model for the efficiency definition is equivalent. Moreover, Roll and Golany (1993) suggested a common set of weights model based on the MOP problem, then, the sum weighted method implemented to solve it. The model is obtained as follows:

$$Max \quad \frac{1}{n}\sum_{j=1}^{n}E_j$$

$$s.t. \quad E_j = \frac{\sum_{r=1}^{s}u_r y_{rj}}{\sum_{i=1}^{m}v_i x_{ij}} \leq 1, \qquad j = 1,...,n, \qquad\qquad (41)$$

$$v_i \geq \varepsilon, \qquad i = 1,...,m,$$

$$u_r \geq \varepsilon, \qquad r = 1,...,s,$$

Model (41) is proposed a true common weights, because it does not need to predicate of neither the reference point nor the weights which are the advantage for Model (41). However, the assumption of the same weight for all DMUs is more restrictive which a disadvantage is for Model (41). Also, Jahanshaloo et al. (2005) introduced a MOP problem based on the proposed MOLP problem in Roll and Golany (1993) to obtain common weights in T_V as follows:

$$Max \quad \left\{ \frac{\sum_{r=1}^{s}u_r y_{r1} + u_0}{\sum_{i=1}^{m}v_i x_{i1}}, ..., \frac{\sum_{r=1}^{s}u_r y_{rn} + u_0}{\sum_{i=1}^{m}v_i x_{in}} \right\}$$

$$s.t. \quad \frac{\sum_{r=1}^{s}u_r y_{rj} + u_0}{\sum_{i=1}^{m}v_i x_{ij}} \leq 1, \qquad j = 1,...,n \qquad (42)$$

$$v_i \geq \varepsilon, \qquad i = 1,...,m,$$

$$u_r \geq \varepsilon, \qquad r = 1,...,s,$$

To solve MOP (42), they implemented the maxmin formulation, then, convert it to the nonlinear programming that is obtained as follows:

$Max \quad z$

$s.t. \quad \displaystyle\sum_{r=1}^{s} u_r y_{rj} + u_0 - z \sum_{i=1}^{m} v_i x_{ij} \geq 0, \qquad j = 1, \ldots, n,$

$\displaystyle\sum_{r=1}^{s} u_r y_{rj} + u_0 - \sum_{i=1}^{m} v_i x_{ij} \leq 0, \qquad j = 1, \ldots, n, \qquad\qquad (43)$

$z \geq 0,$

$v_i \geq \varepsilon, \qquad i = 1, \ldots, m,$

$u_r \geq \varepsilon, \qquad r = 1, \ldots, s,$

As a result, in calculating efficiency scores one nonlinear model is used instead of n linear DEA models to obtain efficiencies of all DMUs based on common weights. In order to show the results of Model (43) is acceptable, they proved the following theorem as follows:

Theorem 5: If DMU_o is efficient in Model (42), then, it is efficient in the input oriented BCC model.

Proof: See Jahanshahloo et al (2005).

At last, they (Jahanshahloo et al 2005) proposed a method to rank all efficient DMUs by solving only two problems instead of n linear standard DEA models. Also, Jahanshahloo et al. (2011) introduced a ranking common weight model based on the general MOLP problem (16). They (Jahanshahloo et al 2011) suggested the Zionts-Wallenius' method (Zionts & Wallenius 1976) to solve it. Moreover, they specified a proper set of the preference weights that reflect the relative degree of decision maker's underlying value structure about inputs and outputs. In other words, they produced a preference common weights, then, the efficiency score of

$DMU_j \left(j = 1, \ldots, n\right)$ is obtained as $\dfrac{\displaystyle\sum_{r=1}^{s} u_r^* y_{rj}}{\displaystyle\sum_{i=1}^{m} v_i^* x_{ij}}$. Roll et al. (1991) argued that the

general requirement for the common set of weights models is that at least one DMU must attain efficiency 1. For this reason, they (Jahanshahloo et al 2011) established the following theorem.

Theorem 6: There is a $DMU_o, o \in \{1, \ldots, n\}$ where $\dfrac{\displaystyle\sum_{r=1}^{s} u_r^* y_{ro}}{\displaystyle\sum_{i=1}^{m} v_i^* x_{io}} = 1$.

Proof: See Jahanshahloo et al (2011).

The interactive method incorporates preference structures of the decision maker into the common set of weights model. Therefore, this method (Jahanshahloo et al 2011) has an advantage over the previous common set of weights models. Also, Kao and Hung (2005) presented a true common weights model based on the MOP problem and solved it using the compromise solution method as follows:

$$Min \quad D_0 = \left[\sum_{j=1}^{n} \left(E_j^* - E_j \right) \right]^{p} \bigg/_{p}$$

$$s.t. \quad E_j = \frac{\displaystyle\sum_{r=1}^{s} u_r y_{rj}}{\displaystyle\sum_{i=1}^{m} v_i x_{rj}} \leq 1, \qquad j = 1, ..., n, \tag{44}$$

$$v_i \geq \varepsilon, \qquad i = 1, ..., m,$$

$$u_r \geq \varepsilon, \qquad r = 1, ..., s.$$

In Model (44), the efficiency scores calculated from the CCR model are concerned as the ideal solution for DMUs to achieve. The objective function of Model (44) implies the efficiency vector $E\left(u, v\right) = \left(E_1\left(u, v\right), ..., E_n\left(u, v\right) \right)$ is calculated from the closest to the ideal solution E_j^*, by norm $p = 1, ..., +\infty$. In Model (44), the smallest value of $p = 1$, every deviation $E_j^* - E_j$ is being weighted equally. As p increases, more weights are given to the large deviation, and when $p = +\infty$ the largest deviation completely dominates. Three important drawbacks of this method include; solving $n + 1$ optimization problems, determining the best norm, and obtaining nonlinear programming. Also, an advantage of this model is that no additional prior information is needed. Then, several common set of weights models are presented to improve Kao and Hung's model (2005). Also, Liu and Peng (2008) introduced a common set of weights model to maximize the group's efficiency score. They considered the virtual DMUs $\left(\sum_{i=1}^{m} v_i x_{ij}, \sum_{r=1}^{s} u_r y_{rj} \right), j \in E$ (E is the set of efficient DMUs) and introduced the score unity as a benchmark for these virtual DMUs such as $\dfrac{\displaystyle\sum_{r=1}^{s} u_r y_{rj}}{\displaystyle\sum_{i=1}^{m} v_i x_{ij}} \leq 1, \left(j \in E \right)$. As a geometrical interpretation,

$\left(\sum_{i=1}^{m} v_i x_{ij}, \sum_{r=1}^{s} u_r y_{rj}\right), j \in E$ are points in $\mathbb{R}^2$ and the benchmark is a straight line that passes through the original with gradient one. The presented model by Liu and Peng (2008) for ranking DMUs based on the common set of weights is as follows:

$$Min \quad \sum_{j \in E}\left(\Delta_j^O + \Delta_j^I\right)$$

$$s.t. \quad E_j = \frac{\sum_{r=1}^{s} u_r y_{rj} + \Delta_j^O}{\sum_{i=1}^{m} v_i x_{ij} - \Delta_j^I} = 1, \qquad j \in E,$$

$$\Delta_j^I, \Delta_j^O \geq 0, \qquad j \in E, \qquad (45)$$

$$v_i \geq \varepsilon, \qquad i = 1, \dots, m,$$

$$u_r \geq \varepsilon, \qquad r = 1, \dots, s,$$

where Δ_j^O and Δ_j^I are the distance measures by vertical and horizontal gaps for the benchmark line. After several appropriated changes, the equivalent model is as follows:

$$-\Delta^* = Max \quad \sum_{r=1}^{s} u_r y_r - \sum_{i=1}^{m} v_i x_i$$

$$s.t. \quad \sum_{r=1}^{s} u_r y_{rj} - \sum_{i=1}^{m} v_i x_{ij} \leq 1, \qquad j \in E, \qquad (46)$$

$$v_i \geq \varepsilon, \qquad i = 1, \dots, m,$$

$$u_r \geq \varepsilon, \qquad r = 1, \dots, s,$$

where $x_i = \sum_{j \in E} v_i x_{ij} \, (i = 1, \dots, m)$ and $y_r = \sum_{j \in E} u_r y_{rj} \, (r = 1, \dots, s)$. The optimal solution of Model (46) $\left(v_1^*, \dots, v_m^*, u_1^*, \dots, u_s^*\right)$, is considered as the common weights. For ranking DMUs, Liu and Peng (2008) defined $g_j^* = \sum_{r=1}^{s} u_r^* y_{rj} - \sum_{i=1}^{m} v_i^* x_{ij} \, (j \in E)$, then, presented the following conditions,

1. If $g_j^* > g_i^*$, then, the performance of DMU_j is better than DMU_i.

2. If $g_j^* = g_i^* < 1$ and $\Delta_j^* < \Delta_i^*$, then, the performance of DMU_j is better than DMU_i, where $\Delta^* = \sum_{i=1}^{m} v_i^* x_{ij} - \sum_{r=1}^{s} u_r^* y_{rj}$ is the horizontal gap between virtual DMU_j and the benchmark line.

3. If $g_j^* = g_i^* = 1$ and $\lambda_j^* > \lambda_i^*$, then, the performance of DMU_j is better than of DMU_i, where λ_j^* $(j \in E)$ are the shadow prices of Model (46). Yet, the proposed model has two difficulties; it may have the alternative solutions, more than one DMU may be efficient. Then, these problems were removed by other researchers. Moreover, Davoodi and Zhiani Rezai (2012) used the MOP problem addressed in Roll and Golany (1993), Hosseinzadeh Lotfi et al. (2000), Chiang and Tzeng (2000) and Jahanshahloo et al. (2005) to provide the common set of weights. They used the goal programming method to solve MOP (42). Since the goal of all objective functions in MOP (42) is 1, it is converted to the following model,

$$
\begin{aligned}
Min \quad & \sum_{j=1}^{n} \eta_j \\
s.t. \quad & \frac{\sum_{r=1}^{s} u_r y_{rj} + u_0}{\sum_{i=1}^{m} v_i x_{ij}} + \eta_j = 1, \qquad j = 1,...,n \\
& \frac{\sum_{r=1}^{s} u_r y_{rj} + u_0}{\sum_{i=1}^{m} v_i x_{ij}} \leq 1, \qquad j = 1,...,n \\
& \eta_j \geq 0 \qquad j = 1,...,n, \\
& v_i \geq \varepsilon, \qquad i = 1,...,m, \\
& u_r \geq \varepsilon, \qquad r = 1,...,s.
\end{aligned}
\tag{47}
$$

Unlike previous methods, they converted MOP (42) into the linear problem after some changes. However, the obtained linear programming may have the alternative optimal solutions, therefore, to determine the efficiency of each DMU the following secondary goal DEA model is proposed,

$$Min \quad \mu_0 + \sum_{r=1}^{n} \mu_r - \sum_{i=1}^{m} \omega_i$$

$$s.t. \quad \sum_{j=1}^{n} \sum_{i=1}^{m} \gamma_i^j = z^*,$$

$$\mu_0 + \sum_{r=1}^{s} \mu_r y_{rj} + \sum_{i=1}^{m} \gamma_i^j x_{ij} - \sum_{i=1}^{m} \omega_i x_{ij} = 0, \qquad j = 1,...,n$$

$$\sum_{i=1}^{m} \omega_i = 1, \qquad\qquad\qquad\qquad\qquad\qquad (48)$$

$$\gamma_i^j \geq 0 \qquad i = 1,...,m, j = 1,...,n,$$

$$\omega_i \geq \varepsilon, \qquad i = 1,...,m,$$

$$\mu_r \geq \varepsilon, \qquad r = 1,...,s,$$

where z^* is the optimal value of Model (47). Model (48) is based on the models of Obata et al. (2003) and Liu and Peng (2008) where it minimized the output weights and maximized the input weights, simultaneously. This common set of weights method is calculated by the efficiency scores all DMUs using the optimal solutions of Model (48), then, the complete ranking is obtained by the definition as follows:

1. If $e_k^* = e_p^* < 1$, DMU_k is better than DMU_p if $\gamma^{k*} < 1.\gamma^{p*}$,

2. If $e_k^* = e_p^* = 1$, DMU_k is better than DMU_P if $\lambda_k^* < \lambda_p^*$,

where $k, p \in \{1,...,n\}$, also, e_j^*, γ^{j*} and λ_j^* are the efficiency scores of DMU_j by Model (48), the optimal solution of Model (48) and the shadow price of the j th constraint at the second set of constraints in Model (48), respectively. Indeed, Sun et al. (2013) proposed two approaches to generate a set of common weights by introducing the two virtual DMUs, the ideal DMU and the anti ideal DMU. The first one determines the weights by minimizing the distance of all DMUs from the ideal DMU. The above mentioned model is constructed as follows:

$$Min \quad D_I = \sum_{j=1}^{n} \delta_j$$

$$s.t. \quad \sum_{i=1}^{m} v_i x_{ij} - \delta_j = \sum_{r=1}^{s} u_r y_{rj}, \qquad j = 1, ..., n,$$

$$\sum_{i=1}^{m} v_i x_{\min} = 1,$$

$$\sum_{r=1}^{s} u_r y_{\max} = 1, \tag{49}$$

$$v_i \geq \varepsilon, \qquad i = 1, ..., m,$$

$$u_r \geq \varepsilon, \qquad r = 1, ..., s,$$

$$d_j \geq 0, \qquad j = 1, ..., n,$$

Model (49) makes an attempt to short the distance between the weighted sum of outputs and the weighted sum of inputs for all DMUs. Generally, the optimal solutions of Model (49) are not unique. This problem reduces its usefulness. To solve this problem, the secondary goal formulation based on Euclidean distance is constructed as follows:

$$Max \quad \sum_{i=1}^{m} v_i^2 + \sum_{r=1}^{s} u_r^2$$

$$s.t. \quad \sum_{j=1}^{n} \left(\sum_{i=1}^{m} v_i x_{ij} - \sum_{r=1}^{s} u_r y_{rj} \right) = D_I^*$$

$$\sum_{i=1}^{m} v_i x_{ij} - \sum_{r=1}^{s} u_r y_{rj} \geq 0, \qquad j = 1, ..., n,$$

$$\sum_{i=1}^{m} v_i x_{\min} = 1, \tag{50}$$

$$\sum_{r=1}^{s} u_r y_{\max} = 1,$$

$$v_i \geq \varepsilon, \qquad i = 1, ..., m,$$

$$u_r \geq \varepsilon, \qquad r = 1, ..., s,$$

where D_I^* is the optimal objective value of Model (49). It is very natural that the weights of Model (50) are expected to be as far away from zero weight as possible. Also, they proved the following theorem in order to indicate the advantage of their proposed model.

Theorem 7: Model (50) has a unique solution.

Proof: SeeSun, Wu, and Guo (2013).

The second proposed model by Sun et al. (2013) determines the weights by maximizing the distance of all DMUs from the anti ideal DMU. Note that, two different sets of optimal weights may generate different efficiency for DMUs. As a result, they would have two different ranks. However, they find that two kinds of ranking orders are the same, but they could not prove it. Also, Jafarian-Moghaddam and Ghoseiri (2011) introduced a fuzzy dynamic multi objective DEA model in which data are changed in T periods. Then, the proposed MOLP problem will have $n \times T$ objectives. The constructed MOLP problem is solved by Zimmerman's method (Zimmerman 1991 and 1998), as a result, the final model is nonlinear and using the optimal common weights the efficiency score of all DMUs is obtained in the same time. Then, Wang et al. (2014) extended the model of Jafarian-Moghaddam and Ghoseiri (2011) to the two stage fuzzy dynamic multi objective DEA model. Assume, each DMU_j $\left(j = 1, ..., n\right)$, in the first process with m inputs x_{ij} $\left(i = 1, ..., m\right)$ are consumed to produce intermediate products z_{pj} $\left(p = 1, ..., q\right)$, and then in the second process to generate s outputs y_{ij} $\left(r = 1, ..., s\right)$ consume q intermediate products z_{pj} $\left(p = 1, ..., q\right)$. Then, the following MOP problem is constructed,

$$
Max \quad \left\{ \frac{\sum\limits_{r=1}^{s} u_r y_{r1}}{\sum\limits_{i=1}^{m} v_i x_{i1}}, ..., \frac{\sum\limits_{r=1}^{s} u_r y_{rn}}{\sum\limits_{i=1}^{m} v_i x_{in}} \right\}
$$

$$
s.t. \quad \frac{\sum\limits_{r=1}^{s} u_r y_{rj}}{\sum\limits_{i=1}^{m} v_i x_{ij}} \leq 1, \qquad j = 1, ..., n,
$$

$$
\frac{\sum\limits_{p=1}^{q} \eta_p z_{pj}}{\sum\limits_{i=1}^{m} v_i x_{ij}} \leq 1, \qquad j = 1, ..., n, \tag{51}
$$

$$
\frac{\sum\limits_{r=1}^{s} u_r y_{rj}}{\sum\limits_{p=1}^{q} \eta_p z_{pj}} \leq 1, \qquad j = 1, ..., n,
$$

$$
u_r, \eta_p, v_i \geq \varepsilon, \qquad r = 1, ..., s, \; p = 1, ..., q, \; i = 1, ..., m.
$$

Similarly, they used the Zimmerman's fuzzy method (1978) to solve MOP (51) and consequently it is converted to the nonlinear model. The efficiency score of each $DMU_j \, (j = 1, ..., n)$ is obtained as follows:

$$\theta_j^F = \frac{\sum\limits_{r=1}^{s} u_r^* y_{rj}}{\sum\limits_{i=1}^{m} v_i^* x_{ij}} = \frac{\sum\limits_{p=1}^{q} \eta_p^* z_{pj}}{\sum\limits_{i=1}^{m} v_i^* x_{ij}} \times \frac{\sum\limits_{r=1}^{s} u_r^* y_{rj}}{\sum\limits_{p=1}^{q} \eta_p^* z_{pj}} = \theta_j^{F1} \times \theta_j^{F2}, \qquad j = 1, ..., n, \tag{52}$$

where $\left(u_r^*, \eta_p^*, v_i^* \right), \left(\forall r, p, i \right)$ are the optimal solutions in the above mentioned nonlinear programming. As a result, the fuzzy multi objective two stage DEA model provides a common weight for comparing performance, where it increases the discriminating power and simplifies the calculation process in comparing with the traditional two stage DEA model.

The standard DEA models classify all DMUs into two sets: efficient and inefficient. However, in the evaluation of DMUs using the standard DEA models often more than one DMU may be recognized as efficient. Hence, these models fail to provide more information about the efficient DMUs. Also, in some studies, the main concern is to find a single efficient DMU, called the most efficient DMU, instead of ranking all efficient DMUs. Yet, in the all proposed models for obtaining most efficient DMU there exist no common criteria to specify the best one, similar to problems of ranking models.

Li and Reeves (1999) presented a multiple criteria DEA model without prior information about the weights. The proposed MOLP problem applied three objective functions; therefore, its discrimination power is improved in comparing with the standard DEA models. The multiple criteria DEA model is proposed as follows:

$$Min \quad d_o \left(Max \sum_{r=1}^{s} u_r y_{ro} \right)$$

$$Min \quad M$$

$$Min \quad \sum_{j=1}^{n} d_j$$

$$s.t. \quad \sum_{i=1}^{m} v_i x_{io} = 1,$$

$$\sum_{r=1}^{s} u_r y_{rj} - \sum_{i=1}^{m} v_i x_{ij} + d_j = 0, \qquad j = 1,...,n, \qquad (53)$$

$$M - d_j \geq 0, \qquad j = 1,...,n,$$

$$v_i \geq 0, \qquad i = 1,...,m,$$

$$u_r \geq 0, \qquad r = 1,...,s,$$

$$d_j \geq 0, \qquad j = 1,...,n.$$

MOLP (53) find the non-dominated solutions and helps the selection of a most preferred one. The first objective of Model (53) is similar to the CCR model in multiplier form. The variable M in the second objective represents the maximum quantity among all deviation variables d_j $(j = 1,...,n)$. The third objective function is a straightforward representation of the deviation sum. Decision space of this model is the same as that in the CCR model in multiplier form, because the constraints $M - d_j \geq 0 (j = 1,...,n)$ do not change the decision space of Model (53). However, Li and Reeves's model (1999) fail optimize all objectives, simultaneously. To resolve this problem, Bal et al. (2010) proposed a model by integrating the goal programming method and the CCR model as follows:

$$Min \quad \left\{ d_1^- + d_1^+ + d_2^+ + \sum_{j=1}^{n} d_{3j}^- + \sum_{j=1}^{n} d_j \right\}$$

$$s.t. \quad \sum_{i=1}^{m} v_i x_{io} + d_1^- - d_1^+ = 1,$$

$$\sum_{r=1}^{s} u_r y_{rj} - \sum_{i=1}^{m} v_i x_{ij} + d_j = 0, \qquad j = 1,...,n,$$

$$\sum_{r=1}^{s} u_r y_{ro} + d_2^- - d_2^+ = 1, \qquad\qquad\qquad (54)$$

$$M - d_j + d_{3j}^- - d_{3j}^+ = 0, \qquad j = 1,...,n,$$

$$v_i \geq 0, \qquad i = 1,...,m,$$

$$u_r \geq 0, \qquad r = 1,...,s,$$

$$d_j \geq 0, \qquad j = 1,...,n.$$

$$d_1^-, d_1^+, d_2^-, d_2^+ \geq 0,$$

$$d_{3j}^-, d_{3j}^+ \geq 0, \qquad j = 1,...,n.$$

In Model (54), minimizing the unwanted deviations from the goal values is desired and also all deviations have been given equal weights. However, this model enjoys some drawbacks such as; creating zero weights for variables in some DMUs, not achieving the similar results with Li and Reeves's model, investigating the case of variable returns to scale and creating zero weight for all DMUs. To remove these problems another researcher proposed some DEA models based on Models (53) and (54). Moreover, Karask and Ahiska (2005) proposed an algorithm based on the parametric common set of weights DEA model to obtain the most efficient DMU. The proposed algorithm is:

Step 1: To determine the set of DMUs and select the appropriate outputs and inputs that are to be considered in the evaluation process.

Step 2: To solve the following minimax MCDM model to identify the minimax efficient DMU(s):

$Min \quad M$

$s.t. \quad M \geq d_j, \qquad\qquad\qquad\qquad j = 1, ..., n,$

$$\frac{\sum\limits_{r=1}^{s} u_r y_{rj}}{x_j} + d_j = 1, \qquad\qquad j = 1, ..., n, \qquad\qquad (55)$$

$\qquad\quad u_r \geq \varepsilon, \qquad r = 1, ..., s,$

$\qquad\quad d_j \geq 0, \qquad j = 1, ..., n,$

where M is the maximum deviation from efficiency and $M \geq d_j$ are the constraints that are added to the model to assure that $M = \max d_j, (j = 1, ..., n)$. If there is a single minimax efficient DMU, stop; otherwise, go to step 3.

Step 3: To solve the proposed MCDM Model (56),

$Min \quad M - k \sum\limits_{j \in EF} d_j$

$s.t. \quad M \geq d_j, \qquad\qquad\qquad\qquad j = 1, ..., n,$

$$\frac{\sum\limits_{r=1}^{s} u_r y_{rj}}{x_j} + d_j = 1, \qquad\qquad j = 1, ..., n, \qquad\qquad (56)$$

$\qquad\quad u_r \geq \varepsilon, \qquad r = 1, ..., s,$

$\qquad\quad d_j \geq 0, \qquad j = 1, ..., n,$

where $k \in [0,1]$ is a predetermined step size and EF is the set of DMUs that are obtained as efficient using Model (55). To repeat step 3 until single DMU remains efficient. They claimed that the proposed algorithm is convergent to a single efficient DMU. This method saves much computation comparing with the cross efficiency method. Later, they stated this claim is not always true. Then, in order to determine the most CCR efficient DMU, Amin and Toloo (2007) introduced a common weights DEA model which has less computation than other previous methods in obtaining most efficient DMU as follows:

$Min \quad M$

$s.t. \quad M - d_j \geq 0, \hspace{5cm} j = 1,...,n,$

$$\sum_{i=1}^{m} v_i x_{ij} \leq 1, \hspace{4cm} j = 1,...,n,$$

$$\sum_{r=1}^{s} u_r y_{rj} - \sum_{i=1}^{m} v_i x_{ij} + d_j - \beta_j = 0, \hspace{1.5cm} j = 1,...,n,$$

$$\sum_{j=1}^{n} d_j = n - 1, \hspace{5cm} (57)$$

$0 \leq \beta_j \leq 1, \hspace{1cm} j = 1,...,n,$

$d_j \in \{0,1\}, \hspace{1cm} j = 1,...,n,$

$v_i \geq \varepsilon^*, \hspace{1cm} i = 1,...,m,$

$u_r \geq \varepsilon^*, \hspace{1cm} r = 1,...,s.$

Unlike previous parametric models to obtain most efficient DMU this model has no parameter. However, the proposed model is useful only for constant returns to scale technology. The nonparametric linear programming (57) makes an effort to find a single efficient DMU without solving n linear programming using the standard DEA models. The constraint $\sum_{j=1}^{n} d_j = n - 1, \left(d_j \in \{0,1\}, j = 1,...,n \right)$ implies that among all DMUs only one efficient DMU is obtained. In Model (57), ε^* is the maximum non-Archimedean, which is obtained from the linear programming as follows:

$Max \quad \varepsilon$

$$s.t. \quad \sum_{i=1}^{m} v_i x_{ij} \leq 1, \hspace{4cm} j = 1,...,n,$$

$$\sum_{r=1}^{s} u_r y_{rj} - \sum_{i=1}^{m} v_i x_{ij} \leq 0, \hspace{2cm} j = 1,...,n, \hspace{1cm} (58)$$

$v_i - \varepsilon \geq 0, \hspace{1cm} i = 1,...,m,$

$u_r - \varepsilon \geq 0, \hspace{1cm} r = 1,...,s.$

Theorem 8: Model (57) is feasible.
Proof: See Amin and Toloo (2007).

Considering, two pessimistic and optimistic approaches are considered in Camanho and Dyson for dealing with the cost efficiency in situations of price uncertainty.

Based on this research, Toloo and Ertay (2014) suggested two mixed integer linear programming models to find the most cost efficient DMU with price uncertainty in pessimistic and optimistic situations. They proposed the following integrated optimistic cost efficiency model to determine the most cost efficient candidate(s) with the common set of weights under optimistic point of view as follows:

$$Min \quad \sum_{j=1}^{n} d_j$$

$$s.t. \quad \sum_{i=1}^{m} v_i x_{ij} \leq 1, \qquad\qquad j = 1,...,n,$$

$$\sum_{r=1}^{s} u_r y_{rj} - \sum_{i=1}^{m} v_i x_{ij} + d_j = 0, \qquad j = 1,...,n,$$

$$v_{i^a} p_{i^b}^{\min} - v_{i^b} p_{i^a}^{\max} \leq 0, \qquad 1 \leq i^a < i^b \leq m,$$

$$v_{i^a} p_{i^b}^{\max} - v_{i^b} p_{i^a}^{\min} \geq 0, \qquad 1 \leq i^a < i^b \leq m,$$

$$d_j \geq 0, \qquad j = 1,...,n,$$

$$u_r \geq \varepsilon^*, \qquad r = 1,...,s,$$

(59)

where v_{i^a} is the common weight for input i^a and also $p_{i^a}^{\min}$ and $p_{i^a}^{\max}$ are the minimum and maximum bounds estimated for the price of input i^a (only the maximal and minimal bounds of input and output prices for all DMUs are available).

Definition 6: DMU_o is the optimistic cost efficient with the common set of weights and price uncertainty if and only if $d_o^* = 0$.

In the Model (59), ε^* is obtained from the following LP,

$$Max \quad \varepsilon$$

$$s.t. \quad \sum_{i=1}^{m} v_i x_{ij} \leq 1, \qquad\qquad j = 1,...,n,$$

$$\sum_{r=1}^{s} u_r y_{rj} - \sum_{i=1}^{m} v_i x_{ij} \leq 0, \qquad j = 1,...,n,$$

$$v_{i^a} p_{i^b}^{\min} - v_{i^b} p_{i^a}^{\max} \leq 0 \qquad 1 \leq i^a < i^b \leq m,$$

$$v_{i^a} p_{i^b}^{\max} - v_{i^b} p_{i^a}^{\min} \geq 0 \qquad 1 \leq i^a < i^b \leq m,$$

$$u_r - \varepsilon \geq 0, \qquad r = 1,...,s.$$

(60)

Let $E^{opt} = \left\{ j \middle| d_j^* = 0 \right\}$. If E^{opt} is singleton and $k \in E^{opt}$, Model (59) is determined DMU_o as the most cost efficient DMU in optimistic perspective. Otherwise, the following mixed integer linear programming to the find most cost efficient DMU is proposed,

$$
\begin{aligned}
Min \quad & \sum_{j=1}^{n} d_j \\
s.t. \quad & \sum_{i=1}^{m} v_i x_{ij} \leq 1, & j = 1, \ldots, n, \\
& \sum_{r=1}^{s} u_r y_{rj} - \sum_{i=1}^{m} v_i x_{ij} + d_j = 0, & j = 1, \ldots, n, \\
& v_{i^a} p_{i^b}^{\min} - v_{i^b} p_{i^a}^{\max} \leq 0, & 1 \leq i^a < i^b \leq m, \\
& v_{i^a} p_{i^b}^{\max} - v_{i^b} p_{i^a}^{\min} \geq 0, & 1 \leq i^a < i^b \leq m, \quad\quad (61) \\
& \sum_{j=1}^{n} \theta_j = n - 1, \\
& d_j \leq M\theta_j, & j = 1, \ldots, n, \\
& \theta_j \leq N d_j, & j = 1, \ldots, n, \\
& \theta_j \in \left\{ 0, 1 \right\}, & j = 1, \ldots, n, \\
& u_r \geq \varepsilon^*, & r = 1, \ldots, s,
\end{aligned}
$$

where M and N are large enough positive numbers and ε^* is obtained from Model (60). The constraint $\sum_{j=1}^{n} \theta_j = n - 1$ that imposed only one DMU is most cost efficient. Similarly, to find the least favorable price pessimistic perspective models are constructed by converting the objective function of Models (59) and (61) to the maximization.

Discriminant analysis (DA) is an originally statistical tool which predict group membership of a newly sampled observation. In other words, DA is a decision making method to predict group membership of newly sampled observation. In these regards, several researchers proposed some nonparametric DA approaches that provide a set of weights of linear discriminant functions that specify the situation of new observation. These models are a kind of the common set of weights models. At first, Retzlaff-Roberts (1996) investigated the relationships between two unrelated linear programming techniques, DEA and DA. Also, the concept of the goal programming method is common for both of these methodologies. Therefore, most of the proposed nonparametric DEA-DA models are based on the goal programming method. In DA, the membership all observations $z_j = \left(x_j, y_j \right)$ $j = 1, ..., n$ are specified and each observation have k independent factors $\left(i = 1, ..., k \right)$ to characterize its performance, then, they are classified into two groups (G_1 and G_2) which have n_1 and n_2 members $\left(n = n_1 + n_2 \right)$. A discriminant function estimates weights or parameters by minimizing their group misclassification, then, through using it new observation are classified.

To overcome the problem of the parametric goal programming DA models, Sueyoshi and Kirihara (1998) proposed a type of nonparametric goal programming DA model. Because of the similarity between the additive model and the minimum sum of deviations model (Freed & Glover 1986), Sueyoshi (1999) proposed the two stage method based on the additive model, referred to the DEA-DA method. This method proceeds as follows:

Stage 1: The classification and overlap identification:

Proposed DEA-DA model in stage 1 is formulated as follows:

$$
\begin{aligned}
Min \quad & \sum_{j \in G_1} s_{1j}^+ + \sum_{j \in G_2} s_{2j}^- \\
s.t. \quad & \sum_{i=1}^{k} \alpha_i z_{ij} + s_{1j}^+ - s_{1j}^- = d, & j \in G_1, \\
& \sum_{i=1}^{k} \beta_i z_{ij} + s_{2j}^+ - s_{2j}^- = d - \eta, & j \in G_2, \\
& \sum_{i=1}^{k} \alpha_i = 1, & \quad (62) \\
& \sum_{i=1}^{k} \beta_i = 1, \\
& s_{1j}^+, s_{1j}^- \geq 0, & j \in G_1, \\
& s_{2j}^+, s_{2j}^- \geq 0, & j \in G_2, \\
& \alpha_i, \beta_i \geq 0, & i = 1, ..., k,
\end{aligned}
$$

where α^*, β^* and d^* are optimal solutions of Model (62). This stage classification and overlap identification are as follows:

1. If $\sum_{i=1}^{k} \alpha_i^* z_{im} > d^* \geq \sum_{i=1}^{k} \beta_i^* z_{im}$ or $\sum_{i=1}^{k} \alpha_i^* z_{im} \leq d^* < \sum_{i=1}^{k} \beta_i^* z_{im}$ is identified

    for the newly sampled m th observation (DMU), then, DEA-DA concludes that there is an overlap and the observation belongs to $G_1 \cap G_2$.

2. If $\sum_{i=1}^{k} \alpha_i^* z_{im} \geq d^*$ and $\sum_{i=1}^{k} \beta_i^* z_{im} \geq d^*$ including $\sum_{i=1}^{k} \alpha_i^* z_{im} = \sum_{i=1}^{k} \beta_i^* z_{im} = d^*$

    are identified for the observation, then, DEA-DA concludes that there is no overlap and the observation belongs to G_1.

3. If $\sum_{i=1}^{k} \alpha_i^* z_{im} < d^*$ and $\sum_{i=1}^{k} \beta_i^* z_{im} < d^*$ is identified for the observation, then,

    DEA-DA concludes that there is no overlap and the observation belongs to G_2.

Stage 2: Handling overlap:

If there exist an overlap, to handle it the following linear programming model is utilized,

$$
\begin{aligned}
Min \quad & \sum_{j \in G_1} s_{1j}^+ + \sum_{j \in G_2} s_{2j}^- \\
s.t. \quad & \sum_{i=1}^{k} \alpha_i z_{ij} + s_{1j}^+ - s_{1j}^- = d, && j \in G_1, \\
& \sum_{i=1}^{k} \alpha_i z_{ij} + s_{2j}^+ - s_{2j}^- = d - \eta, && j \in G_2, \\
& \sum_{i=1}^{k} \alpha_i = 1, && \\
& s_{1j}^+, s_{1j}^- \geq 0, && j \in G_1, \\
& s_{2j}^+, s_{2j}^- \geq 0, && j \in G_2, \\
& \alpha_i \geq 0, && i = 1, ..., k,
\end{aligned}
\tag{63}
$$

where α^* is the optimum solution of above models. As a result, we have following cases:

if $\sum_{i=1}^{k} \alpha_i^* z_{im} \geq d^*$, $j \in G_1 \cap G_2$, then $j \in G_1$, or if $\sum_{i=1}^{k} \alpha_i^* z_{im} < d^*$, $j \in G_1 \cap G_2$, then $j \in G_2$.

Unfortunately, the proposed DEA-DA method have three major drawbacks, include; it can not deal with a negative data, produces two separate hyperplanes for discrimination and fails implement any large scale simulation study. In these regards, to overcome some drawbacks of this methods several methods are proposed by the DEA researchers.

Efficient Units and Efficient Hyperplane

One of the approaches to find efficient hyperplanes of PPS in DEA is the implementation of MOP problems. In some cases, researchers modify the proposed algorithms in obtaining efficient faces of MOLP problems into the DEA context for obtaining efficient hyperplanes of the PPS, see Hosseinzadeh Lotfi et al. (2011). Note that, specifying efficient hyperplanes of PPS using MCDM methodology is discussed only in T_V.

To specify all extreme efficient DMUs in T_V, Hosseinzadeh Lotfi et al. (2009) proposed a method based on the following MOLP as:

$$
\begin{aligned}
Max \quad & \left\{ -x_1, \ldots, -x_m, y_1, \ldots, y_s \right\} \\
s.t. \quad & \sum_{i=1}^{n} \lambda_j \bar{x}_{ij} \leq x_i, & j = 1, \ldots, m, \\
& \sum_{j=1}^{n} \lambda_j \bar{y}_{ij} \geq y_r, & r = 1, \ldots, s, \\
& \sum_{j=1}^{n} \lambda_j = 1, \\
& \lambda_j \geq 0, & j = 1, \ldots, n, \\
& x_i, y_r \geq 0, & i = 1, \ldots, m, \ r = 1, \ldots, s,
\end{aligned}
\tag{64}
$$

where $\left(\bar{X}_j, \bar{Y}_j \right)$, $j = 1, \ldots, n$ are input and output vectors. MOLP (64) is obtained based on MOLP (16). The multicriteria simplex method is utilized to solve MOLP (64). Then, they proved the following Theorem 9 to obtain efficient DMUs.

Theorem 9: Each Parato optimal solution of MOLP (64) is corresponding to an efficient production possibility in T_V and vice versa.

Proof: See See Hosseinzadeh et al (2009).

As a result, each efficient simplex table is corresponding to the extreme efficient DMU in T_V. Note that, generation of all extreme efficient DMUs using this method has less computational process than the classical DEA models. Then, they extended their method to generate efficient hyperplanes of T_V. For this reason, they defined the set of weights to solve MOLP (64) drawing on the sum weighted method as follows:

$$W = \left\{ \left(w_1, ..., w_m, w_1', ..., w_s' \right) \middle| \sum_{i=1}^{m} w_i + \sum_{r=1}^{s} w_r' = 1, \ w_i > 0, w_r' > 0 \right\} \tag{65}$$

According to weights of W, MOLP (64) is converted to the following linear model as follows:

$$
\begin{aligned}
Min \quad & \sum_{i=1}^{m} \omega_i x_i - \sum_{r=1}^{s} \omega_r' y_r \\
s.t. \quad & -\sum_{j=1}^{n} \lambda_j \bar{x}_{ij} + x_i \geq 0, && i = 1, ..., m, \\
& \sum_{j=1}^{n} \lambda_j \bar{y}_{rj} - y_r \geq 0, && r = 1, ..., s, \\
& \sum_{j=1}^{n} \lambda_j = 1, \\
& \lambda_j \geq 0, && j = 1, ..., n, \\
& x_i, y_r \geq 0, && i = 1, ..., n, \\
& \left(\omega_i, \omega_r' \right) \in W, && i = 1, ..., m, \ r = 1, ..., s.
\end{aligned}
\tag{66}
$$

They proved the following theorem to show that this method obtains all efficient hyperplanes of T_V.

Theorem 10: Suppose all components of the input and output vectors are positive, then, the weights chosen from W are gradient vectors of the efficient hyperplane in T_V.

Proof: See Hosseinzadeh et al (2009)

Moreover, Zamani and Hosseinzadeh Lotfi (2013) obtained all of efficient points in T_V drawing on parametric programming and the sum weighted method. The constructed parametric program is as follows:

$$Max \quad (1-\alpha)(-X\lambda) + \alpha(Y\lambda)$$
$$s.t. \quad e\lambda = 1, \tag{67}$$
$$\lambda \geq 0,$$

where $\alpha \in (-\infty, +\infty)$. This method got all efficient DMUs by solving a parametric linear programming instead of solving n linear programming. However, solving a parametric linear programming problem requires high calculation. Also, for large amount of n, solving parametric linear programming is better than solving n linear programming. Therefore, the proposed model (67) is used for finding the efficient points in T_V with one input and output.

DISCUSSION AND CONCLUSION

This research classified the usage of MODM techniques in DEA methodology and also reviewed some available papers in this field. Since MODM enjoys the powerful theoretical framework, the implementation of MODM techniques in DEA play key role to propose the robust theatrical models in DEA. Applying the MODM concepts in DEA has begun from the first DEA paper presented by Charnes, Cooper and Rhodes (1978). In other words, DEA was introduced based on the MODM concepts. This research classified DEA methodology based on the MODM techniques into six groups. As mentioned in the previous section, the two phase process model is the first directly usage of the MODM techniques in DEA methodology and comparing conditions between the efficient DMU and the Pareto optimal solution is indirectly usage of the MODM concepts in DEA methodology. Also, the common set of weights models in DEA are the highest usage of the MODM techniques in DEA methodology. In conclusion, authors argue that DEA was introduced based on the MODM concepts and the robust DEA problems have been constructed based on the MODM techniques. The authors propose that the DEA researchers should apply the MODM techniques in DEA problems, as a result, will be obtained robust DEA models.

REFERENCES

Ali, A. I., & Seiford, L. M. (1990). Translation invariance in data envelopment analysis. *Operations Research Letters*, 9(6), 403–405. doi:10.1016/0167-6377(90)90061-9

Amin, G. R., & Toloo, M. (2007). Finding the most efficient DMUs in DEA: An improved integrated model. *Computers & Industrial Engineering, 52*(1), 71–77. doi:10.1016/j.cie.2006.10.003

Bal, H., Orkcu, H. H., & Celebioglu, S. (2010). Improving the discrimination power and weights dispersion in the data envelopment analysis. *Computers & Operations Research, 37*(1), 99–107. doi:10.1016/j.cor.2009.03.028

Banker, R. D., Charnes, A., & Cooper, W. W. (1984). Some models for estimating technical and scale inefficiency in data envelopment analysis. *Management Science, 30*(9), 1078–1092. doi:10.1287/mnsc.30.9.1078

Banker, R. D., & Morey, R. C. (1986). Efficiency analysis for exogenously fixed inputs and outputs. Operations Research Society of America.

Belton, V., & Vickers, S. P. (1993). Demystifyin DEA-A visual interactive approach based on Multiple Criteria Analysis. *The Journal of the Operational Research Society, 44*, 883–896.

Benayoun, R., Montgolfier, J., Tergny, J., & Laritchev, O. (1971). Linear programming with multiple objective functions: Step method (STEM). *Mathematical Programming, 1*(1), 366–375. doi:10.1007/BF01584098

Camanho, A. S., & Dyson, R. (2005). Cost efficiency measurement: DEA application to bank branch assessment. *European Journal of Operational Research, 161*, 432–446. doi:10.1016/j.ejor.2003.07.018

Chambers, R. G., Chung, Y., & Fare, R. (1998). Profit, directional distance functions, and nerlovian efficency. *Journal of Optimization Theory and Applications, 98*(2), 1078–1092. doi:10.1023/A:1022637501082

Charens, A., Cooper, W. W., Wei, Q. L., & Huang, Z. M. (1989). Cone ratio data envelopment analysis and multi objective programming. *International Journal of Systems Science, 20*(7), 1099–1118. doi:10.1080/00207728908910197

Charnes, A., & Cooper, W. W. (1985). Preference to topics in data envelopment analysis. *Annals of Operations Research, 2*(1), 59–94. doi:10.1007/BF01874733

Charnes, A., Cooper, W. W., Golany, B., Seiford, L., & Stutz, J. (1985). Foundation of data envelopment analysis for Pareto-Koopmans efficient empirical production function. *Journal of Econometrics, 30*(1-2), 91–107. doi:10.1016/0304-4076(85)90133-2

Charnes, A., Cooper, W. W., Golany, B., Seiford, L., & Stutz, J. (1985). Foundations of data envelopment analysis for Pareto-Koopmans efficient empirical production functions. *Journal of Econometrics, 30*(1-2), 91–107. doi:10.1016/0304-4076(85)90133-2

Charnes, A., Cooper, W. W., & Rhodes, E. (1978). Measuring the efficiency of decision making unit. *European Journal of Operational Research, 2*(6), 429–444. doi:10.1016/0377-2217(78)90138-8

Charnes, A., Cooper, W. W., & Rhodes, E. (1979). Short Communication Measuring the efficiency of decision making unit. *European Journal of Operational Research, 3*, 339. doi:10.1016/0377-2217(79)90229-7

Chiang, C. I., & Tzeng, G. H. (2000). A new efficiency measure for DEA: Efficiency achievement measure established on fuzzy multiple objectives programming.[in Chinese]. *Journal of Management, 17*, 369–388.

Cooper, W. W. (2005). Origins, Uses of, and Relations Between Goal Programming and Data Envelopment Analysis. *Journal of Multi-Criteria Decision Analysis., 13*(1), 3–11. doi:10.1002/mcda.370

Cooper, W. W., Seiford, L. M., & Tone, K. (2007). *Introduction to Data Envelopment Analysis and Its Uses with DEA-Solver Software and References* (2nd ed.). Springer.

Davoodi, A., & Zhiani Rezai, H. (2012). Common set of weights in data envelopment analysis: A linear programming problem. *Central European Journal of Operations Research, 20*(2), 355–365. doi:10.1007/s10100-011-0195-6

Dimitrov, S., & Sutton, W. (2010). Promoting symmetric weight selection in data envelopment analysis: A penalty function approach. *European Journal of Operational Research, 200*(1), 281–288. doi:10.1016/j.ejor.2008.11.043

Doyle, J., & Green, R. (1994). Efficiency and cross-efficiency in DEA: Derivations, meanings and uses. *The Journal of the Operational Research Society, 45*(5), 567–578. doi:10.1057/jors.1994.84

Dyson, R. G., & Thanassoulis, E. (1998). Reducing weight flexiblity in data envelopment analysis. *J. Opl Res. Q., 41*, 829–835.

Estellita Lins, M. P., Angulo-Meza, L., & Moreila da Silva, A. C. (2004). A multi-objective approach to determine alternative targets in data envelopment analysis. *The Journal of the Operational Research Society, 55*(10), 1090–1101. doi:10.1057/palgrave.jors.2601788

Farrell, M. J. (1957). The measurement of productive efficiency. *Journal of the Royal Statistical Society. Series A (General), 120*(3), 253–281. doi:10.2307/2343100

Freed, N., & Glover, F. (1986). Evaluating alternative linear programming models to solve the two-group discriminant problem. *Decision Sciences, 17*(2), 151–162. doi:10.1111/j.1540-5915.1986.tb00218.x

Geoffrion, A. M., Dyer, J. S., & Feinberg, A. (1972). An interactive approach for multi-criterion optimization with an application to the operation of an academic department. Part I. *Management Science, 19*(4-part-1), 357–368. doi:10.1287/mnsc.19.4.357

Golany, B. (1988). An Interactive MOLP Procedure for the Extension of DEA to Effectiveness Analysis. *The Journal of the Operational Research Society, 39*(8), 725–734. doi:10.1057/jors.1988.127

Halme, M., Joro, T., Korhonen, P., Salo, S., & Wallenius, J. (1999). A value efficiency approach to incorporating performance information in Data Envelopment Analysis. *Management Science, 45*(1), 103–115. doi:10.1287/mnsc.45.1.103

Halme, M., & Korhonen, P. (2000). Restricting weights in value efficiency analysis. *European Journal of Operational Research, 126*(1), 175–188. doi:10.1016/S0377-2217(99)00290-8

Hosseinzadeh Lotfi, F., Jahanshahloo, G. R., Ebrahimnejad, A., Soltanifar, M., & Mansourzadeh, S. M. (2010). Target setting in the general combined-oriented CCR model using an interactive MOLP method. *Journal of Computational and Applied Mathematics, 234*(1), 1–9. doi:10.1016/j.cam.2009.11.045

Hosseinzadeh Lotfi, F., Jahanshahloo, G. R., & Memariani, A. (2000). A Method for Finding Common Set of Weights by Multiple Objective Programming in Data Envelopment Analysis. *Southwest Journal of Pure and Applied Mathematics., 1*, 44–54.

Hosseinzadeh Lotfi, F., Jahanshahloo, G. R., Mozzaffari, M. R., & Gerami, J. (2011). Finding DEA-efficient hyperplanes using MOLP efficient faces. *Journal of Computational and Applied Mathematics, 235*(5), 1227–1231. doi:10.1016/j.cam.2010.08.007

Hosseinzadeh Lotfi, F., Noora, A. A., Jahanshahloo, G. R., Jablonsky, J., Mozaffari, M. R., & Gerami, J. (2009). An MOLP based procedure for finding efficient units in DEA models. *Central European Journal of Operations Research, 17*(1), 1–11. doi:10.1007/s10100-008-0071-1

Hwang, C. L., & Masud, A. S. M. d. (1979). *Multiple objective Decision Making: Methods and Applications*. Springer-Verlag. doi:10.1007/978-3-642-45511-7

Jafarinan-Moghaddam, A. R., & Ghoseiri, K. (2011). Fuzzy dynamic multi-objective Data Envelopment Analysis model. *Expert Systems with Applications, 38*(1), 850–855. doi:10.1016/j.eswa.2010.07.045

Jahanshahloo, G. R., Hosseinzadeh Lotfi, F., Jafari, Y., & Maddahi, R. (2011). Selecting symmetric weights as a secondary goal in DEA cross-efficiency evaluation. *Applied Mathematical Modelling, 35*(1), 544–549. doi:10.1016/j.apm.2010.07.020

Jahanshahloo, G. R., Memariani, A., Hosseinzadeh Lotfi, F., & Rezai, H. Z. (2005). A note on some of DEA models and finding efficiency and complete ranking using common set of weights. *Applied Mathematics and Computation, 166*(2), 265–281. doi:10.1016/j.amc.2004.04.088

Jahanshahloo, G. R., Zohrehbandian, M., Alinezhad, A., Abbasian Naghneh, S., Abbasian, H., & Kiani Mavi, R. (2011). Finding common weights based on the DM's preference information. *The Journal of the Operational Research Society, 62*(10), 1796–1800. doi:10.1057/jors.2010.156

Joro, T., Korhonen, P., & Wallenius, J. (1998). Structural Comparison of Data Envelopment Analysis and Multiple Objective Linear Programming. *Management Science, 44*(7), 962–970. doi:10.1287/mnsc.44.7.962

Kao, C., & Hung, H. T. (2005). Data envelopment analysis with common weights: The compromise solution approach. *The Journal of the Operational Research Society, 56*(10), 1196–1203. doi:10.1057/palgrave.jors.2601924

Karsak, E. E., & Ahishka, S. S. (2005). Practical common weight multi-criteria decision-making approach with an improved discriminating power for technology selection. *International Journal of Production Research, 43*(8), 1437–1554. doi:10.1080/13528160412331326478

Korenbluth, J. S. H. (1991). Analysing policy effectiveness using cone Restricted DEA. *European Journal of Operational Research, 42*, 1097–1104. doi:10.1057/jors.1991.203

Li, X. B., & Reeves, G. R. (1999). A multiple criteria approach to data envelopment analysis. *European Journal of Operational Research, 115*(3), 507–517. doi:10.1016/S0377-2217(98)00130-1

Liang, L., Wu, J., Cook, W. D., & Zhu, J. (2008). Alternative secondary goals in DEA crossefficiency evaluation. *International Journal of Production Economics, 113*(2), 1025–1030. doi:10.1016/j.ijpe.2007.12.006

Liu, F. H. F., & Peng, H. H. (2008). Ranking of units on the DEA frontier with common weight. *Computers & Operations Research, 35*(5), 1624–1637. doi:10.1016/j.cor.2006.09.006

Nykowski, I., & Zolkiewski, Z. (1985). A compromise produce for the multiple objective linear fractional programming problem. *European Journal of Operational Research, 19*(1), 91–97. doi:10.1016/0377-2217(85)90312-1

Obata, T., & Ishii, H. (2003). A method for discriminating efficient candidates with ranked voting data. *European Journal of Operational Research, 151*(1), 233–237. doi:10.1016/S0377-2217(02)00597-0

Pastor, J. T., Ruiz, J. L., & Sirvent, I. (1999). An enhanced DEA Russell graph efficiency measure. *The Journal of the Operational Research Society, 115*(3), 596–607. doi:10.1016/S0377-2217(98)00098-8

Retzlaff-Roberts, D. L. (1996). Relating discriminant analysis and data envelopment analysis to one another. *Computers & Operations Research, 23*(4), 311–322. doi:10.1016/0305-0548(95)00041-0

Roll, Y., Cook, W. D., & Golany, Y. (1991). Controlling factor weights in data envelopment analysis. *IIE, 23*, 1–9.

Roll, Y., & Golany, B. (1993). Alternative methods of treating factor weights in DEA. *Omega, 21*(1), 99–103. doi:10.1016/0305-0483(93)90042-J

Sexton, T. R., Silkman, R. H., & Hogan, R. (1986). Data envelopment analysis: critique and extension. In R. H. Silkman (Ed.), *Measuring Efficiency: An Assessment of Data Envelopment Analysis Jossey-Bass* (pp. 73–105).

Steuer, R.E. (1977). An interactive multiple objective linear programming procedure. *TIMS Studies in Management Science, 6.*

Steuer, R. E., & Choo, E. U. (1983). An interactive weighted Tchebycheff procedure for multiple objective programming. *Mathematical Programming, 26*(3), 326–344. doi:10.1007/BF02591870

Stewart, T. J. (1996). Relationships between Data Envelopment Analysis and Multi Criteria Decision Analysis. *The Journal of the Operational Research Society, 47*(5), 654–665. doi:10.1057/jors.1996.77

Stuere, R. E. (1986). *Multiple criteria optimization: theory, computation, and application.* New York: Wiley.

Sueyoshi, T. (1999). DEA-discriminant analysis in the view of goal programming. *European Journal of Operational Research, 115*(3), 564–582. doi:10.1016/S0377-2217(98)00014-9

Sueyoshi, T., & Kirihara, Y. (1998). Efficiency measurement and strategic classification of Japanese banking institutions. *International Journal of Systems Science, 29*(11), 1249–1263. doi:10.1080/00207729808929613

Sun, J., Wu, J., & Guo, D. (2013). Performance ranking of units considering ideal and anti-ideal DMU with common weights. *Applied Mathematical Modelling, 37*(9), 6301–6310. doi:10.1016/j.apm.2013.01.010

Thanassoulis, E., & Dyson, R. G. (1992). Estimating preferred target input-output levels using data envelopment analysis. *European Journal of Operational Research, 56*(1), 80–97. doi:10.1016/0377-2217(92)90294-J

Toloo, M., & Ertay, T. (2014). The most cost efficient automotive vendor with price uncertainty: A new DEA approach. *Measurement., 52*, 135–144. doi:10.1016/j.measurement.2014.03.002

Wang, W. K., Lu, W. M., & Liu, P. Y. (2014). A fuzzy multi-objective two-stage DEA model for evaluating the performance of US bank holding companies. *Expert Systems with Applications, 41*(9), 4290–4297. doi:10.1016/j.eswa.2014.01.004

Wang, Y. M., & Chin, K. S. (2010). A neutral DEA model for cross-efficiency evaluation and its extension. *Expert Systems with Applications, 37*(5), 3666–3675. doi:10.1016/j.eswa.2009.10.024

Wei, Q. L., & Yu, G. (1993). *Analyzing the properties of K-cone in a generalized Data Envelopment Analysis model. CCS Research Report 700.* The University of Texas at Austin.

Wei, Q. L., Yu, G., & Lu, J. S. (1993). *Necessary and sufficient conditions for return-to-scale properties in generalized Data Envelopment Analysis models. CCS Research Report 708.* The University of Texas at Austin.

Wei, Q. L., Zhang, J., & Zhang, X. (2000). An inverse DEA model for inputs/outputs estimate. *European Journal of Operational Research, 121*(1), 151–163. doi:10.1016/S0377-2217(99)00007-7

Wierzbicki, A. (1980). The use of reference objectives in multiobjective optimization. In G. Fandel & T. Gal (Eds.), *Multiple Objective Decision Making. Theory and Application.* New York: Springer-Verlag. doi:10.1007/978-3-642-48782-8_32

Wong, B. Y. H., Luquec, M., & Yang, J. B. (2009). Using interactive multiobjective methods to solve DEA problems with value judgements. *Computers & Operations Research, 36*(2), 623–636. doi:10.1016/j.cor.2007.10.020

Wu, J., Liang, L., Zha, Y., & Yang, F. (2009). Determination of cross-efficiency under the principle of rank priority in cross evaluation. *Expert Systems with Applications*, *36*(3), 4826–4829. doi:10.1016/j.eswa.2008.05.042

Yang, J. B. (1999). Gradient projection and local region search for multi-objective optimisation. *European Journal of Operational Research*, *112*(2), 432–459. doi:10.1016/S0377-2217(97)00451-7

Yang, J. B., & Li, D. (2002). Normal vector identification and interactive tradeoff analysis using minimax formulation in multi-objective optimization. *IEEE Transactions on Systems, Man, and Cybernetics. Part A, Systems and Humans*, *32*(3), 305–319. doi:10.1109/TSMCA.2002.802806

Yang, J. B., & Sen, P. (1996). Preference modelling by estimating local utility functions for multi-objective optimization. *European Journal of Operational Research*, *95*(1), 115–138. doi:10.1016/0377-2217(96)00300-1

Yang, J. B., Wong, B. Y. H., Xu, D. L., & Stewart, T. J. (2009). Integrating DEA-oriented performance assessment and target setting using interactive MOLP methods. *European Journal of Operational Research*, *195*(1), 205–222. doi:10.1016/j.ejor.2008.01.013

Yu, G., Wei, Q. L., & Brockett, P. (1996). A Generalized Data Envelopment Analysis model: A unification and extension of existing methods for efficiency analysis of decision making units. *Annals of Operations Research*, *66*.

Zamani, P., & Hosseinzadeh Lotfi, F. (2013). Using MOLP based procedures to solve DEA problems.International Journal of Data Envelopment Analysis, 1.

Zhang, X., & Cui, J. (1996). A project evaluation system in the state economic information system of China. Presented at IFORS'96 Conference, Vancouver, Canada.

Zhu, J. (1996). Data envelopment analysis with preference structure. *The Journal of the Operational Research Society*, *47*(1), 136–150. doi:10.1057/jors.1996.12

Zimmerman, H. J. (1991). *Fuzzy set theory and its applications* (2nd ed.). Boston: Kluwer Academic Publishers. doi:10.1007/978-94-015-7949-0

Zimmermann, H. (1978). Fuzzy programming and linear programming with several objective function. *Fuzzy Sets and Systems*, *1*(1), 45–55. doi:10.1016/0165-0114(78)90031-3

Zionts, S., & Wallenius, J. (1976). An interactive programming method for solving the multiple criteria problem. *Management Science*, 22(6), 625–663. doi:10.1287/mnsc.22.6.652

Zohrebandian, M. (2011). Using Ziants-Wallenius method to improve estimate of value efficiency in DEA. *Applied Mathematical Modelling*, *35*(8), 3769–3776. doi:10.1016/j.apm.2011.02.027

Chapter 2
A Survey on Models and Methods for Preference Voting and Aggregation

Ali Ebrahimnejad
Islamic Azad University, Iran

Farhad Hosseinzadeh Lotfi
Islamic Azad University, Iran

ABSTRACT

A key issue in the preferential voting framework is how voters express their preferences on a set of candidates. In the existing voting systems, each voter selects a subset of candidates and ranks them from most to least preferred. The obtained preference score of each candidate is the weighted sum of votes receives in different places. Thus, one of the most important issues for aggregating preferences rankings is the determination of the weights associated with the different ranking places. To avoid the subjectivity in determining the weights, various models based on Data Envelopment Analysis (DEA) have been appeared in the literature to determine the most favorable weights for each candidate. This work presents a survey on models and methods to assess the weights in voting systems. The existing voting systems are divided into two areas. In the first area it is assumed that the votes of all the voters to have equal importance and in the second area voters are classifies into different groups and assumed that each group is assigned a different voting power. In this contribution, some of the most common models and procedures for determining the most favorable weights for each candidate are analyzed.

DOI: 10.4018/978-1-5225-0596-9.ch002

INTRODUCTION

It is often necessary in decision making to rank a group of candidates using a voting system. In a typical ranked voting method, each voter selects a subset of candidates and ranks them from most to least preferred. Among these methods, a popular procedure for obtaining a group consensus ranking is the scoring method where fixed scores are assigned to different places. In this way, the score obtained by each candidate is the weighted sum of the scores he or she receives in different places. The plurality and Borda methods are the most widely used scoring methods. In the plurality method, the selected candidate is the one who obtains the most votes in the first place. In other words, in this method, the first place receives an importance weight of 100% while all other places receive a weight of zero. In Borda's method, the weight assigned to the first place equals to the number of candidates and each subsequent place receives one unit less than its preceding place. Although Borda's method has interesting properties, the utilization of a fixed scoring vector implies that the choice of the winner may depend upon which scoring vector is used (Brams & Fishburn, 2002).

To avoid this problem, Cook et al. (Cook & Kress, 1990) suggested evaluating each candidate with the most favorable scoring vector for him/her. With this purpose, they introduced Data Envelopment Analysis (DEA) in this context. DEA determines the most favorable weights for each candidate. Different candidates utilize different sets of weights to calculate their total scores, which are referred to as the best relative total scores and are all restricted to be less than or equal to one. The candidate with the biggest relative total score of unity is said to be efficient candidate and may be considered as a winner. The principal drawback of this method is very often leads to more than one candidate to be efficient candidate. We can judge that the set of efficient candidates is the top group of candidates, but cannot single out only one winner among them. To avoid this weakness, Cook et al. (Cook & Kress, 1990), proposed to maximize the gap between consecutive weights of the scoring vector. However, Green et al. (Green, Doyle, & Cook, 1996) noticed two important drawbacks of the previous procedure. The first one is that the choice of the intensify functions used in their model is not obvious, and that choice determines the winner. The second one is that for an important class of discrimination intensity functions the previous procedure is equivalent to imposing a common set of scores on all candidates. Therefore, when Cook and Kress's model is used with this class of discrimination intensity functions, the aim pursued by these authors (evaluating each candidate with the most favorable scoring vector for him/her) is not reached.

Due to the drawbacks mentioned above, other procedures to discriminate efficient candidates have appeared in the literature. Green et al. (Green, Doyle, & Cook, 1996) proposed to use the cross evaluation method, introduced by Sexton et al. (Silkman,

1986) to discriminate efficient candidates. Hashimoto (Hashimoto, 1997) used the DEA exclusion method (see Andersen et al. (Andersen & Petersen, 1993) to Cook and Kress's model. Hashimoto's model is useful to discriminate efficient candidates, but it is unstable with respect to inefficient candidates too. Noguchi et al. (Noguchi, 2002) criticized the choice of discrimination intensity functions in Green et al.'s model. In their model, the weight assigned to a certain rank may be zero and, consequently, the votes granted to that rank are not considered. Furthermore, the weights corresponding to two different ranks may be equal and, therefore, the rank votes lose their meaning. To avoid the previous drawbacks, Noguchi et al. (Noguchi, 2002) gave a strong ordering constraint condition on weights. Besides the previous condition on the scoring vectors, Noguchi et al. (Noguchi, 2002) introduced two other modifications in the model of Green et al. (Green, Doyle, & Cook, 1996). On the one hand, in the cross-evaluation matrix each candidate utilizes the same scoring vector to evaluate each of the remaining candidates. However, Noguchi et al.'s model maintains the problems of Green et al.'s model. Obata et al. (Obata & Ishii, 2003) proposed another model that does not use any information about inefficient candidates. To obtain a fair approach, they used weight vectors of the same size, by normalizing the most favorable weight vectors. But it presents other drawbacks. In their model it is necessary to determine the norm and the discrimination intensity functions to use. If these functions are zero and the L1-norm is used, the winning candidate coincides with the one obtained by means of a scoring rule. If L1-norm is replaced by L1-norm, the outcome could be considered unfair by some candidates. Foroghi et al (Foroughi & Tamiz, 2005) and Foroghi et al. (Foroughi & Tamiz, 2005) extended and simplified their model with fewer constraints and also used it for ranking inefficient as well as efficient candidates. Llamazares and Pena (Llamazares, 2009) analyzed the principal ranking methods proposed in the literature to discriminate efficient candidates and by solving several examples showed that none of the previous proposed procedures was fully convincing. Moreover, Llamazares et al. (Llamazares, Aggregating preferences rankings with variable weights, 2013) proposed a model that allows each candidate to be evaluated with the most favorable weighting vector for him/her and avoids the mentioned drawback of all existing procedures. Also, in some cases, they found a closed expression for the score assigned with their model to each candidate.

Wang et al. (Wang & Chin, 2007) discriminated efficient candidates by considering their least relative total scores. But the least relative total scores and the best relative total scores are not measured within the same range. The obtained conclusion was not persuasive. They also proposed a model in which the total scores are measured within an interval. The upper bound of the interval was set to be one, but they failed to determine the value of the lower bound for the interval. After that, Wang et al. (Wang & Liu, 2008) proposed a method to rank multiple efficient candidates, which often happens in DEA method, by comparing the least relative total scores for each efficient candidate with the best and the least relative total scores measured in the same range.

Wang et al. (Wang, Chin, & Yang, 2007) proposed three new models to assess the weights associated with different ranking places in preference voting and aggregation. Two of them are linear programming models which determine a common set of weights for all the candidates considered and the other is a non-linear programming model that determines the most favorable weights for each candidate. Hadi-Vencheh et al. (Hadi-Vencheh & Mokhtarian) presented three counter examples to show that the three new models developed by Wang et al. (Wang, Chin, & Yang, 2007) for preference voting and aggregation may produce a zero weight for the last ranking place and may sometimes identify two candidates as the winner in some specific situations. After that, Wang et al. (Wang, Chin, & Yang, Improved linear programming models for preference voting and aggregation: Reply to Hadi-Vencheh and Mokhtarian, 2009) presented two modified linear programming models for preference voting and aggregation to avoid the zero weight for the last ranking place. In addition, Hadi-Vencheh (Hadi-Vencheh, 2014) proposed two improved DEA models to determine the weights of ranking places that each of them can lead to a stable full ranking for all the candidates considered and avoid the mentioned shortcoming. Wu et al. (Wu, Liang, & Zha, 105-111) considered a preferential voting system using DEA game cross efficiency model, in which each candidate is viewed as a player that seeks to maximize its own efficiency, under the condition that the cross efficiencies of each of other DMU's does not deteriorate. Jahanshaloo et al. (Jahanshahloo, Hosseinzadeh Lotfi, Khanmohammadi, & Kazemimanesh, 2012) reviewed ranked voting data and its analysis with DEA and proposed a model based on the ranking of units using common weights. Their model gives one common set of weights that is the most favorable for determining the absolute efficiency of all candidates at the same time. In addition, other models have appeared in the literature in order to deal with this kind of problems (Ebrahimnejad, 2012) (Foroughi & Aouni, 2012) (Soltanifar, Ebrahimnejad, & Farrokhi, 2010).

It is worth noting that, all previous models are based on Cook and Kress's model in which the votes of all voters have equal importance and there is no preference among them. To overcome this problem, Ebrahimnejad (Ebrahimnejad, 2015) a new voting system that assumed voters are classified into several categories in which the vote of voters in a higher category is more important than the ones in a lower category. Then, he generalized an existing ranking method to rank multiple efficient candidates based on comparing the least preference scores for each efficient candidate with the best and the least preference scores measured in the same range. After that Ebrahimnejad et al. (Ebrahimnejad & Bagherzadeh, 2016) introduced two models to measure the best preference scores of the target candidate from the virtual best candidate and the virtual worst candidate point of view. After that, they aggregated two obtained preference scores together in order to obtain an overall ranking. In addition, Ebrahimnejad et al. (Ebrahimnejad & Santos-Arteaga, 2016) have used simulation to analyze the rankings and synthesize existing ranking methods into one overall group ranking of the candidates.

The purpose of this chapter is to shortly describe models and methods following the above voting systems, in order to provide the reader a clear view of the main results produced along the last 25 years on this key research area.

PRELIMINARIES

In this section, DEA based models in order to determine the most favorable weights of candidates in voting systems are reviewed (Ebrahimnejad & Bagherzadeh, 2016).

Ranked Voting Systems with Equal Voting Power to Voters

In this section, we consider a ranked voting problem where each voter selects a subset of k candidates from a set of $m(m \geq k)$ candidates $\left\{A_1, A_2, \ldots, A_m\right\}$ and ranks them from the top to the place k, and each place is associated with a relative important weight $w_i^r (i = 1, 2, \ldots, k)$. Let v_i^r be the number of votes for candidate r being ranked in the place i. The total score of each candidate in ranked voting systems with equal voting power to voters is defined as follows:

$$z_r = \sum_{i=1}^{k} w_i^r v_i^r, \ r = 1, 2, \ldots, m \tag{1}$$

This is a linear function of the relative importance weights. Once the weights are determined, each candidate can be ranked in terms of its total score. To avoid subjectivity in obtaining the relative importance weights, Cook et al. (Cook & Kress, 1990) have suggested the following DEA/AR which determines the most appropriate weights for candidate p :

$$z_p^* = \max \; z_p = \sum_{i=1}^{k} w_i^p v_i^p$$

s.t.

$$\sum_{i=1}^{k} w_i^p v_{\,i}^r \leq 1, \qquad\qquad r = 1, 2, \ldots, m, \tag{2}$$

$$w_i^p - w_{i+1}^p \geq d\left(i, \varepsilon\right), \quad i = 1, 2, \ldots, k - 1,$$

$$w_k^p \geq d\left(k, \varepsilon\right).$$

where $d\left(., \varepsilon\right)$ is called the discrimination intensify function that is non-negative and monotonically increasing in a non-negative ε and satisfies $d\left(., 0\right) = 0$.

Cook et al. (Cook & Kress, 1990) showed that the choice of the discrimination intensify function form has a significant impact on the winner. Also, Noguchi et al. (Llamazares & Pena, 2013) showed that the choice of the winner depends upon the value of ε. To overcome these difficulties, Noguchi et al. (Noguchi, 2002) used the following strong ordering DEA model:

$$z_p^* = \max \; z_p = \sum_{i=1}^{k} w_i^p v_i^p$$

s.t.

$$\sum_{i=1}^{k} w_i^p v_{\,i}^r \leq 1, \qquad\qquad r = 1, 2, \ldots, m, \tag{3}$$

$$w_1^p \geq 2 w_2^p \geq \ldots \geq k w_k^p,$$

$$w_k^p \geq \varepsilon = 2 \, / \, Nk\left(k + 1\right).$$

where *N* is the number of voters.

Remark 1: As argued by Hashimoto (Hashimoto, 1997), in ranked voting system each candidate is regarded as a decision making unit (DMU) in DEA and each DMU is considered to have m outputs (ranked votes) and only one input with amount unity, i.e. the pure output DEA model. This means that problems (2) and (3) are equivalent to the well-known DEA/AR model in which the first constraints are the usual DEA constraints (no candidate should have a preference score or an efficiency score greater than 1) and the remaining constraints represent the assurance region (AR).

Ranked Voting Systems with Different Voting Power to Voters

In a ranked voting system with different voting power to voters, it is assumed that voters are classified into t distinct groups. The voters in each group select k candidates among $m(m \geq k)$ candidates $\{A_1, A_2, ..., A_m\}$ and rank them from the top to the place k, each place is associated with a relative importance weight $w_i^r \left(i = 1, 2, ..., k\right)$ and each group is associated with a relative importance weight $u_j^r (j = 1, 2, ..., t)$. Let v_{ij}^r be the number of votes for candidate r being ranked in the place i from the group j. The preference score of candidate r in the place i is equal to $\sum_{j=1}^{t} u_j^r v_{ij}^r$. Thus, the total score for each candidate in ranked voting systems with different voting power to voters is determined as follows (Ebrahimnejad A, 2015):

$$z_r = \sum_{i=1}^{k} \left(w_i^r \sum_{j=1}^{t} u_j^r v_{ij}^r \right) = \sum_{i=1}^{k} \sum_{j=1}^{t} w_i^r u_j^r v_{ij}^r \ , r = 1, 2, ..., m \tag{4}$$

However to obtain a total ranking of candidates, similar to assurance region of model (2), it is required the weight vectors satisfy the following conditions:

$$\begin{aligned} u_j^r - u_{j+1}^r &\geq \bar{d}\left(j, \varepsilon\right), \quad j = 1, 2, ..., t - 1, \\ u_t^r &\geq \bar{d}\left(t, \varepsilon\right). \end{aligned} \tag{5}$$

$$\begin{aligned} w_i^r - w_{i+1}^r &\geq \bar{\bar{d}}\left(i, \varepsilon\right), \quad i = 1, 2, ..., k - 1, \\ w_k^r &\geq \bar{\bar{d}}\left(k, \varepsilon\right). \end{aligned} \tag{6}$$

In a similar way, similar to assurance region of model (3), it is required the weight vectors satisfy the following conditions:

$$u_1^r \geq 2u_2^r \geq ... \geq tu_t^r, \ u_t^r \geq \varepsilon_1'. \tag{7}$$

$$w_1^r \geq 2w_2^r \geq ... \geq kw_k^r, \ w_k^r \geq \varepsilon_2'. \tag{8}$$

Remark 2: The constraints (5) and (7) ensure that the vote of voters in a higher category has a greater importance than that in a lower category. In addition, the constraints (6) and (8) show that the vote of the higher place may has a greater importance than that of the lower place.

The following nonlinear model evaluates candidate p with the most favorable weight vectors according to the assurance region constraints given in (5) and (6):

$$z_p^* = \max \ z_p = \sum_{i=1}^{k}\sum_{j=1}^{t} w_i^p u_j^p v_{ij}^p$$

$s.t.$

$$
\begin{aligned}
&\sum_{i=1}^{k}\sum_{j=1}^{t} w_i^p u_j^p v_{ij}^r \leq 1, && r = 1,2,\dots,m, \\
&u_j^p - u_{j+1}^p \geq \overline{d}\left(j,\varepsilon\right), && j = 1,2,\dots,t-1, \\
&u_t^p \geq \overline{d}\left(t,\varepsilon\right), \\
&w_i^p - w_{i+1}^p \geq \overline{\overline{d}}\left(i,\varepsilon\right), && i = 1,2,\dots,k-1, \\
&w_k^p \geq \overline{\overline{d}}\left(k,\varepsilon\right).
\end{aligned}
\tag{9}
$$

Ebrahimnejad et al (Ebrahimnejad & Bagherzadeh, 2016) proved that the nonlinear model (9) can be transformed into the following linear model by assuming $m_{ij}^p = w_i^p u_j^p$:

$$z_p^* = \max \ z_p = \sum_{i=1}^{k}\sum_{j=1}^{t} m_{ij}^p v_{ij}^p$$

$s.t.$

$$
\begin{aligned}
&\sum_{i=1}^{k}\sum_{j=1}^{t} m_{ij}^p v_{ij}^r \leq 1, && r = 1,2,\dots,m, \\
&m_{ij}^p - m_{i,j+1}^p \geq \overline{d}\left(j,\varepsilon\right), && j = 1,2,\dots,t-1, \ i = 1,2,\dots,k, \\
&m_{it}^p \geq d\left(t,\varepsilon\right), && i = 1,2,\dots,k, \\
&m_{ij}^p - m_{i+1,j}^p \geq \overline{\overline{d}}\left(i,\varepsilon\right), && i = 1,2,\dots,k-1, j = 1,2,\dots,t, \\
&m_{kj}^p \geq \overline{\overline{d}}\left(k,\varepsilon\right), j = 1,2,\dots,t.
\end{aligned}
\tag{10}
$$

A similar procedure adopted for the assurance region constraints given in (7) and (8) results in the following model that evaluates candidate p with the most favorable weight vectors (Ebrahimnejad, Tavana, & Santos-Arteaga, 2016):

$$z_p^* = \max \ z_p = \sum_{i=1}^{k} \sum_{j=1}^{t} m_{ij}^p v_{ij}^p$$

s.t.

$$\sum_{i=1}^{k} \sum_{j=1}^{t} m_{ij}^p v_{ij}^r \leq 1, \qquad\qquad r = 1, 2, \ldots, m, \qquad\qquad (11)$$

$$m_{i1}^p \geq 2 m_{i2}^p \geq \ldots \geq t m_{it}^p, \quad m_{it}^p \geq \varepsilon, i = 1, 2, \ldots, k,$$

$$m_{1j}^p \geq 2 m_{2j}^p \geq \ldots \geq k m_{kj}^p, \ m_{kj}^p \geq \varepsilon, j = 1, 2, \ldots, t.$$

In this model, as argued by Ebrahimnejad et al. (Ebrahimnejad, Tavana, & Santos-Arteaga, 2016), the value of ε can be chosen as follows, in a similar way to Noguchi's model given in (3):

$$\varepsilon = \min \left\{ 2 / Nt(t+1), 2 / Nk(k+1) \right\}$$

Remark 3: It is worth noting that in models (10) and (11), m_{ij}^p can be regarded as the relative importance weight of candidate p being ranked in the place i by group j.

It should be noted that models (2), (3), (10) and (11) are solved for each candidate p, $p = 1, 2, \ldots, k$ and the resulting score z_p^* represents the preference score of the candidate in the corresponding model. The candidates with the biggest preference score ($z_p^* = 1$) are called efficient candidates.

DISCRIMINATING EFFICIENT CANDIDATES

It is worth noting that the use of procedures discussed in the previous section often cause several candidates to be efficient, i.e., they achieve the maximum preference score. For this reason, several methods to discriminate among efficient candidates have been proposed in the literature. In this section, we review some well-known ranking methods to discriminate the efficient candidate.

Ranking the Candidates of Model (2)

Cook et al. (Cook & Kress, 1990) proposed the following model for discriminating efficient candidates by maximizing the gap between consecutive weights of the scoring vector:

$$\varepsilon^{*}_{\max} = \max \; \varepsilon$$

$s.t.$

$$\sum_{i=1}^{k} w_i^p v_i^r \le 1, \qquad\qquad r = 1, 2, \ldots, m, \tag{12}$$

$$w_i^p - w_{i+1}^p \ge d\left(i,\varepsilon\right), \quad i = 1, 2, \ldots, k-1,$$

$$w_k^p \ge d\left(k,\varepsilon\right).$$

Cook et al. (Cook & Kress, 1990) proved that at optimality, there exists at least one candidate p such that $\sum_{i=1}^{k} w_i^p v_i^p = 1$. All of such candidates are the wining candidates. The candidates in second place can be found by resolving model (12) after deleting the constraint(s) corresponding to candidates in the first place. This process can be repeated until the order of all candidates is fixed.

The main drawback of the ranking method by Cook et al. (Cook & Kress, 1990) is the choice of discrimination intensity functions that determine the winner. To avoid of this problem, Green et al. (R.H, Doyle, & Cook, 1996) consider $d\left(i,\varepsilon\right) = 0$ for all $i = 1, 2, \ldots, k$. Moreover, they applied the cross-evaluation method, introduced by Sexton et al. (Sexton, Silkman, & Hogan), to discriminate efficient candidates.

Hashimoto (Hashimoto, 1997) applied the DEA exclusion method introduced by Andersen et al. (Andersen & Petersen, 1993) to Cook and Kress's model given in (2). The proposed model based on this procedure is given as follows:

$$z_{p}^{*} = \max \; z_{p} = \sum_{i=1}^{k} w_i^p v_i^p$$

$s.t.$

$$\sum_{i=1}^{k} w_i^p v_i^r \le 1, \qquad\qquad r = 1, 2, \ldots, m, r \ne p \tag{13}$$

$$w_i^p - w_{i+1}^p \ge \varepsilon, \qquad\qquad i = 1, 2, \ldots, k-1,$$

$$w_i^p - 2w_{i+1}^p + w_{i+2}^p \ge \varepsilon, \quad i = 1, 2, \ldots, k-2.$$

The last $k-2$ constraints of model (13) assure the convex sequence of weights. Also, it can be seen that according to this procedure $d\left(i,\varepsilon\right) = \varepsilon$ for all $i = 1, 2, \ldots, k$.

Obata and Ishii (Obata & Ishii, 2003) demonstrated based on the existing ranking methods the order of efficient candidates may be changed by existence of an inefficient candidate. So they proposed a new method that does not use information about inefficient candidates to discriminate efficient candidates. Their proposed model that normalizes the most favorable weight vectors of the same size is as follows:

$$z_p^* = \max \frac{1}{\|w^p\|}$$

s.t.

$$\sum_{i=1}^{k} w_i^p v_i^p = 1, \tag{14}$$

$$\sum_{i=1}^{k} w_i^p v_i^r \leq 1, \qquad r = 1, 2, \ldots, m, r \neq p$$

$$w_i^p - w_{i+1}^p \geq d(i, \varepsilon), \qquad i = 1, 2, \ldots, k-1,$$

$$w_k^p \geq d(k, \varepsilon).$$

Llamazares et al. (Llamazares B., 2013) proved that if $d(i, \varepsilon) = 0$ for all $i = 1, 2, \ldots, k$ and $L_1 -$ norm or $L_\infty -$ norm are used in model (14), then the winner could be obtained without solving any model.

Foroughi et al. (Foroughi & Tamiz, 2005) demonstrated that solving (14) is not necessary for many candidates, and also many of the constraints in the model are redundant, so the number of problems to be solved as well as the number of constraints can be decreased. They set $\overline{w}_i^p = w_i^p - w_{i+1}^p, i = 1, 2, \ldots, k-1$ and $\overline{w}_k^p = w_k^p$ or equivalently $\overline{w}^p = Aw^p$, in which A is a $k \times k$ matrix with $a_{ii} = 1, a_{i,i+1} = -1$ for all j, and zeros elsewhere. Now, by assuming $d(i, \varepsilon) = \varepsilon$ for all $i = 1, 2, \ldots, k$, they transformed model (14) into the following equivalent model:

$$z_p^* = \max \frac{1}{\|A^{-1}\overline{w}^p\|}$$

s.t.

$$\sum_{i=1}^{k} w_i^p v_i^p = 1, \tag{15}$$

$$\sum_{i=1}^{k} w_i^p v_i^r \leq 1, \qquad r = 1, 2, \ldots, m, r \neq p$$

$$\overline{w}_i^p \geq \varepsilon, \qquad i = 1, 2, \ldots, k.$$

Foroughi et al. (Foroughi & Tamiz,, 2005) proved that model (15) is infeasible for each inefficient candidate and also all constraints corresponding to inefficient candidates are redundant in the model. Hence, they reduced the number of constraints as well as the number of problems to be solved by determining inefficient candidates before solving the model using some interesting tests and without solving any model. In fact, they reformulated model (15) as follows in which E is the index set of all efficient candidates and $p \in E$:

$$z_p^* = \max \frac{1}{\left\| A^{-1} \overline{w}^p \right\|}$$

$s.t.$

$$\sum_{i=1}^{k} w_i^p v_i^p = 1, \qquad\qquad\qquad (16)$$

$$\sum_{i=1}^{k} w_i^p v_i^r \leq 1, \qquad r \in E, r \neq p$$

$$\overline{w}_i^p \geq \varepsilon, \qquad\qquad i = 1, 2, \ldots, k.$$

A similar approach has been adopted by Foroughi et al. (Foroughi & Tamiz, 2005) for ranking inefficient as well as efficient candidates.

Llamazares et al. (Llamazares B. a, 2009) analyzed the principal ranking methods proposed in the literature to discriminate efficient candidates and by solving several examples showed that none of the previous proposed procedures was fully convincing. In fact, although all the previous methods do not require predetermine the weights subjectively, some of them have a serious drawback: the relative order between two candidates may be altered when the number of first, second,..., kth ranks obtained by other candidates changes, although there is not any variation in the number of first, second, ..., kth ranks obtained by both candidates. Thus, Llamazares et al. (Llamazares & Pena, 2013) proposed a model that allows each candidate to be evaluated with the most favorable weighting vector for him/her and avoids the mentioned drawback. Moreover, in some cases, they found a closed expression for the score assigned with their model to each candidate.

Ranking the Candidates of Model (3)

In this section, the ranking methods in order to choose a winner from among the efficient candidates of model (3) are analyzed.

It is worth noting that the model (3) computed the best relative preference score of each candidate. This score represents the score each candidate receives in the most favorable situation. Wang and Chin (Wang & Chin, Discriminating DEA efficient candidates by considering their least relative total scores, 2007) proposed a new method that discriminates the efficient candidates of model (3) by considering their least relative preference score. They proposed the following model to compute the least preference score of each efficient candidate of model (3):

$$\bar{z}_p^* = \min \ \bar{z}_p = \sum_{i=1}^{k} w_i^p v_i^p$$

s.t.

$$\sum_{i=1}^{k} w_i^p v_i^r \geq 1, \qquad r = 1, 2, \ldots, m, \qquad (17)$$

$$w_1^p \geq 2 w_2^p \geq \ldots \geq k w_k^p,$$

$$w_k^p \geq \varepsilon.$$

In this case the efficient candidate of model (3) with the largest least relative preference score is chosen as the winner.

The principal drawback of the ranking method proposed by Wang et al. (Wang, 2007) is that the least relative total scores and the best relative total scores are not measured within the same range and so the obtained conclusion is not persuasive. To avoid this weakness, Wang et al. (Wang & Chin, 2007) defined a concept of virtual worst candidate (VWC). VWC is a candidate which does not exist in the voting. But he/she receives the least votes in each place among all m candidates. The vote for VWC is denoted by $v^{\min} = (v_1^{\min}, v_2^{\min}, \ldots, v_m^{\min})$ in which the vote of each place is determined as $v_r^{\min} = \min_{i} \{v_i^r\}$. In this case, the best preference score of VWC is determined by solving the following model:

$$\alpha^* = \max \ \alpha = \sum_{i=1}^{k} w_i^{\min} v_i^{\min}$$

s.t.

$$\sum_{i=1}^{k} w_i^{\min} v_i^r \leq 1, \qquad r = 1, 2, \ldots, m, \qquad (18)$$

$$w_1^{\min} \geq 2 w_2^{\min} \geq \ldots \geq k w_k^{\min},$$

$$w_k^{\min} \geq \varepsilon.$$

In this case, Wang et al. (Wang & Liu, 2008) proposed two following model to evaluate the best and least preference scores of each candidate, respectively:

$$\max \quad z_p^{\max} = \sum_{i=1}^{k} w_i^p v_i^p$$

s.t.

$$\alpha^* \leq \sum_{i=1}^{k} w_i^p v_i^r \leq 1, \qquad r = 1, 2, \ldots, m, \qquad (19)$$

$$w_1^p \geq 2 w_2^p \geq \ldots \geq k w_k^p,$$

$$w_k^p \geq \varepsilon.$$

$$\min \quad z_p^{\min} = \sum_{i=1}^{k} w_i^p v_i^p$$

s.t.

$$\alpha^* \leq \sum_{i=1}^{k} w_i^p v_i^r \leq 1, \qquad r = 1, 2, \ldots, m, \qquad (20)$$

$$w_1^p \geq 2 w_2^p \geq \ldots \geq k w_k^p,$$

$$w_k^p \geq \varepsilon.$$

It should be note that each candidate can obtain an interval total score, whose upper bound is the optimal value of model (19) and the lower bound is that of model (20). According to the comparison rule of interval numbers, if two positive interval numbers have the same upper bound, then the one with bigger lower bound is more preferred to the other one.

Wang et al. (Wang, Chin, & Yang, 2007) proposed three models to determine the weights of ranking place that not only choose a winner, but also give a full ranking of all the candidates. The first model proposed by Wang et al. (Wang, Chin, & Yang, 2007) is given as follows:

$$\max \alpha$$

s.t.

$$z_r = \sum_{i=1}^{k} w_i v_i^r \geq 1, \qquad r = 1, 2, \ldots, m, \qquad (21)$$

$$w_1 \geq 2 w_2 \geq \ldots \geq k w_k \geq 0,$$

$$\sum_{i=1}^{k} w_i = 1.$$

Their second model is given as follows:

$\max \alpha$

s.t.

$$\alpha \leq z_r = \sum_{i=1}^{k} w_i v_i^r \leq 1, \qquad r = 1, 2, \ldots, m, \qquad (22)$$

$$w_1 \geq 2 w_2 \geq \ldots \geq k w_k \geq 0.$$

Finally, the third model is formulated as follows:

$$\max \ z_r = \sum_{i=1}^{k} w_i v_i^r$$

s.t.

$$w_1 \geq 2 w_2 \geq \ldots \geq k w_k \geq 0, \qquad (23)$$

$$\sum_{i=1}^{k} w_i^2 = 1.$$

It should be note that models (21)-(23) determine a common set of weights for all the candidates. Once the weights are determined, the preference score of each candidate can be computed by equation (2) and the winner can be selected.

After that Hadi-Vencheh et al. (Hadi-Vencheh & Mokhtarian, 2009) by the help of some counterexamples demonstrated the weight of the last ranking place is zero in models (21)-(23), which means that the vote of such place does not have any meaning. Therefore, these models are not appropriate or applicable. However, Wang et al. (Wang, Chin, & Yang, 2009) presented two modified linear programming models for preference voting and aggregation to avoid the zero weight for the last ranking place. In fact they replaced the objective function of models (21) and (22) with $\alpha - (w_1 - w_m)$ which maximizes α and minimizes the gap between the maximum weight w_1 and the minimum weight w_m at the same time.

It can be seen that from the constraints of model (21), Wang et al. (Wang, Chin, & Yang, 2007) consider $\varepsilon = 0$ causing to produce the zero weight for some ranking places. To avoid producing a zero weight for a certain place vote and make full use of all the data, Hadi-Vencheh (Hadi-Vencheh, 2014) modified the model (22) as follows:

$$\max \ \alpha$$

$$s.t.$$

$$\alpha \le z_r = \sum_{i=1}^{k} w_i v_i^r \le 1, \qquad r = 1, 2, \ldots, m, \qquad (24)$$

$$w_1 \ge 2w_2 \ge \ldots \ge kw_k,$$

$$w_k \ge \varepsilon.$$

As a theoretical construct, ε provides a lower bound for scoring of grades to keep them away from zero. Hence, he proposed the following LP to determine the value of ε :

$$\varepsilon^* = \max \ \varepsilon$$

$$s.t.$$

$$\sum_{i=1}^{k} w_i v_i^r \le 1, \qquad r = 1, 2, \ldots, m, \qquad (25)$$

$$w_1 \ge 2w_2 \ge \ldots \ge kw_k,$$

$$w_k - \varepsilon \ge 0.$$

According to this procedure, the optimal value of model (25), ε^*, is employed to solve model (24). Once the optimal weights of model (24) are determined, the preference score of each candidate can be computed by equation (2) and the winner can be selected.

Ranking the Candidates of Model (10)

Ebrahimnejad et al. (Ebrahimnejad & Bagherzadeh, 2016) proposed a procedure based on TOPSIS idea and the concepts of virtual best candidate (VBC) and virtual worst candidate (VWC) in order to discriminate the efficient candidates of model (10). In this section, their proposed approach is summarized.

Definition 1: The virtual best candidate (VBC) is a virtual candidate that receives the most votes in each place among all candidates.

According to this definition, we denote by $V_i^{\max} = (v_{i1}^{\max}, v_{i2}^{\max}, \ldots, v_{it}^{\max})$ the number votes of VBC in place i, in which the votes of each category in this place are determined by $v_{ij}^{\max} = \max_r \left\{ v_{ij}^r \right\}$.

Definition 2: The virtual worst candidate (VWC) is a virtual candidate that receives the least votes in each place among all candidates.

According to this definition, we denote by $V_i^{\min} = (v_{i1}^{\min}, v_{i2}^{\min}, \ldots, v_{it}^{\min})$ the number votes of VBC in place i, in which the votes of each category in this place are determined by $v_{ij}^{\min} = \min_r \{v_{ij}^r\}$.

The best preference score of VBC denoted as ϕ_{VBC}^* is determined by the following model (Ebrahimnejad & Bagherzadeh, 2016):

$$\phi_{VBC}^* = \max \ \phi_{VBC} = \sum_{i=1}^{k} \sum_{j=1}^{t} m_{ij}^{VBC} v_{ij}^{VBC}$$

s.t.

$$
\begin{aligned}
&\sum_{i=1}^{k} \sum_{j=1}^{t} m_{ij}^{VBC} v_{ij}^r \leq 1, && r = 1, 2, \ldots, m, \\
&m_{ij}^{VBC} - m_{i,j+1}^{VBC} \geq \bar{d}\left(j, \varepsilon\right), && j = 1, 2, \ldots, t-1, \ i = 1, 2, \ldots, k, \\
&m_{it}^{VBC} \geq d\left(t, \varepsilon\right), && i = 1, 2, \ldots, k, \\
&m_{ij}^{VBC} - m_{i+1,j}^{VBC} \geq \bar{\bar{d}}\left(i, \varepsilon\right), && i = 1, 2, \ldots, k-1, j = 1, 2, \ldots, t, \\
&m_{kj}^{VBC} \geq \bar{\bar{d}}\left(k, \varepsilon\right), j = 1, 2, \ldots, t.
\end{aligned}
\tag{26}
$$

Now, the best preference score of candidate p under the condition that the best possible preference score of the VBC remains unchanged is determined by use of the following model:

$$\phi_p^* = \max \ \phi_p = \sum_{i=1}^{k} \sum_{j=1}^{t} m_{ij}^{VBC} v_{ij}^{VBC}$$

s.t. $\displaystyle\sum_{i=1}^{k} \sum_{j=1}^{t} m_{ij}^{VBC} v_{ij}^{VBC} = \phi_{VBC}^*$

$$
\begin{aligned}
&\sum_{i=1}^{k} \sum_{j=1}^{t} m_{ij}^p v_{ij}^r \leq 1, && r = 1, 2, \ldots, m, \\
&m_{ij}^p - m_{i,j+1}^p \geq \bar{d}\left(j, \varepsilon\right), && j = 1, 2, \ldots, t-1, \ i = 1, 2, \ldots, k, \\
&m_{it}^p \geq d\left(t, \varepsilon\right), && i = 1, 2, \ldots, k, \\
&m_{ij}^p - m_{i+1,j}^p \geq \bar{\bar{d}}\left(i, \varepsilon\right), && i = 1, 2, \ldots, k-1, j = 1, 2, \ldots, t, \\
&m_{kj}^p \geq \bar{\bar{d}}\left(k, \varepsilon\right), j = 1, 2, \ldots, t.
\end{aligned}
\tag{26}
$$

In a similar way, the worst preference score of VWC denoted as φ_{VWC}^* is determined by the following model (Ebrahimnejad & Bagherzadeh, 2016) (Wu D. A., 819-830):

$$\varphi_{VWC}^* = \min \ \varphi_{VWC} = \sum_{i=1}^{k} \sum_{j=1}^{t} m_{ij}^{VWC} v_{ij}^{\min}$$

s.t.

$$\sum_{i=1}^{k} \sum_{j=1}^{t} m_{ij}^{VBC} v_{ij}^{\max} = 1, \qquad\qquad r = 1,2,\dots,m,$$

$$m_{ij}^{VWC} - m_{i,j+1}^{VWC} \geq \bar{d}\left(j,\varepsilon\right), \quad j = 1,2,\dots,t-1, \ \ i = 1,2,\dots,k, \qquad (27)$$

$$m_{it}^{VWC} \geq d\left(t,\varepsilon\right), \qquad\qquad i = 1,2,\dots,k,$$

$$m_{ij}^{VWC} - m_{i+1,j}^{VWC} \geq \bar{\bar{d}}\left(i,\varepsilon\right), \quad i = 1,2,\dots,k-1, j = 1,2,\dots,t,$$

$$m_{kj}^{VWC} \geq \bar{\bar{d}}\left(k,\varepsilon\right), j = 1,2,\dots,t.$$

Now, the worst preference score of candidate p under the condition that the worst possible preference score of the VWC remains unchanged is determined by use of the following model:

$$\varphi_{p}^* = \min \ \varphi_{VWC} = \sum_{i=1}^{k} \sum_{j=1}^{t} m_{ij}^{p} v_{ij}^{p}$$

s.t.

$$\sum_{i=1}^{k} \sum_{j=1}^{t} m_{ij}^{VWC} v_{ij}^{\min} = \varphi_{VWC}^*,$$

$$\sum_{i=1}^{k} \sum_{j=1}^{t} m_{ij}^{p} v_{ij}^{r} \leq 1, \qquad\qquad r = 1,2,\dots,m, \qquad (28)$$

$$m_{ij}^{p} - m_{i,j+1}^{p} \geq \bar{d}\left(j,\varepsilon\right), \quad j = 1,2,\dots,t-1, \ \ i = 1,2,\dots,k,$$

$$m_{it}^{p} \geq d\left(t,\varepsilon\right), \qquad\qquad i = 1,2,\dots,k,$$

$$m_{ij}^{p} - m_{i+1,j}^{p} \geq \bar{\bar{d}}\left(i,\varepsilon\right), \quad i = 1,2,\dots,k-1, j = 1,2,\dots,t,$$

$$m_{kj}^{p} \geq \bar{\bar{d}}\left(k,\varepsilon\right), j = 1,2,\dots,t.$$

In this case, Ebrahimnejad et al. (Ebrahimnejad & Bagherzadeh, 2016) have used the following relative closeness (RC) (Wang & Luo, 2006) to give an overall assessment of each candidate by combining the optimal objective values of models (25)-(28):

$$RC_p = \frac{\varphi_p^* - \varphi_{VWC}^*}{(\varphi_p^* - \varphi_{VWC}^*) + (\phi_{VBC}^* - \phi_p^*)} \tag{29}$$

Ranking the Candidates of Model (11)

Ebrahimnejad et al. (Ebrahimnejad, Tavana, & Santos-Arteaga, 2016) extended several current ranking methods in DEA and voting systems to discriminate among the efficient candidates of model (11). Then they used simulation to obtain a group consensus ranking for the efficient candidates.

Ebrahimnejad et al. (Ebrahimnejad, Tavana, & Santos-Arteaga, 2016) applied Obata et al. (Obata & Ishii, 2003) method to model (11) and suggested the following model to rank the efficient candidates when the $L_1 - $ norm is used:

$$\frac{1}{\bar{z}_p^*} = \min \ z_p = \sum_{i=1}^{k}\sum_{j=1}^{t} m_{ij}^p$$

$s.t.$

$$\sum_{i=1}^{k}\sum_{j=1}^{t} m_{ij}^p v_{ij}^p = 1, \tag{30}$$

$$\sum_{i=1}^{k}\sum_{j=1}^{t} m_{ij}^p v_{ij}^r \leq 1, \qquad r \in E, r \neq p$$

$$m_{i1}^p \geq 2m_{i2}^p \geq \ldots \geq tm_{it}^p, \quad m_{it}^p \geq \varepsilon, i = 1,2,\ldots,k,$$

$$m_{1j}^p \geq 2m_{2j}^p \geq \ldots \geq km_{kj}^p, \ m_{kj}^p \geq \varepsilon, j = 1,2,\ldots,t.$$

They have also extended Hashimoto's (Hashimoto, 1997) to model (11) and proposed the following model to rank the efficient candidates:

$$\bar{z}_p^* = \max \ z_p = \sum_{i=1}^{k}\sum_{j=1}^{t} m_{ij}^p v_{ij}^p$$

$s.t.$

$$\sum_{i=1}^{k}\sum_{j=1}^{t} m_{ij}^p v_{ij}^r \leq 1, \qquad r = 1,2,\ldots,m, r \neq p \tag{30}$$

$$m_{i1}^p \geq 2m_{i2}^p \geq \ldots \geq tm_{it}^p, \quad m_{it}^p \geq \varepsilon, i = 1,2,\ldots,k,$$

$$m_{1j}^p \geq 2m_{2j}^p \geq \ldots \geq km_{kj}^p, \ m_{kj}^p \geq \varepsilon, j = 1,2,\ldots,t.$$

In order to extend a ranking with a common set of weights (Ramazani-Tarkhorani, Khodabakhshi, Mehrabian, & Nuri-Bahmani, 2014), Ebrahimnejad et al. (Ebrahim-nejad, Tavana, & Santos-Arteaga, 2016) defined an ideal point as the multiplier bundle for which every candidate is efficient. Then, they used a multiple objective linear programming (MOLP) problem in order to minimize the measure of deviation of each candidate from the efficiency score of one in terms of a multiplier bundle of an ideal point. Hence, they have used the following three models for solving the corresponding MOLP model:

$$\min \sum_{r \in E} \alpha_r$$

s.t.

$$\sum_{i=1}^{k}\sum_{j=1}^{t} m_{ij}^{p} v_{ij}^{r} + \alpha_r = 1, \qquad r \in E, \qquad\qquad (31)$$

$$\alpha_r \geq 0, \qquad r \in E,$$

$$m_{i1}^{p} \geq 2 m_{i2}^{p} \geq \ldots \geq t m_{it}^{p}, \quad m_{it}^{p} \geq \varepsilon, \mathrm{i} = 1,2,\ldots,k,$$

$$m_{1j}^{p} \geq 2 m_{2j}^{p} \geq \ldots \geq k m_{kj}^{p}, \ m_{kj}^{p} \geq \varepsilon, \mathrm{j} = 1,2,\ldots,t.$$

$$\min \ \alpha$$

s.t.

$$\sum_{i=1}^{k}\sum_{j=1}^{t} m_{ij}^{p} v_{ij}^{r} + \alpha \geq 1, \qquad r \in E,$$

$$\sum_{i=1}^{k}\sum_{j=1}^{t} m_{ij}^{p} v_{ij}^{r} \leq 1, \qquad r \in E, \qquad\qquad (32)$$

$$m_{i1}^{p} \geq 2 m_{i2}^{p} \geq \ldots \geq t m_{it}^{p}, \quad m_{it}^{p} \geq \varepsilon, \mathrm{i} = 1,2,\ldots,k,$$

$$m_{1j}^{p} \geq 2 m_{2j}^{p} \geq \ldots \geq k m_{kj}^{p}, \ m_{kj}^{p} \geq \varepsilon, \mathrm{j} = 1,2,\ldots,t.$$

$$\min \ \frac{1}{n} \sum_{r \in E} \left(a_r + b_r \right)$$

$s.t.$

$$\sum_{i=1}^{k} \sum_{j=1}^{t} m_{ij}^{p} v_{ij}^{r} + \alpha_r = 1, \qquad r \in E,$$

$$a_r - b_r = \alpha_r - \frac{1}{n} \sum_{r \in E} \alpha_r, \qquad r \in E, \qquad\qquad (33)$$

$$a_r, b_r, \ \alpha_r \geq 0, \qquad\qquad r \in E,$$

$$m_{i1}^{p} \geq 2 m_{i2}^{p} \geq \ldots \geq t m_{it}^{p}, \qquad m_{it}^{p} \geq \varepsilon, i = 1, 2, \ldots, k,$$

$$m_{1j}^{p} \geq 2 m_{2j}^{p} \geq \ldots \geq k m_{kj}^{p}, \ m_{kj}^{p} \geq \varepsilon, j = 1, 2, \ldots, t.$$

Finally, they generalize a model such that a manager can choose the most favorable weights for the group that comprises all candidates under his/her governance. In other words, a set of weights that maximizes the group comprehensive score is used as the common set of weights for all the units to obtain each individual's comprehensive score. Their extended model according to this procedure is formulated as follows (Ebrahimnejad, Tavana, & Santos-Arteaga, 2016):

$$\min \ \sum_{i=1}^{k} \sum_{j=1}^{t} m_{ij}^{p} \left(\sum_{r=1}^{m} v_{ij}^{r} \right)$$

$s.t.$

$$\sum_{i=1}^{k} \sum_{j=1}^{t} m_{ij}^{p} v_{ij}^{r} \leq 1, \qquad\qquad r \in E, \qquad\qquad (34)$$

$$m_{i1}^{p} \geq 2 m_{i2}^{p} \geq \ldots \geq t m_{it}^{p}, \qquad m_{it}^{p} \geq \varepsilon, i = 1, 2, \ldots, k,$$

$$m_{1j}^{p} \geq 2 m_{2j}^{p} \geq \ldots \geq k m_{kj}^{p}, \ m_{kj}^{p} \geq \varepsilon, j = 1, 2, \ldots, t.$$

Once the optimal weights are determined by solving models (29)-(34), the preference score of each candidate can be computed by $\bar{z}_p^* = \sum_{i=1}^{k} \sum_{j=1}^{t} m_{ij}^{p,*} v_{ij}^{p}$ and the winner can be selected. As a final point, despite the wealth of information provided to the decision maker(s), different extended ranking models (29)-(34) may produce different rankings. Thus, Ebrahimnejad et al. (Ebrahimnejad, Tavana, & Santos-Arteaga, 2016) used simulation to analyze these rankings and synthesize them into one overall group ranking.

It is worth noting that In addition, the extension of some other ranking methods to rank of decision making units in DEA framework (Gholam Abri, G.R, F, Shoja, & M., 2013) can be interesting for ranking of efficient candidates in voting systems as a research work.

CONCLUSION

Different methods have been proposed to allow voters to express their preferences on a set of candidates. In ranked voting methods, each voter selects a subset of candidates and ranks them from the most to the least preferred one. The score obtained by each candidate is the weighted sum of the scores received from the different voters. In this contribution, a taxonomy and review of some of techniques based on data envelopment analysis for estimating the preference scores of the candidate without imposing a fixed weight to each place from the outset was provided. The existing voting systems were divided into two general areas. In the first area it is assumed that the votes of all the voters to have equal importance and in the second area voters are classifies into different groups and assumed that each group is assigned a different voting power. We analyzed some of the most common models and procedures for determining the most favorable weights for each candidate in this contribution.

REFERENCES

Amin, G. R., & Sadeghi, H. (2010). Application of prioritized aggregation operators in preference voting. *International Journal of Intelligent Systems*, *25*(10), 1027–1034. doi:10.1002/int.20437

Amirteimoori, A. and Kordrostami, S.A Euclidean distance-based measure of efficiency in data envelopment analysis, Optimization: A Journal of Mathematical Programming and Operations Research 59 (7), 985-996, 2010.

Amirteimoori, A. and Kordrostami, S. An alternative clustering approach: a DEA-based procedure, Optimization: A Journal of Mathematical Programming and Operations Research 62 (2), 227-240, 2013.

Andersen, P., & Petersen, N. C. (1993). A procedure for ranking efficient units in data envelopment analysis. *Management Science*, *39*(10), 1261–1264. doi:10.1287/mnsc.39.10.1261

Brams, S. J., & Fishburn, P. C. (2002). Voting procedures. In K. J. Arrow, A. K. Sen, & K. Suzumura (Eds.), *Handbook of Social, Choice andWelfare* (Vol. 1, pp. 173–236). Amsterdam: Elsevier. doi:10.1016/S1574-0110(02)80008-X

Cook, W. D., & Kress, M. (1990). A data envelopment model for aggregating preference rankings. *Management Science*, *36*(11), 1302–1310. doi:10.1287/mnsc.36.11.1302

Ebrahimnejad, A. (2012). A new approach for ranking of candidates in voting systems. *OPSEARCH*, *49*(2), 103–115. doi:10.1007/s12597-012-0070-9

Ebrahimnejad, A. (2015). A novel approach for discriminating efficient candidates by classifying voters in the preferential voting framework. *Japan Journal of Industrial and Applied Mathematics*, *32*(2), 513–527. doi:10.1007/s13160-015-0172-x

Ebrahimnejad, A., & Bagherzadeh, M. A. (2016). Data envelopment analysis approach for discriminating efficient candidates in voting systems by considering the priority of voters. *Hacettepe Journal of Mathematics and Statistics*, *45*(1), 165–180.

Ebrahimnejad, A., Tavana, M., & Santos-Arteaga, F. J. (2016). An integrated data envelopment analysis and simulation method for group consensus ranking. *Mathematics and Computers in Simulation*, *119*, 1–17. doi:10.1016/j.matcom.2015.08.022

Foroughi, A. A., & Aouni, B. (2012). New approaches for determining a common set of weights for a voting system. *International Transactions in Operational Research*, *19*(4), 521–530. doi:10.1111/j.1475-3995.2011.00832.x

Foroughi, A. A., Jones, D. F., & Tamiz, M. (2005). A selection method for a preferential election. *Applied Mathematics and Computation*, *163*(1), 107–116. doi:10.1016/j.amc.2003.10.055

Foroughi, A. A., & Tamiz, M. (2005). An effective total ranking model for a ranked voting system. *Omega*, *33*(6), 491–496. doi:10.1016/j.omega.2004.07.013

Gholam Abri, A., Jahanshahloo, G. R., Hosseinzadeh Lotfi, F., Shoja, N., & Fallah Jelodar, M. (2013). A new method for ranking non-extreme efficient units in data envelopment analysis. *Optimization Letters*, *7*(2), 309–324. doi:10.1007/s11590-011-0420-1

Green, R. H., Doyle, J. R., & Cook, W. D. (1996). Preference voting and project ranking using DEA and cross-evaluation. *European Journal of Operational Research*, *90*(3), 461–472. doi:10.1016/0377-2217(95)00039-9

Hadi-Vencheh, A. (2014). Two effective total ranking models for preference voting and aggregation. *Mathematical Sciences*, *8*(115), 1–4.

Hadi-Vencheh, A., & Mokhtarian, M. N. (2009). Three new models for preference voting and aggregation: A note. *The Journal of the Operational Research Society*, *60*(7), 1036–1037. doi:10.1057/jors.2008.153

Hashimoto, A. (1997). A ranked voting system using a DEA/AR exclusion model: A note. *European Journal of Operational Research*, *97*(3), 600–604. doi:10.1016/S0377-2217(96)00281-0

Hosseinzadeh Lotfi, F., & Fallahnejad, R. (2011). A note on A solution method to the problem proposed by Wang in voting systems. *Applied Mathematical Sciences*, *5*, 3051–3055.

Hosseinzadeh Lotfi, F., Hatami-Marbini, A., Agrell, P. J., Aghayi, N., & Gholami, K. (2013). Allocating fixed resources and setting targets using a common-weights DEA approach. *Computers & Industrial Engineering*, *64*(2), 631–640. doi:10.1016/j.cie.2012.12.006

Hosseinzadeh Lotfi, F., Rostamy-Malkhalifeh, M., Aghayi, N., Ghelej Beigi, Z., & Gholami, K. (2013). An improved method for ranking alternatives in multiple criteria decision analysis. *Applied Mathematical Modelling*, *37*(1-2), 25–33. doi:10.1016/j.apm.2011.09.074

Jahanshahloo, G. R., Hosseinzadeh Lotfi, F., Khanmohammadi, M., & Kazemimanesh, M. (2012). A method for discriminating efficient candidates with ranked voting data by common weights. *Mathematical and Computational Applications*, *17*(3), 1–8. doi:10.3390/mca17010001

Jahanshahloo, G. R., Hosseinzadeh Lotfi, F., Khanmohammadi, M., Kazemimanesh, M., & Rezaie, V. (2010). Ranking of units by positive ideal DMU with common weights. *Expert Systems with Applications*, *37*(12), 7483–7488. doi:10.1016/j.eswa.2010.04.011

Jahanshahloo, G. R., Khodabakhshi, M., Hosseinzadeh Lotfi, F., & Moazami Goudarzi, M. R. (2011). A cross-efficiency model based on super-efficiency for ranking units through the TOPSIS approach and its extension to the interval case. *Mathematical and Computer Modelling*, *53*(9-10), 1946–1955. doi:10.1016/j.mcm.2011.01.025

Kordrostami, S., & Bakhoda Bijarkani, Z. (2013). A new method to measure efficiency in parallel production systems with shared sourced in natural life. *International Journal of Biomathematics*, *6*(6), 1–18. doi:10.1142/S1793524513500459

Llamazares, B., & Pena, T. (2009). Preference aggregation and DEA: An analysis of the methods proposed to discriminate efficient candidates. *European Journal of Operational Research*, *197*(2), 714–721. doi:10.1016/j.ejor.2008.06.031

Llamazares, B., & Pena, T. (2013). Aggregating preferences rankings with variable weights. *European Journal of Operational Research*, *230*(2), 348–355. doi:10.1016/j. ejor.2013.04.013

Noguchi, H., Ogawa, M., & Ishii, H. (2002). The appropriate total ranking method using DEA for multiple categorized purposes. *Journal of Computational and Applied Mathematics*, *146*(1), 155–166. doi:10.1016/S0377-0427(02)00425-9

Obata, T., & Ishii, H. (2003). A method for discriminating efficient candidates with ranked voting data. *European Journal of Operational Research*, *151*(1), 233–237. doi:10.1016/S0377-2217(02)00597-0

Ramazani-Tarkhorani, S., Khodabakhshi, M., Mehrabian, S., & Nuri-Bahmani, F. (2014). Ranking decision making units with Common Weights in DEA. *Applied Mathematical Modelling*, *38*(15-16), 3890–3896. doi:10.1016/j.apm.2013.08.029

Saati, S., Hatami-Marbini, A., Agrell, P. J., & Tavana, M. (2012). A common set of weight approach using an ideal decision making unit in data envelopment analysis. *Journal of Industrial and Management Optimization*, *8*(3), 623–637. doi:10.3934/jimo.2012.8.623

Sexton, T. R., Silkman, R. H., & Hogan, A. J. Data envelopment Analysis: Critique and extensions, In: Silkman R H (1986) (Ed.), Measuring Efficiency: An Assessment of Data Envelopment Analysis, Jossey-bass, San Francisco, pp 73-105, 1986.

Shokouhi, A. H., Hatami-Marbini, A., Tavana, M., & Saati, S. (2010). A robust optimization approach for imprecise data envelopment analysis. *Computers & Industrial Engineering*, *59*(3), 387–397. doi:10.1016/j.cie.2010.05.011

Soltanifar, M., Ebrahimnejad, A., & Farrokhi, M. M. (2010). Ranking of different ranking models using a voting model and its application in determining efficient candidates. *International Journal of Society Systems Science.*, *2*(4), 375–389. doi:10.1504/IJSSS.2010.035570

Stein, W. E., Mizzi, P. J., & Pfaffenberger, R. C. (1994). A stochastic dominance analysis of ranked voting systems with scoring. *European Journal of Operational Research*, *74*(1), 78–85. doi:10.1016/0377-2217(94)90205-4

Tavana, M., & Hatami-Marbini, A. (2011). A group AHP-TOPSIS framework for human space flight mission planning at NASA. *Expert Systems with Applications*, *38*, 13588–13603.

Tavana, M., Khalili-Damaghani, K., & Sadi-Nezhad, S. (2013). A fuzzy group data envelopment analysis model for high-technology project selection: A case study at NASA. *Computers & Industrial Engineering*, *66*(1), 10–23. doi:10.1016/j.cie.2013.06.002

Tavana, M., Mirzagholtabar, H., Mirhedayatian, S. M., Farzipoor Saen, R., & Azadi, M. (2013). A new network epsilon-based DEA model for supply chain performance evaluation. *Computers & Industrial Engineering*, *66*(2), 501–513. doi:10.1016/j.cie.2013.07.016

Wang, N., Yi, R., & Liu, D. (2008). A solution method to the problem proposed by Wang in voting systems. *Journal of Computational and Applied Mathematics*, *221*(1), 106–113. doi:10.1016/j.cam.2007.10.006

Wang, Y. M., & Chin, K. S. (2007). Discriminating DEA efficient candidates by considering their least relative total scores. *Journal of Computational and Applied Mathematics*, *206*(1), 209–215. doi:10.1016/j.cam.2006.06.012

Wang, Y. M., Chin, K. S., & Yang, J. B. (2007). Three new models for preference voting and aggregation. *The Journal of the Operational Research Society*, *58*(10), 1389–1393. doi:10.1057/palgrave.jors.2602295

Wang, Y. M., Chin, K. S., & Yang, J. B. (2009). Improved linear programming models for preference voting and aggregation: Reply to Hadi-Vencheh and Mokhtarian. *The Journal of the Operational Research Society*, *58*(7), 1037–1038. doi:10.1057/jors.2008.156

Wang, Y. M., & Luo, Y. (2006). DEA efficiency assessment using ideal and anti-ideal decision making units. *Applied Mathematics and Computation*, *173*(2), 902–915. doi:10.1016/j.amc.2005.04.023

Wu, D. (2006). A note on DEA efficiency assessment using ideal point: An improvement of Wang and Luo's model. *Applied Mathematics and Computation*, *183*(2), 819–830. doi:10.1016/j.amc.2006.06.030

Wu, J., Liang, L., & Zha, Y. (2009). Preference voting and ranking using DEA game cross efficiency model. *Journal of the Operations Research Society of Japan*, *52*, 105–111.

Chapter 3
Application of Malmquist Productivity Index in Integrated Units of Power Plant

Elahe Shariatmadari Serkani
Islamic Azad University, Iran

Seyed Esmaeil Najafi
Islamic Azad University, Iran

Arash Nejadi
Tehran Polytechnic, Iran

ABSTRACT

The Malmquist Productivity Index (MPI) evaluates the productivity change of a Decision Making Unit (DMU) between two time periods. DEA considers performance analysis at a given point of time. Classic Malmquist Productivity Index shows regress and progress of a DMU in different periods with efficiency and technology variations without considering the present value of money. In this chapter Application of Malmquist productivity index in integrated units of power plant is discussed. Four units of one of the power plants are assessed & the data of its five successive years are supplied. Also application of Malmquist productivity index (precise data) in Safa Rolling and pipe plants for the time period of 2007 – 2012 is studied.

DOI: 10.4018/978-1-5225-0596-9.ch003

INTRODUCTION

The Malmquist index (MI) is one of the most frequently used techniques to measure productivity changes overtime. The concept of Malmquist productivity index was first introduced by Malmquist (1953), and has further been studied and developed in the non-parametric framework by several authors. Malmquist productivity index (MPI) is usually to measure the productivity growth over the time and is product of efficiency change and technological change. The main disadvantage of the Malmquist index is the necessity to compute the distance function. The Malmquist index can be further decomposed by disaggregating changes in technical efficiency into changes in scale efficiency and input congestion (Fare et al.,1994).

Farell (1957) determined a suitable method to evaluate experimental production function for several inputs and outputs with using linear programming technique and Data Envelopment Analysis (DEA). By applying DEA, the best efficiency frontier will be calculated with a set of DMUs and omitting of any priority for inputs and outputs. The DMUs of efficiency frontier are the units with the maximum output and/or the minimum input levels. Using the efficient units and efficiency frontier, is the analysis of other inefficiency units possible.

Fare in the 1992-1994 developed Malmquist productivity index based on DEA in order to measure productivity by time shift. Malmquist index was used as a quantitative index for using in the analysis of input consumption in 1953.

BACKGROUND

Table 1 is showing some researches in relationships between DEA and Malmquist.

Malmquist Productivity Index

Malmquist productivity index can be calculated via several functions, such as distance function:

$$D\left(X_o, \; Y_o\right) \;=\; inf \; \{\theta \mid \left(\theta X_o, Y_o\right) \in PPS\} \tag{1}$$

This equation shows in special conditions, only the efficiency frontier change in period t+1 related to t; that could not be a suitable criterion to calculate the technology change. If $D_K\left(X_K, \; Y_K\right) = 1$, then kth unit is hypothesized as efficient. Production function in period t and t + 1 is given. Calculation of the MPI requires four linear programming problems as below:

Table 1. Researches DEA-Malmquist

Authors	Methodology and Results
Abbott (2006)	They integrated Data envelopment analysis (DEA) models with MI to estimate total factor productivity (TFP) of the electricity supply industry, broken down into its state-based constituent parts over the long term (1969 to 1999).
Aghdam (2011)	This paper examines the dynamics of productivity changes in the Australian electricity industry and conducts several hypotheses-testing to identify whether industry's efficiency measures are truly improved as a result of the reform-driven changes. Malmquist Total Factor Productivity Index approach and ANOVA are used for this purpose.
Arabi et al. (2015)	In this study they introduced the Malmquist–Luenberger index and developed a new slacks-based measure to eliminate the infeasibility problem encountered in applying this index.
Babalos et al. (2012)	This study assesses the relative performance of Greek equity funds employing a non-parametric method, namely DEA. They evaluate the funds' total productivity change using the DEA-based Malmquist Index Productivity measurement using DEA and Malmiquest index.
Charnes et al. (1978).	They represented a revision of earlier versions entitled, respectively, 'Exposition: Interpretations, and Extensions of the Farrell Efficiency Measure', and 'Measuring the Efficiency of DMUs With Some New Production Functions and Estimation Methods'.
Chang et al. (2008)	In this article, multi criteria are considered by applying the data envelopment analysis to evaluate the relative efficiencies of all the manufacturing processes to help to assess the allocation of a company's resources.
Chang et al.(2009)	They investigated changes in productive efficiency for 62 US public accounting firms between the periods (2000–2001) and (2003–2004). DEA was used to calculate Malmquist indexes of productivity and efficiency changes.
Chowdhurya et al.(2014)	They compared productivity, efficiency and technological changes with and without case-mix as output categories using panel data on Ontario hospitals for the period 2002–2006. They use the MPI, DEA, and non-parametric density estimation and related statistical tests. They also decompose MPI into efficiency change (ECH) and technological change (TCH).
Fuentes & Lillo-Banuls (2015).	This paper analyses the productivity growth of the SUMA tax offices located in Spain evolved between 2004 and 2006 by using Malmquist Index based on DEA models.
Hermans et al. (2013)	In this study, a DEA based Malmquist index model was developed to assess the relative efficiency and productivity of U.S. states in decreasing the number of road fatalities. Based on the model output, the good and bad aspects of road safety are identified for each country.
Hwang and Chang (2003)	Hwang and Chang adopted the DEA model and the Malmquist productivity index to measure the managerial performance of 45 international tourist hotels in 1998 and the efficiency change of 45 international tourist hotels From 1994 to 1998 in Taiwan.
Kao (2010)	Kao presented Malmquist productivity index based on common-weights DEA. This study proposes a common-weights DEA model for time-series evaluations to calculate the global Malmquist productivity index (MPI) so that the productivity changes of all DMUs have a common basis for comparison.
Krishnasamy (2003)	Krishnasamy used both DEA and Malmquist total factor productivity index (MPI) to evaluate bank efficiency and productivity changes in Malaysia over the period 2000-2001.
Lee (2013)	Lee analyzed the efficiency, productivity, growth, and stability of Korean SMS shipyards using the DEA model and Malmquist index in order to classify competitive and uncompetitive SMS shipyards.
Liu and Wang (2008)	In this research they employed DEA to measure the Malmquist productivity of semiconductor packaging and testing firms in Taiwan from 2000 to 2003.
Ma et al. (2002)	In this paper the technical efficiency and Malmquist productivity indexes of a sample of 88 enterprises producing 72 percent of the industry's output were determined for the period 1989–1997, with the aim of gaining some insights into the policy options likely to achieve this.

continued on following page

Table 1. Continued

Authors	Methodology and Results
Ouellette & Vierstraete (2004)	They proposed a DEA method, introducing quasi-fixed inputs to evaluate the productivity change of a DMU in the context of the Malmquist indices.
Pires & Fernandes, (2012)	This article discusses the financial efficiency of 42 airlines from 25 countries, in 2001 (the year of the September 11 terrorist attack in the United States), and their profitability in the following year. The Malmquist index was used to indicate the airlines' capital structure changes from 2001 to 2002.
Pilyavsky and Staat (2008)	They conducted a study to investigate technical efficiency and efficiency changes of hospitals and polyclinics. The DEA and Malmquist productivity index methods were employed upon the data set for the five-year period 1997-2001.
Portela,& Thanassoulis (2010)	In this paper they develop an index and an indicator of productivity change that can be used with negative data. For that purpose the range directional model (RDM), a particular case of the directional distance function, is used for computing efficiency in the presence of negative data. They used RDM efficiency measures to arrive at a Malmquist-type index.
Sueyoshi and Goto (2013b)	They proposed a DEA method by using the Malmquist index to examine the degree of a frontier shift among multiple periods. They utilized the proposed approach in an empirical application and identified the relationship between fuel mix, electricity and CO_2 among ten industrial nations.
Tanase & Tidor (2012)	This paper examines the efficiency and productivity of enterprises (more than 250 employees) in machinery industry which are part of emerging markets. Techniques selected for evaluation of progress efficiency and changing productivity studied are DEA and the MPI.
Worthington (1999)	Worthington used Non parametric frontier analysis, employed Malmquist indices (MALMQUIST–DEA) to investigate productivity growth in credit unions, the productivity growth is decomposed into technical efficiency change and technological efficiency change for 269 Australian credit unions.
Yang & Zeng (2014).	This study examine the trends of productivity, efficiency and quality changes of hospitals in Shenzhen city over the period 2006–2010 and explore whether there is a trade-off between efficiency and quality in the hospital production. A three-stage DEA based Malmquist productivity index is used to estimate the changes of productivity, efficiency and quality.
Zhou et al. (2010)	This paper introduces a Malmquist CO2 emission performance index (MCPI) for measuring changes in total factor carbon emission performance over time. The MCPI is derived by solving several data envelopment analysis models.

$$D_o^t(X_o^t, Y_o^t) = Min\theta$$
$$s.t. \sum_{j=1}^{n} \lambda_j x_{ij}^t \leq \theta x_{io}^t, \quad i = 1, ..., m,$$
$$\sum_{j=1}^{n} \lambda_j y_{rj}^t \geq y_{ro}^t, \quad r = 1, ..., s,$$
$$\lambda_i \geq 0, \quad j = 1, ..., n.$$

(2)

x_{io}^t is i[th] input and y_{ro}^t is r[th] output of DMU$_O$ in period t. The value of efficiency ($D_o^t \left(X_o^t, Y_o^t \right) = \theta_o^*$) shows that how much can be decrease inputs of DMU$_O$ to production that output.

Instead of t, CCR problem, is calculated in period t+1 and is equal $D_o^{t+1} \left(X_o^{t+1}, Y_o^{t+1} \right)$ and is the technical efficiency for DMU$_O$ in period t + 1. The value of $D_o^t \left(X_o^{t+1}, Y_o^{t+1} \right)$ for DMU$_O$ is the distance of DMU$_O$ at t + 1 with the frontier of time t, calculated by below problem:

$$D_o^t(X_o^{t+1}, Y_o^{t+1}) = Min\theta$$

$$s.t. \sum_{j=1}^{n} \lambda_j x_{ij}^t \leq \theta x_{io}^{t+1}, \qquad i = 1, ..., m$$

$$\sum_{j=1}^{n} \lambda_j y_{rj}^t \geq y_{ro}^{t+1}, \qquad r = 1, ..., s,$$

$$\lambda_i \geq 0, \qquad j = 1, ..., n. \tag{3}$$

$$D_o^{(t+1)}(X_o^{(t+1)}, Y_o^{(t+1)}) = Min\theta$$

$$s.t. \sum_{j=1}^{n} \lambda_j x_{ij}^{t+1} \leq \theta x_{io}^{t+1}, \qquad i = 1, ..., m,$$

$$\sum_{j=1}^{n} \lambda_j y_{rj}^{t+1} \leq \theta y_{ro}^{t+1}, \qquad r = 1, ..., s,$$

$$\lambda_i \geq 0, \qquad j = 1, ..., n. \tag{4}$$

Similarly $D_o^{t+1} \left(X_o^t, Y_o^t \right)$ of DMU$_O$ distance with period t is calculated by the time efficiency frontier which is required for computing the efficiency index of Malmquist in input oriented model. This value is the optimum answer of the following linear programming problem:

$$D_o^{t+1}(X_o^t, Y_o^t) = Min\theta$$

$$s.t. \sum_{j=1}^{n} \lambda_j x_{ij}^{t+1} \leq \theta x_{io}^t, \qquad i = 1, ..., m,$$

$$\sum_{j=1}^{n} \lambda_j y_{rj}^{t+1} \geq y_{ro}^t, \qquad r = 1, ..., s,$$

$$\lambda_i \geq 0, \qquad j = 1, ..., n. \tag{5}$$

Fare assumed that $D_o^t\left(X_o^t, Y_o^t\right), D_o^{t+1}\left(X_o^{t+1}, Y_o^{t+1}\right)$ for being effective should be equal to 1. The relative efficiency change is defined as:

$$TEC_o = \frac{D_o^{t+1}(X_o^{t+1}, Y_o^{t+1})}{D_o^t(X_o^t, Y_o^t)} \tag{6}$$

Definition 1: A piece of the frontier has had a positive move, if and only if the piece in period t+1 in comparison to the corresponding point in time t, expand & enlarge production possibility set (PPS).

Definition 2: A piece of the frontier has a negative move, if and only if the piece in period t + 1 in comparison to the corresponding point in time t of set make the PPS smaller and move inward.

Fare described one geometric compotation to determine technology change between t and t + 1:

$$FS_o = \left[\frac{D_o^t\left(X_o^{t+1}, Y_o^{t+1}\right)}{D_o^{t+1}\left(X_o^{t+1}, Y_o^{t+1}\right)} \cdot \frac{D_o^t\left(X_o^t, Y_o^t\right)}{D_o^{t+1}\left(X_o^t, Y_o^t\right)} \right]^{\frac{1}{2}} \tag{7}$$

Three conditions occur:

1. $FS_o > 1$, the frontier movement is positive and or progress can be observed.
2. $FS_o < 1$, the frontier movement is negative or retrogression can be observed.
3. $FS_o = 1$ shows the motion is not required or the frontier does not change.

MPI will be calculated from multiplication efficiency change and technology change for each input oriented DMU_o in period's t and t + 1:

$$MI_o = \frac{D_o^{t+1}\left(X_o^{t+1}, Y_o^{t+1}\right)}{D_o^t\left(X_o^t, Y_o^t\right)} \left[\frac{D_o^t\left(X_o^{t+1}, Y_o^{t+1}\right)}{D_o^{t+1}\left(X_o^{t+1}, Y_o^{t+1}\right)} \cdot \frac{D_o^t\left(X_o^t, Y_o^t\right)}{D_o^{t+1}\left(X_o^t, Y_o^t\right)} \right]^{\frac{1}{2}} \tag{8}$$

The simple form of above equation is:

$$MI_o = \left[\frac{D_o^t \left(X_o^{t+1}, Y_o^{t+1} \right)}{D_o^t \left(X_o^t, Y_o^t \right)} \cdot \frac{D_o^{t+1} \left(X_o^{t+1}, Y_o^{t+1} \right)}{D_o^{t+1} \left(X_o^t, Y_o^t \right)} \right]^{\frac{1}{2}} \tag{9}$$

This value defines geometric convex compotation, because it specified the smallest decrease of efficiencies and any small change in each efficiency effects in MPI. Three conditions are available:

1. $MI_o > 1$, Increase productivity and observe progress.
2. $MI_o < 1$, Decrease productivity and observe regress.
3. $MI_o = 1$, No change in productivity in period t + 1 in comparison to t.

Non-Radial Malmquist Productivity Index

DEA models which are used in the radial Malmquist productivity index, can be input or output oriented. When outputs are fixed, this index can be defined in input oriented and when inputs are fixed, this index can be defined in output-oriented.

Because Malmquist productivity index of bearing only on the degree of radial efficiency, nonzero slack variables are not considered in the input oriented (nonzero output slack variables in output oriented), The productivity change cannot be determined accurately and if inputs and outputs are only effective in improving the results, this index will fail.So non-radial model is considered for the Malmquist productivity index. In addition, a dedicated excellence of inputs and outputs can be taken on implementation progress.

It assumes that $\alpha_i (i = 1,...,n)$ the certain weights are based on a dedicated excellence of input in improvement of inputs. According to α_i DEA model is as follow model:

$$\theta_o^t (X_o^t, Y_o^t) = \frac{1}{\sum_{i=1}^m \alpha_i} \underset{(\theta_o^i, \lambda_j)}{Min} \sum_{i=1}^m \alpha_i \theta_o^i$$

$$s.t. \sum_{j=1}^n \lambda_j x_{ij}^t \leq {}_o^i x_{io}^t, \quad i = 1,...,m,$$

$$\sum_{j=1}^n \lambda_j y_{rj}^t \geq y_{ro}^t, \quad r = 1,...,s, \tag{12}$$

$$\lambda_i \geq 0, \quad j = 1,...,n.$$

$$\theta_o^i \quad free$$

Model (12) measures relative efficiency of DMU_o in period t in terms of α_i weights. If $\alpha_i = 0$ then θ_o^i is considered to be equal to one. Enlargement of α_i raises the priority reduction of input i.

Theorem: in any optimal solution of model (12) always all of the input slacks variables and at least one output slack variable is zero.

Proof: proof by contradiction, let us assume that slack variable input k is not zero. In this case:

$$i = k \Rightarrow \sum_{j=1}^{n} \lambda_j x_{ij}^t \leq, _o^{k^*} x_{ko}^t \Rightarrow, _o^{k^*} \geq \frac{\sum_{j=1}^{n} \lambda_j x_{ij}^t}{x_{ko}^t} = \hat{\theta}_o^k \Rightarrow \theta_o^{i^*} \geq \hat{\theta} \tag{13}$$

In model (12) if the time t+ 1 be instead of the time t, $D_o^{t+1}\left(X_o^{t+1}, Y_o^{t+1}\right)$ will be achieved.

The productivity index of non-radial Malmquist by using the aforementioned level of specified non radial efficiency in input oriented is equal to:

$$PI_o = \frac{D_o^{t+1}\left(X_o^{t+1}, Y_o^{t+1}\right)}{D_o^t\left(X_o^t, Y_o^t\right)} \left[\frac{D_o^t\left(X_o^{t+1}, Y_o^{t+1}\right)}{D_o^{t+1}\left(X_o^{t+1}, Y_o^{t+1}\right)} \cdot \frac{D_o^t\left(X_o^t, Y_o^t\right)}{D_o^{t+1}\left(X_o^t, Y_o^t\right)}\right]^{\frac{1}{2}} \tag{14}$$

Modified Malmquist Productivity Index by Russell Model

A non-radial model was introduced in the previous section. In that model it was tried by defining efficiency in any input component by the θ_i. All possible inefficiency that a decision making unit may have in each of its inputs, can omitted by the objective function like $\frac{1}{m} \sum_{i=1}^{m} \theta_i$. But if the DMU under evaluation of inefficiency in some outputs have (s_r^+) it will have no effect on the value of efficiency. To solve this problem, the modified Russell model will be used.

The purpose is calculated the efficiency index of DMU_O is in period t + 1 in comparison with the period t. In this case, the four efficiencies of $R_{e_o}^t(X_o^t, Y_o^t), R_{e_o}^t(X_o^{t+1}, Y_o^{t+1}), R_{e_o}^{t+1}(X_o^t, Y_o^t), R_{e_o}^{t+1}(X_o^{t+1}, Y_o^{t+1})$ are calculated. These efficiencies are obtained by solving four models & by the change of t and t + 1 in model (15).

It is assumed that α_i & β_r sequentially are the importance of ith ($i=1,\ldots,m$) input & r^{th} ($r=1,\ldots,s$) output. α_i & β_r are known parameters that are provided by the decision-maker and management. The modified Russell model for calculating efficiencies is as follow:

$$
R_{e_o}^t(X_o^t, Y_o^t) = \min \frac{\dfrac{1}{\sum_{i=1}^m \alpha_i} \sum_{i=1}^m \alpha_i \theta_i}{\dfrac{1}{\sum_{r=1}^s \beta_r} \sum_{r=1}^s \beta_r \varphi_r}
$$

$$
s.t. \sum_{j=1}^n \lambda_j x_{ij}^t \le \theta_i x_{io}^t,, \qquad i = 1,\ldots,m,
$$

$$
\sum_{j=1}^n \lambda_j y_{rj}^t \ge \varphi_r y_{ro}^t, \qquad r = 1,\ldots,s,
$$

$$
0 \le \theta_i \le 1, \qquad i = 1,\ldots,m,
$$

$$
\varphi_r \ge 0, \qquad j = 1,\ldots,n,
$$

$$
\lambda_j \ge 0, \qquad j = 1,\ldots,n.
$$

(15)

Problem (15) is a fractional programming that can be converted into a linear programming problem and $0 \le R_{e_o}^t(X_o^t, Y_o^t) \le 1$.

To calculating $R_{e_o}^{t+1}(X_o^t, Y_o^t)$, it is sufficient to compare DMU_O in period t than period t+1 to all the DMUs and the value of this efficiency is non-negative.

$R_{e_o}^{t+1}(X_o^{t+1}, Y_o^{t+1})$ is obtained with shift of t and t + 1 in the model (15), this efficiency is a value between zero and one. DMU_O is obtained with the time coordinates t+1 in comparison with all DMUs with t coordinates and the value of this efficiency is non-negative. Malmquist productivity index is defined as follow:

$$
M_{\text{Re}}^{t,t+1} = \frac{R_{e_o}^{t+1}(X_o^{t+1}, Y_o^{t+1})}{R_{e_o}^t(X_o^t, Y_o^t)} \left[\frac{R_{e_o}^t(X_o^t, Y_o^t)}{R_{e_o}^{t+1}(X_o^t, Y_o^t)} \cdot \frac{R_{e_o}^t(X_o^{t+1}, Y_o^{t+1})}{R_{e_o}^{t+1}(X_o^{t+1}, Y_o^{t+1})} \right]^{\frac{1}{2}}
$$

(16)

In formulation (16), $M_{\text{Re}}^{t,t+1} > 1$ represents a progress, $M_{\text{Re}}^{t,t+1} < 1$ represents a regress of DMU_O and if $M_{\text{Re}}^{t,t+1} = 1$, this means that in this section has not progress, nor regress.

Assumptions of Cost Malmquist Productivity Index (CM)

Malmquist productivity index in the input oriented is an index to determine progress or regress of a unit. The cost Malmquist productivity index is an index for regression or progression of one unit of input price point of view.

Suppose in period t to produce each unit of output $Y^t \in \mathbf{R}^s_+$, input $X^t \in \mathbf{R}^m_+$ $X^t \in \mathbf{R}^m_+$ is needed.

Production technology in period t is defined by a set of input demand:

$$L^t(Y^t) = \left\{ X^t | X^t \text{ can produce } Y^t \right\} \tag{17}$$

$L^t(Y^t)$ Specifies all input vectors that can produce the output Y^t. $L^t(Y^t)$ is assumed non-empty, closed, convex and bounded set and all inputs and outputs are true in it. $L^t(Y^t)$ is bounded from below. Its bound is shown by an input requirement set.

$$I_{soq} L^t(Y^t) = \left\{ X^t | X^t \in L^t\left(Y^t\right), \lambda X^t \notin L^t\left(Y^t\right) for \lambda < 1 \right\} \tag{18}$$

This makes boundary collection for $L^t(Y^t)$. It means that the radial contraction for input vectors on the frontier is not possible. Input distance function based on the technology is defined as follows:

$$D^t_i(X^t, Y^t) = \sup \left\{ \theta : \left(\frac{X^t}{\theta}\right) \in L^t\left(Y^t\right), \theta > 0 \right\} \tag{19}$$

Index i specifies the input oriented. $D^t_i(X^t, Y^t)$ is the most coefficient that X^t factor can be divided on it and still remain in $L^t(Y^t)$.

If $D^t_i\left(X^t, Y^t\right) > 1$ then $X^t \in L^t(Y^t)$ and if $D^t_i\left(X^t, Y^t\right) = 1$ then $X^t \in I_{soq}L^t(Y^t)$, it's exactly the same as technical efficiency input oriented:

$$TE^t_i\left(X^t, Y^t\right) = Min \left\{ \varphi | \varphi X^t \in L^t\left(Y^t\right), \varphi > 0 \right\} \tag{20}$$

When the price of inputs is achievable, the cost function $P^t \in R^m_+$ is obtained.

$$C^t\left(Y^t, P^t\right) = Min\left\{P^t X^t | X^t \in L^t\left(Y^t\right), P^t > 0\right\} \tag{21}$$

Formulate (21) specifies the lowest production cost of the output vector Y^t with the input price of P^t in period t.

Set of input vectors X^t corresponding to the numerical value $C^t(Y^t, P^t)$, which are on the isoquant line called cost frontier & is shown as follows:

$$I_{soq} C^t\left(Y^t, P^t\right) = \left\{X^t | P^t X^t = C^t(Y^t, P^t)\right\} \tag{22}$$

This specifies input vectors set which can produce output Y^t with the lowest cost. Given that the technical efficiency for each unit is the same with the defined distance function and the technical efficiency is more than the overall efficiency (cost) for per unit;

$$0E_i^t\left(Y^t, X^t, P^t\right) \leq D_i^t(Y^t, X^t) \tag{23}$$

Based on Farrell definition for overall efficiency, $0E_i^t\left(Y^t, X^t, P^t\right) = \dfrac{C^t\left(Y^t, P^t\right)}{P^t X^t}$

$$0E_i^t\left(Y^t, X^t, P^t\right) = \frac{C^t(Y^t, P^t)}{P^t X^t} \tag{24}$$

The below unequal is resulted:

$$\frac{C^t(Y^t, P^t)}{P^t X^t} \leq D_i^t(Y^t, X^t) \tag{25}$$

The overall efficiency compares the production cost $C^t(Y^t, P^t)$ which is the lowest production cost with the production cost of unit in period t.

If overall efficiency is less than one or more input is used for output production Y^t, or input cost $\left(P^t X^t\right)$, X^t is not a pleasure cost, or both, the first problem is recognizable by the technical efficiency (20) and the second one by the defined allocative efficiency in below.

Allocative efficiency is the proportion of the overall efficiency changes to the technical efficiency (the technical efficiency is the same with the distance function).

$$AE_i^t\left(Y^t, X^t, P^t\right) = \frac{C(Y^t, P^t)}{P^t X^t D_i^t(Y^t, X^t)} \tag{26}$$

Allocative efficiency is equal to one if & only if the overall & technical efficiency are equal. Malmquist productivity index with distance function is defined as follows.

Suppose that time t and t + 1 are given. Malmquist index in the nature of input for time t is equal to:

$$IM^t = \left[\frac{D_i^t(Y^{t+1}, X^{t+1})}{D_i^t(Y^t, X^t)}\right] \tag{27}$$

IM^t Compares the DMU under evaluation between two periods of t & t+1 in comparison to frontier of t under constant return to scale (CRS). Similarly IM^{t+1} is the distance of $(X^t, Y^t), (X^{t+1}, Y^{t+1})$ with CRS under frontier of t+1.

$$IM^{t+1} = \left[\frac{D_i^{t+1}(Y^{t+1}, X^{t+1})}{D_i^{t+1}(Y^t, X^t)}\right] \tag{28}$$

MPI which is a geometric combination of two above indices (27) & (28) is defined as follows:

$$IM = \left[\frac{D_i^t(Y^{t+1}, X^{t+1})}{D_i^{t+1}(Y^t, X^t)} \cdot \frac{D_i^{t+1}(Y^{t+1}, X^{t+1})}{D_i^t(Y^t, X^t)}\right]^{\frac{1}{2}} \tag{29}$$

Here is assumed that is CRS based because the reference points are clearly marked. Variable Return to scale (VRS) is similarly discussed and this assumption is to simplify the content.

Cost Malmquist Productivity Index

Productivity changes are discussed according to the changes in allocative efficiency & technical efficiency in production technology & input cost. According to the Malmquist productivity index in relations (26) to (28), cost Malmquist is defined for periods of t and t + 1 are as follows:

$$CM^t = \left[\frac{\dfrac{C^t(Y^{t+1}, P^t)}{P^t X^{t+1}}}{\dfrac{C^t(Y^t, P^t)}{P^t X^t}} \right] \tag{30}$$

$$CM^{t+1} = \left[\frac{\dfrac{C^{t+1}(Y^{t+1}, P^{t+1})}{P^{t+1} X^{t+1}}}{\dfrac{C^{t+1}(Y^t, P^{t+1})}{P^{t+1} X^t}} \right] \tag{31}$$

$$CM = \left[\frac{\dfrac{C^t(Y^{t+1}, P^t)}{P^t X^{t+1}}}{\dfrac{C^t(Y^t, P^t)}{P^t X^t}} \cdot \frac{\dfrac{C^{t+1}(Y^{t+1}, P^{t+1})}{P^{t+1} X^{t+1}}}{\dfrac{C^{t+1}(Y^t, P^{t+1})}{P^{t+1} X^t}} \right]^{\frac{1}{2}} \tag{32}$$

Such that:

$$P^t X^t = \sum_{N=1}^{n} P_N^t x_N^t \tag{33}$$

In equation (33), N is defined as the Nth input and $C^t(Y^t, P^t)$ is the least cost that has been calculated at (21).

The fraction of $\dfrac{C^t(Y^t, P^t)}{P^t X^t}$ is the efficiency of production cost of vector Y^t in period of t with input price P^t. This fraction is the distance ratio between the price of $P^t X^t$ and the lowest consumer price. The value of this fraction cannot be larger than one. If DMU under evaluation consumes the least cost for Y^t, the value of fraction equals to one, and when the value of fraction is less than one, it means that cost of inputs can be reduced. This fraction is precisely the definition of over-all efficiency which is denoted by (20).

CM Index shows that which input price can be reduced to reach cost border. There are three following conditions for CM index.

1.   CM> 1 means productivity has increased.
2.   CM <1 productivity dropped.
3.   CM = 1 productivity has not changed.

Decomposition of CM Index

CM index decomposed into two factors overall efficiency change (OEC) and the cost technical change (CTC) as follows:

$$
CM = \frac{\dfrac{C^{t+1}(Y^{t+1},P^{t+1})}{P^{t+1}X^{t+1}}}{\dfrac{C^{t}(Y^{t},P^{t})}{P^{t}X^{t}}} \left[\frac{\dfrac{C^{t}(Y^{t+1},P^{t})}{P^{t}X^{t+1}}}{\dfrac{C^{t+1}(Y^{t+1},P^{t+1})}{P^{t+1}X^{t+1}}} \cdot \frac{\dfrac{C^{t}(Y^{t},P^{t})}{P^{t}X^{t}}}{\dfrac{C^{t+1}(Y^{t},P^{t+1})}{P^{t+1}X^{t}}} \right]^{\frac{1}{2}}
\tag{34}
$$

In the model (34) numerator and denominator are analyzed, which are out of square root and indicate the overall efficiency changes that is the shown in (24). In fact, it shows the value of OEC between two periods of t, t + 1 and represents the nearness of the two DMU to the cost frontier at the same time and a factor that is taken square root, reflects the CTC value. This value shows the value of cost boundary changes.

OEC index is decomposed itself into the Technical Efficiency Changes (TEC) & Allocative Efficiency Changes (AEC).

$$
OEC = \frac{D_{i}^{t+1}(Y^{t+1},X^{t+1})}{D_{i}^{t}(Y^{t},X^{t})} \cdot \left[\frac{\dfrac{C^{t+1}(Y^{t+1},P^{t+1})}{P^{t+1}X^{t+1}D_{i}^{t+1}(Y^{t+1},X^{t+1})}}{\dfrac{C^{t+1}(Y^{t},P^{t+1})}{P^{t+1}X^{t}D_{i}^{t}(Y^{t},X^{t})}} \right]
\tag{35}
$$

CTC index is also biodegradable as follows:

$$
CTC =
$$

$$
\left[\frac{D_{i}^{t}(Y^{t+1},X^{t+1})}{D_{i}^{t+1}(Y^{t+1},X^{t+1})} \cdot \frac{D_{i}^{t}(Y^{t},X^{t})}{D_{i}^{t+1}(Y^{t},X^{t})} \right]^{\frac{1}{2}} \left[\frac{AE_{i}^{t}(X_{p}^{t+1},Y^{t+1},P^{t})}{AE_{i}^{t+1}(X_{p}^{t+1},Y^{t+1},P^{t+1})} \cdot \frac{AE_{i}^{t}(X_{p}^{t},Y^{t},P^{t})}{AE_{i}^{t+1}(X_{p}^{t},Y^{t},P^{t+1})} \right]^{\frac{1}{2}}
\tag{36}
$$

The first fraction indicates TEC and the second one shows the AEC cost.

Calculation of CM Index and Analyzed Its Factors

Input distance and cost functions are required to calculate the allocative and technical efficiency. These factors can be calculated by using the non-parametric programming and DEA techniques. To get the CM index, it will be done as follows:

$DMU_j (j = 1,...,n)$ are available at any time.

At the unit of time t, k^{th} unit will be shown with $x_{ik}^t (i = 1,...,m)$ is used for producing r^{th} output $Y_{rk}^t (r = 1,...,s)$.

The cost of the unit j with $P^t x^t$ is calculated as $P^t X^t = \sum_{j=1}^{n} p_{ij}^t x_{ij}^t$ & similarly, the costs of $P^{t+1}X^{t+1}, P^{t+1}X^t, P^t X^{t+1}$ are obtained by sum of $\sum_{j=1}^{n} P^{t+1}X^{t+1}, \sum_{j=1}^{n} P^{t+1}X^t, \sum_{j=1}^{n} P^t X^{t+1}$. The value of $C^t(Y^t, P^t)$ is calculated for j^{th} unit by using of the following model and λ_j is coefficients of linear combination of inputs and outputs.

$$C^t(Y^t, P^t) = Min \sum_{i=1}^{m} p_{ik}^t x_i$$

$$s.t. \sum_{j=1}^{n} \lambda_j x_{ij}^t \leq x_i \qquad i = 1,...,m,$$

$$\sum_{j=1}^{n} \lambda_j y_{rj}^t \geq y_{rk}^t \qquad r = 1,...,s, \tag{37}$$

$$\lambda_j \geq 0 \qquad j = 1,...,n,$$

$$x_i \geq 0 \qquad i = 1,...,m.$$

$C^t(Y^{t+1}, P^t)$ is obtained as same as above with the following model.

$$C^t(Y^{t+1}, P^t) = Min \sum_{i=1}^{m} p_{ik}^t x_i$$

$$s.t. \sum_{j=1}^{n} \lambda_j x_{ij}^t \leq x_i \qquad i = 1, ..., m,$$

$$\sum_{j=1}^{n} \lambda_j y_{rj}^t \geq y_{rk}^{t+1} \qquad r = 1, ..., s, \tag{38}$$

$$\lambda_j \geq 0 \qquad\qquad j = 1, ..., n,$$

$$x_i \geq 0 \qquad\qquad i = 1, ..., m.$$

Values of $C^{t+1}(Y^{t+1}, P^{t+1}), C^{t+1}(Y^t, P^{t+1})$ are obtained by transfer in periods t to t + 1 and t+1 to t, according to the above models.

The value of distance function is needed to calculate CM index. In period t, the function value is determined by using the following models.

$$D_i^t(Y^t, X^t) = Min\theta$$

$$s.t. \sum_{j=1}^{n} \lambda_j x_{ij}^t \leq \theta x_{ik}^t \qquad i = 1, ..., m,$$

$$\sum_{j=1}^{n} \lambda_j y_{rj}^t \geq y_{rk}^t \qquad r = 1, ..., s, \tag{39}$$

$$\lambda_j \geq 0 \qquad\qquad j = 1, ..., n.$$

$$D_i^t(Y^{t+1}, X^{t+1}) = Min\theta$$

$$s.t. \sum_{j=1}^{n} \lambda_j x_{ij}^t \leq \theta x_{ik}^{t+1} \qquad i = 1, ..., m,$$

$$\sum_{j=1}^{n} \lambda_j y_{rj}^t \geq y_{rk}^{t+1} \qquad r = 1, ..., s, \tag{40}$$

$$\lambda_j \geq 0 \qquad\qquad j = 1, ..., n.$$

The values of $D_i^{t+1}(Y^{t+1}, X^{t+1}), D_i^{t+1}(Y^t, X^t)$ obtained by replacing t instead of t + 1 & t + 1 instead of t in (39) and (40).

Revenue Malmquist Productivity Index (RM)

Revenue Malmquist Productivity Index (RM) is an index for signification progress and regress each unit based on consideration benefit as product Y^t.

Suppose in period t, with consumption per input unit $X^t \in R^m$, product output $Y^t \in R^s$ is produced.

The production technology in period t is defined as output offer set which is:

$$L^t(Y^t) = \left\{ Y^t | Y^t \text{ can product } X^t \right\} \tag{41}$$

$L^t(Y^t)$ contains all output vectors which is produced from X^t. This set is non-empty, closed, and convex, bounded, and satisfies strong disposability of inputs and outputs. Bound of the set is named as output isoquant, that is:

$$I_{soq} L^t(X^t) = \left\{ Y^t | Y^t \in L^t\left(X^t\right), \ \lambda Y^t \notin L^t\left(X^t\right) \ \text{ for } \lambda > 1 \right\} \tag{42}$$

This set shows a boundary (frontier) to the output offer set in the sense that any radial expansion of output vectors that lie on the frontier is not possible within $L^t(X^t)$. The output distance function is defined as:

$$D_o^t\left(X^t, Y^t\right) = \text{Sup} \left\{ \varphi | \left(\varphi Y^t\right) \in L^t\left(X^t\right), \varphi > 0 \right\} \tag{43}$$

The subscript o denotes output orientation.

$D_o^t\left(X^t, Y^t\right)$ In relation (43) is the highest possible demand, which can be multiplied with Y^t remains in $L^t(X^t)$.

If $D_o^t\left(X^t, Y^t\right) > 1$, then $Y^t \in L^t(X^t)$. if $D_o^t\left(X^t, Y^t\right) = 1$, then $Y^t \in I_{soq} L^t\left(X^t\right)$. $D_o^t\left(X^t, Y^t\right)$ is similar to the definition of technical efficiency in output orientation.

$$TE_o^t(X^t, Y^t) = \text{Max} \left\{ \varphi | \left(\varphi Y^t\right) \in L^t\left(X^t\right), \varphi > 0 \right\} \tag{44}$$

When the output price $W^t \in R_+^s$, are available, the revenue function is defined.

$$R^t\left(X^t, W^t\right) = \text{Max} \left\{ W^t Y^t | Y^t \in L^t\left(X^t\right), W^t > 0 \right\} \tag{45}$$

$R^t\left(X^t, W^t\right)$ is the maximum revenue of producing outputs Y^t. Frontier of this set is:

$$I_{soq} R^t\left(X^t, W^t\right) = \left\{Y^t | W^t Y^t = R^t\left(X^t, W^t\right)\right\} \tag{46}$$

This boundary contains the output vectors that can have the maximum revenue with their price W^t. Therefore technical efficiency and distance function have the same definition. Overall efficiency defines as follows:

$$OE_o^t\left(X^t, Y^t, W^t\right) = \frac{W^t Y^t}{R^t\left(X^t, W^t\right)} \tag{47}$$

Because technical efficiency is less than overall efficiency (revenue) for each unit, then:

$$TE_o^t\left(X^t, Y^t\right) \leq OE_o^t\left(X^t, Y^t, W^t\right) \tag{48}$$

According to technical efficiency is the same as distance function:

$$D_o^t\left(X^t, Y^t\right) \leq \frac{W^t Y^t}{R^t\left(X^t, W^t\right)} \tag{49}$$

Allocative efficiency defines as follows:

$$AE_o^t\left(X^t, Y^t, W^t\right) = \frac{W^t Y^t}{R^t\left(X^t, W^t\right) D_o^t\left(X^t, Y^t\right)} \tag{50}$$

Malmquist productivity index with distance function is defined as follows:

$$OM^t = \left[\frac{D_o^t\left(X^t, Y^t\right)}{D_o^t\left(X^{t+1}, Y^{t+1}\right)}\right] \tag{51}$$

$$OM^{t+1} = \left[\frac{D_0^{t+1}\left(X^t, Y^t\right)}{D_o^{t+1}\left(X^{t+1}, Y^{t+1}\right)} \right] \tag{52}$$

OM^t is composed by DMUs in periods t and t + 1 to frontier t. OM^{t+1} is composed by DMUs in periods t and t + 1 to frontier t + 1. OM is a geometric component of (51) and (52):

$$OM = \left[\frac{D_0^t\left(X^t, Y^t\right)}{D_0^t\left(X^{t+1}, Y^{t+1}\right)} \cdot \frac{D_0^{t+1}\left(X^t, Y^t\right)}{D_0^{t+1}\left(X^{t+1}, Y^{t+1}\right)} \right]^{\frac{1}{2}} \tag{53}$$

Three conditions are exited for OM:

1. OM> 1, observe progress.
2. OM <1, observe regress.
3. OM = 1, do not observe any change in productivity.

By using allocative and technical efficiency, output's price productivity changes are determined. Revenue Malmquist Productivity Index (RM) is calculated as:

$$RM^t = \left[\frac{{W^t Y^t}\Big/{R^t\left(X^t, W^t\right)}}{{W^t Y^{t+1}}\Big/{R^t\left(X^{t+1}, W^t\right)}} \right] \tag{54}$$

$$RM^{t+1} = \left[\frac{{W^{t+1} Y^t}\Big/{R^{t+1}\left(X^t, W^{t+1}\right)}}{{W^{t+1} Y^{t+1}}\Big/{R^{t+1}\left(X^{t+1}, W^{t+1}\right)}} \right] \tag{55}$$

$$RM = \left[\frac{{W^t Y^t}\Big/{R^t\left(X^t, W^t\right)}}{{W^t Y^{t+1}}\Big/{R^t\left(X^{t+1}, W^t\right)}} \cdot \frac{{W^{t+1} Y^t}\Big/{R^{t+1}\left(X^t, W^{t+1}\right)}}{{W^{t+1} Y^{t+1}}\Big/{R^{t+1}\left(X^{t+1}, W^{t+1}\right)}} \right]^{1/2} \tag{56}$$

and $W^t Y^t = \sum_{n=1}^{N} w_n^t y_n^t$, n is the nth output & $R^t\left(X^t, W^t\right)$ is the maximum revenue which is calculated in (45).

Malmquist and CM indices is respectively in related to the quantity of inputs and input costs. OM index discusses outputs quantity and RM index discusses outputs revenue.

$\dfrac{W^t Y^t}{R^t\left(X^t, W^t\right)}$ is the revenue efficiency of product Y^t in period t with output

cost W^t. This fraction compares reverie of output Y^t and the maximum product revenue and its value is not less than one.

1. RM> 1, observe progress and decrease productivity.
2. RM< 1, observe regress and increase productivity.
3. RM = 1, no change in productivity

Analysis of Revenue Malmquist Productivity Index

RM index mentioned in (56) can be decomposed easily in to OM index mentioned in (57). Results of this composition are overall efficiency change (OEC) and revenue technical change (RTC). Each of these components can be self-decomposed as follow:

As mentioned, RM index can be decomposed into OEC and RTC.

$$RM = \frac{W^t Y^t / R^t\left(X^t, W^t\right)}{W^{t+1}Y^{t+1} / R^{t+1}\left(X^{t+1}, W^t\right)} \cdot \left[\frac{W^{t+1}Y^{t+1} / R^{t+1}\left(X^{t+1}, W^{t+1}\right)}{W^t Y^{t+1} / R^t\left(X^{t+1}, W^t\right)} \cdot \frac{W^{t+1}Y^t / R^{t+1}\left(X^t, W^{t+1}\right)}{W^t Y^t / R^t\left(X^t, W^t\right)} \right]^{\frac{1}{2}}$$

(57)

In model (57), the numerator and denominator of the component outside the square brackets are the value of overall efficiency change at two time periods t and t + 1, that is OEC; and it value indicates whether the production unit catches up the revenue boundary when going from period t to period t+ 1 or not.

Decomposition of Overall Efficiency Change (OEC)

It can be decomposed into technical efficiency change (TEC) and allocative efficiency change (AEC).

$$OEC = \left[\frac{D_o^{t+1}(X^{t+1}, Y^{t+1})}{D_o^t(X^t, Y^t)} \cdot \frac{AE_o^t \left(X^t, Y^t, W^t \right)}{AE_o^{t+1} \left(X^{t+1}, Y^{t+1}, W^{t+1} \right)} \right] \qquad (58)$$

The first component on the left of the relation (58) indicates technical efficiency change.

The fraction identifies the distance ratio of $(X^t, Y^t), (X^{t+1}, Y^{t+1})$ with revenue border in periods t and t + 1. The second component in (58) shows allocative efficiency change.

Decomposition of Revenue Technical Change (RTC)

This component can be decomposed as follow:

$$RTC = \left[\frac{D_o^t(X^{t+1}, Y^{t+1})}{D_o^{t+1}(X^{t+1}, Y^{t+1})} \cdot \frac{D_o^t(X^t, Y^t)}{D_o^{t+1}(X^t, Y^t)} \right]^{\frac{1}{2}} \cdot \left[\frac{AE_o^{t+1} \left(X^{t+1}, Y^{t+1}, W^{t+1} \right)}{AE_o^t \left(X^{t+1}, Y^{t+1}, W^t \right)} \cdot \frac{AE_o^{t+1} \left(X^t, Y^t, W^{t+1} \right)}{AE_o^t \left(X^t, Y^t, W^t \right)} \right]^{\frac{1}{2}}$$

$$(59)$$

The first fraction on the left side is the value of technical efficiency change & the second fraction is technology changes of allocative efficiency.

RM Index Calculation and Its Components

Output distance function and revenue distance function are used to calculate the allocative and technical efficiency.

These components are calculated by using the non-parametric programming and it is possible according to the DEA techniques.

The unit (x_{i0}^t, y_{ro}^t) represents the ith input and r^{th} output of unit o^{th} in period t.

Product revenue in period t for r^{th} component is $W^t Y^t$ and is calculated by

$$W^t Y^t = \sum_{r=1}^s w_{ro}^t\, y_{ro}^t \,. \text{ Therefore revenues } W^{t+1} Y^{t+1}, W^{t+1} Y^t, W^t Y^{t+1} \text{ are obtained}$$

with the sum of $\sum_{r=1}^s w_{ro}^{t+1}\, y_{ro}^{t+1}, \sum_{r=1}^s w_{ro}^{t+1}\, y_{ro}^t, \sum_{r=1}^s w_{ro}^t\, y_{ro}^{t+1}$.

$R^t(X^t, W^t)$ is calculated by using the following model that the vectors Y, λ are calculated unknowns.

$$R^t \left(X^t, W^t \right) = \text{Max} \quad \sum_{r=1}^{s} w_{r0}^t Y_r$$

$$s.t. \sum_{j=1}^{n} \lambda_j x_{ij}^t \leq x_{i0}^t, \quad i = 1, ..., m,$$

$$\sum_{j=1}^{n} \lambda_j x_{rj}^t \geq y_r, \quad r = 1, ..., s, \tag{60}$$

$$\lambda_j \geq 0 \qquad j = 1, ..., n,$$

$$y_r \geq 0 \qquad r = 1, ..., s.$$

$R^t \left(X^{t+1}, W^t \right)$ is acquired similar to the above model:

$$R^t \left(X^{t+1}, W^t \right) = \text{Max} \quad \sum_{r=1}^{s} w_{r0}^t Y_r$$

$$s.t. \sum_{j=1}^{n} \lambda_j x_{ij}^t \leq x_{i0}^{t+1}, \quad i = 1, ..., m,$$

$$\sum_{j=1}^{n} \lambda_j x_{rj}^t \geq y_r, \quad r = 1, ..., s, \tag{61}$$

$$\lambda_j \geq 0, \qquad j = 1, ..., n,$$

$$y_r \geq 0, \qquad r = 1, ..., s.$$

$R^{t+1} \left(X^{t+1}, W^{t+1} \right), R^{t+1} \left(X^t, W^{t+1} \right)$ values are obtained with changing t to t + 1 in the aforementioned models. To calculate the RM index, distance functions are required which are acquired in accordance with the following model.

$$D_0^t \left(X^t, Y^t \right) = \text{Max} \quad \varphi$$

$$s.t. \sum_{j=1}^{n} \lambda_j x_{ij}^t \leq x_{ik}^t, \quad i = 1, ..., m,$$

$$\sum_{j=1}^{n} \lambda_j y_{rj}^t \geq \varphi y_{rk}^t, \quad r = 1, ..., s, \tag{62}$$

$$\lambda_j \geq 0, \qquad j = 1, ..., n.$$

$$D_0^t \left(X^{t+1}, Y^{t+1} \right) = \text{Max} \quad \varphi$$

$$s.t. \sum_{j=1}^{n} \lambda_j x_{ij}^t \leq x_{ik}^{t+1}, \qquad i = 1,\dots,m,$$

$$\sum_{j=1}^{n} \lambda_j y_{rj}^t \geq \varphi y_{rk}^{t+1}, \qquad r = 1,\dots,s, \tag{63}$$

$$\lambda_j \geq 0, \qquad j = 1,\dots,n.$$

The values $D_0^{t+1} \left(X^{t+1}, Y^{t+1} \right), D_0^{t+1} \left(X^t, Y^t \right)$ are obtained by using of models (62) and (63) with changing t to t + 1.

Bounded DEA Model (Interval DEA)

For a reasonable set of interval efficiency for any decision-making unit, DEA models is used such as below:

Definition: Anti-ideal DMU is a virtual DMU which consumes the most inputs to produce minimum outputs.

Due to above definition, inputs and outputs of anti-ideal DMU are determined by following equations:

$$x_i^{max} = max_j \left\{ x_{ij} \right\} \quad i = 1,\dots,m$$
$$y_r^{max} = min_j \left\{ y_{rj} \right\} \quad r = 1,\dots,s \tag{64}$$

The best efficiency relations of anti-ideal DMU are calculated based on fractional programming model as follows:

$$Max \quad \theta_{ADMU} = \frac{\sum_{r=1}^{s} u_r y_r^{min}}{\sum_{i=1}^{m} v_i x_i^{max}}$$

$$s.t. \quad \theta_j = \frac{\sum_{r=1}^{s} u_r y_{rj}}{\sum_{i=1}^{m} v_i x_{ij}} \leq 1, \qquad j = 1,\dots,n,$$

$$u_r \geq 0, \qquad\qquad\qquad r = 1,\dots,s, \tag{65}$$

$$v_i \geq 0, \qquad\qquad\qquad i = 1,\dots,m.$$

Model (65) can be moved with the LP model.

$$
\begin{aligned}
Max \quad & \sum_{r=1}^{s} u_r y_r^{min} \\
s.t. & \sum_{r=1}^{s} u_r y_{rj} - \sum_{i=1}^{m} v_i x_{ij} \le 0, \qquad j = 1, \ldots, n, \\
& \sum_{i=1}^{m} v_i x_{ij} = 1, \\
& u_r \ge 0, \qquad\qquad\qquad\qquad r = 1, \ldots, s, \\
& v_i \ge 0, \qquad\qquad\qquad\qquad i = 1, \ldots, m.
\end{aligned}
\tag{66}
$$

Efficiencies of all DMU cannot be less than $\theta_{ADMU}{}^{*}$ and also $\theta_{ADMU}{}^{*}$ is the optimum value of the objective function of above model. Thus the below idea defines the bounded DEA model.

$$
\begin{aligned}
Max \quad & \frac{\sum_{r=1}^{s} u_r y_{ro}}{\sum_{i=1}^{m} v_i x_{io}} \\
s.t. \quad & \theta_{ADMU}{}^{*} \le \frac{\sum_{r=1}^{s} u_r y_{rj}}{\sum_{i=1}^{m} v_i x_{ij}} \le 1, \qquad j = 1, \ldots, n, \\
& u_r \ge 0, \qquad\qquad\qquad\qquad r = 1, \ldots, s, \\
& v_i \ge 0 \qquad\qquad\qquad\qquad i = 1, \ldots, m.
\end{aligned}
\tag{67}
$$

Model (67) can be converted to the following LP models:

$$
\begin{aligned}
Max \;/\; Min \quad & \sum_{r=1}^{s} u_r y_{ro} \\
s.t. \quad & \sum_{r=1}^{s} u_r y_{rj} - \sum_{i=1}^{m} v_i x_{ij} \le 0, \qquad\qquad j = 1, \ldots, n, \\
& \sum_{r=1}^{s} u_r y_{rj} - \sum_{i=1}^{m} v_i (\theta_{ADMU}{}^{*}) x_{ij} \ge 0, \qquad j = 1, \ldots, n, \\
& \sum_{i=1}^{m} v_i x_{ij} = 1, \\
& u_r \ge 0 \qquad\qquad\qquad\qquad\qquad r = 1, \ldots, s, \\
& v_i \ge 0 \qquad\qquad\qquad\qquad\qquad i = 1, \ldots, m.
\end{aligned}
\tag{68}
$$

After solving the above models, the interval efficiency is shown as $\left[\theta_o^{L^*}, \theta_o^{u^*} \right]$ that $\theta_o^{u^*}$ and $\theta_o^{L^*}$ are respectively the maximum and the minimum value of the above objective function.

Malmquist Productivity Index with Interval Data

In this part, Bounded DEA model is used & the Malmquist productivity index will be provided. First is need to evaluate efficiency scores of anti-ideal DMU for each time period t and t + 1. In time period t, for reference time $\theta_{ADMU}^{t^*}$ $\theta_{ADMU}^{t^*}$ obtained from the following model by using values $D_0^t \left(X^t{}_0, Y^t{}_0 \right), D_0^t \left(X^{t+1}{}_0, Y^{t+1}{}_0 \right)$

$$
\max \quad \theta_{ADMU}^t = \sum_{r=1}^{s} u_r y_r^{min,t}
$$

$$
s.t. \sum_{r=1}^{s} u_r y_{rj}^t - \sum_{i=1}^{m} v_i x_{ij}^t \leq 0, \qquad j = 1,...,n,
$$

$$
\sum_{i=1}^{m} v_i x_{ij}^{max,t} = 1, \tag{69}
$$

$$
u_r \geq 0, \qquad\qquad r = 1,...,s,
$$

$$
v_i \geq 0, \qquad\qquad i = 1,...,m.
$$

$x_i^{max,t}, y_r^{min,t}$ respectively are input & output of anti-ideal DMU in period t which is determined as below:

$$
x_i^{max,t} = \frac{\max}{j} \left\{ x_{ij}^t \right\}, \quad i = 1,...,m,
$$

$$
y_r^{min,t} = \frac{\min}{j} \left\{ y_{rj}^t \right\}, \quad r = 1,...,s. \tag{70}
$$

The following model shows interval Efficiency:

$$D_0^t\left(X_0^t, Y_0^t\right) = max \ / \ min \quad \sum_{r=1}^{s} u_r y_{r0}^t$$

$$s.t. \sum_{r=1}^{s} u_r y_{rj}^t - \sum_{i=1}^{m} v_i x_{ij}^t \leq 0, \qquad\qquad j = 1, \ldots, n,$$

$$\sum_{r=1}^{s} u_r y_{rj}^t - \sum_{i=1}^{m} v_i (\theta_{ADMU}^{t^*} x_{ij}^t) \leq 0, \qquad j = 1, \ldots, n,$$

$$\sum_{i=1}^{m} v_i x_{i0}^t = 1,$$

$$u_r \geq 0, \qquad\qquad\qquad\qquad\qquad r = 1, \ldots, s,$$

$$v_i \geq 0. \qquad\qquad\qquad\qquad\qquad i = 1, \ldots, m.$$

$$(71)$$

It is assumed that $D_0^{t,U}\left(X_0^t, Y_0^t\right), D_0^{t,L}\left(X_0^t, Y_0^t\right)$ are respectively the upper & lower value of interval efficiency $D_0^t\left(X_0^t, Y_0^t\right)$ which are respectively obtained from the max & min of model (71). Consequently the interval efficiency is shown as $\left[D_0^{t,L}\left(X_0^t, Y_0^t\right), D_0^{t,U}\left(X_0^t, Y_0^t\right)\right]$.

For mixed periods, interval efficiency is calculated as below:

$$D_0^t\left(X_0^{t+1}, Y_0^{t+1}\right) = max \ / \ min \quad \sum_{r=1}^{s} u_r y_{r0}^{t+1}$$

$$s.t. \sum_{r=1}^{s} u_r y_{rj}^t - \sum_{i=1}^{m} v_i x_{ij}^t \leq 0, \qquad\qquad j = 1, \ldots, n,$$

$$\sum_{r=1}^{s} u_r y_{rj}^t - \sum_{i=1}^{m} v_i (\theta_{ADMU}^{t^*} x_{ij}^t) \leq 0, \qquad j = 1, \ldots, n,$$

$$\sum_{i=1}^{m} v_i x_{i0}^{t+1} = 1,$$

$$u_r \geq 0, \qquad\qquad\qquad\qquad\qquad r = 1, \ldots, s,$$

$$v_i \geq 0. \qquad\qquad\qquad\qquad\qquad i = 1, \ldots, m.$$

$$(72)$$

Malmquist productivity index is defined as follows:

$$MI_0 = \left[\frac{D_0^t\left(X_0^{t+1}, Y_0^{t+1}\right)}{D_0^t\left(X_0^t, Y_0^t\right)} \cdot \frac{D_0^{t+1}\left(X_0^{t+1}, Y_0^{t+1}\right)}{D_0^{t+1}\left(X_0^t, Y_0^t\right)}\right]^{\frac{1}{2}} \qquad (73)$$

Interval Malmquist index for each $DMU_o(o\{1,2,\ldots,n\})$ which the upper & lower of Malmquist productivity index are given as follows:

$$MI_o^L = \left[\frac{D_o^{t,L}\left(X_o^{t+1},Y_o^{t+1}\right)}{D_o^{t,U}\left(X_o^t,Y_o^t\right)} \cdot \frac{D_o^{t+1,L}\left(X_o^{t+1},Y_o^{t+1}\right)}{D_o^{t+1,U}\left(X_o^t,Y_o^t\right)} \right]^{\frac{1}{2}}$$

$$MI_o^U = \left[\frac{D_o^{t,U}\left(X_o^{t+1},Y_o^{t+1}\right)}{D_o^{t,L}\left(X_o^t,Y_o^t\right)} \cdot \frac{D_o^{t+1,U}\left(X_o^{t+1},Y_o^{t+1}\right)}{D_o^{t+1,L}\left(X_o^t,Y_o^t\right)} \right]^{\frac{1}{2}} \tag{74}$$

Therefore interval Malmquist productivity index is shown as $\left[MI_o^L, MI_o^U\right]$. Classification of DMUs to two units of time t and t + 1 and estimation progress & regress is as follows:

$$M^{++} = \{Alternative_i \,\big|\, M.P.I_i^L > 1\}$$
$$M^{-} = \{Alternative_i \,\big|\, M.P.I_i^U < 1\} \tag{75}$$
$$M^{+} = \{Alternative_i \,\big|\, M.P.I_i^L \leq 1,\; M.P.I_i^U \geq 1\}$$

Here two set of M^{++}, M^{+} include units that in time period t and t + 1, respectively were in progress and regress. The following modes are considered to determine the progress or regress of each unit belonging to a set of M^{-}:

1. If $MI_O^U = 1, MI_{OI}^L = 1$, consequently DMU_O has not have progress or regress.
2. If $MI_O^U > 1, MI_{OI}^L = 1$, DMU_O just has progress.
3. If $MI_O^U = 1, MI_{OI}^L < 1$, DMU_O just has regress.
4. If $MI_O^U > 1, MI_{OI}^L < 1$, then use the following index for estimating of progress & regress of DMU_O:

$$\rho = \frac{MI_O^U - 1}{1 - MI_O^L}, \quad 0 < \rho < \infty \tag{76}$$

1. p>1 indicates that DMU_O has a higher progress percentage than regress,
2. p<1 shows that DMU_O has a high regress percentage than progress.

Cost Efficiency with Interval Data

Assume that have n DMU with interval input & output and P_{ij} is i^{th} input cost for DMU_0 such that $p_{ij} \in \left[p_{ij}^{max}, p_{ij}^{min} \right]$. For this purpose the value of cost efficiency is obtained as interval & to calculate it the following models are used:

$$
\begin{aligned}
\text{Min} \quad & \sum_{i=1}^{m} p_{io}^{max} x_i^{o} \\
s.t. \quad & \sum_{j=1, j \neq o}^{n} \lambda_j x_{ij}^{u} + \lambda_o x_{io}^{l} = x_i^{o}, \quad i = 1, \ldots, m, \\
& \sum_{j=1, j \neq o}^{n} \lambda_j y_{rj}^{l} + \lambda_o x_{ro}^{u} \geq y_{ro}^{u}, \quad r = 1, \ldots, s, \\
& \lambda_j \geq 0, \quad\quad\quad\quad j = 1, \ldots, n, \\
& x_i^{o} \geq 0, \quad\quad\quad\quad i = 1, \ldots, m.
\end{aligned}
\tag{77}
$$

$$
\begin{aligned}
\text{Min} \quad & \sum_{i=1}^{m} p_{io}^{min} x_i^{o} \\
s.t. \quad & \sum_{j=1, j \neq o}^{n} \lambda_j x_{ij}^{l} + \lambda_o x_{io}^{u} = x_i^{o}, \quad i = 1, \ldots, m, \\
& \sum_{j=1, j \neq o}^{n} \lambda_j y_{rj}^{u} + \lambda_o x_{ro}^{l} \geq y_{ro}^{l}, \quad r = 1, \ldots, s, \\
& \lambda_j \geq 0, \quad\quad\quad\quad j = 1, \ldots, n, \\
& x_i^{o} \geq 0, \quad\quad\quad\quad i = 1, \ldots, m.
\end{aligned}
\tag{78}
$$

Assume that $\overline{x}_i^{o*}$ & $\underline{x}_i^{o*}$ are respectively the optimum solutions for (77) & (78). The cost efficiencies for DMU_0 are obtained as follows:

$$
\overline{c} = \frac{\sum_{i=1}^{m} p_{io}^{max} \overline{x}_i^{o*}}{\sum_{i=1}^{m} p_{io}^{min} x_{io}}, \underline{c} = \frac{\sum_{i=1}^{m} p_{io}^{min} \underline{x}_i^{o*}}{\sum_{i=1}^{m} p_{io}^{min} x_{io}}
\tag{79}
$$

Theorem: the cost efficiency for DMU_0 is as $c \in [\underline{c}, \overline{c}]$ and also $p_{io} \leq p_{io}^{max}$.

Proof: it is obvious that:

$$x_i^{o^*} = \sum_{j=1}^{n} \lambda_j x_{ij}^* \leq \sum_{j=1}^{n} \lambda_j x_{ij}^{*u} = x_i^{o^{*u}},$$

$$\sum_{i=1}^{m} p_{io} x_i^{o^*} \leq \sum_{i=1}^{m} p_{io}^{max} \bar{x}_i^{o^*}, \tag{a}$$

Also regard to $p_{i0} \geq p_{i0}^{min}$:

$$\sum_{i=1}^{m} p_{io} x_{io} \leq \sum_{i=1}^{m} p_{io}^{min} x_{io}, \tag{b}$$

The Cost Malmquist Productivity Index with Interval Data

In the last sections in calculation of cost Malmquist productivity index is assumed that p_{ij} are constant. But if p_{ij} and inputs & outputs are in interval, following models is needed for calculating cost Malmquist productivity index:

$$
\begin{aligned}
\text{Min} \quad & \sum_{i=1}^{m} p_{io}^{max} x_i^{o} \\
s.t. \quad & \sum_{j=1,j\neq o}^{n} \lambda_j x_{ij}^{t+1,u} + \lambda_o x_{io}^{t+1,u} = x_i^{o}, \qquad i = 1,\ldots,m, \\
& \sum_{j=1,j\neq o}^{n} \lambda_j y_{rj}^{t+1,l} + \lambda_o y_{ro}^{t+1,u} \geq y_{ro}^{t+1,u}, \quad r = 1,\ldots,s, \\
& \lambda_j \geq 0, \qquad\qquad\qquad\qquad j = 1,\ldots,n, \\
& x_i^{o} \geq 0, \qquad\qquad\qquad\qquad i = 1,\ldots,m.
\end{aligned}
\tag{80}
$$

$$
\begin{aligned}
\text{Min} \quad & \sum_{i=1}^{m} p_{io}^{max} x_i^{o} \\
s.t. \quad & \sum_{j=1}^{n} \lambda_j x_{ij}^{t,u} = x_i^{o}, \qquad\qquad i = 1,\ldots,m, \\
& \sum_{j=1}^{n} \lambda_j y_{rj}^{t,l} \geq y_{ro}^{t+1,u}, \qquad\qquad r = 1,\ldots,s, \\
& \lambda_j \geq 0, \qquad\qquad\qquad j = 1,\ldots,n, \\
& x_i^{o} \geq 0, \qquad\qquad\qquad i = 1,\ldots,m.
\end{aligned}
\tag{81}
$$

$$\text{Min} \quad \sum_{i=1}^{m} p_{io}^{\min} x_i^o$$

$$s.t. \sum_{j=1, j \neq o}^{n} \lambda_j x_{ij}^{t,l} + \lambda_o x_{io}^{t,u} = x_i^o, \qquad i = 1, \dots, m \ ,$$

$$\sum_{j=1, j \neq o}^{n} \lambda_j y_{rj}^{t,u} + \lambda_o y_{ro}^{t,l} \geq y_{ro}^{t,l}, \qquad r = 1, \dots, s, \qquad (82)$$

$$\lambda_j \geq 0, \qquad\qquad\qquad j = 1, \dots, n,$$

$$x_i^o \geq 0, \qquad\qquad\qquad i = 1, \dots, m.$$

$$\text{Min} \quad \sum_{i=1}^{m} p_{io}^{\max} x_i^o$$

$$s.t. \sum_{j=1}^{n} »_j x_{ij}^{t+1,l} = x_i^o, \qquad\qquad i = 1, \dots, m \ ,$$

$$\sum_{j=1}^{n} »_j y_{rj}^{t+1,u} \geq y_{ro}^{t,l}, \qquad r = 1, \dots, s, \qquad (83)$$

$$»_j \geq 0, \qquad\qquad\qquad j = 1, \dots, n,$$

$$x_i^o \geq 0, \qquad\qquad\qquad i = 1, \dots, m.$$

According to cost models (80), (81), (82), (83):

$$\overline{c}_{t+1}^{t+1} = \frac{\sum_{i=1}^{m} p_{io}^{\max} \overline{x}_i^{o^*}}{\sum_{i=1}^{m} p_{io}^{\max} x_i^o}, \overline{c}_t^{t+1} = \frac{\sum_{i=1}^{m} p_{io}^{\max} \overline{x}_i^{o^*}}{\sum_{i=1}^{m} p_{io}^{\min} x_i^o}$$

$$\underline{c}_t^t = \frac{\sum_{i=1}^{m} p_{io}^{\min} \underline{x}_i^{o^*}}{\sum_{i=1}^{m} p_{io}^{\max} x_{io}}, \qquad \underline{c}_{t+1}^t = \frac{\sum_{i=1}^{m} p_{io}^{\min} \underline{x}_i^{o^*}}{\sum_{i=1}^{m} p_{io}^{\max} x_{io}} \qquad (84)$$

Regarding to above models $\overline{M}_c, \underline{M}_c$ is calculated as follows:

$$\overline{M}_c = \left[\frac{\overline{c}_t^{t+1}}{\underline{c}_t^t} \cdot \frac{\overline{c}_{t+1}^{t+1}}{\underline{c}_{t+1}^t} \right]^{\frac{1}{2}}, \underline{M}_c = \left[\frac{\underline{c}_t^{t+1}}{\overline{c}_t^t} \cdot \frac{\underline{c}_{t+1}^{t+1}}{\overline{c}_{t+1}^t} \right]^{\frac{1}{2}} \qquad (85)$$

Theorem: $M_c \in \left[\underline{M}_c, \bar{M}_c \right]$ that M_c is cost Malmquist productivity index.

Revenue Efficiency with Interval Data

It assumed that there are n DMU with interval input & output. R_{ri} is a profit of rth output DMU_j, such that $R_{rj} \in \left[R_{rj}^{min}, R_{rj}^{max} \right]$, in order to obtain revenue efficiency which is interval for this type of data, the following models have been offered:

$$
\begin{aligned}
\text{Max} \quad & \sum_{r=1}^{s} R_{ro}^{max} y_r^o \\
\text{s.t.} \quad & \sum_{j=1, j \neq o}^{n} \lambda_j x_{ij}^l + \lambda_o x_{io}^u = x_{io}^u, && i = 1, \ldots, m , \\
& \sum_{j=1}^{n} \lambda_j y_{rj}^u = y_r^o, && r = 1, \ldots, s, \\
& \lambda_j \geq 0, && j = 1, \ldots, n, \\
& y_r^o \geq 0, && r = 1, \ldots, s.
\end{aligned}
\tag{86}
$$

$$
\begin{aligned}
\text{Max} \quad & \sum_{r=1}^{s} R_{ro}^{max} y_r^o \\
\text{s.t.} \quad & \sum_{j=1, j \neq o}^{n} \lambda_j x_{ij}^u + \lambda_o x_{io}^l \leq x_{io}^l, && i = 1, \ldots, m , \\
& \sum_{j=1}^{n} \lambda_j y_{rj}^l = y_r^o, && r = 1, \ldots, s, \\
& \lambda_j \geq 0, && j = 1, \ldots, n, \\
& y_r^o \geq 0, && r = 1, \ldots, s.
\end{aligned}
\tag{87}
$$

It assumed that $\bar{y}^{o^*}, \underline{y}^{o^*}$ are respectively the optimum solutions for models (86) & (87).

The revenues $\underline{R}, \bar{R}$ are calculated for DMU_0 as follows:

$$
\underline{R} = \frac{\sum_{r=1}^{s} R_{ro}^{min} y_{ro}}{\sum_{r=1}^{s} R_{ro}^{max} \bar{y}_r^{o^*}}, \quad \bar{R} = \frac{\sum_{r=1}^{s} R_{ro}^{max} y_{ro}}{\sum_{r=1}^{s} R_{ro}^{min} \underline{y}_r^{o^*}}
\tag{88}
$$

Theorem: the revenue efficiency for DMU_0 is as $R \in \left[\underline{R}, \ \bar{R} \right]$.

Proof: it is clear that $R_{ro} \leq R_{ro}^{\max}$ & also:

$$
\begin{aligned}
\text{Max} \quad & \sum_{r=1}^{s} R_{ro}^{\min} y_r^o \\
s.t. \quad & \sum_{j=1, j \neq o}^{n} \lambda_j x_{ij}^{t,u} + \lambda_o x_{io}^{t,l} \leq x_{io}^{t,l}, & i = 1, \ldots, m \ , \\
& \sum_{j=1}^{n} \lambda_j y_{rj}^{t,l} = y_r^o, & r = 1, \ldots, s, \\
& \lambda_j \geq 0, & j = 1, \ldots, n, \\
& y_r^o \geq 0, & r = 1, \ldots, s.
\end{aligned}
\tag{89}
$$

$$
\begin{aligned}
\text{Max} \quad & \sum_{r=1}^{s} R_{ro}^{\min} y_r^o \\
s.t. \quad & \sum_{j=1}^{n} \lambda_j x_{ij}^{t+1,u} \leq x_{io}^{t,l}, & i = 1, \ldots, m \ , \\
& \sum_{j=1}^{n} \lambda_j y_{rj}^{t+1,l} = y_r^o, & r = 1, \ldots, s, \\
& \lambda_j \geq 0, & j = 1, \ldots, n, \\
& y_r^o \geq 0, & r = 1, \ldots, s.
\end{aligned}
\tag{90}
$$

The revenues of $\underline{R}_{t+1}^{t+1}, \underline{R}_t^{t+1}, \bar{R}_t^t, \bar{R}_{t+1}^t$ are calculated as follows:

$$
\underline{R}_{t+1}^{t+1} = \frac{\sum_{r=1}^{s} R_{ro}^{\min} y_{ro}^l}{\sum_{r=1}^{s} R_{ro}^{\max} \bar{y}_{r1}^{o^*}}
\qquad\qquad
\underline{R}_t^{t+1} = \frac{\sum_{r=1}^{s} R_{ro}^{\min} y_{ro}^l}{\sum_{r=1}^{s} R_{ro}^{\max} \bar{y}_{r2}^{o^*}}
$$

$$
\bar{R}_t^t = \frac{\sum_{r=1}^{s} R_{ro}^{\max} y_{ro}^u}{\sum_{r=1}^{s} R_{ro}^{\min} \bar{y}_{r3}^{o^*}}
\qquad\qquad
\bar{R}_{t+1}^t = \frac{\sum_{r=1}^{s} R_{ro}^{\max} y_{ro}^u}{\sum_{r=1}^{s} R_{ro}^{\min} \bar{y}_{r4}^{o^*}}
\tag{91}
$$

that $\bar{y}_{r1}^{o^*}, \bar{y}_{r2}^{o^*}, \bar{y}_{r3}^{o^*}, \bar{y}_{r4}^{o^*}$ are optimum solutions.

Therefore M_R is obtained by using the above models as follows:

$$M_R = \left[\frac{\underline{R}_t^{t+1}}{\overline{R}_t^t} \cdot \frac{\underline{R}_{t+1}^{t+1}}{\overline{R}_{t+1}^t} \right]^{\frac{1}{2}} \tag{92}$$

Similarly $\overline{M}_R$ is obtained as follows:

$$\overline{M}_R = \left[\frac{\overline{R}_t^{t+1}}{\underline{R}_t^t} \cdot \frac{\overline{R}_{t+1}^{t+1}}{\underline{R}_{t+1}^t} \right]^{\frac{1}{2}} \tag{93}$$

Theorem: $M_R \in \left[\underline{M}_R , \overline{M}_R \right]$ that M_R is revenue Malmquist productivity index.

Application of Malmquist Productivity Index in Integrated Units of Power Plant

This section consider Malmquist productivity index applicably in a thermal power plant consist of four similar 325 megawatt steam units.

Four units of one of the country's power plants are assessed & the data of its five successive years are supplied. For each DMU (power plant unit), the assessment model & inputs and outputs indices are defined as the Figure 1.

Figure 1. DMU of a power plant

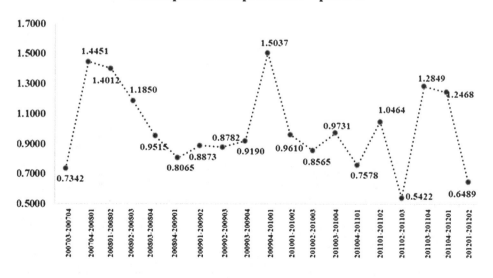

It is confirmed that the data are supplied at five successive years which the data information at 2005 are given in Table 2.

Domestic Consumption

Percentage of per unit production is spending on domestic consumption of same unit. This rate of usage is calculated as a percentage of total production and usually depends on the rate of load unit and the conditions of the unit consumers can be varied between 7-9 percent. It is natural that proper utilization, timely periodic repairs of equipment and observing the optimization rules of energy consumption can help reduce domestic consumption.

Function of Each Unit

The hours that relevant units are settled on electrical energy production cycle. This parameter is not the same for all units. Usually two types of repairs are done on units: Periodic and overhaul repairs.

Readiness Index

Readiness index is defined by the control center (dispatching), which controls the power plant and the higher the index, indicating that the power plant has a good operation. Definition of readiness index is:

The total number of days that the unit has production is divided into the total number of days that can have production.

Fuel Consumption

Fuel consumption in power plants is in form of gas, mazut or combination of them.

Table 2. DMUs Information- 2005

DMU	Inputs						Outputs	
	Domestic Consumption	Function of Per Unit	Fuel Consumption Mazut (Cubic Meters)	Gas Consumption (Cubic Meters 1000)	Non-Functioning Unit	Readiness Index	Net Production	Production to Forecast Ratio %
1	169661	7571	143517	326227	3	86.42%	1927417	104/16%
2	169584	8146	135346	359955	8	92.99%	2034628	101/44%
3	170236	8071	173567	330010	3	92.13%	2077532	106/95%
4	160849	8121	162031	319718	1	92.70%	1999199	103/23%

Dysfunction of Unit without a Plan

Due to technical problems power plant units gets out from the production circuit with planned or unplanned (emergency exit). In planned condition, problem is pre-identified and in coordination with the control center unit gets out of circuit in a specific time, and at the appointed time becomes parallel with network. But sometimes circumstances arise that due to technical limitation, individual mistakes or natural disasters it is impossible to coordinate with the control center, say that there is emergency exit that high rate of emergency exit is a negative rating for each power plant unit.

Gross Domestic Product (GDP)

The concept of GDP is to be deducted from the total production per unit of domestic consumption of that unit

GDP= total production - Domestic consumption

Production Percentage in Comparison with the Annual Forecast

Since the power plants contract with the regional electric company at the beginning of the year & are committed to a level of production according to the situation of units by the end of the year which is known forecast, the index is usually expressed in terms of percentage. The Production rate than annual forecast can be considered one of the most important indicators in the unit's evaluation and pricing.

The Results of Model

Relevant information in five consecutive years (2003-2007) collected & Malmquist productivity index is calculated by using gams software.

As mentioned in the theory of this section, productivity index calculation is examined by Malmquist index over time and in dynamic conditions namely (means that efficiency frontier is calculated in period $t + 1$ than efficiency frontier in period t. Therefore, by having information of five consecutive years, Malmquist indices can be calculated for each DMU.

Malmquist index has been calculated in years 2003 and 2004. The year 2003 and 2004 indicates respectively the frontier of t & $t + 1$.

At the first column in Table 3 DMUs are marked, second column indicates efficiency of per DMU in period t to time border of t. The value of efficiency is obtained with regard to the under evaluation unit and the rest of DMU_j from in period t. DMU_2 in the Table 3 is efficient with respect to this border and the rest of the DMUs are inefficient. The third column shows the efficiency of each unit in period t to the border of time t + 1. For the calculation DMU_j is considered in period t and under evaluation DMU in period t + 1.

The fourth column compares each DMU in time period t +1 to t that the maximum efficiency in this case is 1. DMU_j are considered in time period t + 1 and the DMU under evaluation (DMU_p) in period t.

In the fifth column efficiency of per DMU is estimated in period t+1 than the border of t+1. Malmquist index of years 2004 & 2005 has been calculated. Year of 2004 & 2005 shows t & t+1 border respectively. Table 4 indicates Malmquist productivity index of years 2004-2005.

As noted above, Malmquist index measures the productivity change of all DMUs factors from period t to t+1 by using distance function. The first part of the mentioned index measures the technical efficiency changes of DMUs from time period t to t+1 (movement along frontier function) and the second component calculate the technology efficiency changes of DMUs from time period t to the t+1 (transfer of frontier function).

In case of change in technology efficiency becomes clear that if a DMU has the input in period t, by occurring changes in the technology when meet the time period t +1, what changes in efficiency value and or if the inputs of period t+1 are available what changes will be created by technology change in the value of the efficiency.

Table 3. Malmquist productivity index (years: 2003-2004)

DMU	$D^t(t)$	$D^{t+1}(t)$	$D^t(t+1)$	$D^{t+1}(t+1)$	Efficiency Progress	Technology Progress	Malmquist Index
1	0.8804	0.9798	1	0.9193	1.0441	0.9886	1.0323
2	1	1.1226	1	0.8971	0.8971	0.9929	0.8971
3	0.7644	0.8524	0.8283	0.7443	0.9737	0.9989	0.9727
4	0.7480	0.8324	0.9839	0.8841	1.1819	1	1.1819

Table 4. Malmquist productivity index (years: 2004-2005)

DMU	$D^t(t)$	$D^{t+1}(t)$	$D^t(t+1)$	$D^{t+1}(t+1)$	Efficiency Progress	Technology Progress	Malmquist Index
1	1	0.8877	1.1139	1	1	1.1201	1.1201
2	1	0.9104	0.7947	0.7219	0.7219	1.099	0.7938
3	0.8283	0.7541	1.0877	0.9549	1.1528	1.1185	1.2894
4	0.9839	0.8958	1.5345	1	1.0163	1.2982	1.3194

In Table 4, the DMU_1, did not progress in terms of efficiency, but the technology progress has caused the DMU to be faced with increased productivity.

The most technology progress is related to the DMU_4 that despite of very small changes in the value of efficiency, the tangible progress can be seen in the value of efficiency.

In Table 5 Malmquist index in years 2005 and 2006 are calculated and years 2005 & 2006 indicates t & t + 1 border respectively.

According to the Table 5 the least efficiency in period's t & t+1 is related to the DMU_2, but by comparing the value of both values and calculating their ratio obvious that the efficiency of this DMU is ascending while the DMU_4 with higher efficiency has the descending trend.

In Table 6 Malmquist index in years 2006 and 2007 has been calculated since years 2006 & 2007 indicates the t & t+1 border respectively.

According to the Table 6, by constant efficiency of the DMU_1 in time periods t & t+1 technology changes has a descend trend, hence, the productivity index is descending.

As it can be seen from the above Tables:

1. If efficiency & technology changes are more than one, the index will become more than one and progress can be observed and if both are less than one, the productivity index has been less than one & regress can be observed. Otherwise,

Table 5. Malmquist productivity index (years: 2005-2006)

DMU	$D^t(t)$	$D^{t+1}(t)$	$D^t(t+1)$	$D^{t+1}(t+1)$	Efficiency Progress	Technology Progress	Malmquist Index
1	1	1.0322	0.9696	1	1	0.9691	0.9691
2	0.7219	0.745	0.7442	0.7678	1.0635	0.9691	1.03
3	0.9549	1.0122	0.9569	0.9872	1.0338	0.9344	0.9685
4	1	1.4452	0.8553	0.9334	0.9334	0.7962	0.7432

Table 6. Malmquist productivity index (years: 2006-2007)

DMU	$D^t(t)$	$D^{t+1}(t)$	$D^t(t+1)$	$D^{t+1}(t+1)$	Efficiency progress	Technology progress	Malmquist index
1	1	1.0898	0.9340	1	1	0.9257	0.9257
2	0.7678	0.8296	0.7657	0.8273	1.0774	0.9252	0.9947
3	0.9872	1.0758	0.8524	0.9210	0.9329	0.9156	0.8577
4	0.9334	1.0079	0.9313	0.9971	1.0682	0.93	0.9934

if the deficiency in one of the changes can be compensated by another, the DMU has progress.

2. DMU_1 between years of 2004 to 2007 has efficiency equal one which represents a stable condition in comparison with the other DMUs.

The progress in efficiency, technology and Malmquist has been brought distinctly in four power plants in five years.

Figure 2 shows the changes for DMU_1. In the following figures, the periods are indicated as follow:

The period 2003-2004 is indicated by no. 1,
The period of 2004-2005 is indicated by no. 2,
The period of 2005-2006 is indicated by no. 3,
The period of 2006-2007 is indicated by no. 4.

DMU_1 during the periods of 2003-2004 & 2004-2005, has progress in Malmquist index but in next periods is seen regress in the DMU and the main reason is regress in technology efficiency. Figure 3 indicates Malmquist, efficiency and technology changes for the DMU_2.

Unlike DMU_1, DMU_2 in the periods of 2003-2004 & 2004-2005 has regress in Malmquist index, but we see progress in this DMU in the next period.

Figure 4 shows Malmquist, efficiency and technology changes for DMU3.

Figure 2. Diagram of efficiency progress and Malmquist related to DMU_1

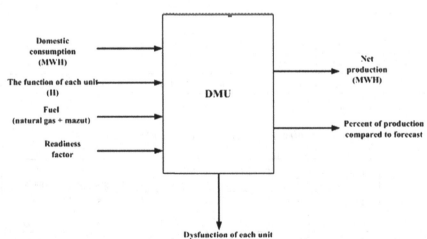

Figure 3. Diagram of efficiency progress and Malmquist – DMU$_2$

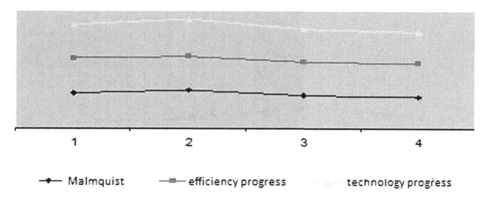

Figure 4 Diagram of efficiency progress and Malmquist – DMU$_3$

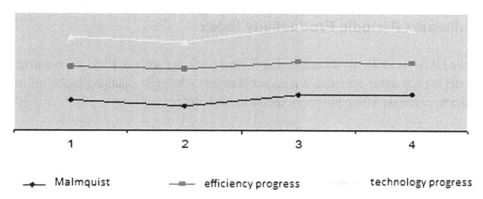

Technology progress is obvious in periods one and two, but in periods three and four is seen regress in the technology that this process is also seen in efficiency and Malmquist. Figure 5 shows Malmquist, efficiency and technology changes for the DMU$_4$.

Severe regress of Technology in the third period led to a sharp decline in the Malmquist index that is quite evident in the third period of Malmquist assessment. Mentioned DMU due to a technical problem (Turbine vibration) has limitation in load production with a maximum of 20 MW, in years between 2003 to 2005 has a high sensitivity, so that the Collections Management, the best operators, the most services & maintenance were assigned to the DMU so the technology progress can be seen in this DMU over the years. In next years, the sensitivity is less and hence technology regress is observed in these years.

Figure 5. Diagram of efficiency progress and Malmquist – DMU$_4$

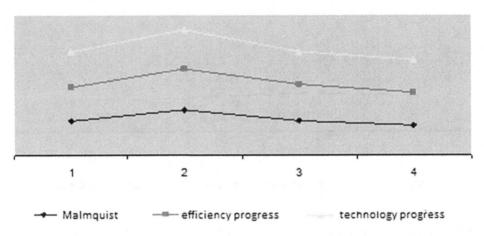

Malmquist Periodic Productivity Index

If the DMU$_p$ is DMU under evaluation in time periods t and t + 1 and the required model is CCR input-oriented, it is required to solve the eight planning problems in order to calculate Malmquist periodic index as follows:

$$D^{t,L}(X_p^t \cdot Y_p^t) = Min\theta$$

$$s.t. \sum_{\substack{j=1 \\ j \neq p}}^{n} \lambda_j x_{ij}^{t,L} + \lambda_p x_{ip}^{t,U} \leq \theta x_{ip}^{t,U}, i = 1,...,m$$

$$\sum_{\substack{j=1 \\ j \neq p}}^{n} \lambda_j y_{rj}^{t,U} + \lambda_p y_{rp}^{t,L} \geq y_{rp}^{t,L}, \quad r = 1,...,s,$$

$$\lambda_j \geq 0, \qquad\qquad j = 1,...,n.$$

(94)

$$D^{t,U}(X_p^t \cdot Y_p^t) = Min\theta$$

$$s.t. \sum_{\substack{j=1 \\ j \neq p}}^{n} \lambda_j x_{ij}^{t,U} + \lambda_p x_{ip}^{t,L} \leq \theta x_{ip}^{t,L}, i = 1,...,m$$

$$\sum_{\substack{j=1 \\ j \neq p}}^{n} \lambda_j y_{rj}^{t,L} + \lambda_p y_{rp}^{t,U} \geq y_{rp}^{t,U}, \quad r = 1,...,s,$$

$$\lambda_j \geq 0, \qquad\qquad j = 1,...,n.$$

(95)

$$D^{t+1,L}(X_p^{t+1} \cdot Y_p^{t+1}) = Min\theta$$

$$s.t. \sum_{\substack{j=1 \\ j\neq p}}^{n} \lambda_j x_{ij}^{t+1,L} + \lambda_p x_{ip}^{t+1,U} \leq \theta x_{ip}^{t+1,U}, i = 1,...,m$$

$$\sum_{\substack{j=1 \\ j\neq p}}^{n} \lambda_j y_{rj}^{t+1,U} + \lambda_p y_{rp}^{t+1,L} \geq y_{rp}^{t+1,L}, \quad r = 1,...,s,$$

$$\lambda_j \geq 0, \qquad\qquad j = 1,...,n.$$

(96)

$$D^{t+1,U}(X_p^{t+1} \cdot Y_p^{t+1}) = Min\theta$$

$$s.t. \sum_{\substack{j=1 \\ j\neq p}}^{n} \lambda_j x_{ij}^{t+1,U} + \lambda_p x_{ip}^{t+1,L} \leq \theta x_{ip}^{t+1,L}, \quad i = 1,...,m$$

$$\sum_{\substack{j=1 \\ j\neq p}}^{n} \lambda_j y_{rj}^{t+1,L} + \lambda_p y_{rp}^{t+1,U} \geq y_{rp}^{t+1,U}, \qquad r = 1,...,s,$$

$$\lambda_j \geq 0, \qquad\qquad j = 1,...,n.$$

(97)

$$D^{t+1,L}(X_p^{t} \cdot Y_p^{t}) = Min\theta$$

$$s.t. \sum_{\substack{j=1 \\ j\neq p}}^{n} \lambda_j x_{ij}^{t+1,L} \leq \theta x_{ip}^{t,U}, \quad i = 1,...,m$$

$$\sum_{\substack{j=1 \\ j\neq p}}^{n} \lambda_j y_{rj}^{t+1,U} \geq y_{rp}^{t,L}, \qquad r = 1,...,s,$$

$$\lambda_j \geq 0, \qquad j = 1,...,n.$$

(98)

$$D^{t+1,U}(X_p^{t} \cdot Y_p^{t}) = Min\theta$$

$$s.t. \sum_{\substack{j=1 \\ j\neq p}}^{n} \lambda_j x_{ij}^{t+1,U} \leq \theta x_{ip}^{t,L}, \quad i = 1,...,m$$

$$\sum_{\substack{j=1 \\ j\neq p}}^{n} \lambda_j y_{rj}^{t+1,L} \geq y_{rp}^{t,U}, \qquad r = 1,...,s,$$

$$\lambda_j \geq 0, \qquad\qquad j = 1,...,n.$$

(99)

$$D^{t,L}(X_p^{t+1} \cdot Y_p^{t+1}) = Min\theta$$

$$s.t. \sum_{\substack{j=1 \\ j \neq p}}^{n} \lambda_j x_{ij}^{t,L} \leq \theta x_{ip}^{t+1,U}, \quad i = 1, \ldots, m$$

$$\sum_{\substack{j=1 \\ j \neq p}}^{n} \lambda_j y_{rj}^{t,U} \geq y_{rp}^{t+1,L}, \quad r = 1, \ldots, s,$$

$$\lambda_j \geq 0, \qquad\qquad j = 1, \ldots, n \ .$$

(100)

$$D^{t,U}(X_p^{t+1} \cdot Y_p^{t+1}) = Min\theta$$

$$s.t. \sum_{\substack{j=1 \\ j \neq p}}^{n} \lambda_j x_{ij}^{t,U} \leq \theta x_{ip}^{t+1,L}, \quad i = 1, \ldots, m$$

$$\sum_{\substack{j=1 \\ j \neq p}}^{n} \lambda_j y_{rj}^{t,L} \geq y_{rp}^{t+1,U}, \quad r = 1, \ldots, s,$$

$$\lambda_j \geq 0, \qquad\qquad j = 1, \ldots, n \ .$$

(101)

After calculating the above values, the Malmquist index calculated for each DMU as the periodic distance (the lower and upper bound) as follows:

$$MI_p^L = \sqrt{\frac{D_p^{t,L}(X_p^{t+1}, Y_p^{t+1}) D_p^{t+1,L}(X_p^{t+1}, Y_p^{t+1})}{D_p^{t,U}(X_p^t, Y_p^t) D_p^{t+1,U}(X_p^t, Y_p^t)}} \ .$$

$$MI_p^U = \sqrt{\frac{D_p^{t,U}(X_p^{t+1} \cdot Y_p^{t+1}) D_p^{t+1,U}(X_p^{t+1}, Y_p^{t+1})}{D_p^{t,L}(X_p^t, Y_p^t) D_p^{t+1,L}(X_p^t, Y_p^t)}}$$

(102)

Thus, for each DMU with periodic data have: $MI_p \in [MI_p^L, MI_p^U]$

$$M^{++} = \{DMU_j \, \big| MI_j^L > 1\}$$
$$M^{-} = \{DMU_j \, \big| MI_j^U < 1\}$$
$$M^{+} = \{DMU_j \, \big| MI_j^L \leq 1, \ MI_j^U \geq 1\}$$

(103)

The set of M^{++} includes DMUs that in all circumstances have progressed from the period t to period t + 1, & the set M^{-} includes DMUs which have regressed in all circumstances & the set of M^+ consists of DMUs that have progressed & regressed in some points from period t to t+1.

So if:

1. If $MI_p^L = MI_p^U = 1$, then the DMU_p has neither progress nor regress.
2. If $MI_p^U > 1$, $MI_p^L = 1$, then DMU_p has progress
3. If $MI_p^L < 1$, $MI_p^U = 1$, then DMU_p has regress.
4. If $MI_p^L < 1$, $MI_p^U > 1$ then the index p is used to measure the progress or regress of DMUp as shown below:

$$\acute{A} = \frac{MI_p^U - 1}{1 - MI_p^L} \quad 0 < \rho < \infty \tag{104}$$

If $\acute{A} > 1$ then percentage of progress is more than regress

If $\acute{A} < 1$, the percentage of regress will be more than progress.

Case Study: Pipe Plants

All activities carried out in this study are in Safa Rolling and pipe plants and data are related to this organization's DMUs. The plant is the largest pipe plant includes four plants, these four plants are considered by abbreviations G, W, R & E. Production method is steel sheet or plate reach into production lines and after going through the various stages & doing production and testing operations, they are changed into the final tube.

These tubes are used depending on the manufacturing process in many industries such as water and sewage, gas & oil.

Each three-month period in each plant is considered as a DMU. The reason of choosing three-months period is that at first, the efficiency computing are fulfilled by organization in a non- systematic way is as a three-month period. Second, if the periods were considered at the longer time periods, therefore calculations become less & easier, but because the possibility of concentration & analysis are more at the smaller time periods with regard to all aspects and management idea, three-month periods were selected. The studied time Period was since the beginning of 2007 to the end of the first half of 2012.

That is due to the three-month periods, there should be 22 periods that with consideration four plants, regularly 88 DMUs should be included in the efficiency calculations, but because of what were stated in general part, three courses at plant

G, two courses at plant E, and one course at the plant W have not been considered because of lack of production or holiday. So in the efficiency calculations, totally 82 DMUs or DMU have been examined without taking into account of these six periods.

Also according to the three months periods, in the discussion of productivity calculations based on Malmquist productivity index, totally 25 courses have been analyzed.

It should be noted that each DMU is known by the company name, the year and the quarter.

For example, G200802 is the second quarter of 2008 at the plant G so that E201004 is the fourth quarter of 2010 at the plant E. In this study is used three input & two output variables that its conceptual model is as follows:

According to the inputs & outputs, it is evident that all variables are quantitative.

The consumption sheets used in kilograms, electricity consumption based on kilowatt hour and one-hour consumption is calculated based on hours. Pipe's length & weight are respectively based on the meter & ton. Sheet as the main raw material, electricity as the most important consumption energy and staff's operation as the most important company's costs were determined as input. The length and weight of the produced pipe as the most important outcome that is the result of all activities of the production and testing were considered as output variables.

Results of Malmquist Productivity Index (Precise Data)

Table 7 shows results of MPI based on accurate data. It's necessary to explain because in the first two periods, plants E & G had not been set up, the calculation of the two periods were based on two DMUs of W and R.

Figure 6. The conceptual model of input & output indices of Safa rolling & pipes

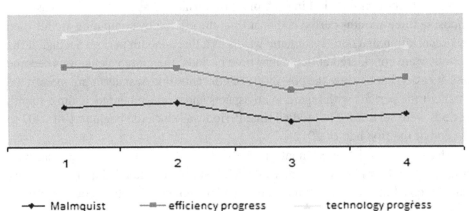

Table 7. Calculations result of Malmquist productivity index (precise data)

Period	DMU_j	$D^t(t)$	$D^{t+1}(t+1)$	$D^{t+1}(t)$	$D^t(t+1)$	Efficiency Progress	Technology Progress	Malmquist Index
200701-200702	G	--------	--------	--------	--------	--------	--------	--------
	W	1.0000	1.0000	0.9945	2.9413	1.0000	1.7198	1.7198
	R	1.0000	1.0000	1.8268	1.2072	1.0000	0.8129	0.8129
	E	--------	--------	--------	--------	--------	--------	--------
200702-200703	G	--------	--------	--------	--------	--------	--------	--------
	W	1.0000	1.0000	0.9945	1.4468	1.0000	1.2061	1.2061
	R	1.0000	1.0000	1.1775	1.5272	1.0000	1.1389	1.1389
	E	--------	--------	--------	--------	--------	--------	--------
200703-200704	G	0.9427	0.9543	0.9537	0.9433	1.0123	0.9885	1.0006
	W	1.0000	1.0000	2.8899	1.1949	1.0000	0.6430	0.6430
	R	1.0000	0.9688	1.4500	0.9540	0.9688	0.8241	0.7984
	E	1.0000	1.0000	1.8213	0.9817	1.0000	0.7342	0.7342
200704-200801	G	0.9543	1.0000	1.0649	0.9535	1.0479	0.9244	0.962007
	W	1.0000	1.0000	1.4022	2.2578	1.0000	1.2689	1.2689
	R	0.9688	1.0000	0.9585	1.1899	1.0322	1.0967	1.1320
	E	1.0000	1.0000	1.0032	2.0950	1.0000	1.4451	1.4451
200801-200802	G	1.0000	1.0000	0.9841	1.5881	1.0000	1.2703	1.2703
	W	1.0000	1.0000	0.9995	1.1719	1.0000	1.0828	1.0828
	R	1.0000	0.9970	0.9818	1.2514	0.9970	1.1307	1.1273
	E	1.0000	1.0000	1.0549	2.0710	1.0000	1.4012	1.4012
200802-200803	G	1.0000	1.0000	1.2727	1.0515	1.0000	0.9090	0.9090
	W	1.0000	1.0000	1.0068	1.0116	1.0000	1.0024	1.0024
	R	0.9970	0.9911	0.9997	0.9873	0.9941	0.9967	0.9908
	E	1.0000	1.0000	1.1521	1.6178	1.0000	1.1850	1.1850
200803-200804	G	--------	--------	--------	--------	--------	--------	--------
	W	1.0000	1.0000	1.0074	1.0054	1.0000	0.9990	0.9990
	R	0.9911	1.0000	0.9883	2.0417	1.0090	1.4309	1.4438
	E	1.0000	1.0000	2.0788	1.8820	1.0000	0.9515	0.9515
200804-200901	G	--------	--------	--------	--------	--------	--------	--------
	W	1.0000	1.0000	1.0039	1.0056	1.0000	1.0008	1.0008
	R	1.0000	1.0000	1.6893	1.0099	1.0000	0.7732	0.7732
	E	1.0000	1.0000	1.8316	1.1912	1.0000	0.8065	0.8065
200901-200902	G	1.0000	0.9816	1.0688	0.9931	0.9816	0.9729	0.9551
	W	1.0000	0.9881	0.9927	1.0029	0.9881	1.0112	0.9991
	R	1.0000	1.0000	0.9808	1.3135	1.0000	1.1573	1.1573
	E	1.0000	1.0000	1.2809	1.0085	1.0000	0.8873	0.8873

continued on following page

Table 7. Continued

Period	DMU_j	$D^t(t)$	$D^{t+1}(t+1)$	$D^{t+1}(t)$	$D^t(t+1)$	Efficiency Progress	Technology Progress	Malmquist Index
200902-200903	G	0.9816	0.9884	0.9954	1.2662	1.0069	1.1240	1.1318
	W	0.9881	1.0000	1.0020	1.4336	1.0121	1.1890	1.2033
	R	1.0000	1.0000	1.0170	0.9860	1.0000	0.9847	0.9847
	E	1.0000	1.0000	2.7879	2.1503	1.0000	0.8782	0.8782
200903-200904	G	0.9884	0.9909	1.1157	0.9905	1.0025	0.9411	0.9434
	W	1.0000	1.0000	1.2831	1.1864	1.0000	0.9616	0.9616
	R	1.0000	1.0000	1.0039	1.0339	1.0000	1.0148	1.0148
	E	1.0000	1.0000	2.1431	1.8099	1.0000	0.9190	0.9190
200904-201001	G	0.9909	0.9934	0.9918	1.0324	1.0026	1.0189	1.0216
	W	1.0000	1.0000	1.0020	1.2180	1.0000	1.1025	1.1025
	R	1.0000	0.9547	1.0027	0.9549	0.9547	0.9987	0.9535
	E	1.0000	1.0000	0.9899	2.2384	1.0000	1.5037	1.5037
201001-201002	G	0.9934	0.9896	1.0143	0.9908	0.9962	0.9903	0.9865
	W	1.0000	1.0000	1.5943	1.0010	1.0000	0.7924	0.7924
	R	0.9547	1.0000	0.9491	1.0074	1.0475	1.0066	1.0544
	E	1.0000	1.0000	1.1477	1.0599	1.0000	0.9610	0.9610
201002-201003	G	0.9896	0.9945	1.0729	0.9947	1.0049	0.9605	0.9652
	W	1.0000	1.0000	1.4306	0.9980	1.0000	0.8352	0.8352
	R	1.0000	1.0000	1.1120	1.0013	1.0000	0.9489	0.9489
	E	1.0000	1.0000	1.9149	1.4048	1.0000	0.8565	0.8565
201003-201004	G	0.9945	0.9706	0.9781	0.9875	0.9760	1.0171	0.9926
	W	1.0000	1.0000	0.9954	1.3839	1.0000	1.1791	1.1791
	R	1.0000	1.0000	1.0001	1.0176	1.0000	1.0087	1.0087
	E	1.0000	1.0000	1.5588	1.4762	1.0000	0.9731	0.9731
201004-201101	G	0.9706	1.0000	0.9983	0.9717	1.0303	0.9720	1.0014
	W	1.0000	1.0000	1.0233	1.0004	1.0000	0.9887	0.9887
	R	1.0000	1.0000	1.0298	0.9612	1.0000	0.9661	0.9661
	E	1.0000	1.0000	3.6454	2.0934	1.0000	0.7578	0.7578
201101-201102	G	1.0000	0.9979	0.9953	1.0002	0.9979	1.0035	1.0014
	W	1.0000	1.0000	1.3084	1.1209	1.0000	0.9256	0.9256
	R	1.0000	1.0000	0.9838	1.0206	1.0000	1.0185	1.0185
	E	1.0000	1.0000	1.6572	1.8144	1.0000	1.0464	1.0464
201102-201103	G	0.9979	1.0000	1.2938	0.9970	1.0021	0.8769	0.8788
	W	1.0000	1.0000	2.8717	1.0004	1.0000	0.5902	0.5902
	R	1.0000	1.0000	0.9989	0.9844	1.0000	0.9927	0.9927
	E	1.0000	1.0000	5.7266	1.6837	1.0000	0.5422	0.5422

continued on following page

Table 7. Continued

Period	DMU_j	$D^t(t)$	$D^{t+1}(t+1)$	$D^{t+1}(t)$	$D^t(t+1)$	Efficiency Progress	Technology Progress	Malmquist Index
201103-201104	G	1.0000	1.0000	0.9996	1.5809	1.0000	1.2576	1.2576
	W	--------	--------	--------	--------	--------	--------	--------
	R	1.0000	1.0000	0.9867	2.2033	1.0000	1.4943	1.4943
	E	1.0000	1.0000	1.1918	1.9676	1.0000	1.2849	1.2849
201104-201201	G	1.0000	0.9930	1.1422	1.0015	0.9930	0.9397	0.9331
	W	--------	--------	--------	--------	--------	--------	--------
	R	1.0000	1.0000	1.5919	1.3754	1.0000	0.9295	0.9295
	E	1.0000	1.0000	0.9807	1.5245	1.0000	1.2468	1.2468
201201-201202	G	0.9930	1.0000	0.9866	0.9945	1.0070	1.0005	1.0075
	W	1.0000	1.0000	0.9892	1.3084	1.0000	1.1501	1.1501
	R	1.0000	1.0000	1.0146	1.0196	1.0000	1.0025	1.0025
	E	1.0000	1.0000	2.3090	0.9722	1.0000	0.6489	0.6489
Mean						1.001	1.021	1.022

Also, due to closure of plant G in period 200804 and plant W in period 201104, there was no possibility to compare the productivity of these periods with the before and after period & there is not registered any number for the two plants in forenamed periods.

The results indicate that totally productivity of Safa Rolling and Pipe plants grew by 2.2% during this period. The most share in productivity growth is related to the technology changes factor of 2.1% and efficiency changes are poor & about 0.1% (see Figures 7 and 8).

Figure 7. The process of the output1 index (length of pipe)

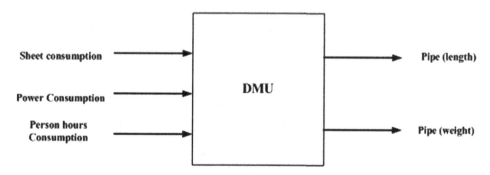

Figure 8. The process of the output 2 indicator (Weight of pipe)

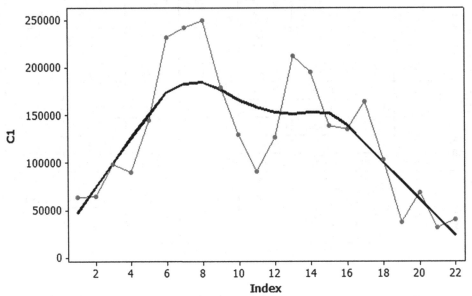

The two indicators process show that the both outputs have decreased sharply in the recent periods and the mentality with regard to outputs alone is not unreasonable, but as calculations showed that Productivity growth has been positive in the organization.

In other words, this organization has been able to achieve this issue by controlling inputs.

One of the most important works in this field is the use and distribution of manpower in other companies (because of the similarity of the production process).

Among the four plants, plant R with average productivity growth of 3.5% has had the most growth and then plant W and G with average productivity growth of 3.4% & 1.3% respectively are second and third plants and at the end plant E with 0.15% has had the lowest growth.

In Figure 9, productivity index average has come during the quarter and their growth or decline is determined.

Totally in 21 quarters investigated studied, the period of 201103-201104 had the highest growth. It can be seen that in this period, the efficiency did not change and the total rate of productivity growth has been due to technology changes.

In this period, the productivity of all DMUs had a considerable growth. After the periods 201103-201104, periods 200701-200702 had the highest growth in productivity that has been due to technology changes. The reason factor of high

Figure 9. Malmquist index average during the quarter (Total plant) (precise data)

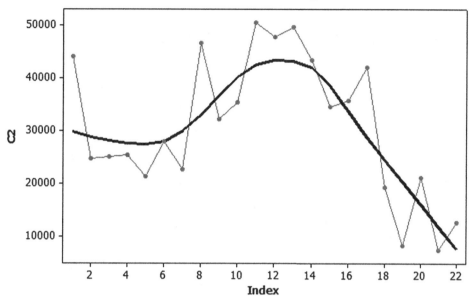

productivity of period is the high productivity of the plant W with the value 1.72 that this number has the highest productivity growth among plants and despite the fact that during this period, productivity of plant R has decreased 0.81 but the average of productivity in this period is high. The period 201102-201103 has the lowest growth with the rate of 0.751.

In this period the efficiency didn't almost change & falling in productivity is related to the technology decrease. Also all DMUs efficiency in this period is less than one (Figure 10.).

Average growth of Plant G is 1.3%.

The third and fifteenth periods had the highest productivity growth. In both periods, there is no change in efficiency and productivity growth has been related to technology changes.

The greatest decrease in productivity was in the fourth & fourteenth periods namely 201102-201103 and 200802-200803 periods.

In periods 201102-201103 in spite of efficiency growth, technology changes have been negative and productivity number has been decreased to 0.8788.

In periods 200802-200803, the efficiency has no change, but with the decrease in technology index, productivity has decreased too.

As can be seen due to the closure of the plant in period of 200804 is not possible to compare this time with the previous and next time.

Figure 10. The Malmquist index procedure in plant G (precise data)

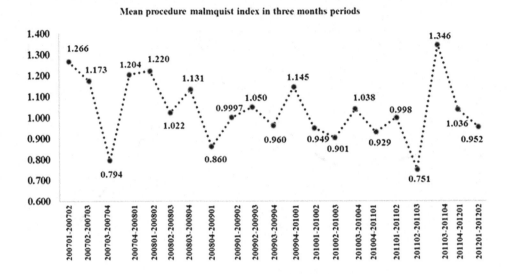

The reason of the plant closure at this time has been to do some changes in forming machine welding systems as the bottleneck for the production and its promotion of S5 to S7 system is in order to increase production speed and possible smart troubleshooting.

These changes have shown their effectiveness in the period 200902-200903 and with the progress of technological change; productivity has been increased in this period (Figure 11.).

Average growth of this index in the plant W is 3.4%. The highest growth was in the first period, the total share of growth is related to technology changes and this value of growth 1.7198 was unprecedented across all plants and all courses. The lowest value of Malmquist index is 201102-201103 periods with the rate of 0.59 that this decrease factor is technology changes & efficiency has no changes.

But in the next period with changes especially in relation to the Hydro test machine promotion as a bottleneck, is seen the growth of this index (Figure 12.).

Plant R with an average growth of 3.5 percent had the highest increase in productivity between plants.

The highest growth is in periods 201103-201104 & 200803-200804 which was also caused by technology changes.The greatest decrease in productivity occurred in the periods 200804-200901 & 200703-200704 which in the first one just technology changes were involved, but in the latter both efficiency and technology were involved & their fall reduced productivity (Figure 13.).

Figure 11. Malmquist index process in plant W (precise data)

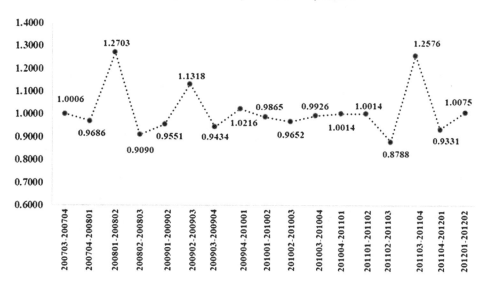

Figure 12. The process of Malmquist index in plant R (precise data)

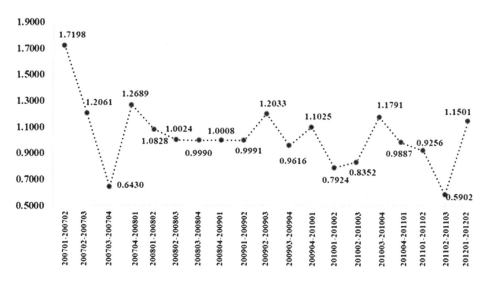

Figure 13. The process of Malmquist index in plant E (precise data)

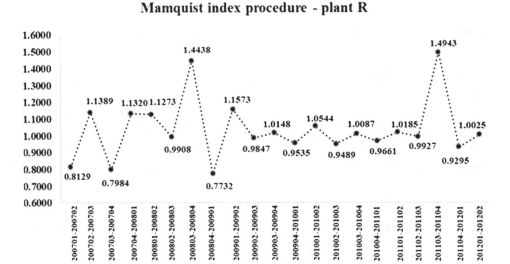

Plant E has the lowest growth rate with productivity growth of 0.15 among four plants, while with regard to production process technology, has the latest technology.

Periods of 200904-201001 & 200704-200801 have the highest productivity growth & periods of 201102-201103 & 201201-201202 have the highest level of productivity fall that in these total periods, technology changes play a main role and efficiency has no role.

REFERENCES

Abbott, M. (2006). The productivity and efficiency of the Australian electricity supply industry. *Energy Economics*, *28*(4), 444–454. doi:10.1016/j.eneco.2005.10.007

Aghdam, R. F. (2011). Dynamics of productivity change in the Australian electricity industry: Assessing the impacts of electricity reform. *Energy Policy*, *39*(6), 3281–3295. doi:10.1016/j.enpol.2011.03.019

Arabi, B., Munisamy, S., & Emrouznejad, A. (2015). A new slacks-based measure of Malmquist–Luenberger index in the presence of undesirable outputs. *Omega*, *51*, 29–37. doi:10.1016/j.omega.2014.08.006

Babalos, V., Caporale, G. M., & Philippas, N. (2012). Efficiency evaluation of Greek equity funds. *Research in International Business and Finance*, *26*(2), 317–333. doi:10.1016/j.ribaf.2012.01.003

Chang, D. S., Chun Kuo, Y., & Chen, T. Y. (2008). Productivity measurement of the manufacturing process for outsourcing decisions: The case of a Taiwanese printed circuit board manufacturer. *International Journal of Production Research*, *46*(24), 6981–6995. doi:10.1080/00207540701429934

Chang, H., Choy, H. L., Cooper, W. W., Parker, B. R., & Ruefli, T. W. (2009). "Measuring Productivity Growth, Technical Progress, and Efficiency Changes of CPA Firms Prior to, and Following the Sarbanes-Oxley Act." Socio-Economic Planning Sciences. *The International Journal of Public Sector Decision-Making.*, *43*(4), 221–228.

Chang, H., Choy, H. L., Cooper, W. W., & Ruefli, T. W. (2009). Using Malmquist Indexes to measure changes in the productivity and efficiency of US accounting firms before and after the Sarbanes Oxley Act. *Omega*, *37*(5), 951–960. doi:10.1016/j.omega.2008.08.004

Charnes, A., Cooper, W. W., Lewin, A. Y., & Seiford, L. M. (1994). *Data envelopment analysis: theory, methodology, and applications* (pp. 253–272). Boston: Kluwer Academic Publishers. doi:10.1007/978-94-011-0637-5

Charnes, A., Cooper, W. W., & Rhodes, E. L. (1978). Measuring the efficiency of decision making units. *European Journal of Operational Research*, *2*(6), 429–444. doi:10.1016/0377-2217(78)90138-8

Chowdhurya, H., Zelenyukb, V., Laportec, A., & Walter, P. (2014). Analysis of productivity, efficiency and technological changes in hospital services in Ontario: How does case-mix matter? *International Journal of Production Economics*, *150*, 74–82. doi:10.1016/j.ijpe.2013.12.003

Fare, R., Grosskof, S., Lindgren, B., & Roos, P. (1992). *Productivity Developments in Swedish Hospital: A Malmquist Output Index Approach. In Data Envelopment Analysis*. Boston: Kluwer Academic Publishers.

Fare, R., Grosskof, S., Lindgren, B., & Ross, P. (1994). *Productivity Developments in Swendish Hospital: A Malmquist Output Index Approach* (pp. 253–272). Boston: Kluwer.

Fare, R., Grosskof, S., Norris, M., & Zhang, Z. (1994). Productivity growth, Technical progress and Efficiency Changes in Industrialized Countries. *The American Economic Review*, *1*, 66–83.

Farrell, M. J. (1957). The measurement of productive efficiency. *Journal of the Royal Statistical Society. Series A (General)*, *120*(3), 253–281. doi:10.2307/2343100

Fuentes, R., & Lillo-Banuls, A. (2015). Smoothed bootstrap Malmquist index based on DEA model to compute productivity of tax offices. *Expert Systems with Applications*, *42*(5), 2442–2450. doi:10.1016/j.eswa.2014.11.002

Hermans, E., Brijs, T., Wets, G., & Vanhoof, K. (2009). Benchmarking road safety: Lessons to learn from a data envelopment analysis, Transportation Research Institute, Hasselt University. *Accident; Analysis and Prevention*, *41*(1), 174–182. doi:10.1016/j.aap.2008.10.010 PMID:19114152

Hwang, S., & Chang, T. (2003). Using data envelopment analysis to measure hotel managerial efficiency change in Taiwan. *Tourism Management*, *24*(4), 357–369. doi:10.1016/S0261-5177(02)00112-7

Kao, C. (2010). Malmquist productivity index based on common-weights DEA: The case of Taiwan forests after reorganization. *Omega*, *38*(6), 484–491. doi:10.1016/j.omega.2009.12.005

Krishnasamy, G., Hanuum Ridzwa, A., & Perumal, V. (2003). Malaysian post-merger banks' productivity: Application of Malmquist productivity index. *Managerial Finance*, *30*(4), 63–74. doi:10.1108/03074350410769038

Lee, J. (2013). Directions for the Sustainable Development of Korean Small and Medium Sized Shipyards. *The Asian Journal of Shipping and Logistics, 29*(3), 335–60.

Liu, F. H. F., & Wang, P. H. (2008). DEA Malmquist productivity measure: Taiwanese semiconductor companies. *International Journal of Production Economics*, *112*(1), 367–379. doi:10.1016/j.ijpe.2007.03.015

Ma, J. L., Evans, D. G., Fuller, R. J., & Stewart, D. F. (2002). Technical efficiency and productivity change of China's iron and steel industry. *International Journal of Production Economics*, *76*(3), 293–312. doi:10.1016/S0925-5273(01)00195-5

Malmquist, S. (1953). Index numbers and indifference surfaces. *Trabajos de Estatistica*, *4*(2), 209–242. doi:10.1007/BF03006863

Ouellette, P., & Vierstraete, V. (2005). An evaluation of the efficiency of Quebec's school boards using the data envelopment analysis method. *Applied Economics*, *37*(14), 1643–1653. doi:10.1080/00036840500173247

Pilyavsky, A., & Staat, M. (2008). The Analysis of Technical Efficiency for Small Dairy Farms in Southern Chile: A Stochastic Frontier. *Journal of Productivity Analysis*, *29*(2), 143–154. doi:10.1007/s11123-007-0070-6

Pires, H. M., & Fernandes, E. (2012). Malmquist financial efficiency analysis for airlines. *Transportation Research Part E, Logistics and Transportation Review*, *48*(5), 1049–1055. doi:10.1016/j.tre.2012.03.007

Portela, M. C. A. S., & Thanassoulis, E. (2010). Malmquist-type indices in the presence of negative data:an application to bank branches. *Journal of Banking & Finance*, *34*(7), 1472–1483. doi:10.1016/j.jbankfin.2010.01.004

Sueyoshi, T., & Goto, M. (2013). DEA environmental assessment in a time horizon: Malmquist index on fuel mix, electricity and CO_2 of industrial nations. *Energy Economics*, *40*, 370–382. doi:10.1016/j.eneco.2013.07.013

Tanase, L., & Tidor, A. (2012). Efficiency Progress and Productivity Change in Romania Machinery Industry 2001–2010. *Procedia Economics and Finance*, *3*, 1055–1062. doi:10.1016/S2212-5671(12)00273-0

Worthington, A. (1999). Malmquist Indices of Productivity Change in Australian Financial Services. *Journal of International Financial Markets, Institutions and Money*, *9*(3), 303–320. doi:10.1016/S1042-4431(99)00013-X

Yang, J., & Zeng, W. (2014). The trade-offs between efficiency and quality in the hospital production: Some evidence from Shenzhen, China. *China Economic Review*, *31*(C), 166–184. doi:10.1016/j.chieco.2014.09.005

Zhou, P., Ang, B. W., & Han, J. Y. (2010). Total factor carbon emission performance: A Malmquist index analysis. *Energy Economics*, *32*(1), 194–201. doi:10.1016/j.eneco.2009.10.003

Chapter 4
Evaluation of Faculties by DEA–ANP Hybrid Algorithm of Chapter:
Educational–Research Performance

Elahe Shariatmadari Serkani
Islamic Azad University, Iran

ABSTRACT

One of the fundamental issues facing universities, research centers and institutes of higher education is the absence of an integrated system for performance evaluation. Data Envelopment Analysis (DEA) is a mathematical and management technique for evaluation of Decision Making Units (DMUs) with multiple input and output. The original DEA does not perform full-ranking; instead, it merely provides classification into two groups: efficient and inefficient. Among the available multi-attribute decision-making methods only Analytic Network Process (ANP) can be used to evaluate performance systematically due to the dependencies and feedbacks caused by the mutual effects of the criteria. The DEA-ANP hybrid algorithm, is designed to eliminate the disadvantage of full-ranking in the DEA method, as well as the disadvantage of subjective evaluation in the ANP method. The goal of this chapter is measuring educational and research performance of seventeen faculties, for the academic year 2009-2010, by using the DEA-ANP hybrid algorithm.

DOI: 10.4018/978-1-5225-0596-9.ch004

INTRODUCTION

Evaluating the performance of educational and Research groups is a part of the difficult process of resource allocation at universities. Primary duties and mission of universities is the development and transfer of knowledge that the first one is obtained through research and the second one through education (Kao, Hung, 2008).

The issue of decision making units (DMUs) performance evaluation attracts the manager's attention initially. Measurement and performance evaluation of the processes helps in achieving the objectives of each process and together determine the organization's objectives. Hence the more efficient DMUs can help scientific & economic growth in society, bad performance can have big cultural, social and economic crisis.

Efficiency means not wasting resources and measurement of efficiency has been of great attention of researchers because of its importance in evaluating the performance of a company or organization and requires the output & input comparison of a DMU. In the simplest case which there is only one input and one output, efficiency can be achieved by dividing the output into input. The efficiency is often confused with effectiveness and productivity & until the end of the nineteenth century, the words efficiency & effectiveness were almost as synonymous terms.

Effectiveness is indicative of the amount of "doing right things". Effectiveness refers to the using method of resources to achieve the specified goals. Productivity is a mix of effectiveness and efficiency, because the effectiveness with the performance & efficiency is associated with the use of resources.

DEA method has a public deficit that it is just mathematical & therefore there is no ability to incorporate qualitative, subjective and intuitive indicators in it. Some of the multi criteria Decision-making techniques such as ANP can eliminate this contradiction with its special features. Many decide issues can't have a hierarchical structure, because of interdependencies or feedback system, preferably ANP method is used. Priorities derived from ANP algorithm based on DEA is two-stage approach. In first stage, paired comparison of DMUs, regardless of other DMUs is done based on data envelopment & paired comparison matrix is formed at this stage. Then in the second stage, the results of the first phase are entered in ANP model to full ranking.

BACKGROUND

The issue of performance evaluation and efficiency assessment of universities that have multiple inputs and outputs, in the past few decades has attracted many attentions (Bobe, 2009). Most notably in the area of evaluating the universities performance is as follows:

Bessent (1980) compared the efficiency between faculties by using data envelopment analysis techniques and also in 1983 he used the DEA method to measure the relative efficiency of training programs in the social science faculty. Inputs include contact hours (students contact), each school area of land (training center) and direct educational expenses (Bessent, Bessent, 1980).

Charnes, Arnold, Cooper, Ahn (1989) examined governmental institutes performance by using the technique DEA at the level of higher education in Texas, America. The results published by the nonprofit institutes and public researches. Comparison of the university departments was done by Beasley (1990). Beasley (1995) measured and compared the efficiency of physics and chemistry education and research departments throughout the University of British

Ahn and Seiford (1993) applied DEA method to analyze the relative performance of 153 institutions with doctorate, in the graduate-level. Among these 153 institutions, 104 institutions were public & 49 institutions were private. Johns & Johns measured the relative efficiency of economic sectors' universities in Britain. They used potential issues in determining the output and input & it is interesting that Bessel and Johns and Johns (1995), used the research revenue as input.

Coelli (1996) assessed the technical efficiency the 36 universities in Australia with three DEA model. Sinuany-Stern et al. (1994) used DEA method to determine the relative efficiency of 21 Sections of Ben-Gurion university. Breu & Raab (1994) used the statistical data relevant to a ranking in which 25 national universities were ranked for calculating the relative efficiency.

Athanassopoulos & shale (1997) according to statistics information of 1992-3 examined the technical efficiency of 45 UK experienced university.

Friedman and Sinuany-Sterm (1998) ranked academic DMUs by using DEA and discriminant analysis.

Colbert et al., (1999) check the relative efficiency of MBA programs among 24 universities in America & rooted the inefficiencies stemming from the different outputs in three categories.

Vargass et al. (2000) combined DEA and factor analysis methods for the assessment improvement of the outcomes of academic educational groups.

Avkiran (2001) evaluated the technical and scale efficiency and scale of 3630 Australian university DMUs by using the DEA model. Korhonen et al. (2001) analyzed the research performance of 18 research unit of the Helsinki Economics Faculties & studied to provide a model for engaging the decision makers views in identifying and selecting the best performance, optimal combination of inputs and outputs & their preferences over each other.

Lopez and Lanzer (2002) evaluated the 58 Brazilian universities performance, their research outputs were classified in four groups: quantitative, qualitative, research and services.

Protela and Thanassoulis (2001) analyzed the faculties performance in different ways of 122 faculties in England and in that due to student & school performance and the performance of public and private faculties they offered a kind of DEA model for the inefficiencies causes root.

Martin (2003) examined the performance of Zaragoza University groups. He classified inputs into three categories of financial, human, physical, and outputs into two level of educational and research. Thursby and Kemp (2002) examined the growth and productivity of 112 universities in the field of efficient developing in creating the covered branches.

Banker et al. (2003) analyzed the created changes in the technical & allocative efficiency of the Texas public faculties. In this study, in terms of performance, faculties in the West, Southeast and North of Texas were recognized as the first to third grades. The results of this research indicate a direct correlation between inefficiency and variable costs.

Abbot and Doucouliagos (2003) used DEA and clustering algorithm to measure the efficiency of 36 public universities of Australia. The results showed that the Australian universities have a high level of efficiency compared with each other & there are similar performances in the universities system.

Othman Joumady and Catherine Ris (2005) examined the performance of 209 high school institutions in eight European countries. Kao & Hung (2008) evaluated the relative efficiency of six academic departments (41 educational group) related to Cheng Chung National University of Taiwan with output-oriented DEA model. Among the models of the DEA, output -oriented BCC model with weight control were chosen.

Antonio and Santos (2008) evaluated the relative efficiency of Portugal public universities by using the DEA model. They selected two input & output variables for their model. The findings showed universities that had competence to be promoted.

The idea of combination two methods of AHP and DEA is not new, a great deal of research has been done on combining these two methods. Shang and Sueyoshi (1995) used a combination of methods DEA and AHP for decision-making DMUs ranking.

Cai and Wu (2001) in a study used the hybrid method of AHP and DEA in the financial assessment. Wang et al. (2007) conducted a study to assess the risk of 20 bridge structures by using a DEA/AHP method. They formed Hierarchical structure by using AHP method to determine the weighting of criteria and levels of the risk used this procedure.

But hybrid method of DEA-ANP is being used less by researchers. Daneshvar & Serpil Erol (2010) presented hybrid algorithm DEA-ANP to evaluate the university performance. They carried out a complete ranking for the AUT departments by using this algorithm, regardless of its efficiency or inefficiency.

In addition to the studies mentioned above, another study carried out in DEA-ANP areas that are included.

Bowen (1990), Zhang and Cui (1999), Yang & Kuo (2003), Saen et al.(2005), Ramanathan (2006).

DEA-ANP HYBRID ALGORITHM APPROACH

Data envelopment analysis method is a method based on mathematical programming to evaluate efficiency.

Charnez, Cooper, Rhodes developed Farrell view and provide a model that can measure efficiency of multiple inputs and multiple outputs. This pattern is known as data envelopment analysis or CCR and was used for the first time in the doctoral dissertation of Edward Rhodes at Carnegie University guided by Cooper to assess student achievement of national faculties of America in 1976. The drawback with the CCR model is that it compares DMU's only based on overall efficiency assuming constant returns to scale. It ignores the fact that different DMU's could be operating at different scales. To overcome this drawback, Banker, Charnez and Cooper (1984) developed the BCC model.

DEA determines the weights so that the efficiency of the DMU will be maximized to the other DMUs.

Suppose the set under evaluation includes n decision-making unit of DMU_j (j=1,2,...n) where consumes m input $x_{1j}, x_{2j}, ..., x_{mj}$ to produce s output $y_{1j}, y_{2j}, ..., y_{sj}$. $v_i (i = 1, ..., m)$ and $u_r (r = 1, ..., s)$ are respectively corresponding weight of inputs and outputs. Efficiency is defined as follows:

$$Efficiency = \frac{\sum_{r=1}^{s} u_r y_{rj}}{\sum_{i=1}^{m} v_i x_{ij}} \qquad (1)$$

Another principle of the DEA models is the relationship between the number of inputs and outputs and DMUs. In DEA restrictions are applied such as $n \geq 3(m + s)$

or $n \geq 2(m + s)$ that n, m and s are respectively the number of DMUs, inputs and outputs.

If we have n DMUs that each one has the same m input & s output, the relative efficiency of jth DMU $(DMU_j, j = 1,2,...,n)$ is defined as the following mathematical model (Doyle, Green, 1994).

$$e_k = Max \sum_{r=1}^{s} u_r y_{rk} \Big/ \sum_{i=1}^{m} v_i x_{ik}$$

$s.t.$ $x_{ij} = input \ i \ for \ DMU \ j$

$$\sum_{r=1}^{s} u_r y_{rj} \Big/ \sum_{i=1}^{m} v_i x_{ij} \leq 1, j = 1,...,n \qquad y_{rj} = output \ r \ for \ DMU \ j$$

$u_r \geq 0, r = 1,...,s$ $u_r = weight \ of \ output \ r$

$v_i \geq 0, i = 1,...,m$ $v_i = weight \ of \ input \ i$

(2)

In DEA for each DMU efficiency score is calculated that is between zero and one & divides the DMUs under evaluation into two groups of the efficient and inefficient ones.

The DMU that its score is one, $(e_k = 1)$, is efficient & the DMU that is less than one, $(e_k < 1)$, is inefficient.

CCR Models

Suppose that $(DMU_j, j = 1,2,...,n)$ are n DMU that by using the input vector of $X_j \ (j = 1,\cdots,n)$ produces output vector of $Y_j \ (j = 1,\cdots,n)$ and the objective is to evaluate performance of DMU_k. (Tables 1 and 2)

If θ^* is the optimal value of the objective function, it is proved that $0 \leq \theta^* \leq 1$.

If ϕ^* is the optimal value, it is proved that $\phi^* \geq 1$. If $\phi_o^* = 1$ in this case DMU_k is efficient, otherwise it's inefficient. In this model ϕ^* does not show efficiency. Efficiency is obtained from $\dfrac{1}{\phi^*}$.

Analytic Network Process (ANP) is one of the Multi Attribute Decision Making techniques that are suggested as a proper alternative to AHP in 1996 by the Thomas L. Saaty. ANP provides a comprehensive and powerful method for precise decision making by using experimental data or personal judgments of the decision maker.

Both methods DEA and ANP are used in the operation. Both methods have their limitations, but the hybrid algorithm of DEA-ANP has the benefits of both methods, since like ANP method does not use subjective evaluation, in fact, paired

Table 1. Input oriented CCR model

Multiplier Form	Envelopment Form
Linear Form Multiplier Form	**Linear Form**

Multiplier Form

$$Max \frac{\sum_{r=1}^{s} u_r y_{rk}}{\sum_{i=1}^{m} v_i x_{ik}}$$

$$s.t.:$$

$$\frac{\sum_{r=1}^{s} u_r y_{rj}}{\sum_{i=1}^{m} v_i x_{ij}} \leq 1$$

$$u_r, v_i \geq 0$$

$$Max \sum_{r=1}^{s} u_r y_{rk}$$

$$s.t.:$$

$$\sum_{i=1}^{m} v_i x_{ik} = 1,$$

$$\sum_{r=1}^{s} u_r y_{rj} - \sum_{i=1}^{m} v_i x_{ij} \leq 0, j = 1,...,n$$

$$u_r \geq 0, r = 1,...,s,$$

$$v_i \geq 0, i = 1,...,m.$$

Envelopment Form

$$Min \ \theta$$

$$s.t.:$$

$$\sum_{j=1}^{n} \lambda_j x_{ij} \leq \theta x_{ik}, i = 1,...,m$$

$$\sum_{j=1}^{n} \lambda_j y_{rj} \geq y_{rk}, r = 1,...,s$$

$$\lambda_j \geq 0, j = 1,...,n$$

Table 2. output oriented CCR model

Multiplier Form	Envelopment Form
$Min \sum\limits_{i=1}^{m} v_i x_{ik}$ $s.t :$ $\sum\limits_{r=1}^{s} u_r y_{rk} = 1,$ $\sum\limits_{r=1}^{s} u_r y_{rj} - \sum\limits_{i=1}^{m} v_i x_{ij} \leq 0, j = 1,...,n$ $u_r \geq 0, \quad r = 1,...,s$ $v_i \geq 0, \quad i = 1,...,m$	$Max \ \phi$ $s.t :$ $\sum\limits_{j=1}^{n} \lambda_j x_{ij} \leq x_{ik}, i = 1,...,m$ $\sum\limits_{j=1}^{n} \lambda_j y_{rj} \geq \phi y_{rk}, r = 1,...,s$ $\lambda_j \geq 0, j = 1,...,n$

comparisons are created by DEA model & purely mathematical & as well as DEA doesn't only divide DMUs into two categories, but does full ranking.

In this chapter, the interaction and dependencies between different faculties have caused to use the hybrid algorithm of DEA-ANP for evaluating efficiency of departments.

DEA-ANP hybrid algorithm designed to eliminate the problem of the full ranking of DEA and the consequences of mental evaluations of ANP method. The other purpose of this study is to eliminate ranking problems in hybrid model, and dependency problems of alternatives or criteria. Therefore, the issues of ranking and interdependence of alternatives or criteria are incorporated this method. The stages of the algorithm DEA-ANP is as follows:

Stage 1: To Obtain a Pairwise Comparisons Matrix Based on DEA.

At this stage of hybrid algorithm, evaluation of DMUs is done by binary comparison of DMUs (comparing each DMU with another one).

Suppose k (k=1,...,n) DMU must be assessed. Each DMU consumes m type of inputs to produce s type of output.

For example DMU_k consumes $Xjk \ (i = 1,...,m)$ input to produce $Yrk \ (r = 1,...,s)$ output. In this case, the $X(m \times n)$ & $Y(s \times n)$, respectively, are the input and output matrices.

$$E_{K,K'} = Max \sum_{r=1}^{s} u_r y_{rk}$$

$$s.t : \sum_{i=1}^{m} v_i x_{ik} = 1$$

$$\sum_{r=1}^{s} u_r y_{rk} - \sum_{i=1}^{m} v_i x_{ik} \leq 0, \tag{3}$$

$$\sum_{r=1}^{s} u_r y_{rk'} - \sum_{i=1}^{m} v_i x_{ik'} \leq 0, \quad j = 1,...,n$$

$$u_r \geq 0, \qquad\qquad r = 1,...,s$$

$$v_i \geq 0, \qquad\qquad i = 1,...,m.$$

By Solving the mathematical model (3) for the entire DMUs, the values $e_{k,k'}(k' = 1,...,n, \ k = 1,...,n, k \neq k'$ obtained and the matrix E is created with k rows & k' columns that the all elements of its original diagonal is 1. Pairwise comparisons matrix E is like as Table 3.

After formation of pairwise comparisons of matrix E, the first stage is continued by the following four steps:

Step 1: Calculate the pairwise comparisons of matrix A, according to the pairwise comparisons matrix of E.

The values of matrix A from organizations' paired comparisons are obtained from $a_{k'k} = \dfrac{e_{kk'}}{e_{k'k}}$ (This formula shows the k decision unit efficiency, and the k' decision unit.

Pairwise comparisons matrix of A is as Table 4.

Table 3. E Matrix by solving model

	1	2	3	...	N
1	1	$e_{1,2}$	$e_{1,3}$	...	$e_{1,N}$
2	$e_{2,1}$	1	$e_{2,3}$	...	$e_{2,N}$
3	$e_{3,1}$	$e_{3,2}$	1	...	$e_{3,N}$
.	.	.	.	.	.
.	.	.	.	.	.
.	.	.	.	.	.
N	$e_{N,1}$	$e_{N,2}$	$e_{N,3}$	...	1

Table 4. Pairwise comparisons matrix (A)

	1	2	3	...	N
1	1	$a_{1,2}$	$a_{1,3}$	...	$a_{1,N}$
2	$a_{2,1}$	1	$a_{2,3}$	...	$a_{2,N}$
3	$a_{3,1}$	$a_{3,2}$	1	...	$a_{3,N}$
.	.	.	.	.	.
.	.	.	.	.	.
.	.	.	.	.	.
N	$a_{N,1}$	$a_{N,2}$	$a_{N,3}$	...	1

Step 2: Calculate pairwise comparisons matrix (A')

After obtaining matrix A, each component of the matrix A is divided by that column's total value as follow as $a'_{k'k} = \dfrac{a_{kk'}}{\sum\limits_{k=1}^{n} a_{kk'}}$. The obtained matrix is a normalized. Normalized pairwise comparisons matrix (A') is as Table 5.

Step 3: Calculate column vector A″

Here, the column vector elements are found by summation over the rows. Column vector A″ is as Table 6.

Step 4: Calculate column vector A‴

The vector A‴ which is a complete ranking of organizational DMUs is obtained from normalization of column vector A″ from the relationship of $a'''_{kk'} = \dfrac{a''_k}{\sum\limits_{k=1}^{n} a''_k}$. The obtained column vector A‴ is based on Table 7.

Stage 2: Ranking by ANP

Based on the pair-wise comparison of matrix E and after developing the hierarchy of ANP has been developed.

Table 5. Normalized pairwise comparisons matrix (A')

	1	2	3	...	N
1	1	$a'_{1,2}$	$a'_{1,3}$	...	$a'_{1,N}$
2	$a'_{2,1}$	1	$a'_{2,3}$	...	$a'_{2,N}$
3	$a'_{3,1}$	$a'_{3,2}$	1	...	$a'_{3,N}$
.	.	.	.	.	.
.	.	.	.	.	.
.	.	.	.	.	.
N	$a'_{N,1}$	$a'_{N,2}$	$a'_{N,3}$	...	1

Table 6. Column vector (A")   *Table 7. Column vector (A''')*

	1
1	a_1''
2	a_2''
3	a_3''
. . .	. . .
N	a_N''

	1
1	a_1'''
2	a_2'''
3	a_3'''
. . .	. . .
N	a_N'''

After defining the relationships and interactions between faculties in the view point of educational administrators of departments, super matrix is obtained by Super decision software.

Finally, the $a_{kk'}'''$ and w_k^* are multiplied, and the relative dependent priorities of factors obtained.

Thus the final result of the algorithm DEA-ANP will be achieved.

It should be noted that the software Lindo & Super decision were used to solve the models and the results will be provided & described in Tables.

Indicators which are evaluated to assess efficiency in the two field, are respectively displayed in Figure 1 and Figure 2.

In this study, number of conditional student is undesirable outputs therefore its reverse has been used.

Figure 1. Assessed indicators in the evaluation of educational performance of faculties

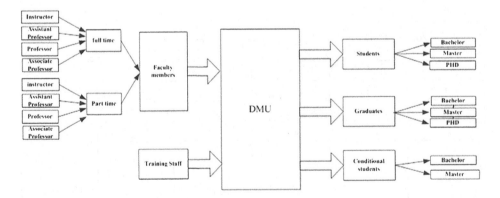

Figure 2. Assessed indicators in the evaluation of research performance of faculties

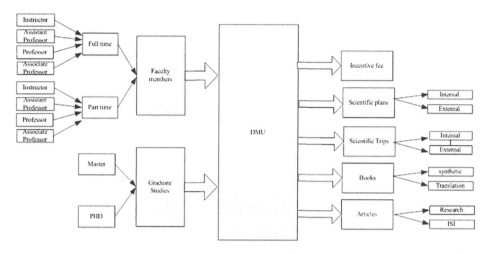

INTEGRATION OF INPUT AND OUTPUT VARIABLES

Combine the input and output variables with predetermined weighting coefficients to reduce their number through this combination and achieved precise results.

Weight factors used in this research are extracted from previous articles & conducted research & promotion of faculty members' regulation, which are as follows:

Entrance students= 4*(PhD) + 2*(Master) + Bachelor

Full-time faculty member (Part time faculty) = 5*(Professor) + 4*(Associate professor) + 3*(Assistant professor) +2*(Instructor)

Faculty member = 2*(Full-time faculty) + (Part time faculty)

Books = 5*(Synthetic) + 3*(Translated)

Scientific plans = 3*(External plans) + 2*(Internal plans)

Scientific Trips = 1.5 (Foreign Trips) + Domestic trips

Articles = 3* (ISI articles) + 2* (Scientific-Research articles)

After applying these factors, we used two input variables (Faculty member and Training staff) and three output variables (Entrance students, graduated, conditional student) for examining the educational efficiency & two input variables (graduated students and Faculty member) & five output variables (the incentive fee, plans, trips, articles, books) to assess research efficiency in Figure 3.

In the study, research efficiency has two input variables and three output variables and 17 DMUs.

$$n \geq 3(m + n)$$
$$17 \geq 3(2 + 5)$$

$$(4)$$

As you can see the value of left side inequality is not more than the right side & there is probability of bias efficiency. Therefore weight restrictions have been used to solve the present study models.

After determining indicators, collection of data in 17 department will be done in order to assess efficiency in the field of education and research. Information is related to years 2009-2010 that the results of this information collection are gathered with the indicators weights in the Tables 8, 9.

After studying & consulting with a number of training directors of various colleges, it was found that there are communications and interactions between various faculties of the university & faculties have a mutual influence on each other.

Typically exchange between faculty members occurs between different faculties. Because of the existence of these communications and creating the network between colleges it was decided to inevitably use network tool that between the multi criteria decision making methods, only ANP method has usability and influence in such networks. For this reason, the ANP method is used. Communications & interactions between faculties were specified like the Figure 4.

Figure 3. Input and output components

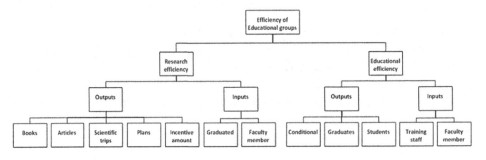

Table 8. Basic input and output indicators

DMU	Graduated				Students				Full time faculty member					Part time faculty member				
	Bachelor	Master	Ph.D	Total	Bachelor	Master	Ph.D.	Total	Instructor	Assistant	professor	Associate	Total	Instructor	Assistant	professor	Associate	Total
1	42	310	219	571		431	211	642		8	5	5	18		9	8	2	19
2	32		12	44		47	392	439		6	12	5	23	2	13	6	3	24
3		97		97	395	698	232	1325		3	2		5	1	13	8	3	25
4		92	141	233		1551	484	2035		2	10	2	14	2	15	13	6	36
5		30	20	50		248	51	299	1	1	1		3		4		1	5
6	246	397	45	688	1180	1696	510	3386		5	18	10	33	1	48	1	3	53
7		225	39	264	1646			1646	1	3	4	2	10	5	9		3	17
8	8	270	69	347	220	1364	406	1990		3	10	4	17		33	13	9	55
9	92	33	98	223	973	224	103	1300		7	7	2	16	3	12		1	16
10		437	129	566	353	2220	298	2871		3	6	3	12	3	30	7	10	50
11	382			382	803	190	43	1036		6	3	6	15	4	9			13
12		170	72	242		1514	162	1676		6	7	5	18	3	19	2	1	25
13	80	70	5	155	800	174	15	989			3	6	9	1	7	1		9
14	62	70	100	232	30	314	115	459		5		1	6		7	1	1	9
15		187	57	244	2	473	694	1169		7	2	7	16	4	20	6	2	32
16	132	3	40	175	481	1586	587	2654			8	3	11		20	10	10	40
17	240	50	15	305	1107	142	50	1299		1	1	3	5	3	13	2	4	22

Table 9. Basic input and output indicators

DMU	Incentive fee	Training staff	Articles			Scientific Plans			Scientific Trips			Books			Conditional Students		
			ISI	Research	Total	Internal	External	Total	Domestic	Foreign	Total	Synthetic	Translation	Total	Bachelor	Master	Total
1	9070000	9		3	3	1			6	4	10	1		1	134	50	184
2	50570000	30	27	48	75					2	2				28		28
3	25250000	20		15	15					2	2				14		14
4	91540000	13	10	85	95					2	2	1	2	3	8	36	44
5	4600000	5	4		4					1	1				15	10	25
6	296442500	16	133	49	182	1	19	20	3	20	23		2	2	844	238	1082
7	19650000	30	4	10	14		7	7								70	70
8	333770000	16	123	189	312		1	1		22	22	2	1	3	58	70	128
9	17500000	10	10	5	15	1				2	2				32	23	55
10	1305100000	22	11	93	104	1	1	1	4	4	8	5	3	8	118	166	284
11	15820000	30	8	3	11		1	1							354		354
12	74940000	22	59	32	91		9	9		5	5	•	1	1	24	178	202
13	3710000	28	7	3	10		3	3	1		1				60	10	70
14	8590000	8	2	17	19					1	1				50	5	55
15	19550000	12		20	20					2	2					26	26
16	382523500	11	267	148	415	1			5	17	22	2		2	202	12	214
17	1008900000	40	58	8	66	1				7	7		3	3	136	112	248

Figure 4. Communications and interactions between faculties

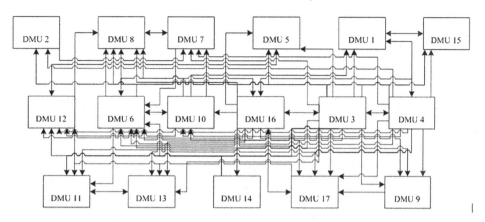

Educational indicators are as follows:

Students (BA, MA, Ph.D.)

Graduated (BA, MA, Ph.D.)

Conditional (BA, MA)

Faculty member{full time (Instructor, Assistant Professor, Professor, Associate Professor), part-time (Instructor, Assistant Professor, Associate Professor)}

Training staff

Due to the high number of variables we have to combine them with different weights. After integration in indicators, ultimately, evaluating the educational efficiency is done with two input variables (students and training staff) and three output variables (faculty member, graduated, conditionals).

In the questionnaire, the importance of each variable was expressed in determining the value of educational efficiency compared with each other in a qualitative form in a range of 7-option (ineffective, very less important, less important, average, high, very high, extremely) & distributed among experts.

The results of this questionnaire specify the importance of each indicator.

The data obtained from input and output indicators are determined by educational district is gathered by their weight allocation in Table 10:

In order to be comparable different measurements scales, dimensionless must be used by which the elements of converted indicators n_{ij} are measured without dimension.

Table 10. Input and output indicators related to the field of education & the allocative weight

Weight	0.824	0.645	0.587	0.491	0.619
DMU	Inputs		Outputs		
	Faculty Member	Training Staff	Students	Graduated	Conditional Students[1]
1	219	9	1706	1538	0.0043
2	268	30	1662	80	0.0357
3	205	20	2719	194	0.0714
4	340	13	5038	748	0.0125
5	42	5	700	140	0.0286
6	471	66	6612	1220	0.0007
7	137	30	1646	606	0.0071
8	475	16	4572	824	0.005
9	156	10	1833	550	0.0128
10	393	22	5985	1390	0.0022
11	127	30	1355	382	0.0028
12	227	22	3676	628	0.0026
13	95	28	1208	240	0.0125
14	79	8	1118	220	0.0167
15	271	12	3722	602	0.0192
16	352	11	6001	298	0.0044
17	162	40	1591	400	0.0028

In this study linear dimensionless is used, meaning that each value of r_{ij} is divided into the maximum value in the column as $n_{ij} = \dfrac{r_{ij}}{r_j^*}$ such that $r_j^* = \max r_{ij}$ where $0 \leq n_{ij} \leq 1$.

And the advantage of dimensionless is that it's linear and all results are converted into a linear proportionally. As a result, the relative order from the existing result remains the same. Thus we will make dimensionless the input and output indicators that results are given in Table 11:

Ranking faculties by using the DEA classic model – Educational scope

Multiplier form of the CCR Input oriented model has been used to obtain relative efficiency. By solving this model, departments divided into two efficient and inefficient groups.

Table 11. Dimensionless of input - output indicators related to education scope

Weight	0.824	0.645	0.587	0.491	0.619
DMU	Inputs		Outputs		
	Faculty Member	Training Staff	Students	Graduated	Conditional Students
1	0.461	0.1364	0.258	1	0.0602
2	0.5642	0.4545	0.2514	0.052	0.5
3	0.4316	0.303	0.4112	0.1261	1
4	0.7158	0.197	0.7619	0.4863	0.1751
5	0.0884	0.0757	0.1059	0.091	0.1633
6	0.9916	1	1	0.7932	0.0098
7	0.2884	0.4545	0.2489	0.394	0.0994
8	1	0.2424	0.6915	0.5358	0.07
9	0.3284	0.1515	0.2772	0.3576	0.1793
10	0.8274	0.3333	0.9052	0.9038	0.0308
11	0.2674	0.4545	0.2049	0.2484	0.0392
12	0.4779	0.3333	0.5559	0.4083	0.0364
13	0.2	0.4242	0.1827	0.156	0.1751
14	0.1663	0.1212	0.1691	0.143	0.2339
15	0.5705	0.1818	0.5629	0.3914	0.2689
16	0.741	0.1667	0.9076	0.1937	0.0616
17	0.341	0.606	0.2406	0.2601	0.0392

Inefficient DMUs can be easily ranked but efficient DMUs are ranked by using the efficient ranking methods. In this study, Anderson - Peterson is used for ranking efficient DMUs (Anderson, Peterson, 1993).

$$Max \quad \sum_{r=1}^{s} u_r y_{rk}$$

$$S.t. \quad \sum_{i=1}^{m} v_i x_{ik} = 1$$

$$\sum_{r=1}^{s} u_r y_{rj} - \sum_{i=1}^{s} v_i x_{ij} \leq \circ \quad , \quad j = 1, \cdots n , j \neq k \tag{5}$$

$$u_r \geq 0 \quad , \quad r = 1, \cdots, s$$

$$v_i \geq 0 \quad , \quad i = 1, \cdots, m$$

X and y respectively are the input and output's vectors. V and u are weights of model of input and output vectors.

Input oriented of CCR model with the multiplier form is used to rank DMUs. For instance, for DMU_3 we have:

max 0.4112u1+0.1261u2+u3

subject to

0.4316v1+0.303v2=1

0.258u1+u2+0.0602u3-0.461v1-0.1364v2<=0

0.2514u1+0.052u2+0.5u3-0.5642v1-0.4545v2<=0

0.4112u1+0.1261u2+u3-0.4316v1-0.303v2<=0

0.7619u1+0.4863u2+0.1751u3-0.7158v1-0.197v2<=0

0.1059u1+0.091u2+0.1633u3-0.0884v1-0.0757v2<=0

u1+0.7932u2+0.0098u3-0.9916v1-v2<=0

0.2489u1+0.394u2+0.0994u3-0.2884v1-0.4545v2<=0

0.6915u1+0.5358u2+0.0700u3-v1-0.2424v2<=0

0.2772u1+0.277u2+0.1793u3-0.3284v1-0.1515v2<=0

0.9052u1+0.9038u2+0.0308u3-0.8274v1-0.3333v2<=0

0.2049u1+0.2484u2+0.0392u3-0.2674v1-0.4545v2<=0

0.5559u1+0.4083u2+0.0364u3-0.4779v1-0.3333v2<=0

0.1827u1+0.156u2+0.1751u3-0.2v1-0.4242v2<=0

0.1691u1+0.143u2+0.2339u3-0.1663v1-0.1212v2<=0

0.5629u1+0.3914u2+0.2689u3-0.5705v1-0.1818v2<=0

0.9076u1+0.1937u2+0.0616u3-0.741v1-0.1667v2<=0

0.2406u1+0.2601u2+0.0392u3-0.341v1-0.606v2<=0

0.619u1-0.587u3<=0

0.587u2-0.491u1<=0

0.824v2-0.645v1<=0

u1>=0.000001

u2>=0.000001

u3>=0.000001

v1>=0.000001

v2>=0.000001

(6)

This model is solved for the rest of the DMUs and DMUs ranking is done by the results. Anderson - Peterson model is used for ranking efficient DMUs. For instance, Anderson-Peterson model for DMU_3 is known as an efficient DMU with efficiency score one:

max $0.4112u1+0.1261u2+u3$

subject to

$0.4316v1+0.303v2=1$

$0.258u1+u2+0.0602u3-0.461v1-0.1364v2<=0$

$0.2514u1+0.052u2+0.5u3-0.5642v1-0.4545v2<=0$

$0.7619u1+0.4863u2+0.1751u3-0.7158v1-0.197v2<=0$

$0.1059u1+0.091u2+0.1633u3-0.0884v1-0.0757v2<=0$

$u1+0.7932u2+0.0098u3-0.9916v1-v2<=0$

$0.2489u1+0.394u2+0.0994u3-0.2884v1-0.4545v2<=0$

$0.6915u1+0.5358u2+0.0700u3-v1-0.2424v2<=0$

$0.2772u1+0.277u2+0.1793u3-0.3284v1-0.1515v2<=0$

$0.9052u1+0.9038u2+0.0308u3-0.8274v1-0.3333v2<=0$

$0.2049u1+0.2484u2+0.0392u3-0.2674v1-0.4545v2<=0$

$0.5559u1+0.4083u2+0.0364u3-0.4779v1-0.3333v2<=0$

$0.1827u1+0.156u2+0.1751u3-0.2v1-0.4242v2<=0$

$0.1691u1+0.143u2+0.2339u3-0.1663v1-0.1212v2<=0$

$0.5629u1+0.3914u2+0.2689u3-0.5705v1-0.1818v2<=0$

$0.9076u1+0.1937u2+0.0616u3-0.741v1-0.1667v2<=0$

$0.2406u1+0.2601u2+0.0392u3-0.341v1-0.606v2<=0$

$0.619u1-0.587u3<=0$

$0.587u2-0.491u1<=0$

$0.824v2-0.645v1<=0$

$u1>=0.000001$

$u2>=0.000001$

$u3>=0.000001$

$v1>=0.000001$

$v2>=0.000001$

(7)

The results of the ranking in method of classic DEA are like Table 12:

As the results of Table 12, DMU_3, DMU_5 are efficient and the rest of the DMUs are inefficient, and after using the AP ranking for two efficient DMU_3 and DMU_5, DMU_3 with the efficient score 1.352 is as the most efficient DMU & DMU_{17} with the efficient score 0.3656 is as the most inefficient DMU which were identified in the field of education.

RANKING OF FACULTIES BY DEA-ANP: EDUCATIONAL SCOPE

Stage 1: The binary comparison of DMUs occurs regardless of other DMUs by using the model (9) with weight restriction and the matrix E is obtained.

For example, a couple comparison of DMUs one and two, $e_{1,2}$ with considered weight restrictions for input and output can be calculated in accordance with the model (9):

Table 12. The efficiency of the classic DEA method – Educational scope

DMU	DEA		
	Efficiency Score	**Anderson Peterson Model**	**Rank**
3	1	1.352	1
4	0.6484		8
16	0.5483		11
6	0.4212		15
10	0.6487		7
15	0.6865		5
14	0.8545		3
17	0.3656		17
5	1	1.1007	2
12	0.528		12
9	0.6509		6
7	0.5913		10
1	0.8501		4
2	0.4064		16
13	0.6212		9
11	0.4237		14
8	0.4252		13

$e_{1,2} = \max 0.258u1 + u2 + 0.0602u3$

subject to

$0.461v1 + 0.1364v2 = 1$

$0.258u1 + u2 + 0.0602u3 - 0.461v1 - 0.1364v2 <= 0$

$0.2514u1 + 0.052u2 + 0.5u3 - 0.5642v1 - 0.4545v2 <= 0$

$0.619u1 - 0.587u3 <= 0$ 　　　　　　　　　　　　　　　　　　(9)

$0.587u2 - 0.491u1 <= 0$

$0.824v2 - 0.645v1 <= 0$

$u_i >= 0.000001$

$v_i >= 0.000001$

So the paired comparison matrix E is achieved by solving the model for the rest of the DMUs as Table 13.

Step 1: Calculate the pairwise comparisons of matrix A, according to the pairwise comparisons matrix of E.

Pairwise comparisons matrix of A is as Table 14.

Step 2: The normalized matrix is obtained by $a'_{k'k} = \dfrac{a_{kk'}}{\sum\limits_{k=1}^{n} a_{kk'}}$ as Table 15.

Step 3: Column vector A'' are found by summation over the rows. Column vector A'' is calculated by $a''_{kk'} = \sum\limits_{k=1}^{n} a'_{kk'}$ as Table 16.

Step 4: The column vector A''' which is calculated from the relationship of $a'''_{kk'} = \dfrac{a''_k}{\sum\limits_{k=1}^{n} a''_k}$ as Table 17.

Stage 2: Ranking by ANP

Super matrix is obtained by Super decision software (Table 18).

Finally, the $a'''_{kk'}$ and w^*_k are multiplied, and the relative dependent priorities of factors obtained.

Thus the final result of the algorithm DEA-ANP will be achieved (Table 19).

Table 13. Pairwise comparison matrix (E) – Educational scope

	1	2	3	4	5	6	7	8	9	10	11	12	13	14	15	16	17
1	1	1	1	1	1	1	1	1	1	1	1	1	1	1	1	1	1
2	1	1	0.4064	1	0.51	1	1	1	1	1	1	1	1	0.6301	1	1	1
3	1	1	1	1	1	1	1	1	1	1	1	1	1	1	1	1	1
4	1	1	1	1	1	1	1	1	1	1	1	1	1	1	1	1	1
5	1	1	1	1	1	1	1	1	1	1	1	1	1	1	1	1	1
6	1	1	0.4637	0.8928	0.4212	1	1	1	0.7942	0.8991	1	0.862	1	0.3627	0.8204	1	1
7	1	1	0.6508	1	0.5913	1	1	1	1	1	1	1	1	0.7359	1	0.842	1
8	1	1	0.9654	0.7287	1	1	1	1	1	1	1	1	1	1	0.7753	1	1
9	1	1	0.8885	1	0.9846	1	1	1	1	1	1	1	1	1	0.9948	1	1
10	1	1	0.9799	1	1	1	1	1	1	1	1	1	1	1	0.9948	1	1
11	1	1	0.4664	0.898	0.4237	1	0.7508	1	0.7989	1	1	1	0.8512	0.5274	0.8252	1	1
12	1	1	0.5414	1	0.6	1	1	1	0.9213	1	1	1	1	0.6356	0.9517	1	1
13	1	1	0.6838	1	0.6212	1	1	1	1	1	1	1	1	0.7732	1	1	1
14	1	1	0.8843	1	0.944	1	1	1	1	1	1	1	1	1	1	1	1
15	1	1	1	1	1	1	1	1	1	1	1	1	1	1	1	1	1
16	1	1	1	1	1	1	1	1	1	1	1	1	1	1	1	1	1
17	1	1	0.4024	0.7748	0.3656	1	0.6741	1	0.6892	1	0.8978	1	0.7023	0.455	0.7119	1	1

Table 14. Pairwise comparison matrix (A) – Educational scope

	1	2	3	4	5	6	7	8	9	10	11	12	13	14	15	16	17
1	1	1	1	1	1	1	1	1	1	1	1	1	1	1	1	1	1
2	1	1	0.4064	1	0.51	1	1	1	1	1	1	1	1	0.6301	1	1	1
3	1	2.4606	1	1	1	2.1566	1.5366	1.0358	1.1255	1.0205	2.1441	1.8471	1.4624	1.1308	1	1	2.4851
4	1	1	1	1	1	1.1201	1	1.3723	1	1	1.1136	1.6667	1.6098	1.0593	1	1	1.2906
5	1	1.9608	1	1	1	2.3742	1.6912	1	1.0156	1	2.3602	1	1	1	1	1	2.7352
6	1	1	0.4637	0.8928	0.4212	1	1	1	0.7942	0.8991	1	0.862	1	0.3627	0.8204	1	1
7	1	1	0.6508	1	0.5913	1	1	1	1	1	1.3319	1	1	0.7359	1	1	1.4834
8	1	1	0.9654	0.7287	1	1	1	1	1	1	1	1	1	1	0.7753	0.842	1
9	1	1	0.8885	1	0.9846	1.2591	1	1	1	1	1.2517	1.0854	1	1	1	1	1.4509
10	1	1	0.9799	1	0.4237	1.1122	0.7508	1	1	1	1	1	1	1	0.9948	1	1
11	1	1	0.4664	0.898	0.6	1	1	1	0.7989	1	1	1	0.8512	0.5274	0.8252	1	1.1138
12	1	1	0.5414	1	0.6212	1.1601	1	1	0.9213	1	1	1	1	0.6356	0.9517	1	1
13	1	1	0.6838	1	0.944	1	1.3589	1	1	1	1.1748	1	1	0.7732	1	1	1.4239
14	1	1	0.8843	1	1	2.7571	1	1.2898	1	1	1.8961	1.5733	1.2933	1	1	1	2.1978
15	1	1.587	1	1	1	1.2189	1	1.1876	1	1.0052	1.2118	1.0507	1	1	1	1	1.4047
16	1	1	1	1	1	1	1	1	1	1	1	1	1	1	1	1	1
17	1	1	0.4024	0.7748	0.3656	1	0.6741	1	0.6892	1	0.8978	1	0.7023	0.455	0.7119	1	1

Table 15. Normalized matrix (A✓) – Educational scope

	1	2	3	4	5	6	7	8	9	10	11	12	13	14	15	16	17
1	0.0588	0.05	0.075	0.0614	0.0743	0.0451	0.0555	0.0559	0.0612	0.0591	0.0468	0.0524	0.0558	0.0699	0.0622	0.0594	0.0424
2	0.0588	0.05	0.0305	0.0614	0.0379	0.0451	0.0555	0.0559	0.0612	0.0591	0.0468	0.0524	0.0558	0.044	0.0622	0.0594	0.0424
3	0.0588	0.123	0.075	0.0614	0.0743	0.0973	0.0853	0.0579	0.0689	0.0603	0.1003	0.0968	0.0816	0.079	0.0622	0.0594	0.1054
4	0.0588	0.05	0.075	0.0614	0.0743	0.0505	0.0555	0.0767	0.0612	0.0591	0.0521	0.0524	0.0558	0.0699	0.0622	0.0594	0.0547
5	0.0588	0.098	0.075	0.0614	0.0743	0.1071	0.0939	0.0559	0.0621	0.0591	0.1104	0.0873	0.0898	0.074	0.0622	0.0594	0.116
6	0.0588	0.05	0.0348	0.0548	0.03129	0.0451	0.0555	0.0559	0.0486	0.0531	0.0468	0.0452	0.0558	0.0253	0.051	0.0594	0.0424
7	0.0588	0.05	0.0488	0.0614	0.0439	0.0451	0.0555	0.0559	0.0612	0.0591	0.0623	0.0524	0.0558	0.0514	0.0622	0.0594	0.0629
8	0.0588	0.05	0.0724	0.0447	0.0743	0.0451	0.0555	0.0559	0.0612	0.0591	0.0468	0.0524	0.0558	0.0699	0.0482	0.05	0.0424
9	0.0588	0.05	0.0666	0.0614	0.0731	0.0568	0.0555	0.0559	0.0612	0.0591	0.0585	0.0569	0.0558	0.0699	0.0622	0.0594	0.0615
10	0.0588	0.05	0.0735	0.0614	0.0743	0.0502	0.0555	0.0559	0.0612	0.0591	0.0468	0.0524	0.0558	0.0699	0.0619	0.0594	0.0424
11	0.0588	0.05	0.035	0.0551	0.0315	0.0451	0.0417	0.0559	0.0489	0.0591	0.0468	0.0524	0.0475	0.0368	0.0513	0.0594	0.0472
12	0.0588	0.05	0.0406	0.0614	0.0446	0.0523	0.0555	0.0559	0.0564	0.0591	0.0468	0.0524	0.0558	0.0444	0.0592	0.0594	0.0424
13	0.0588	0.05	0.0513	0.0614	0.0461	0.0451	0.0555	0.0559	0.0612	0.0591	0.0549	0.0524	0.0558	0.054	0.0622	0.0594	0.0604
14	0.0588	0.0793	0.0663	0.0614	0.0701	0.1244	0.0754	0.0559	0.0612	0.0591	0.0887	0.0824	0.0722	0.0699	0.0622	0.0594	0.0932
15	0.0588	0.05	0.075	0.0614	0.0743	0.055	0.0555	0.0721	0.0612	0.0594	0.0567	0.055	0.0558	0.0699	0.0622	0.0594	0.0595
16	0.0588	0.05	0.075	0.0614	0.0743	0.0451	0.0555	0.0664	0.0612	0.0591	0.0468	0.0524	0.0558	0.0699	0.0622	0.0594	0.0424
17	0.0588	0.05	0.0302	0.0475	0.0271	0.0451	0.0374	0.0559	0.0422	0.0591	0.042	0.0524	0.0392	0.0318	0.0443	0.0594	0.0424

Table 16. Column vector (A″) – Educational scope

Table 17. Column vector (A‴) – Educational scope

DMU	Efficiency Score
1	0.9852
2	0.8784
3	1.3469
4	1.029
5	1.3447
6	0.81379
7	0.9461
8	0.9425
9	1.0226
10	0.9885
11	0.8225
12	0.895
13	0.9435
14	1.2399
15	1.0412
16	0.9957
17	0.7648

DMU	Efficiency Score
1	0.0579
2	0.0517
3	0.0792
4	0.0605
5	0.0791
6	0.0479
7	0.0556
8	0.0554
9	0.0601
10	0.0581
11	0.0484
12	0.053
13	0.0555
14	0.0729
15	0.0612
16	0.0586
17	0.045

In Figure 5 educational efficiency scores of hybrid algorithm DEA-ANP is shown and sorted scores is shown in Figure 6.

COMPARISON BETWEEN RESULTS OF DEA-ANP AND DEA: EDUCATIONAL SCOPE

In this section, the results of DEA-ANP and DEA are gathered in Table 20.

As you can see the differences are in the results and ranking results from the two methods of DEA-ANP and DEA that indicate the incompatibility of these two methods.

Non-parametric Mann- Whitney U test is used to measure these two methods compatibility.

Man – Whitney test is used to measure the difference hypothesis between two independent (non- related) societies when the data are in nominal or ordinal scale. In this case two scores are compared by probable assessing of ranking distribution.

Table 18. Relations between faculties (w_k^*)

	1	2	3	4	5	6	7	8	9	10	11	12	13	14	15	16	17
1	0.5234	0	0	0	0	0	0	0	0	0	0	0	0	0	0.097	0	0
2	0	0.5499	0	0	0	0	0.1131	0	0	0	0	0	0	0	0	0	0
3	0.1153	0.2098	0.5499	0.1078	0.1095	0.0748	0.1185	0.0657	0.1028	0.1036	0.0933	0.0849	0.0849	0.1562	0.1001	0.0934	0.0876
4	0.1204	0.2403	0.2403	0.7891	0	0.0734	0.1095	0.0678	0.1055	0.1074	0	0.0825	0.0795	0	0.1042	0.1025	0.0898
5	0	0	0	0	0.5403	0	0	0	0	0	0	0.0795	0	0	0	0	0
6	0	0	0	0	0.1185	0.5544	0	0.0667	0.1148	0.1008	0.1006	0	0.0825	0.1852	0	0.0956	0.086
7	0	0	0	0	0	0.0767	0.5402	0.0657	0	0	0	0	0	0	0	0	0
8	0	0	0	0	0	0	0	0.5321	0	0	0	0	0	0	0	0	0
9	0	0	0	0	0	0	0	0	0.5622	0	0	0	0	0	0	0	0.0974
10	0.1118	0	0	0	0	0.0723	0.1185	0.0667	0	0.5751	0	0.0825	0	0	0	0	0
11	0	0	0	0	0	0	0	0	0	0	0.5255	0	0.0808	0	0	0	0
12	0	0	0	0	0.1131	0	0	0.0694	0	0	0	0.5049	0	0	0	0	0
13	0	0	0	0	0	0	0	0	0	0	0.0962	0	0.5049	0	0	0	0
14	0	0	0	0	0	0	0	0	0	0	0	0	0	0.6587	0	0	0
15	0.1291	0	0	0	0	0	0	0	0	0	0	0	0	0	0.6987	0	0
16	0	0	0.2098	0.1031	0.1185	0.0734	0	0.0657	0.1148	0.1131	0.0912	0.0849	0.0849	0	0	0.606	0.0898
17	0	0	0	0	0	0.0748	0	0	0	0	0.0933	0.0808	0.0825	0	0	0.1025	0.5494

Table 19. Final result educational efficiency $\left(w_k^* \times a_{kk'}'''\right)$

DMU	Efficiency Score DEA-ANP	Rank
1	0.0362	13
2	0.0347	14
3	0.1429	1
4	0.1373	2
5	0.0469	8
6	0.0848	4
7	0.0373	12
8	0.0295	17
9	0.0382	11
10	0.058	6
11	0.03	16
12	0.0395	10
13	0.0327	15
14	0.048	7
15	0.0502	5
16	0.106	3
17	0.0458	9

Test "Man-Whitney" is one of the most powerful non-parametric tests. This test with the amount of p-value less than 0.05 rejected hypothesis (H_0) "compatibility of DEA & DEA-ANP" & the opposite hypothesis (H_1) accepts "incompatibility of the two methods DEA & DEA-ANP".

Figure 5. Educational efficiency score by DEA-ANP

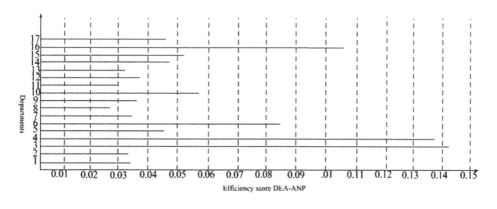

Figure 6. Sorted educational efficiency score by DEA-ANP

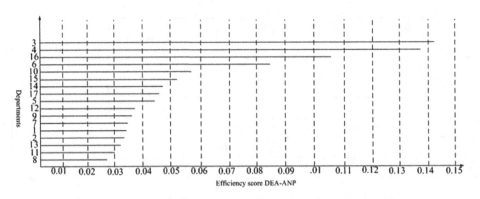

Table 20. Comparison educational efficiency between DEA and DEA-ANP

DMU	Models				
	DEA-ANP		DEA		
	Efficiency Score	Rank	Efficiency Score	Anderson Peterson Model	Rank
3	0.1429	1	1	1.352	1
4	0.1373	2	0.6484		8
16	0.106	3	0.5483		11
6	0.0848	4	0.4212		15
10	0.058	5	0.6487		7
15	0.0502	6	0.6865		5
14	0.048	7	0.8545		3
17	0.0477	8	0.3656		17
5	0.0469	9	1	1.1007	2
12	0.0395	10	0.528		12
9	0.0382	11	0.6509		6
7	0.0373	12	0.5913		10
1	0.0362	13	0.8501		4
2	0.0347	14	0.4064		16
13	0.0327	15	0.6212		9
11	0.03	16	0.4237		14
8	0.0295	17	0.4252		13

Indicators which were considered for the field of research, include the following instances:

- Graduate students (BA, PHD)
- Faculty member {full time (Instructor, Assistant Professor, Professor, Associate Professor), part-time (instructor, assistant professor, professor, associate professor)}
- Incentive fee
- The academic plans (the projects within university, outside university projects)
- Scientific trips (domestic, foreign)
- Articles (ISI, research papers)
- Books (Synthetic, translated)

Due to the high number of indicators, integration was done by considering their weight importance.

Finally, evaluating the research efficiency occurs with two input variables (graduated students and faculty member) and five output variables (incentive fee, academic plans, scientific trips, articles, books).

The information of input and output parameters determined by their weight allocation, as well as the results of the linear dimensionless in the field of research are as shown in the Tables 21, 22.

RANKING FACULTIES BY USING THE DEA CLASSIC METHODS: RESEARCH SCOPE

Multiplier form of the CCR Input oriented model is used to rank DMUs. For instance for DMU_6:

Table 21. Input and output indicators related to the field of research and allocative weight

Weight	0.824	0.685	0.917	0.845	0.868	0.851	0.906
DMU	Inputs		Outputs				
	Faculty Member	Students	Incentive Fee	Articles	Academic Plans	Trips	Books
1	219	1706	9070000	6	0	0	5
2	268	1662	50570000	177	2	12	0
3	205	2324	25250000	30	0	3	0
4	340	5038	91540000	200	0	3	11

continued on following page

Table 21. Continued

Weight	0.824	0.685	0.917	0.845	0.868	0.851	0.906
DMU	Inputs		Outputs				
	Faculty Member	Students	Incentive Fee	Articles	Academic Plans	Trips	Books
5	42	700	4600000	12	0	1.5	0
6	471	5432	296442500	497	58	33	6
7	137	0	19650000	32	21	0	0
8	475	4352	333770000	747	3	33	13
9	156	860	17500000	40	2	3	0
10	393	5632	130510000	219	5	3	34
11	127	552	15820000	30	3	6	0
12	227	3676	74940000	241	27	7.5	3
13	95	408	3710000	27	9	0	0
14	79	1088	8590000	40	0	1.5	0
15	271	3722	19550000	40	0	3	0
16	352	5520	382523500	1097	2	30.5	10
17	162	484	100890000	190	2	10.5	9

Table 22. The dimensionless of input-output indicators related to the field of research

Weight	0.824	0.685	0.917	0.845	0.868	0.851	0.906
DMU	Inputs		Outputs				
	Faculty Member	Students	Incentive Fee	Articles	Academic Plans	Trips	Books
1	0.4611	0.3029	0.0237	0.0055	0	0	0.147
2	0.5642	0.2951	0.1322	0.1613	0.0345	0.3636	0
3	0.4316	0.4126	0.066	0.0273	0	0.0909	0
4	0.7158	0.8945	0.2393	0.1823	0	0.0909	0.3235
5	0.0884	0.1243	0.012	0.0109	0	0.0454	0
6	0.9916	0.9645	0.775	0.453	1	1	0.1765
7	0.2884	0	0.0514	0.0292	0.3621	0	0
8	1	0.7727	0.8725	0.6809	0.0517	1	0.3823
9	0.3284	0.1527	0.0457	0.0365	0.0345	0.0909	0
10	0.8274	1	0.3412	0.1996	0.0862	0.0909	1
11	0.2674	0.098	0.0413	0.0273	0.0517	0.1818	0
12	0.4779	0.6527	0.1959	0.2197	0.4138	0.2273	0.0882
13	0.2	0.0724	0.0097	0.0246	0.1552	0	0
14	0.1663	0.1932	0.0224	0.0365	0	0.0454	0
15	0.5705	0.6609	0.0511	0.0365	0	0.0909	0
16	0.741	0.9801	1	1	0.0345	0.9242	0.2941
17	0.341	0.0859	0.2637	0.1732	0.0345	0.3182	0.2647

max 0.775u1+0.453u2+u3+u4+0.1765u5

subject to

0.9916v1+0.9645v2=1

0.0237u1+0.0055u2+0.147u5-0.4611v1-0.3029v2<=0

0.1322u1+0.1613u2+0.0345u3+0.3636u4-0.5642v1-0.2951v2<=0

0.066u1+0.0273u2+0.0909u4-0.4316v1-0.4126v2<=0

0.2393u1+0.1823u2+0.0909u4+0.3235u5-0.7158v1-0.8945v2<=0

0.012u1+0.0109u2+0.0454u4-0.0884v1-0.1243v2<=0

0.775u1+0.453u2+u3+u4+0.1765u5-0.9916v1-0.9645v2<=0

0.0514u1+0.0292u2+0.3621u3-0.2884v1<=0

0.8725u1+0.6809u2+0.0517u3+u4+0.3823u5-v1-0.7727**v2**<=0

0.0457u1+0.0365u2+0.0345u3+0.0909u4-0.3284v1-0.1527v2<=0

0.3412u1+0.1996u2+0.0862**u3**+0.0909u4+u5-0.8274v1-v2<=0

0.0413u1+0.0273u2+0.0517u3+0.1818u4-0.2674v1-0.098v2<=0

0.1959u1+0.2197u2+0.4138u3+0.2273u4+0.0882u5-0.4779v1-0.6**527**v2<=0

0.0097u1+0.0246u2+0.1552u3-0.2v1-0.0724v2<=0

0.0224u1+0.0365u2+0.0454u4-0.1663**v1**-0.1932v2<=0

0.0511u1+0.0365u2+0.0909u4-0.5705v1-0.6609v2<=0

u1+u2+0.0345u3-0.9242u4+0.2941u5-0.741v1-0.9801v2<=0

0.2637u1+0.1732u2+0.0345u3+0.3182u4+0.2647u5-0.341v1-0.0859v2<=0

0.917u5-0.906u1<=0

0.906u3-0.868u5<=0

0.868u4-0.851u3<=0

0.851u2-0.845u4<=0

0.824v2-0.685v1<=0

u1>=0.000001

u2>=0.000001

u3>=0.000001

u4>=0.000001

u5>=0.000001

v1>=0.000001

v2>=0.000001

(10)

This model apply for the rest of DMUs and ranking of DMUs occurs through the results. Since the efficient DMUs cannot be ranked by using DEA model so the Anderson - Peterson model is used. Anderson - Peterson model for DMU_6 which is known as an efficient DMU with efficiency score one is as follows:

max 0.775u1+0.453u2+u3+u4+0.1765u5

subject to

0.9916v1+0.9645v2=1

0.0237u1+0.0055u2+0.147u5-0.4611v1-0.3029v2<=0

0.1322u1+0.1613u2+0.0345u3+0.3636u4-0.5642v1-0.2951v2<=0

0.066u1+0.0273u2+0.0909u4-0.4316v1-0.4126v2<=0

0.2393u1+0.1823u2+0.0909u4+0.3235u5-0.7158v1-0.8945v2<=0

0.012u1+0.0109u2+0.0454u4-0.0884v1-0.1243v2<=0

0.0514u1+0.0292u2+0.3621u3-0.2884v1<=0

0.8725u1+0.6809u2+0.0517u3+u4+0.3823u5-v1-**0**.7727v2<=0

0.0457u1+0.0365u2+0.0345u3+0.0909u4-0.3284v1-0.1527v2<=0

0.3412u1+0.1996u2+0.0862u3+0.0909u4+u5-0.8274v1-v2<=0

0.0413u1+0.0273u2+0.0517u3+0.1818u4-0.2674v1-0.098v2<=0

0.1959u1+0.2197u2+0.4138u3+0.2273u4+0.0882u5-0.4779**v**1-0.6527v2<=0

0.0097u1+0.0246u2+0.1552u3-0.2v1-0.0724**v**2<=0

0.0224u1+0.0365u2+0.0454u4-0.1663v1-0.1932v2<=0

0.0511u1+0.0365u2+0.0909u4-0.5705v1-0.6609v2<=0

u1+u2+0.0345u3-0.9242u4+0.2941u5-0.741v1-0.9801v2<=0

0.2637u1+0.1732u2+0.0345u3+0.3182u4+0.2647u5-0.34**1**v1-0.0859v2<=0

0.917u5-0.906u1<=0

0.906u3-0.868u5<=0

0.868u4-0.851u3<=0

0.851u2-0.845u4<=0

0.824v2-0.685v1<=0

u1>=0.000001

u2>=0.000001

u3>=0.000001

u4>=0.000001

u5>=0.000001

v1>=0.000001

v2>=0.000001

$$(11)$$

Table 23. Efficiency of DEA model - Research scope

Department	DEA		
	Efficiency Score	**Anderson Peterson Model**	**Rank**
4	0.485		8
3	0.162		16
6	1	1.1647	3
16	1	1.5467	2
17	1	1.6633	1
10	1	1.0031	5
8	0.9856		6
7	1	1.0103	4
12	0.7384		7
1	0.2266		12
2	0.3743		11
9	0.1955		14
11	0.3787		10
13	0.4666		9
5	0.2221		13
15	0.0995		17
14	0.1806		15

The results of the ranking in form of DEA classic method is as follows in Table 23:

As the above table shows the results of the DMUs 6, 16, 17, 10, 7 are efficient & rest of them are inefficient.

After applying AP ranking, for the efficient DMUs, DMU_{17} was known as the most efficient DMU with achieving the efficiency value 1.6633 & DMU_{15} with efficiency value 0.0995 was known as the most efficient DMU in the research area.

RANKING FACULTIES BY THE HYBRID ALGORITHM DEA-ANP: RESEARCH SCOPE

First Stage: The binary comparison of DMUs occurs by using the following model in company with weight restriction & matrix E is achieved. For instance $e_{1,2}$ is to do a paired compare of DMUs 1 & 2.

max 0.0237u1+0.0055u2+0.147u5

subject to

0.4611v1+0.3029v2=1

0.0237u1+0.0055u2+0.147u5-0.4611v1-0.3029v2<=0

0.1322u1+0.1613u2+0.0345u3+0.3636u4-0.5642v1-0.2951v2<=0

0.906u1-0.917u5>=0

0.868u5-0.906u3>=0

0.851u3-0.868u4>=0

0.845u4-0.851u2>=0   (12)

0.824v2-0.685v1<=0

u1>=0.000001

u2>=0.000001

u3>=0.000001

u4>=0.000001

u5>=0.000001

v1>=0.000001

v2>=0.000001

It will done the same for the rest of DMUs & thus E- pairwise comparisons matrix of solving the models is obtained in form of Table 24:

Step 1: A- paired comparisons matrix is obtained from the paired comparison matrix E by the relationship $a_{k'k} = \dfrac{e_{kk'}}{e_{k'k}}$ according to Table 25:

Step 2: the normalized matrix A′ is obtained from the relationship $a'_{kk'} = \dfrac{a_{kk'}}{\sum_{k=1}^{n} a_{kk'}}$ as Table 26:

Step 3: the values of column vector A″ are calculated from the relation $a''_{kk'} = \sum_{k=1}^{n} a'_{kk'}$ as Table 27.

Step 4: The normalized vector A‴ is achieved from the relation $a'''_{kk'} = \dfrac{a''_k}{\sum_{k=1}^{n} a''_k}$ as Table 28.

Table 24. Pairwise matrix (E) –Research scope

	1	2	3	4	5	6	7	8	9	10	11	12	13	14	15	16	17
1	1	1	1	0.8926	1	0.5666	1	0.3447	1	0.4196	1	1	1	1	1	-	0.2379
2	1	1	1	1	1	0.6563	1	0.5971	1		1	1	1	1	1	-	0.3884
3	1	0.6526	1	0.5979	1	0.1991	0.858	0.1753	1	0.4688	0.9901	0.5329	1	1	1	0.7672	0.1977
4	1	1	1	1	1	0.8155	1	0.6245	1	0.8107	1	1	1	1	1	-	0.5069
5	1	0.6878	1	0.6814	1	0.2221	0.7616	0.2749	1	0.3577	0.8789	0.3311	1	1	1	0.9747	0.2447
6	1	1	1	1	1	1	1	1	1	1	1	1	1	1	1	-	-
7	1	1	1	1	1	1	1	1	1	1	1	1	1	1	1	-	-
8	1	1	1	1	1	1	1	1	1	1	1	1	1	1	1	-	-
9	1	0.9185	1	1	1	0.3826	0.7808	0.3697	1	0.8771	0.901	0.9971	1	1	1	-	0.2013
10	1	1	1	1	1	1	1	1	1	1	1	1	1	1	1	-	-
11	1	1	1	1	1	0.9025	0.8666	0.9167	1	1	1	1	1	1	1	-	0.387
12	1	1	1	1	1	0.7384	1	1	1	1	1	1	1	1	1	-	0.863
13	1	1	1	1	1	1	0.614	1	1	1	1	1	1	1	1	-	-
14	1	0.5748	1	0.5602	1	0.1806	0.7558	0.2068	0.9873	0.3398	0.8721	0.3863	1	1	1	0.7032	0.4786
15	1	0.3823	0.7288	0.289	0.8009	0.1146	0.5026	0.1066	0.6436	0.2266	0.5799	0.2576	1	0.6669	1	0.4315	0.1987
16	1	1	1	1	1	1	1	1	1	1	1	1	1	1	1	-	0.1158
17	1	1	1	1	1	1	1	1	1	1	1	1	1	1	1	-	-

Table 25. Pairwise comparison matrix (A) – Research scope

	1	2	3	4	5	6	7	8	9	10	11	12	13	14	15	16	17
1	1	1	1	0.8926	1	0.5666	1	0.3447	1	0.4196	1	1	1	1	1	1	0.2379
2	1	1	1.5323	1	1.4539	0.6563	1	0.5971	1.0887	1	1	1	1	1.7397	2.6157	1	0.3884
3	1	0.6526	1	0.5979	1	0.1991	0.858	0.1753	1	0.4688	0.9901	0.5329	1	1	1.3721	0.7672	0.1977
4	1.1203	1	1.6725	1	1.4676	0.8155	1	0.6245	1	0.8107	1	1	1	1.7851	3.4602	1	0.5069
5	1	0.6878	1	0.6814	1	0.2221	0.7616	0.2749	1	0.3577	0.8789	0.3311	1	1	1.2486	0.9747	0.2447
6	1.7649	1.5237	5.0226	1.2262	4.5025	1	1	1	2.6137	1	1.108	1.3543	1	5.5371	8.726	1	1
7	1	1	1.1655	1	1.313	1	1	1	1.2807	1	1.1539	1	1.6287	1.3231	1.9896	1	1
8	2.9011	1.6748	5.7045	1.6013	3.6377	1	1	1	2.7049	1	1.0909	1	1	4.8356	9.3809	1	1
9	1	0.9185	1	1	1	0.3826	0.7808	0.3697	1	0.8771	0.901	0.9971	1	1.0129	1.5538	1	0.2013
10	2.3832	1	2.1331	1.2335	2.7956	1	1	1	1.1401	1	1	1	1	2.9429	4.4131	1	1
11	1	1	1.01	1	1.1378	0.9025	0.8666	0.9167	1.1099	1	1	1	1	1.1466	1.7244	1	0.387
12	1	1	1.8765	1	3.0202	0.7384	0.614	1	1.0029	1	1	1	1	2.5887	3.882	1	0.863
13	1	1	1	1	1	1	1	1	1	1	1	1	1	1	1	1	0.4786
14	1	0.5748	1	0.5602	1	0.1806	0.7558	0.2068	0.9873	0.3398	0.8721	0.3863	1	1	1.4995	0.7032	0.1987
15	1	0.3823	0.7288	0.289	0.8009	0.1146	0.5026	0.1066	0.6436	0.2266	0.5799	0.2576	1	0.6669	1	0.4315	0.1158
16	1	1	1.3034	1	1.0259	1	1	1	1	1	1	1	1	1.4221	2.3175	1	1
17	4.2034	2.5747	5.0582	1.9728	4.0866	1	1	1	4.9677	1	2.584	1.1587	2.0894	5.0327	8.6356	1	1

Table 26. Normalized matrix (A✓) - Research scope

	1	2	3	4	5	6	7	8	9	10	11	12	13	14	15	16	17
1	0.041	0.0556	0.0301	0.0523	0.032	0.0481	0.066	0.0297	0.0407	0.0311	0.0551	0.0666	0.0534	0.0285	0.0179	0.063	0.0242
2	0.041	0.0556	0.0461	0.0586	0.0465	0.0557	0.066	0.0514	0.0444	0.0741	0.0551	0.0666	0.0534	0.0496	0.0469	0.063	0.0395
3	0.041	0.0363	0.0301	0.035	0.032	0.0169	0.0567	0.0151	0.0407	0.0347	0.0545	0.0355	0.0534	0.0285	0.0246	0.0483	0.0201
4	0.046	0.0556	0.0504	0.0586	0.047	0.0692	0.066	0.0538	0.0407	0.06	0.0551	0.0666	0.0534	0.0509	0.062	0.063	0.0516
5	0.041	0.0382	0.0301	0.0399	0.032	0.0188	0.0503	0.0237	0.0407	0.0265	0.0484	0.022	0.0534	0.0285	0.0224	0.0614	0.0249
6	0.0724	0.0847	0.1512	0.0719	0.1441	0.0849	0.066	0.0861	0.1065	0.0741	0.061	0.0902	0.0534	0.158	0.1563	0.063	0.1018
7	0.041	0.0556	0.0351	0.0586	0.042	0.0849	0.066	0.0861	0.0522	0.0741	0.0635	0.0666	0.0534	0.0378	0.0356	0.063	0.1018
8	0.119	0.0931	0.1718	0.0939	0.1164	0.0849	0.066	0.0861	0.1102	0.0741	0.0601	0.0666	0.0534	0.138	0.168	0.063	0.1018
9	0.041	0.051	0.0301	0.0586	0.032	0.0325	0.0516	0.0318	0.0407	0.065	0.0496	0.0664	0.0534	0.0289	0.0278	0.063	0.0205
10	0.0978	0.0556	0.0642	0.0723	0.0895	0.0849	0.066	0.0861	0.0464	0.0741	0.0551	0.0666	0.0534	0.084	0.0791	0.063	0.1018
11	0.041	0.0556	0.0304	0.0586	0.0364	0.0766	0.0572	0.0789	0.0452	0.0741	0.0551	0.0666	0.0534	0.0327	0.0309	0.063	0.0394
12	0.041	0.0556	0.0565	0.0586	0.0967	0.0627	0.066	0.0861	0.0409	0.0741	0.0551	0.0666	0.0534	0.0739	0.0695	0.063	0.0879
13	0.041	0.0556	0.0301	0.0586	0.032	0.0849	0.066	0.0861	0.0407	0.0741	0.0551	0.0666	0.0534	0.0285	0.0179	0.063	0.0487
14	0.041	0.0319	0.0301	0.0328	0.032	0.0153	0.0405	0.0178	0.0402	0.0252	0.048	0.0257	0.0534	0.0285	0.0269	0.0443	0.0202
15	0.041	0.0212	0.0219	0.0169	0.0256	0.0097	0.0332	0.0092	0.0262	0.0168	0.0319	0.0171	0.0534	0.019	0.0179	0.0272	0.0118
16	0.041	0.0556	0.0392	0.0586	0.0328	0.0849	0.066	0.0861	0.0407	0.0741	0.0551	0.0666	0.0534	0.0406	0.0415	0.063	0.1018
17	0.1725	0.1431	0.1523	0.1157	0.1308	0.0849	0.066	0.0861	0.2024	0.0741	0.1423	0.0771	0.1116	0.1436	0.1547	0.063	0.1018

Table 27. Column vector (A") - research scope

Table 28. Column vector (A''') - research scope

Department	Efficiency Score
1	0.7353
2	0.9135
3	0.6034
4	0.9499
5	0.6022
6	1.6256
7	1.0509
8	1.6664
9	0.7439
10	1.2399
11	0.8951
12	1.1076
13	0.8768
14	0.5632
15	0.4
16	1.001
17	2.022

Department	Efficiency Score
1	0.0433
2	0.0537
3	0.0355
4	0.0559
5	0.0354
6	0.0956
7	0.0618
8	0.098
9	0.0438
10	0.0729
11	0.0527
12	0.0652
13	0.0516
14	0.0331
15	0.0235
16	0.0589
17	0.119

The final result is obtained from the complete ranking of faculties by multiplying $(w_k^* \times a_{kk'}''')$ that the super matrix is shown. At Table 29 these results are brought with their ranking,

As it is clear from the above table a complete ranking are obtained.

The faculties' efficiency is in ascending order 14,15,5,13,11,9,2,1, 12,7,8, 10,17,16, 6,3,4 that the DMU_4 with efficiency value 0.1323 is as the most efficient faculty & DMU_{14} with calculating of efficiency value 0.0218 has been known as the most inefficient faculty in the research area that Figure 7 and Figure 8 express it:

COMPARISONS BETWEEN RESULTS OF DEA AND DEA-ANP: RESEARCH SCOPE

In this part the ranking results of DEA, DEA-ANP are gathered in Table 30.

As it can be observed there are differences in the results of two methods, for instance according to DEA-ANP methodology the DMU_4 has the first grade with

Table 29. Final result educational efficiency $(w_k^* \times a_{kk'}''')$

DMU	Efficiency Score DEA-ANP	Rank
1	0.0433	10
2	0.0365	11
3	0.1169	2
4	0.1323	1
5	0.0243	15
6	0.1077	3
7	0.0471	8
8	0.0521	7
9	0.0362	12
10	0.0729	6
11	0.0319	13
12	0.0437	9
13	0.0311	14
14	0.0218	17
15	0.022	16
16	0.1052	4
17	0.093	5

Figure 7. Research efficiency score by hybrid algorithm DEA-ANP

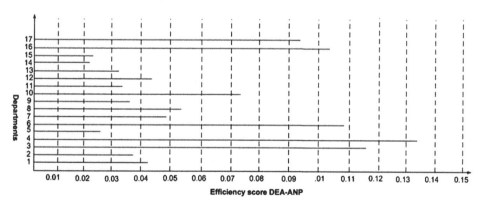

Figure 8. Sorted Research efficiency score by hybrid algorithm DEA-ANP

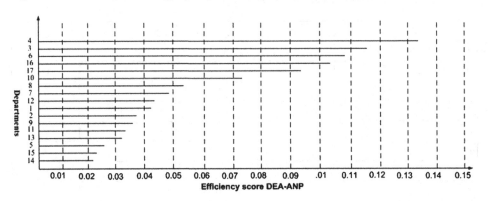

Table 30. Comparison research efficiency between DEA and DEA-ANP

Department	DEA-ANP		DEA		
	Efficiency Score	Rank	Efficiency Score	Anderson Peterson Model	Rank
4	0.1323	1	0.485		8
3	0.1169	2	0.162		16
6	0.1077	3	1	1.1647	3
16	0.1052	4	1	1.5467	2
17	0.093	5	1	1.6633	1
10	0.0729	6	1	1.0031	5
8	0.0521	7	0.9856		6
7	0.0471	8	1	1.0103	4
12	0.0437	9	0.7384		7
1	0.0433	10	0.2266		12
2	0.0365	11	0.3743		11
9	0.0362	12	0.1955		14
11	0.0319	13	0.3787		10
13	0.0311	14	0.4666		9
5	0.0243	15	0.2221		13
15	0.022	16	0.0995		17
14	0.0218	17	0.1806		15

the efficiency value 0.1323 but DMU_7 is known as an efficient DMU & DMU_8 is known as an inefficient DMU by the DEA method, but, the DMU_7 has a lower grade than DMU_8 by using DEA-ANP method. Thus this difference is noticeable in the other results of faculties. Then it is concluded that there is a significant difference between the two classic methods of DEA, DEA-ANP that this incompatibility has been confirmed by Man-Whitney U test with the value p-value less than 0.05 & consequently alternative hypothesis (H_1) "two methods' incompatibility" is accepted.

CONCLUSION

In an educational system, there is always a direct relationship between educational & research efficiency. Weakness in each of these two areas concludes weakness in another one. Typically if performance is calculated low in the research area, the performance result is weak in the education area & vice versa. The results from the hybrid algorithm DEA-ANP have been brought together in two education & research areas in a diagram as the Figure 9. Faculties is distributed into four areas by achieving Geometric mean of education and research performance rates.

First Area: Educational: inefficient, Research: inefficient
Second Area: Educational: inefficient, Research:efficient
Third Area: Educational: efficient, Research:efficient
Fourth Area: Educational: efficient, Research: inefficient

The dotted lines in the Figure 9 represents the above average, the faculties were placed in four districts. In Table 31 Education and research effectiveness - ineffectiveness average has been conducted in each area.

Table 31. Comparison between efficiency of educational and research scope

	Average Efficient-Inefficient of Research	Average Efficient-Inefficient of Educational	DMUs in Area
First area	0.0351	0.03817	1, 2, 5, 7, 9, 11, 12, 13, 14
Second area	0.07255	0.0386	8, 17
Third area	0.107	0.1058	3, 4, 6, 10, 16
Fourth area	0.022	0.0502	15

Figure 9. The scattering plot of the efficiency scores of education and research

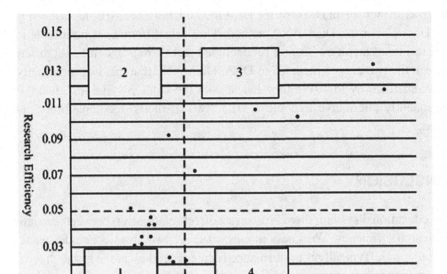

The highest concentration of faculties is in the first area which suggests faculty education and research inefficiency. After the first area, the faculties concentration has occurred in the third area which has a reasonable efficiency in both training and research requirements. In the second area there are only two faculties and in the fourth one there is only one faculty.

With regard to the direct relationship between education and research, placing the faculties in these two areas isn't somewhat logical that it may be the lack of health information which has been gathered. It should be noted that the DMUs located in these two areas are near the first and third areas.

REFERENCES

Ahn, D., & Seiford, L.M. (1993). Determining of impact differentiation output on the ranking, in public and private universities. *Socio Economic Journal, 7*(8).

Ahn, T., Arnold, V., Charnes, A., & Cooper, W. W. (1989). DEA and ratio efficiency analyses for public institutions of higher learning in Texas. *Research in Governmental and Nonprofit Accounting, 5*, 165–185.

Anderson, P., & Peterson, N. C. (1993). A procedure for ranking efficient units in DEA. *Management Science, 39*(10), 1261–1264. doi:10.1287/mnsc.39.10.1261

Antonio, A., & Santos, M. (2008). *Students and Teachers: A DEA Approach to the Relative Efficiency of Portuguese Public Universitie*. Academic Press.

Athanassopoulos, A., & Shale, E. (1997). Assessing the Comparative Efficiency of Higher Education in the U.K by Means of DEA. *Education Economics, 5*(2), 117–134. doi:10.1080/09645299700000011

Avkiran, N. (2001). Investigating technical and scale efficiencies of Australian Universities through data envelopment analysis. *Socio-Economic Planning Sciences, 35*(1), 57–80. doi:10.1016/S0038-0121(00)00010-0

Banker, R. D., Charnes, A., & Cooper, W. W. (1984). Some models for estimating technical and scale efficiencies in data envelopment analysis. *Management Science, 30*(9), 1078–1092. doi:10.1287/mnsc.30.9.1078

Banker, R. D., Janakiramang, S., & Natarajan, R. (2003). (Article in Press). Analysis of trends in technical and allocative efficiency: An application to Texas public school districts. *European Journal of Operational Research*.

Banker, R. D., & Thrall, R. M. (1992). Estimation of Returns to Scale Using Data Envelopment Analysis. *European Journal of Operational Research, 62*(1), 74–84. doi:10.1016/0377-2217(92)90178-C

Beasley, J. E. (1990). Comparing university departments. *Omega-International Journal, 18*(2), 171-183.

Beasley, J. E. (1995). Determining Teaching and Research Efficiencies. *The Journal of the Operational Research Society, 46*(4), 441–452. doi:10.1057/jors.1995.63

Bessent, A. M., & Bessent, E. W. (1980). Determining the comparative efficiency of schools through data envelopment analysis. *Educational Administration Quarterly, 16*(2), 57–75. doi:10.1177/0013161X8001600207

Bobe, B. (2009). Evaluating the efficiencies of university faculties: Adjusted data envelopment analysis. Paper for Accounting and Finance Association of Australia and New Zealand (AFAANZ) 2009 Conference, Adelaide, Australia.

Bowen, W. M. (1990). Subjective judgements and data envelopment analysis in site selection. *Computers, Environment and Urban Systems, 14*(2), 133–144. doi:10.1016/0198-9715(90)90018-O

Breu, T. M., & Raab, R. L. (1994). Efficiency and perceived quality of the nation's "top 25" national universities and national liberal arts colleges: An application of data envelopment analysis to higher education. *Socio-Economic Planning Sciences, 28*(1), 33–45. doi:10.1016/0038-0121(94)90023-X

Cai, Y., & Wu, W. (2001). Synthetic financial evaluation by a method of combining DEA with AHP. *International Transactions in Operational Research, 8*.

Coelli, T. (1996). *Assessing the performance of Australian universities using data envelopment analysis. internal report.* Center for Efficiency and Productivity Analysis, University of New England.

Colbert, A., Levary, R., & Shaner, C. (1999). Determining the relative efficiency of MBA programs using DEA. *European Journal of Operation Research.*

Daneshvar Royendegh, B., & Erol, S. (2010). A DEA – ANP hybrid Algorithm Approach to Evaluate a University's Performance. *International Journal of Basic & Applied Sciences IJBAS, 9*(10).

Doyle, J. R., & Green, R. (1994). Efficiency and cross efficiency in DEA:Derivations, meanings and the uses. *The Journal of the Operational Research Society, 45*(5), 567–578. doi:10.1057/jors.1994.84

Farrell, M. J. (1957). The measurement of productive efficiency. *Journal of the Royal Statistical Society, Series A, 120*(3), 253-281.

Friedman, L., & Sinuany-Sterm, Z. (1998). DEA and the discriminate analysis of ratio for ranking units. *Journal of Operational Research, 111*, 470-478.

Joumady, O., & Ris, C. (2005). Performance in European Higher Education: A Non-Parametric Production Frontier Approach. *Education Economics, 13*(2), 189–205. doi:10.1080/09645290500031215

Kao, C., & Hung, H.T. (2008). Efficiency analysis of university departments: An empirical study. *Omega, 36*(4), 653-664.

Korhonen, P., Tainio, R., & Wallenius, J. (2001). Value efficiency analysis academic research. *European Journal of Operational Research, 130*(1), 121–132. doi:10.1016/S0377-2217(00)00050-3

Martin, E. (2003). *An Application of the Data Envelopment Analysis Methodology in the Performance Assessment of Zaragoza University Departments.* Available: www.google.com

Protela, A.S., Thanassoulis, E. (2001). Decomposing school and school-type efficiency. *European of Operational Research, 132*.

Ramanathan, R. (2006). Data Envelopment Analysis for Weight Derivation and Aggregation in the Analytic Hierarchy Process. *Journal of Computer and Operation Research, 33*(5), 1289–1307. doi:10.1016/j.cor.2004.09.020

Saaty, T. L. (1996). *The analytic network process-decision making with dependence and feedback*. Pittsburgh, PA: RWS.

Saen, R. F., Memariani, A., & Lot, F. H. (2005). Determining Relative Efficiency of Slightly Non-Homogeneous Decision-Making Units by Data Envelopment Analysis: A Case Study in IROST. Journal of Applied Mathematics and. *Computation, 165*(2), 313–328.

Shang, J., & Sueyoshi, T. (1995). A United Framework for the Selection of a Flexible Manufacturing System. *European Journal of Operational Research, 85*(2), 297–31. doi:10.1016/0377-2217(94)00041-A

Sinuany-Stern, Z., Mehrez, A., & Barboy, A. (1994). Academic Departments Efficiency Via DEA. *Computers & Operations Research, 21*(5), 543–556. doi:10.1016/0305-0548(94)90103-1

Thursby, G., & Kemp, S. (2002). Growth and productive efficiency of university intellectual property licensing. *Research Policy*, 31.

Vargass. (2000). Combining DEA and factor analysis to improve evaluation of academic departments given uncertaing about the output constructs. Departments of industrial Eng. University of Iowa.

Wang, Y.M., Liu, J., & Elhag, T.M.S. (2007). An integrated AHP-DEA methodology for bridge risk assessment. *Journal of Computer and Industrial Engineering*, 1-13.

Yang, T., & Kuo, C. (2003). A Hierarchical AHP/DEA Methodology for the Facilities Layout Design Problem. *European Journal of Operational Research, 147*(1), 128–136. doi:10.1016/S0377-2217(02)00251-5

Zhang, X. S., & Cui, J. C. (1999). A Project Evaluation System in the State Economic Information System of China: An Operations Research Practice in Public Sectors. *International Transactions in Operational Research, 6*(5), 441–452. doi:10.1111/j.1475-3995.1999.tb00166.x

Chapter 5
Evaluation of Supplier Performance and Efficiency:
A Critical Analysis

Chandra Sekhar Patro
GVP College of Engineering (Autonomous), India

ABSTRACT

In the present competitive business environment, it is essential for the management of any organisation to take wise decisions regarding supplier evaluation. It plays a vital role in establishing an effective supply chain for any organisation. Most of the experts agreed that there is no one best way to evaluate the suppliers and different organizations use different approaches for evaluating supplier efficiency. The overall objective of any approach is to reduce purchase risk and maximize overall value to the purchaser. In this paper Data Envelopment Analysis (DEA) technique is developed to evaluate the supplier efficiency for an organisation. DEA is a multifactor productivity technique to measure the relative efficiency of the decision making units. The super efficiency method of DEA provides a way, which indicates the extent to which the efficient suppliers exceed the efficient frontier formed by other efficient suppliers. A case study is undertaken to evaluate the supplier performance and efficiency using DEA approach.

DOI: 10.4018/978-1-5225-0596-9.ch005

INTRODUCTION

Over the past decade, the traditional purchasing and logistics functions have evolved into a broader strategic approach to materials and distribution management system known as Supply Chain Management. Supply chain management involves the flow of material, information and finance in a network consisting of customers, suppliers, manufacturers, and distributors. It begins with raw materials, continues through internal operations, and ends with distribution of finished goods to the ultimate users. The main aim of supply chain management is to integrate various suppliers to satisfy market demand. The short-term objective of supply chain management is primarily to increase the productivity and reduce the entire inventory along with the total cycle time. Whereas the long-term objective is to increase customer satisfaction, increase the market share, and profits for all members of the supply chain (Tan, 2001).

In supply chain management, coordination between a manufacturer and a supplier is typically a difficult and important link in the channels of distribution. Since suppliers are manufacturer's external links, the coordination with the suppliers is not easy unless the systems for cooperation and information exchange are properly integrated. The coordination between a manufacturer and suppliers is important because, the failure of non-coordination results in excessive delays which ultimately lead to poor customer services. Consequently, inventories of incoming parts from suppliers or those of finished goods at the manufacturer and distribution centres (DCs) may accumulate. Hence, the total cost of the entire supply chains will rise. Manufacturers are able to assist their suppliers by providing knowledge, skills, and experience, and to benefit in turn from suppliers' improved delivery performance and from fewer production disruptions that are caused by poor quality materials. The suppliers also can benefit by becoming more competitive than other suppliers as performance improves and costs go down. Thus, supplier development is a vehicle that can be used to increase the competitiveness of the entire supply chains.

Supplier evaluation is one of the fundamental steps to evaluate a supplier's efficiency on the adaptability towards one's organization. Supplier evaluation techniques adopted in an organisation are mainly based on simple, weighted scoring methods which primarily rely on subjective judgments and opinions of purchasing managers or staff involved in the supplier evaluation process. In this approach, the experience and contextual knowledge of purchasing staff is utilized to assign weightages arbitrarily to the supplier performance attributes. Consequently, the final ranking of the suppliers is heavily dependent on the assignment of these weights, which are often difficult to specify in an objective manner. It is the major limitation of the weighted scoring method for supplier evaluation.

Companies usually spend a large amount of their sales revenue on purchasing of raw material and components. So, decision on selecting a competent supplier is important for successful implementation of supply chain management. Supplier evaluation is one of the most critical activities of purchasing management in a supply chain, because of the key role of supplier's performance on cost, quality, delivery and service in achieving the objectives of a supply chain. The cost of raw materials, component parts and services purchased from external vendors or suppliers is significant for most manufacturing firms.

In the actual business scenario, there are two problems encountered in evaluating suppliers. Supplier evaluations are usually done in a group setting. In group evaluations, although it is relatively easy to get concurrence on the importance rankings for the first little supplier performance attributes, it is difficult to reach consensus beyond the first few attributes of performance. Secondly, in most of the firms, the evaluation process is based only on supplier performance outcomes such as price, quality and delivery. While these outcome measures are important in evaluating supplier performance, they only deal with part of the supplier evaluation problem. For example, a supplier may be achieving high levels of performance by utilizing enormous amounts of resources and thus be an inefficient performer. Thus, in order to comprehensively evaluate the performance of suppliers, it is also necessary to consider the type and amount of input resources utilized in generating performance outcomes.

DATA ENVELOPMENT ANALYSIS

Data Envelopment Analysis (DEA) was developed by Charnes Cooper and Rhodes in the year 1978. It is a non-parametric, multi-factor productivity analysis model that evaluates linear programming based technique used to determine the relative efficiencies of a set of homogenous organizational units called Decision Making Units (DMUs). These DMUs utilize multiple inputs to produce multiple outputs and their efficiency is measured by the ratio of multiple outputs to multiple inputs. Data envelopment analysis is a linear programming based decision technique designed specifically to measure relative efficiency using multiple inputs and outputs without a prior information regarding which inputs and outputs are the most important in determining an efficiency score. DEA considers n decision making units (DMUs) to be evaluated, where each DMU consumes varying amounts of m different inputs to produce s different outputs.

DEA is a very flexible method of comparing the efficiency performance of various decision-making units (DMUs). DMUs can be individuals, branches of an organization, or entire organizations. What is important is not the scale, but that all DMUs exist in the same basic environment and convert the same set inputs into the same set of outputs. The relative efficiency of a DMU is defined as the ratio of its total weighted output to its total weighted input. In mathematical programming terms, this ratio, which is to be maximized, forms the objective function for the particular DMU being evaluated. A set of normalizing constraints is required to reflect the condition that the output to input ratio of every DMU be less than or equal to unity. As a non-parametric method, DEA does not require or assume any functional relationship between the inputs and outputs. The method can successfully be applied to profit and nonprofit making organizations as well as data envelopment analysis can handle multiple inputs and multiple outputs as opposed to other techniques such as ratio analysis or regression.

The aim of data envelopment analysis is to quantify the distance of the efficient frontier for every decision making unit. The measure of performance is expressed in the form of efficiency score. The efficiency score is measured as a ratio between weighted outputs and weighted inputs, even if the production function is unknown. After the evaluation of the relative efficiency of the present set of units, the analysis shows how inputs and outputs have to be change in order to maximize the efficiency of the target decision making unit. Data envelopment analysis suggests the benchmark for each in-efficient decision making unit at the level of its individual mix of inputs and outputs. The weights are chosen so as to find the best advantage for each unit to maximize its relative efficiency, under the restriction that this score is bound by 100% efficiency. If a unit with its optimal weights receives the efficiency score of 100%, it is efficient, while a score of less than 100% is considered inefficient.

FUNDAMENTAL CONCEPTS OF DEA TECHNIQUE

Data Envelopment Analysis technique is concerned with the efficiency of the individual unit, which can be defined as the 'Unit of Assessment' or the 'Decision Making Unit' (DMU) that is responsible for controlling the process of production and making decisions at various levels including daily operation, short-term tactics and long-term strategy. DEA is used to measure the relative productivity of a DMU by comparing it with other homogeneous units transforming the same group of measurable positive inputs into the same types of measurable positive outputs. The schematic diagram for DMU and homogeneous units is shown in Figure 1.

The input and output data can be expressed as matrixes X and Y.

Figure 1. Schematic Diagram for DMU and Homogeneous units

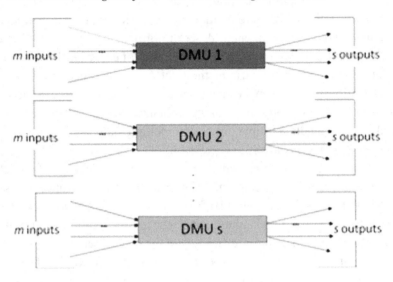

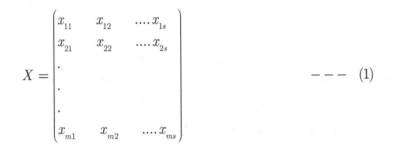

$$--- (1)$$

$$---(2)$$

where,

x_{ij} = the jth input data of DMU i,

y_{ki} = the kth output of DMU $_i$

DEA technique has been used to evaluate and compare educational departments (schools, Libraries, US Air Force wings, colleges and universities), health care sector, agricultural production, banking, armed forces, sports, market research transportation sector etc. In the present days, the DEA approach is extended to supply chain management issues also. In this study, the DEA technique is employed to evaluate supplier's efficiency of an organisation.

RANKING METHODS IN DEA

There are several ranking methods in Data Envelopment Analysis technique. Sexton *et.al.* (1986) developed a method to fully rank both efficient and inefficient DMUs. The first group evaluates Cross Efficiencies (CE) by which DMUs are self and peer evaluated and the second group measures the Super Efficiencies (SE) in which the evaluated unit is excluded from the reference set. However, it may be noticed that each of these techniques may be useful in a specific area. In this paper both these methods are used for ranking the DMUs. Super efficiency method is used to rank the efficient suppliers whereas cross efficiency method is employed to rank the performance of the suppliers. These methods are discussed as follows:

Super Efficiency Method (SE)

Super Efficiency model of Data Envelopment Analysis technique can be used in ranking the performance of efficient DMUs. The efficiency model allows for effective ranking of efficient Decision Making units. The Decision Making unit being evaluated is removed from the constraint set thereby allowing its efficiency score to exceed a value of 1.00. A fractional programming to determine the efficiency score of each of the DMUs in a data set of comparable units. This model determines the best set of weights for each DMU when the problem is solved for each DMU under consideration. The objective function maximizes the efficiency of the DMU using the weights u_j and v_k for the outputs and the inputs respectively. The mathematical programming model formulation is as follows:

Objective function:

Maximize $\quad Z = \sum_{k=1}^{s} v_k y_{kp}$

Subjected to constraints:

$$\sum_{k=1}^{s} v_k y_{ki} - \sum_{j=1}^{m} u_j x_{ji} \leq 0 \ \forall i \neq p$$

$$\sum_{j=1}^{m} u_j x_{jp} = 1$$

$$v_k, \ u_j \geq \ 0 \ \forall k, j$$

where,

i = Number of DMUs (suppliers);
p = DMU (supplier) being evaluated
j = Inputs (1 to m),
k = Outputs (1 to s),
y_{ki}= amount of input j utilized by supplier i,
x_{ji}= amount of output k produced by supplier i,
v_k= weight given to output k,
$u_{j=}$ weight given to input j.

The efficiency score in the presence of multiple input and output factors is computed as follows:

$$\text{Efficiency} = \frac{\text{Weighted sum of outputs}}{\text{Weighted sum of inputs}}$$

As per the efficiency scores, the DMUs are ranked. The difference between the weighted sum of the outputs and the weighted sum of the inputs should be less than zero.

Cross Efficiency Method (CE)

Cross efficiency evaluation has long been suggested as an alternative method for ranking decision making units (DMUs) in data envelopment analysis (DEA). This thesis proposes DEA model for cross efficiency evaluation. Unlike the aggressive and benevolent formulations in cross-efficiency evaluation, the DEA model determines one set of input and output weights for each DMU from its own point of view without being aggressive or benevolent to the other DMUs. As a result, the cross efficiencies computed in this way are more neutral, neither aggressive nor benevolent. A mathematical model is formulated through DEA using cross efficiency method, which given below.

Objective function:

$$\text{Maximize} \quad Z = \sum_{k=1}^{s} \left[v_k \sum_{i \neq p}^{s} y_{ki} \right]$$

Subjected to constraints:

$$\sum_{j=1}^{m} \left[u_j \sum_{i \neq p}^{s} x_{ji} \right] = 1$$

$$\sum_{k=1}^{s} v_k y_{ki} - \sum_{j=1}^{m} u_j x_{ji} \leq 0 \, \forall \, i \neq p$$

$$\sum_{k=1}^{s} v_k y_{kp} - \theta_p \sum_{j=1}^{m} u_j x_{jp} = 0 \qquad v_k, u_j \geq 0 \qquad \forall \, k, j$$

where,

θ_p = Relative efficiency score of DMU p

Cross efficiency provides the information on the performance of a particular DMU with the optimal DEA weights of other DMUs. The Cross Efficiency score of DMUs is also determined by using the ratio of weighted sum of outputs to the weighted sum of inputs.

SUPPLIER CLASSIFICATION

The supplier evaluation process consists of performance and efficiency. Performance reflects the relationship between suppliers and the organisations. The better performance, the better services can suppliers provide, such as accurate delivery time, preferential price, enough goods, and so on. The organisations can build the robust supply chain, which helps an organisation to operate normally and gain more profit. Efficiency reflects the competitiveness of the suppliers' own. The higher the efficiency, the stronger will be the competitiveness for a supplier to occupy the market position. According to Jiang et al., the division for supplier clusters which shows the relationship of performance and efficiency, concerning four classifications is described and shown in Figure 2.

1. **High Performance and Efficient (HPE):** These kinds of suppliers have miraculous industry, positive credit and healthy development. They are the best choice for an organisation. In the long-term cooperation, the organisations need a supplier with high performance, who have perfect operation system and supply system to provide services. They both make the profit balance which can keep the health cooperation and harmonious development to obtain win-win results.

2. **High Performance and In-efficient (HPI):** The supplier of this class is also suitable for the organisations, but when they provide service, they also consume a lot of resources, like more human resource. From a view of long-term trend, it will undermine the cooperation between them, breaking the organisations supply chain, so they are not the best options for any organisations.

3. **Low Performance and Efficient (LPE):** This class of supplier is competitive enough, but it does not provide a good service and thus is not conducive to the supply chain. In the long term cooperation, they will affect the development of the whole supply chain in an organisation.

Figure 2. Performance and Efficiency of Suppliers

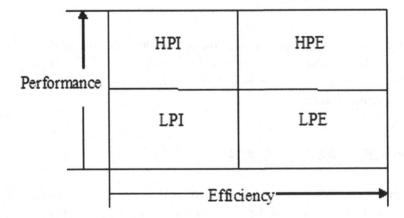

4. **Low Performance and In-efficient (LPI):** This type of supplier is not competitive and they cannot provide great services for the enterprise. The organisation should consider giving up the cooperative relationship with their suppliers.

OBJECTIVES OF THE CHAPTER

1. The paper aims to review the literature related to the application of DEA method for supplier evaluation.
2. The main objective of the study is to employ DEA technique to evaluate the supplier's efficiency of an organisation.
3. To identify the list of suppliers who are efficient and possess high performance using super efficiency and cross efficiency methods of DEA.

IMPORTANCE OF SUPPLIER EVALUATION

Purchasing managers need to periodically evaluate supplier performance in order to retain those suppliers which meet their requirements in terms of several performance criteria. Traditionally, the price and the cost are used to be the predominant dimensions in the evaluation of supplier performance. Dickson conducted a study that investigated the importance of supplier evaluation criteria for industrial purchasing managers. The study concluded that cost, quality and delivery performance were the most important criteria in supplier evaluation (Srinivas & Narasimhan, 2004). Over the years, a number of supplier selection criteria have been developed to meet the objectives of the respective organizations. In comparison to the traditional hardnosed way of procurement, the ideas of sharing information and assisting vendor to improve quality, quantity, delivery, price and service performance are more prevalent nowadays.

In most of the manufacturing organisations the cost of raw materials and component parts constitute the main cost of the product, which is in the range of 50-70%, depending on type of industry. Naturally industries are focusing on the major cost contributing factor so as to produce their products at the lowest prices possible at the same time improving all its characteristics such as quality, technical capability, etc., by giving due attention to supply chain management. Supplier evaluation is an area of tremendous importance for an effective supply chain management. Supplier evaluation decisions have a significant impact on the competitiveness of a firm. By choosing good/services at lower cost, due to better quality of material being received resulting in less lateral rejections and reworks, due to lower lead time and prompt delivery from the supplier resulting in avoidance of production delays/ stoppages and the necessity of keeping high inventories, due to good supplier relations which are critical in these days of Total quality Management arena. Thus by selecting good supplier, the company can gain by reduced product prices and at the same time additional monetary saving in course of time due to increased quality levels of products, increased after sales services, improves technical collaborative capacities and by processing trusted partners who can help in meeting emergency requirement in any emergency situations.

The Supplier evaluation decisions determine better amongst available sources and incase of split orders how much quantity of items are to be ordered to each. The main focus is on tangible elements of the supplier's proposals, such as quality levels, cost of product, after sales service levels, technical competencies, long term business relations, lead time required for each product to supply and resources available with supplier to meet buyers demand, as all these tangible and intangible elements have considerable impact on the formulation of successful strategic supplier and buyer relationships keeping in mind long-term objectives and gains to both.

PROBLEM RELATED TO SUPPLIER EVALUATION

There are two different features characterize the problem of supplier evaluation and selection. The first aspect is the determination of the number of suppliers and the mode of relations with them. Considering the characteristics of the company, product and market, its strategic plan can encourage a large number of suppliers or not. The company usually seeks a strong co-operation with its principal suppliers. An area of current research focuses on the classification of components or parts or process to externalize, in order to establish a suitable relation with the suppliers of each category.

The second aspect is the critical examination of the suppliers in terms of their performance and efficiency. The suppliers who belong to the category of low performance and inefficient cannot be considered. The set of suppliers under the category of high performance and inefficient, potential long-term risk is associated with them. Even though, they are performing satisfactory now, but most likely they do not have a structure and organizational capabilities that can sustain performance in the near future. Therefore, a company needs to identify the suppliers who possess high performance and efficiency. These are the suppliers with which company needs to develop a long-term relationship. These suppliers are the potential suppliers with high efficiency and star performance. The proposed methodology is demonstrated through a case study in this paper.

LITERATURE REVIEW

Dickson (1966) studied the importance of supplier evaluation criteria for industrial purchasing managers. The study presented over 20 supplier attributes that managers consider in supplier evaluation. Based on the data from 170 purchasing managers, Dickson concluded that cost, quality, and delivery performance were the three most important criteria in supplier evaluation. Banker (1993) conceptualized a convex and monotonic nonparametric frontier with a one-sided disturbance term and showed that the DEA estimator converges in distribution to the maximum likelihood estimators. Anderson and Peterson (1993) developed super efficiency approach for rank-scaling that was followed by other researchers. The ranking in relation to rank scaling has the advantage that it can be tested statistically by a non-parametric analysis. Weber and Desai (1996) have addressed in their article the issue of supplier selection and negotiation. However, the DEA models used in their studies are in a sense only input oriented, i.e., they did not explicitly consider any output variables except for a constant, one unit of product as output. As discussed earlier, in order to obtain a comprehensive evaluation of supplier performance, the use of both input and output variables is important.

Monczka *et al.* (1998) suggested eleven categories that should be used in initial supplier evaluation process: supplier management capability; overall personnel capabilities; cost structure; total quality performance systems and philosophy; process and technological capability, including the supplier's design capability; environ-mental regulation compliance; financial capability and stability; production scheduling and control systems, including supplier delivery performance; information systems capability, supplier purchasing strategies, policies, and techniques and longer-term relationship potential. Lambert & Pohlen (2001) indicated that traditionally many companies use logistics focused metrics to evaluate their current and potential suppliers such as lead time, fill rate, or on-time performance. Narasimhan, Talluri & Mendez (2001) recognizing that business performance based on total performance of suppliers network propose a DEA model for effective supplier performance evaluation, based on eleven critical factors, six inputs and five outputs. The DEA results are combined with managerial performance, rating the suppliers into 4 clusters i.e., High performance and Efficient (HE), High performance and Inefficient (HI), Low performance and Efficient (LE) and Low performance and Inefficient (LI). Based on this categorization firms on HI, LE and LI suppliers clusters could improve their operations across a variety of dimensions by benchmarking and analyzing High performance and Efficient (HE) suppliers.

Forker & Mendez (2001) applied DEA in order to benchmarking the comparative efficiency of suppliers in order to help companies save time and resources by identify the "best peer" supplier(s). "Best peer" suppliers can be imitated by companies with similar organizational structures by paying the least amount of effort. Forker and Mendez method for each supplier calculated the maximum ratio of multiple outputs for each single input and use Cross-Efficiency to filter the total results. Talluri & Baker (2002) present a multi-phase mathematical programming approach for designing effectively supply chain networks. Specifically, they develop and apply a combination of multi-criteria efficiency models, based on Game Theory concepts, and Linear and Integer Programming methods. In first stage, potential suppliers and manufacturers were evaluated separately in two inputs and four outputs using DEA. Based on the results of this phase, at the second phase developed a supply and distribution model of goods in warehouses by identifying the optimal number of suppliers, manufactures and distributors. Finally, the third phase involves the initial deployment plans, which identify the optimal routing of material from selected suppliers to manufacturers by minimizing the total cost.

Kannan and Tan (2002) have identified quality level, on-time delivery; response time and service levels are the most important factors while evaluating suppliers. Talluri & Sarkis (2002) used DEA to formulate a new model for performance monitoring of suppliers. The aims of this paper were to apply a new multi-criteria evaluation model for supplier performance evaluation by considering various performance criteria, such as to serve a monitoring and control mechanism for the performance of suppliers. Juhantila & Virolainen (2003) recognized that the process of managing business relationships during all respective stages is a critical success factor. From their study, good supplier attributes which clearly stand out are: high quality, delivery accuracy, responsiveness and service, low competitive cost and competitive price. Jiuping, Bin, and Desheng (2009) have developed a DEA model with rough parameters. This model can be used to evaluate the performance of supply chain network. In the process of solving the RDEA model, optimistic and pessimistic values of rough variable to transfer the rough model into deterministic liner programming are used and employed an efficiency interval to descript efficiency score for each DMU. This approach is used to rank the efficiency interval, and the DMU with the smallest maximum loss of efficiency is considered the most efficient one. These evaluation results may help decision makers to improve the operation efficiency of the supply chain network.

Alem et al (2009) presented three types of vendor selection models and a decision making scheme for choosing appropriate method for supplier selection under certainly, uncertainly and probabilistic conditions in supply chains. These models are Data Envelopment Analysis (DEA), Fuzzy Data Envelopment Analysis (FDEA), and Chance Constraint Data Envelopment Analysis (CCDEA). Shirouyehzad, Hosseinzadeh, Mir, & Dabestani (2011) developed an approach, how a firm can implement the DEA technique and use DEA modeling for measuring vendors' performance in multiple criteria relative to other vendors competing in the same marketplace. Based on results of the research, companies should consider multi criteria in vendors' evaluation because the vendors which are better at one criterion in compare with others necessarily do not provide the best services in other items. This approach allows the purchasing manager to evaluate effectively each vendor's performance relative to the performance of the "best vendors" in the marketplace. The results derived from DEA model can be used in order to calculate/determine benchmark values to compare with inefficient vendors. DurgaPrasad et al. (2012) employed DEA technique for establishing suppliers' performance-efficiency score grid. They considered a numerical illustration to demonstrate their methodology.

Ertugrul and Mehtap (2013) proposed an approach that enables to incorporate imprecise data into the analysis using linguistic variables. It is apt to consider the impacts of relationships among the purchased product features and supplier selection criteria, and also the inner dependence among supplier selection criteria. The method uses FWA method, which rectifies the problem of loss of information that occurs when integrating imprecise and subjective information, to calculate the upper and lower bounds of the weights of supplier selection criteria. DEA circumvents the possibility of selecting a suboptimal supplier. Finally, the decision approach presented in here avoids the troublesome fuzzy number ranking process, which may yield inconsistent results for different ranking methods. Jiang, Wei, Hua, and Weifeng (2013) proposed an integrated model, which hybridized data envelopment analysis (DEA) and support vector machine (SVM) together, to predict the four-class problem according to their efficiency and performance. The first step groups them into the efficient and the inefficient according to a new metric (i.e., efficient score) computed by DEA and the second step will use efficient score as a new feature introduced into the data set to train SVM model and further to forecast new supplier's classification. The proposed approach shows comparable performance when compared with several existing approaches. Manjari, Prince, Vaibhav, Monark, & Vrijendra (2014) in a study on analysis of DEA are done by measuring supplier performance of two firms: multi-national telecommunication corporation and a manufacturing firm. The firm uses the methodology according to their requirement and criteria for evaluating their suppliers and find best among them.

METHODOLOGY

The evaluation of suppliers is the key aspect in any manufacturing firm. Prior to select a best supplier, it is necessary to evaluate the suppliers. Therefore, the decision taken on the selection of supplier depends on the appropriate evaluation of suppliers. In order to solve the problem related to evaluation a decision model is used in this study using DEA. To demonstrate the proposed approach a study was carried out in a large manufacturing organization in Visakhapatnam City. In order to maintain the confidentiality of the organisation it is referred to as "Case Company" throughout the paper.

The case company operates production plants, research and development facilities, and distribution systems on a global basis. The organisations objectives in procurement and supply management included improving the quality of purchased products/services, reducing lead time and improving on-time delivery, developing long-term relationships with key suppliers, and securing competitive pricing. In order to achieve these objectives, the organisation has focused on improving the supplier reliability by continuous evaluation and feedback of suppliers' performance in order to improve quality, optimize the cost, and decreasing the supplier base by eliminating those suppliers that do not meet standards. This study mainly stress on the evaluating the best, capable and efficient suppliers.

The first step in the study is to collect the required the input and output variables for supplier evaluation. This was done through personal interviews and several meetings with the management. To identify the input and output data, two separate questionnaires were structured i.e. Supplier Capability (for input parameters) and Supplier Performance Assessment (for output parameters). The questionnaires were distributed to 16 different suppliers of the case company and the individual responses were measured on Yes/No scale. Based on the responses the data was analyzed and the methodology was adopted to select the highly efficient suppliers.

Questionnaire for Measuring Supplier Capability

For the purpose of the DEA evaluation, items on the Supplier Capability Questionnaire were grouped into the following categories, constituting the input parameters:

- Quality Management Practices (QMS)
- Documentation and Self-Audit (DSA)
- Freight Capability (FC)
- Cost Reduction Capability (CRC)
- Reliability (RE)
- Management Capability (MC)

Questionnaire for Supplier Performance Assessment

To assess the performance, the items on the Supplier Performance Assessment Questionnaire were grouped into the following categories, constituting the output parameters:

- Quality (Q)
- Price (P)
- Delivery (D)
- Cost Reduction Performance (CRP)
- Service (S)

Supplier Evaluation Process

The step by step procedure to carry out the DEA methodology is shown in Figure 3:

ANALYSIS AND DISCUSSIONS

This paper presents a practical approach for evaluating the suppliers which provide the required services in a procurement situation. This approach uses data envelopment

Figure 3. DEA Methodology for Supplier Evaluation

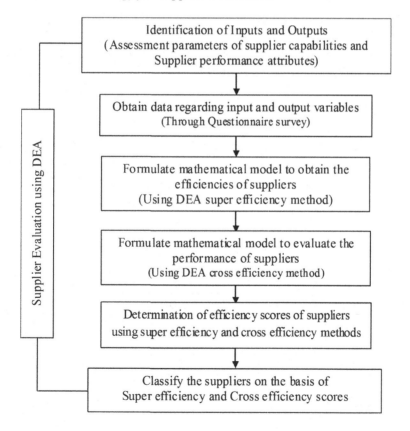

analysis to evaluate the supplier's performance and efficiency. It also provides an appropriate framework for organization to examine the suppliers' efficiency and also choose some effective ways to improve the suppliers' performance. The efficiency is measures based on the questionnaires distributed to suppliers and the purchase manager of an organisation. Based on the information the DEA methodology is applied to identify the efficient supplier.

Identification of Inputs and Outputs

The first step is to identify the inputs and outputs that are strategically important or critical to the buyer. The inputs and outputs are used as the evaluation criteria for the suppliers. Input variables are the assessment parameters of supplier capabilities (comprising the input dimensions of DEA) and the output variables reflects the supplier performance attributes (comprising the output dimension of DEA). In the process of data acquisition, the input and output dimensions to be utilized in the DEA model are defined through focus group discussions.

The focus group includes managers of the different departments of the company. The specific product line to be examined is selected in the initial meetings. In the subsequent meetings, specific input and output dimensions to be used in the analysis were discussed and a final set of dimensions on which to collect data was compiled. After several discussions six input parameters and five output parameters are identified which are shown in Table 1.

Obtain Data of Input and Output Variables

The questionnaire survey is conducted to obtain the responses regarding supplier capability and performance attributes. The assessment parameters of supplier capabilities (Input variables) and the supplier performance attributes (output variables) are identified through the discussions made with the managerial team and the persons

Table 1. Inputs and Output parameters for Supplier Evaluation

Input Parameters	Output Parameters
Quality Management Practices (QMP)	Quality (Q)
Documentation and Self-audit (DSA)	Price (P)
Freight Capability (FC)	Delivery (D)
Cost Reduction Capability (CRC)	Cost Reduction Performance (CRP)
Reliability (RL)	Service (S)
Management Capability (MC)	

of purchasing department of the case company. The supplier capability assessment questionnaires are distributed to the 16 existing suppliers with a view to obtain their responses. In order to maintain the confidentiality of the case company, the 16 suppliers are coded as S_1 to S_{16}.

The response data for input variables is shown in Table 2. To obtain the responses regarding output variables, supplier performance assessment questionnaires are administered to the purchasing personnel of the company are shown in Table 3.

To compute super efficiency and cross efficiency values for all the suppliers, the weightages for input and output parameters are required. The weightages are obtained by solving the mathematical model discussed in methodology chapter. The computation of super efficiency and cross efficiency values are discussed below. For instance, to obtain the weightages for input and output variables and determining the super efficiency and cross efficiency values for supplier-1, the mathematical formulations are enumerated.

Table 2. Data for Input Variables (scores)

Supplier	Input Scores (u_{ji}); $j=1...6$, $i=1...16$					
	QMP	DSA	FC	CRC	RL	MC
S1	0.25	0.75	0.33	0.50	0.00	1.00
S2	0.75	1.00	0.66	0.25	1.00	0.00
S3	0.00	0.25	1.00	0.75	0.33	0.66
S4	1.00	0.00	0.00	1.00	0.66	0.33
S5	0.50	0.25	0.33	0.50	0.00	1.00
S6	1.00	0.25	0.66	0.50	0.33	0.00
S7	0.75	0.75	0.33	1.00	0.00	1.00
S8	0.50	0.25	0.66	0.25	0.33	0.66
S9	1.00	0.00	0.66	1.00	0.66	1.00
S10	0.00	0.25	0.33	0.50	0.66	0.33
S11	0.75	0.00	1.00	0.25	0.33	1.00
S12	0.25	0.75	1.00	0.50	0.66	0.33
S13	0.50	0.00	1.00	0.25	0.33	1.00
S14	1.00	0.75	0.66	0.50	1.00	0.00
S15	0.00	0.25	0.33	1.00	0.33	0.66
S16	0.00	0.75	1.00	0.00	0.66	1.00

Table 3. Data for Output Variables (scores)

Supplier	Output Scores (v_{ki}); $k=1...5$, $i=1...16$				
	Quality	Price	Delivery	CRP	Service
S1	0.25	1.00	0.20	0.00	0.33
S2	1.00	0.25	0.00	0.75	0.00
S3	0.25	0.50	0.00	1.00	1.00
S4	0.50	0.00	1.00	0.50	0.66
S5	1.00	0.25	0.50	0.25	1.00
S6	0.00	0.75	0.25	0.00	0.33
S7	0.50	1.00	0.50	1.00	0.00
S8	0.25	0.00	0.75	0.25	1.00
S9	0.00	0.25	1.00	0.00	0.00
S10	1.00	0.50	0.00	0.50	0.33
S11	0.25	0.00	0.25	0.75	0.66
S12	0.50	1.00	0.50	1.00	1.00
S13	1.00	0.75	0.25	0.00	0.00
S14	0.75	0.25	1.00	1.00	0.33
S15	0.25	0.50	0.00	0.00	0.66
S16	0.75	1.00	0.00	0.50	0.33

Formulation of DEA Super Efficiency Mathematical Model

A mathematical model is formulated through DEA using Super Efficiency Method to obtain the efficiencies of the Suppliers. The amounts of inputs utilized and the amounts of outputs produced are determined using Super Efficiency model as follows:

For Supplier - I (DMU1):

$$\text{Maximize Z} = 0.25x_1 + 1.00x_2 + 0.20x_3 + 0.00x_4 + 0.33x_5 \tag{1}$$

Subjected to

$$0.25y_1 + 0.75y_2 + 0.33y_3 + 0.5y_4 + 0.00y_5 + 1.00y_6 = 1 \tag{2}$$

Evaluation of Supplier Performance and Efficiency

$$\begin{aligned} &\left(1.00x_1 + 0.25x_2 + 0.00x_3 + 0.75x_4 + 0.00x_5\right) - \\ &\left(0.75y_1 + 1.00y_2 + 0.66y_3 + 0.25y_4 + 1.00y_5 + 0.00y_6\right) \le 0 \end{aligned} \tag{3}$$

$$\begin{aligned} &\left(0.25x_1 + 0.50x_2 + 0.00x_3 + 1.00x_4 + 1.00x_5\right) - \\ &\left(0.00y_1 + 0.25y_2 + 1.00y_3 + 0.75y_4 + 0.33y_5 + 0.66y_6\right) \le 0 \end{aligned} \tag{4}$$

$$\begin{aligned} &\left(0.50x_1 + 0.00x_2 + 1.00x_3 + 0.50x_4 + 0.66x_5\right) - \\ &\left(1.00y_1 + 0.00y_2 + 0.00y_3 + 1.00y_4 + 0.66y_5 + 0.33y_6\right) \le 0 \end{aligned} \tag{5}$$

$$\begin{aligned} &\left(1.00x_1 + 0.25x_2 + 0.50x_3 + 0.25x_4 + 1.00x_5\right) - \\ &\left(0.50y_1 + 0.25y_2 + 0.33y_3 + 0.50y_4 + 0.00y_5 + 1.00y_6\right) \le 0 \end{aligned} \tag{6}$$

$$\begin{aligned} &0.00x_1 + 0.75x_2 + 0.25x_3 + 0.00x_4 + 0.33x_5 - \\ &\left(1.00y_1 + 0.25y_2 + 0.66y_3 + 0.5y_4 + 0.33y_5 + 0.00y_6\right) \le \ 0 \end{aligned} \tag{7}$$

$$\begin{aligned} &\left(0.50x_1 + 1.00x_2 + 0.50x_3 + 1.00x_4 + 0.00x_5\right) - \\ &\left(0.75y_1 + 0.75y_2 + 0.33y_3 + 1.00y_4 + 0.00y_5 + 1.00y_6\right) \le 0 \end{aligned} \tag{8}$$

$$\begin{aligned} &\left(0.25x_1 + 0.00x_2 + 0.75x_3 + 0.25x_4 + 1.00x_5\right) - \\ &\left(0.50y_1 + 0.25y_2 + 0.66y_3 + 0.25y_4 + 0.33y_5 + 0.66y_6\right) \le 0 \end{aligned} \tag{9}$$

$$\begin{aligned} &0.00x_1 + 0.25x_2 + 1.00x_3 + 0.00x_4 + 0.00x_5 - \\ &\left(1.00y_1 + 0.00y_2 + 0.66y_3 + 1.00y_4 + 0.66y_5 + 1.00y_6\right) \le \ 0 \end{aligned} \tag{10}$$

$$\left(1.00x_1 + 0.50x_2 + 0.00x_3 + 0.50x_4 + 0.33x_5\right) - \left(0.00y_1 + 0.25y_2 + 0.33y_3 + 0.50y_4 + 0.66y_5 + 0.33y_6\right) \leq 0 \tag{11}$$

$$\left(0.25x_1 + 0.00x_2 + 0.25x_3 + 0.75x_4 + 0.66x_5\right) - \left(0.75y_1 + 0.00y_2 + 1.00y_3 + 0.25y_4 + 0.33y_5 + 1.00y_6\right) \leq 0 \tag{12}$$

$$0.50x_1 + 1.00x_2 + 0.50x_3 + 1.00x_4 + 1.00x_5 - \left(0.25y_1 + 0.75y_2 + 1.00y_3 + 0.50y_4 + 0.66y_5 + 0.33y_6\right) \leq 0 \tag{13}$$

$$\left(1.00x_1 + 0.75x_2 + 0.25x_3 + 0.00x_4 + 0.00x_5\right) - \left(0.50y_1 + 0.00y_2 + 1.00y_3 + 0.25y_4 + 0.33y_5 + 1.00y_6\right) \leq 0 \tag{14}$$

$$0.75x_1 + 0.25x_2 + 1.00x_3 + 1.00x_4 + 0.33x_5 - \left(1.00y_1 + 0.75y_2 + 0.66y_3 + 0.50y_4 + 1.00y_5 + 0.00y_6\right) \leq 0 \tag{15}$$

$$\left(0.25x_1 + 0.50x_2 + 0.00x_3 + 0.00x_4 + 0.66x_5\right) - \left(0.00y_1 + 0.25y_2 + 0.33y_3 + 1.00y_4 + 0.33y_5 + 0.66y_6\right) \leq 0 \tag{16}$$

$$\left(0.75x_1 + 1.00x_2 + 0.00x_3 + 0.50x_4 + 0.33x_5\right) - \left(0.50y_1 + 0.75y_2 + 1.00y_3 + 0.00y_4 + 0.66y_5 + 1.00y_6\right) \leq 0 \tag{17}$$

The equations 1 to 17 are solved using MATLAB and the amounts utilized and amounts produced for supplier - I to determine super efficiency are shown in Table 4. The super efficiency for the supplier – I, is computed as follows:

Table 4. Amounts utilized and produced for Supplier-I to calculate Super Efficiency

Input Variables	Amount Utilized	Output Variables	Amount Produced
QMP $\left(y_1 \right)$	0.6772	Quality $\left(x_1 \right)$	0.0678
DSA $\left(y_2 \right)$	0.9935	Price $\left(x_2 \right)$	1.2352
FC $\left(y_3 \right)$	0.9168	Delivery $\left(x_3 \right)$	1.5200
CR $\left(y_4 \right)$	0.5464	CRP $\left(x_4 \right)$	1.3494
RL $\left(y_5 \right)$	0.0000	Service $\left(x_5 \right)$	0.0024
MC $\left(y_6 \right)$	0.0000		

$$\text{Super Efficiency} = \frac{\left[\left(v_1 \times x_1 \right) + \left(v_2 \times x_2 \right) + \left(v_3 \times x_3 \right) + \left(v_4 \times x_4 \right) + \left(v_5 \times x_5 \right) \right]}{\left[\left(u_1 \times y_1 \right) + \left(u_2 \times y_2 \right) + \left(u_3 \times y_3 \right) + \left(u_4 \times y_4 \right) + \left(u_5 \times y_5 \right) + \left(u_6 \times y_6 \right) \right]}$$

$$\frac{\left[\left(0.25 \times 0.0678 \right) + \left(1.0 \times 1.2352 \right) + \left(0.20 \times 1.5200 \right) + \left(0.00 \times 1.3494 \right) + \left(0.33 \times 0.0024 \right) \right]}{\left[\left(0.25 \times 0.6772 \right) + \left(0.75 \times 0.9935 \right) + \left(0.33 \times 0.9168 \right) + \left(0.50 \times 0.5464 \right) + \left(0.00 \times 0.00 \right) + \left(1.00 \times 0.00 \right) \right]}$$

$= 1.0448$

Formulation of DEA Cross Efficiency Mathematical Model

A mathematical model is formulated through DEA using Cross Efficiency Method to obtain the efficiencies of the Suppliers. The amounts of inputs utilized and the amounts of outputs produced are determined using Cross Efficiency model as follows:

For Supplier - I (DMU 1):

Maximize Z =

$$0.25\left(x_1 + x_2 + x_3 + x_4 + x_5\right) + 1.00\left(x_1 + x_2 + x_3 + x_4 + x_5\right) + 0.20\left(x_1 + x_2 + x_3 + x_4 + x_5\right) +$$
$$0.00\left(x_1 + x_2 + x_3 + x_4 + x_5\right) + 0.33\left(x_1 + x_2 + x_3 + x_4 + x_5\right)$$

(18)

Subjected to

$$0.25\left(y_1 + y_2 + y_3 + y_4 + y_5 + y_6\right) + 0.75\left(y_1 + y_2 + y_3 + y_4 + y_5 + y_6\right) +$$
$$0.33\left(y_1 + y_2 + y_3 + y_4 + y_5 + y_6\right) + 0.50\left(y_1 + y_2 + y_3 + y_4 + y_5 + y_6\right) +$$
$$0.00\left(y_1 + y_2 + y_3 + y_4 + y_5 + y_6\right) + 1.00\left(y_1 + y_2 + y_3 + y_4 + y_5 + y_6\right) = 1$$

(19)

$$\left(1.00x_1 + 0.25x_2 + 0.00x_3 + 0.75x_4 + 0.00x_5\right) -$$
$$\left(0.75y_1 + 1.00y_2 + 0.66y_3 + 0.25y_4 + 1.00y_5 + 0.00y_6\right) \leq 0$$

(20)

$$\left(0.25x_1 + 0.50x_2 + 0.00x_3 + 1.00x_4 + 1.00x_5\right) -$$
$$\left(0.00y_1 + 0.25y_2 + 1.00y_3 + 0.75y_4 + 0.33y_5 + 0.66y_6\right) \leq 0$$

(21)

$$\left(0.50x_1 + 0.00x_2 + 1.00x_3 + 0.50x_4 + 0.66x_5\right) -$$
$$\left(1.00y_1 + 0.00y_2 + 0.00y_3 + 1.00y_4 + 0.66y_5 + 0.33y_6\right) \leq 0$$

(22)

$$\left(1.00x_1 + 0.25x_2 + 0.50x_3 + 0.25x_4 + 1.00x_5\right) -$$
$$\left(0.50y_1 + 0.25y_2 + 0.33y_3 + 0.50y_4 + 0.00y_5 + 1.00y_6\right) \leq 0$$

(23)

$$0.00x_1 + 0.75x_2 + 0.25x_3 + 0.00x_4 + 0.33x_5 -$$
$$\left(1.00y_1 + 0.25y_2 + 0.66y_3 + 0.5y_4 + 0.33y_5 + 0.00y_6\right) \leq 0$$

(24)

Evaluation of Supplier Performance and Efficiency

$$\begin{aligned}&\left(0.50x_1 + 1.00x_2 + 0.50x_3 + 1.00x_4 + 0.00x_5\right) - \\ &\left(0.75y_1 + 0.75y_2 + 0.33y_3 + 1.00y_4 + 0.00y_5 + 1.00y_6\right) \leq 0\end{aligned}$$ (25)

$$\begin{aligned}&\left(0.25x_1 + 0.00x_2 + 0.75x_3 + 0.25x_4 + 1.00x_5\right) - \\ &\left(0.50y_1 + 0.25y_2 + 0.66y_3 + 0.25y_4 + 0.33y_5 + 0.66y_6\right) \leq 0\end{aligned}$$ (26)

$$\begin{aligned}&0.00x_1 + 0.25x_2 + 1.00x_3 + 0.00x_4 + 0.00x_5 - \\ &\left(1.00y_1 + 0.00y_2 + 0.66y_3 + 1.00y_4 + 0.66y_5 + 1.00y_6\right) \leq 0\end{aligned}$$ (27)

$$\begin{aligned}&\left(1.00x_1 + 0.50x_2 + 0.00x_3 + 0.50x_4 + 0.33x_5\right) - \\ &\left(0.00y_1 + 0.25y_2 + 0.33y_3 + 0.50y_4 + 0.66y_5 + 0.33y_6\right) \leq 0\end{aligned}$$ (28)

$$\begin{aligned}&\left(0.25x_1 + 0.00x_2 + 0.25x_3 + 0.75x_4 + 0.66x_5\right) - \\ &\left(0.75y_1 + 0.00y_2 + 1.00y_3 + 0.25y_4 + 0.33y_5 + 1.00y_6\right) \leq 0\end{aligned}$$ (29)

$$\begin{aligned}&\left(0.50x_1 + 1.00x_2 + 0.50x_3 + 1.00x_4 + 1.00x_5\right) - \\ &\left(0.25y_1 + 0.75y_2 + 1.00y_3 + 0.50y_4 + 0.66y_5 + 0.33y_6\right) \leq 0\end{aligned}$$ (30)

$$\begin{aligned}&\left(1.00x_1 + 0.75x_2 + 0.25x_3 + 0.00x_4 + 0.00x_5\right) - \\ &\left(0.50y_1 + 0.00y_2 + 1.00y_3 + 0.25y_4 + 0.33y_5 + 1.00y_6\right) \leq 0\end{aligned}$$ (31)

$$\begin{aligned}&\left(0.75x_1 + 0.25x_2 + 1.00x_3 + 1.00x_4 + 0.33x_5\right) - \\ &\left(1.00y_1 + 0.75y_2 + 0.66y_3 + 0.50y_4 + 1.00y_5 + 0.00y_6\right) \leq 0\end{aligned}$$ (32)

$$0.25x_1 + 0.50_2 + 0.00x_3 + 0.00x_4 + 0.66x_5 -$$
$$\left(0.00y_1 + 0.25y_2 + 0.33y_3 + 1.00y_4 + 0.33y_5 + 0.66y_6\right) \leq 0 \quad (33)$$

$$\left(0.75x_1 + 1.00x_2 + 0.00x_3 + 0.50x_4 + 0.33x_5\right) -$$
$$\left(0.50y_1 + 0.75y_2 + 1.00y_3 + 0.00y_4 + 0.66y_5 + 1.00y_6\right) \leq 0 \quad (34)$$

$$\left(0.25x_1 + 1.00x_2 + 0.20x_3 + 0.00x_4 + 0.33x_5\right) -$$
$$\left(0.25y_1 + 0.75y_2 + 0.33y_3 + 0.50y_4 + 0.00y_5 + 1.00y_6\right) \leq 0 \quad (35)$$

The equations 18 to 35 are solved using Matlab and the amounts utilized and amounts produced for supplier – I to determine cross efficiency are shown in Table 5. The cross efficiency value for supplier - I is computed as follows:

$$\text{Cross Efficiency} = \frac{\left(x_1 + x_2 + x_3 + x_4 + x_5\right)\left[v_1 + v_2 + v_3 + v_4 + v_5\right]}{\left(y_1 + y_2 + y_3 + y_4 + y_5 + y_6\right)\left[u_1 + u_2 + u_3 + u_4 + u_5 + u_6\right]}$$

Table 5. Amounts utilized and produced for Supplier-I to calculate Cross Efficiency

Input variables	Amount utilized	Output variables	Amount produced
QMP $\left(y_1\right)$	2.3362	Quality $\left(x_1\right)$	2.1617
DSA $\left(y_2\right)$	0.7601	Price $\left(x_2\right)$	0.5429
FC $\left(y_3\right)$	2.8599	Delivery $\left(x_3\right)$	1.0064
CR $\left(y_4\right)$	1.3650	CRP $\left(x_4\right)$	1.9954
RL $\left(y_5\right)$	3.1850	Service $\left(x_5\right)$	0.2840
MC $\left(y_6\right)$	2.6159		

$$= \frac{\left(2.1617 + 0.5429 + 1.0064 + 1.9954 + 0.2840\right) \left[0.25 + 1.00 + 0.20 + 0.00 + 0.33\right]}{\left(2.3362 + 0.7601 + 2.8599 + 1.3650 + 3.1850 + 2.6159\right) \left[0.25 + 0.75 + 0.33 + 0.50 + 0.00 + 1.00\right]}$$

$=0.2393$

Determination of Efficiency Scores of Suppliers

The efficiency of each supplier can be computed by determining the ratio of the weighted sum of outputs to weighted sum of inputs. Super Efficiency indicates the extent to which the efficient suppliers exceed the efficient frontier formed by other efficient suppliers. Cross efficiency provides the information on the performance of a particular DMU with the optimal DEA weights of other DMUs. In both these methods, the efficiency of DMUs is determined by using the ratio of weighted sum of outputs to the weighted sum of inputs.

In the similar way, the DEA model equations for the remaining 15 suppliers are developed and solved using Matlab. The super efficiency and cross efficiency for the remaining 15 suppliers are computed and those values for all the suppliers are shown in Table 6.

Classification of Suppliers

On the basis of Super Efficiency and Cross Efficiency scores the Suppliers are classified under the categories such as High Performance & Efficient (HPE), High Performance & Inefficient (HPI), Low Performance & Efficient (LPE), and Low Performance & Inefficient (LPI). The LPI category suppliers are candidates for pruning. The suppliers under the category HPE possesses star performance. These suppliers are the type of suppliers with which company needs to develop a long-term relationship. The classification of suppliers based on their values is shown in Table 7.

The Figure 4 shows the classification of supplier's efficiency and performance based on the evaluations made under cross and supper efficiency models. It is found that there are six suppliers under HPE category, four suppliers under LPE category, six suppliers under LPI category and none of the suppliers are under HPI category.

RESULTS AND DISCUSSION

The HPE category consists of eight suppliers. There are five supplier selection attributes namely quality, price, delivery, cost reduction performance (CRP) and

Table 6. Super efficiency and Cross efficiency values of all the Suppliers

Supplier	Super Efficiency	Cross Efficiency
S1	1.04	0.28
S2	0.64	0.21
S3	1.08	0.58
S4	3.98	0.51
S5	3.05	0.44
S6	1.20	0.18
S7	1.68	0.59
S8	2.70	0.52
S9	0.86	0.11
S10	1.68	0.29
S11	0.66	0.38
S12	1.14	0.56
S13	0.70	0.24
S14	1.99	0.62
S15	1.26	0.20
S16	0.40	0.28

service. The list of supplier evaluation attributes and the output data for the eight suppliers are shown in Table 8.

The objective of the methodology is the evaluation of best supplier in a cluster of efficient and high performance suppliers. The cluster of high performance and efficient suppliers is obtained through Super Efficiency and Cross Efficiency methods of DEA. Table 9 shows the HPE category of the suppliers.

From Table 9, it is observed that the suppliers S3, S4, S7, S8, S12, and S14 possess super efficiency scores are more than 1 and cross efficiency scores are more than 0.5. They are the efficient suppliers with high performance (HPE). But, the decision maker needs to identify the best supplier among all the suppliers with a view to maintain long term relationship. In this approach the best suppliers can be identified for further process of selecting the best supplier.

CONCLUSION

The ultimate objective of dealing with the supplier evaluation problem is to obtain a solution for selecting a best supplier. The best supplier may provide faster deliv-

Table 7. Classification of Suppliers based on the values

Supplier	Super Efficiency	Cross Efficiency	Category of suppliers
S1	1.04	0.28	LPE
S2	0.64	0.21	LPI
S3	1.08	0.58	HPE
S4	3.98	0.51	HPE
S5	3.05	0.44	LPE
S6	1.20	0.18	LPI
S7	1.68	0.59	HPE
S8	2.70	0.52	HPE
S9	0.86	0.11	LPI
S10	1.68	0.29	LPE
S11	0.66	0.38	LPI
S12	1.14	0.56	HPE
S13	0.70	0.24	LPI
S14	1.99	0.62	HPE
S15	1.26	0.20	LPE
S16	0.40	0.28	LPI

Figure 4. Suppliers efficiency and performance chart

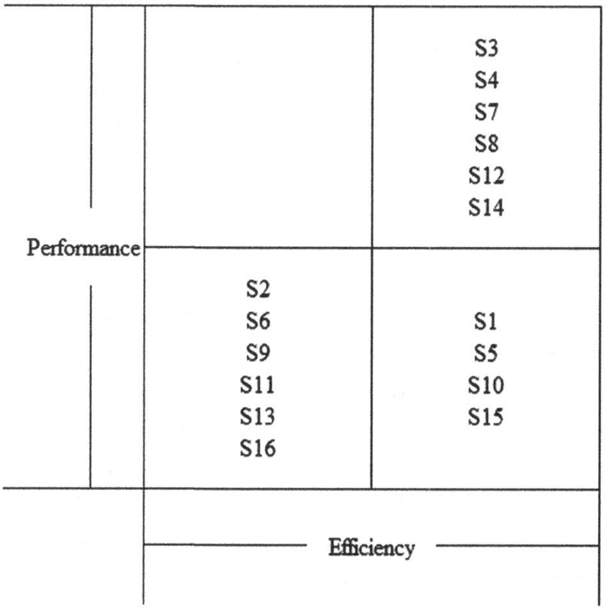

Table 8. The response data on supplier selection attributes

Supplier	Output scores (v_{kl}) ; $k=1...5, i=1...16$				
	Quality	Price	Delivery	CRP	Service
S3	0.25	0.50	0.00	1.00	1.00
S4	0.50	0.00	1.00	0.50	0.66
S7	0.50	1.00	0.50	1.00	0.00
S8	0.25	0.00	0.75	0.25	1.00
S12	0.50	1.00	0.50	1.00	1.00
S14	0.75	0.25	1.00	1.00	0.33

Table 9. List of HPE Category Suppliers (with Super Efficiency and Cross Efficiency Scores)

Super Efficiency	Cross Efficiency	HPE Category of suppliers
1.08	0.58	S3
3.98	0.50	S4
1.68	0.59	S7
2.70	0.52	S8
1.14	0.55	S12
1.99	0.62	S14

ery, reduced cost along with the improved quality in order to increase competitive advantage in the market. Prior to select the best supplier, it is essential to evaluate the existing suppliers.

In this study to demonstrate the DEA, a case study is conducted in an industrial company located at Visakhapatnam. To evaluate the suppliers eleven supplier evaluation attributes are considered, out of which, the six attributes namely Quality management practices and systems (QMP), Documentation and self-audit (DSA), Fright capability (FC), Management capability (MC), Reliability (RL), Cost reduction capability (CRC) are the input variables. The Quality, Price, Delivery, Cost reduction performance (CRP) and Service are the output variables. While evaluating the suppliers for the case company, the super efficiency and cross efficiency methods of DEA are employed to obtain efficiency and performance scores. The mathematical models of super efficiency and cross efficiency are developed and solved using Matlab. On the basis of super efficiency and cross efficiency scores, eight efficient and high performance suppliers are identified.

A variety of extensions to this work can be undertaken. In this study, the DEA approach allowed for complete weight flexibility. In situations where some of the measures are likely to be more important than the others, DEA allows for restricting factor weights through linear constraints. These linear constraints represent ranges for relative preferences among factors based on managerial input. Such an analysis enables effective incorporation of managerial input into the DEA evaluations. A further study can be carried for supplier selection using several other approaches.

REFERENCES

Adler, N., Friedman, L., & Sinuany-Stern, Z. (2002). Review of Ranking Methods in the DEA Context. *European Journal of Operational Research*, *140*, 249–265. doi:10.1016/S0377-2217(02)00068-1

Alem, S. M., Azadeh, A., Shirkouhi, S. N., & Rezaie, K. (2009). A decision making methodology for vendor selection problem based on DEA, FDEA and CCDEA models. *Third Asia International Conference on Modeling & Simulation*. doi:10.1109/AMS.2009.69

Anderson, P., & Peterson, N. C. (1993). A Procedure for Ranking Efficient Units in DEA. *Management Science*, *39*(10), 1261–1264. doi:10.1287/mnsc.39.10.1261

Banker, R. D. (1993). Maximum-Likelihood, Consistency and Data Envelopment Analysis - a Statistical Foundation. *Management Science*, *39*(10), 1265–1273. doi:10.1287/mnsc.39.10.1265

Charnes, A., Cooper, W. W., & Rhodes, E. (1978). Measuring the Efficiency of Decision Making Units. *European Journal of Operational Research*, *2*(4), 429–444. doi:10.1016/0377-2217(78)90138-8

Dickson, G. (1966). An Analysis of Vendor Selection Systems and Decisions. *Journal of Purchasing*, (2), 28-41.

DurgaPrasad, K. G., VenkataSubbaiah, K., VenuGopalaRao, C., & NarayanaRao, K. (2012). Supplier evaluation through Data Envelopment Analysis. *Journal of Supply Chain Management Systems*, *1*(2), 1–11.

Ertugrul, K. E., & Mehtap, D. (2013). An Integrated QFD-DEA Framework with Imprecise Data for Supplier Selection. *Proceedings of the World Congress on Engineering*. WCE.

Farzipoor, S. R. (2010). Developing a new data envelopment analysis methodology for supplier selection in the presence of both undesirable outputs and imprecise data. *International Journal of Advanced Manufacturing Technology, 51*(9-12), 1243–1250. doi:10.1007/s00170-010-2694-3

Forker, L. B., & Mendez, D. (2001). An analytical method for benchmarking best peer suppliers. *International Journal of Operations & Production Management, 21*(1–2), 195–209. doi:10.1108/01443570110358530

Jian, B., Wei, C., Hua, Z., & Weifeng, P. (2013). Supplier's Efficiency and Performance Evaluation using DEA-SVM Approach. *Journal of Software, 8*(1), 25–30. doi:10.4304/jsw.8.1.25-30

Jiuping, X., Bin, L., & Desheng, W. (2009). Rough Data Envelopment Analysis and its Application to Supply Chain Performance Evaluation. *International Journal of Production Economics, 122*(2), 628–638. doi:10.1016/j.ijpe.2009.06.026

Juhantila, O. P., & Virolainen, V. M. (2003). Buyers Expectation from their Suppliers. *19th IMP Conference.*

Kannan, V. R., & Tan, K. C. (2002). Supplier Selection and Assessment: Their Impact on Business Performance. *The Journal of Supply Chain Management, 38*(3), 11–21. doi:10.1111/j.1745-493X.2002.tb00139.x

Lambert, D. M., & Pohlen, T. L. (2001). Supply chain metrics. *International Journal of Logistics Management, 12*(1), 1–19. doi:10.1108/09574090110806190

Manjari, S., Prince, A., Vaibhav, M., Monark, B., & Vrijendra, S. (2014). Supplier Selection through Application of DEA. *International Journal Engineering and Manufacturing, 1*, 1–9. doi:10.5815/ijem.2014.01.01

Monczka, R. M., Kenneth, J. P., Robert, B. H., & Gary, L. R. (1998). Success Factors in Strategic Supplier Alliances: The Buying Company Perspective. *Decision Sciences, 29*(3), 553–577. doi:10.1111/j.1540-5915.1998.tb01354.x

Narasimhan, R., Srinivas, T., & Mendez, D. (2001). Supplier Evaluation and Rationalization via Data Envelopment Analysis: An empirical examination. *The Journal of Supply Chain Management, 37*(3), 28–37. doi:10.1111/j.1745-493X.2001.tb00103.x

Ning-Sheng, W., Rong-Hua, Y., & Wei, W. (2008). Evaluating the performances of decision-making units based on interval efficiencies. *Journal of Computational and Applied Mathematics, 216*(2), 328–343. doi:10.1016/j.cam.2007.05.012

Paradi, J. C., & Yang, X. (2014). Data Envelopment Analysis of Corporate Failure for Non-Manufacturing Firms Using a Slacks-Based Measure. *Journal of Service Science and Management*, *7*(04), 277–290. doi:10.4236/jssm.2014.74025

Seiford, L. M., & Zhu, J. (1999). Infeasibility of super-efficiency data envelopment analysis models. *INFOR*, *37*(2), 174–187.

Sexton, T. R., Silkman, R. H., & Hogan, A. J. (1986). Data Envelopment Analysis: Critique and Extensions. In Measuring Efficiency: An Assessment of Data Envelopment Analysis. Jossey-Bass.

Seydel, J. (2006). Data envelopment analysis for decision support. *Industrial Management & Data Systems*, *106*(1), 81–95. doi:10.1108/02635570610641004

Shimchi-Levi, D., Kaminsky, P., & Shimchi-Levi, E. (2000). *Designing and Managing the Supply chain: Concepts, Strategies and Case studies* (International Edition). Singapore: McGraw Hill.

Shirouyehzad, H., Hosseinzadeh, L. F., Mir, B. A., & Dabestani, R. (2011). Efficiency and Ranking Measurement of Vendors by Data Envelopment Analysis. *International Business Research*, *4*(2), 137–146.

Srinivas, T., & Narasimhan, R. (2004). A methodology for strategic sourcing. *European Journal of Operational Research*, *154*(1), 236–250. doi:10.1016/S0377-2217(02)00649-5

Talluri, S., & Baker, R. C. (2002). A multi-phase mathematical programming approach for effective supply chain design. *European Journal of Operational Research*, *141*(3), 544–558. doi:10.1016/S0377-2217(01)00277-6

Talluri, S., & Sarkis, J. (2002). A model for performance monitoring of suppliers. *International Journal of Production Research*, *40*(16), 4257–4269. doi:10.1080/00207540210152894

Tan, K. C. (2001). A framework of supply chain management literature. *European Journal of Purchasing & Supply Management*, *7*(2), 39–48. doi:10.1016/S0969-7012(00)00020-4

Timmerman, E. (1986). An approach to vendor performance evaluation. *International Journal of Purchasing and Materials Management*, *22*(4), 2–8.

Tracey, M., & Vonderembse, M. A. (2000). Building Supply Chains: A Key to Enhancing Manufacturing Performance. *American Journal of Business*, *15*(2), 11–20. doi:10.1108/19355181200000007

Wang, Y. M., & Luo, Y. (2006). DEA Efficiency assessment using ideal and anti-ideal decision-making units. *Applied Mathematics and Computation*, *173*(2), 902–915. doi:10.1016/j.amc.2005.04.023

Weber, C. A., & Desai, A. (1996). Determination of paths to vendor market Efficiency using parallel co-ordinates representation: A negotiation tool for buyers. *European Journal of Operational Research*, *90*(1), 142–155. doi:10.1016/0377-2217(94)00336-X

Chapter 6
Productivity Assessment in Data Envelopment Analysis

M. Vaez-Ghasemi
Islamic Azad University, Rasht Branch, Iran

Z. Moghaddas
Islamic Azad University, Qazvin Branch, Iran

ABSTRACT

Malmquist Productivity Index (MPI) is taken into consideration by different researchers in different theoretical and scientific fields after S. Malmquist presented it. This index has a profound meaning and is used in a number of applications for performance evaluation. In literature, there exist variety of subjects consider this index, each of which tries to develop it from different points of view. Here, the aim, in accordance to the importance of this index, is to try gathering most of the issues, related to this subject, from the oldest one to the newest one, in a framework of a review chapter.

INTRODUCTION

Data envelopment analysis (DEA) is a mathematical programming technique introduced by Farrell (1957) and then populated by Charnes et al. (1978) and Banker et al. (1984) which introduced the most popular models named after the authors CCR and BCC, respectively. In DEA technique a linear programming problem is

DOI: 10.4018/978-1-5225-0596-9.ch006

formulated with which it is possible to evaluate decision-making units (DMUs). An important issue in this technique is that DMUs can have multiple inputs and outputs and knowing the production function is not necessary. Considering this technique an LP problem solved to each DMU and the relative efficiency of each unit obtained. In this technique, weights are free to get their value to show the under evaluation unit in optimistic viewpoint. IN this relative efficiency evaluation those units with optimal objective function equal to one are called best practice or efficient unit. Considering geometric interpretation, best practice units are located onto the efficient frontier and can be taken as benchmark for other inefficient units. On basis of the CCR and BCC models, based on what Charnes et al. (1978)and Banker et al. (1984) provided, many extensions to DEA models are presented in literature.

Malmquist indexes of productivity are generally estimated using index number techniques or non-parametric frontier approaches. In 1953 Sten Malmquist, introduced a productivity index which now called after his name. On basis what Malmquist provided, Caves et al. (1982) introduced the malmquist index for the first time in productivity analysis utilizing a non-parametric DEA frontier approach. On basis of this index many modifications and improvements are done for introducing further analysis.

In this chapter the aim is to gather some of the existing papers about DEA-based malmquist productivity index. In each of these issues some modifications are performed for better analysis. In the following section a review of the DEA-based malmquist index are briefly summarized. Finally, conclusion ends the chapter.

BACKGROUND

At First Malmquist index is introduced by Malmquist (1953) and then it is used in theory and application by Caves et al.(1982). On basis of what they have provided, later Farell et al.(1989) used DEA technique for estimation the production function. They introduced the malmquist index as the geometric average on bias of what Caves et al presented.

Let us assume there exist n DMUS to be evaluated each which uses m inputs to produce s outputs. Following notification shows the inputs and outputs of DMUj in time t1,

$$x_j^{t1} = (x_{1j}^{t1}, ..., x_{mj}^{t1}), y_j^{t1} = (y_{1j}^{t1}, ..., y_{sj}^{t1}), j = 1, ..., n$$

Considering time t2 the input and output data for each DMUj is as follows,

$$x_j^{t2} = (x_{1j}^{t2}, ..., x_{mj}^{t2}), y_j^{t2} = (y_{1j}^{t2}, ..., y_{sj}^{t2}), j = 1, ..., n$$

Considering the malmquist productivity index for assessing DMUo as following:

$$M_o = \left[\frac{D_o^{t1}(x_o^{t2}, y_o^{t2})}{D_o^{t1}(x_o^{t1}, y_o^{t1})} \times \frac{D_o^{t2}(x_o^{t2}, y_o^{t2})}{D_o^{t2}(x_o^{t1}, y_o^{t1})} \right]^{1/2}$$

$$M_o = \frac{D_o^{t2}(x_o^{t2}, y_o^{t2})}{D_o^{t1}(x_o^{t1}, y_o^{t1})} \left[\frac{D_o^{t1}(x_o^{t2}, y_o^{t2})}{D_o^{t2}(x_o^{t2}, y_o^{t2})} \times \frac{D_o^{t1}(x_o^{t1}, y_o^{t1})}{D_o^{t2}(x_o^{t1}, y_o^{t1})} \right]^{1/2}$$

Note that:

$$D_o^{t1}(x_o^{t1}, y_o^{t1}) = Min \ \theta$$

s.t.
$$\sum_{j=1}^{n} \lambda_j x_{ij}^{t1} \leq \theta x_{io}^{t1}, \qquad i = 1, ..., m$$

$$\sum_{j=1}^{n} \lambda_j y_{rj}^{t1} \geq y_{ro}^{t1}, \qquad r = 1, ..., s$$

$$\lambda_j \geq 0, \qquad\qquad j = 1, ..., n$$

In which DMUo is considered to be in time t1 and technology is in time t.

$$D_o^{t2}(x_o^{t1}, y_o^{t1}) = Min \ \theta$$

s.t.
$$\sum_{j=1}^{n} \lambda_j x_{ij}^{t2} \leq \theta x_{io}^{t1}, \qquad i = 1, ..., m$$

$$\sum_{j=1}^{n} \lambda_j y_{rj}^{t2} \geq y_{ro}^{t1}, \qquad r = 1, ..., s$$

$$\lambda_j \geq 0, j = 1, ..., n$$

Where which DMUo is considered to be in time t1 and technology is in time t2.

Two other LP models can also be considered. One for the DMUo and technology, both in time t2, $D_o^{t2}(x_o^{t2}, y_o^{t2})$, and the other in which DMUo is in time t2 and technology in time t1, $D_o^{t1}(x_o^{t2}, y_o^{t2})$. Corresponding models can be written the same as the above mentioned models.

In the case that the malmquist index for evaluating DMUo is greater than 1 the DMU under evaluation made progress, otherwise it made regress and in the case that it is equal to 1 it neither made regress nor progress.

MAIN FOCUS OF THE CHAPTER

In this section some of the existing subjects in the field of DEA-based malmquist index are reviewed.

Chang et al. (1995) for obtaining the relative changes of decision making units, tried to generalized the use of the data envelopment analysis approach and simultaneously measure relative effectiveness of an organization using malmquist productivity approach. This method is then used in assessing the administrative regions in Taiwan in the time period of 1983 and 1990.

In their paper Grifell-Tatje and Lovell (1995) considered the scale economies and claimed that when non-constant returns to scale exists, the malmquist productivity index bias is considerable and it depends on the magnitude of scale economies.

Grifell-Tatjé and Lovell (1997) in their paper utilized data envelopment analysis technique to panel data in order to evaluate productive efficiency over time. They built a malmquist index using the data envelopment analysis technique and tried to present a new decomposition for this index. An important issue they discussed is that they showed that the in new decomposition productivity changes is divided into productive efficiency, the magnitude of technical change and the bias of technical change. For the purpose of clarity they illustrated the presented method in Spanish savings banks.

In order to estimate and decompose the productivity change, Atkinson and Cornwell (1998) proposed a new econometric framework. They noted that this method does not need a distribution for inefficiency or the uncorrelatedness between inefficiency and the regressors. They declared that the method is used for the US railroads to show the validity of the method.

Grifell-Tatje et al. (1998) in their paper noted that the malmquist productivity index will affected badly when it is based upon the distance functions which obtained from data envelopment analysis models since using radial DEA models true efficiency will overstate.

For considering all the slacks the authors presented a new definition of "one-sided" efficiency in which considering all the slacks non radial efficiency is obtained.

Thus in doing so the quasi-malmquist productivity index is introduced. Also, they illustrated the provided method for assessing the productivity alterations in Spanish banking.

They consider the distance function as follows:

$$D_o^t(x^t, y^t) = inf\{\theta : y^t / \theta \in P^t(x^t)\}$$

Consider $P^t(x^t)$ as the set of all output produced by x^t in the period t.

Grifell-Tatje et al. (1998) defined efficiency of DMU_o at the time t when the technology is also at time t as follows:

$$E_o^t(x^t, y^t) = [D_o^t(x^t, y^t)]^{-1}$$

Thus, you can consider the output-oriented malmquist productivity index when the unit under assessment is in time t as follows:

$$M_o^t(x^t, y^t, x^{t+1}, y^{t+1}) = D_o^t(x^{t+1}, y^{t+1}) / D_o^t(x^t, y^t)$$

Need to mention that:

$$[D_o^t(x^{it}, y^{it})]^{-1} = \min \quad \phi$$

s.t.
$$\sum_{j=1} \lambda^{jt} y^{jt} \geq \phi y^{it},$$
$$\sum_{j=1} \lambda^{jt} x^{it} \leq x^{it},$$
$$\sum_{j=1} \lambda^{jt} = 1, \tag{1}$$
$$\lambda^{jt} \geq \emptyset, \quad j = 1, ..., I^t.$$

In the above model $i = 1, ..., I^t$.

They defined the output slacks in order to acquire nonradial efficiency as follows:

$$S_m^t = (\phi - 1)y_m^t + r_m^t, \quad m = 1, ..., M$$

Note that

$$r_m^t = \sum_{j=1} \lambda^{jt} y_m^{jt} - \phi y_m^t$$

Finally they obtained the output-oriented nonradial technical efficiency as follows:

$$\Omega_o^t =: [1 + (M)^{-1} \sum_m (S_m^t / y_m^t)]$$

A generalization of malmquist productivity index is introduced by Grifell-Tatjé and Lovell (1999). The authors investigated that the product of malmquist productivity index and a malmquist scale index shows the generalized malmquist productivity index. Moreover they investigated that the ratio of a malmquist output quantity index to a malmquist input quantity index shows he generalized malmquist productivity index. They, also, showed that the geometric mean of a pair of malmquist scale indexes and the reciprocal of the Törnqvist scale index are equal to each other.

What Grifell-Tatjé and Lovell (1999) called as generalized malmquist index defined as follows:

$$G_o^t(x^t, y^t, x^{t+1}, y^{t+1}) = M_o^t(x^t, y^t, x^{t+1}, y^{t+1}) E_o^t(x^t, y^t, x^{t+1})$$

$$= M_o^t(x^t, y^t, x^{t+1}, y^{t+1}) \{ \frac{D_{oc}^t(x^{t+1}, y^t) / D_o^t(x^{t+1}, y^t)}{D_{oc}^t(x^t, y^t) / D_o^t(x^t, y^t)} \}$$

Need to be noted that the first term of the following equation is a the malmquist productivity index considering period t and the second one is the malmquist scale index in the period t. As it is shown, the period t malmquist scale index is considered as the ratio of a pair of output-oriented scale efficiency measures.

The authors also showed that:

$$G_o^t(x^t, y^t, x^{t+1}, y^{t+1}) = \frac{D_o^t(x^{t+1}, y^{t+1}) / D_o^t(x^{t+1}, y^t)}{D_{ic}^t(y^t, x^{t+1}) / D_{ic}^t(x^t, y^t)}$$

$$= \frac{O_o^t(y^t, y^{t+1}; x^{t+1})}{I_{ic}^t(x^t, x^{t+1}; y^t)}$$

which means the output-oriented generalized malmquist productivity index in period t can be defined as the ratio of an output-oriented malmquist output quantity index to an input-oriented malmquist input quantity index in period t.

Utilizing data envelopment analysis technique, Worthington (1999) investigated the efficiency assessment and productivity growth in deposit-taking. As a case study, the author considered two hundred and sixty-nine Australian credit unions for assessing using the malmquist index as well as the related decompositions, namely technical efficiency and technological change.

Taking into account the English Family Health Service Authorities, in their paper Giuffrida (1999) tried to evaluate the efficiency measure of such units. For acquiring the malmquist productivity index and its decompositions, such as pure technical efficiency change, scale efficiency change and technological change, the authors considered data envelopment analysis technique.

For solving the problem of measuring the improvements of productivity changes in the periods of time, Arcelus and Arozena (1999) investigated the OECD's International Sectoral Data Bases. In such assessment the authors used generalized malmquist productivity indices based on data envelopment analysis technique.

Rebelo and Mendes (2000) tried to evaluate the productivity change in Portuguese banking in according to the malmquist productivity index.

Uri (2000) presented a paper which provides an approach which considers a measure of the change in productivity. Further, the author mentioned that this index can be decomposed into technical efficiency change and technology change over times.

Odeck (6000) used non-parametric technique of data envelopment analysis in order to obtain the efficiency measure and malmquist productivity index for evaluation of the Norwegian Motor Vehicle Inspection Agencies.

The adjacent malmquist productivity index to the base period malmquist productivity index were compared with each other by Althin (2001). Moreover, Althin examined the Monte Carlo test to check the similarities between these two indexes. Finally, the provided method is applied to a panel of Swedish pharmacy data.

Fuentes (2001) considered an output distance function to show that using the estimated parameters, several radial distance functions can be calculated and combined in order to estimate and decompose the productivity index.

Fuentes (2001) introduced the following relations:

$$M_o^t(x^{i,t}, y^{i,t}, x^{i,t+1}, y^{i,t+1}) = \frac{D_o^{t+1}(x^{i,t+1}, y^{i,t+1})}{D_o^t(x^{i,t}, y^{i,t})} . D_o^t(x^{i,t+1}, y^{i,t+1}) D_o^{t+1}(x^{i,t+1}, y^{i,t+1})$$

$$= \Delta TE(x^{i,t}, y^{i,t}, x^{i,t+1}, y^{i,t+1}). \Delta T(x^{i,t+1}, y^{i,t+1})$$

Note that (ΔTE) stands for the technical efficiency change and (ΔT) stands for the technical change. The author investigated that the technical change can be decomposed into two elements as follows:

$$\Delta T(x^{i,t+1}, y^{i,t+1}) = \left[\frac{D_o^t(x^{i,t+1}, y^{i,t+1})}{D_o^{t+1}(x^{i,t+1}, y^{i,t+1})} \cdot \frac{D_o^{t+1}(x^{i,t}, y^{i,t})}{D_o^t(x^{i,t}, y^{i,t})} \right]$$

$$= \Delta T(x^{i,t}, y^{i,t}) . B(x^{i,t}, y^{i,t}, x^{i,t+1}, y^{i,t+1}) =$$

They finally introduced the first term shows technical change index in time *t* and the second one shows the bias index. The bias index can be further decomposed into the following terms:

$$B(x^{i,t}, y^{i,t}, x^{i,t+1}, y^{i,t+1}) = \left[\frac{D_o^t(x^{i,t+1}, y^{i,t+1})}{D_o^{t+1}(x^{i,t+1}, y^{i,t+1})} \cdot \frac{D_o^{t+1}(x^{i,t+1}, y^{i,t})}{D_o^t(x^{i,t+1}, y^{i,t})} \right] \times$$

$$\left[\frac{D_o^t(x^{i,t+1}, y^{i,t})}{D_o^{t+1}(x^{i,t}, y^{i,t+1})} \cdot \frac{D_o^{t+1}(x^{i,t}, y^{i,t})}{D_o^t(x^{i,t}, y^{i,t})} \right]$$

$$= [OB(y^{i,t}, x^{i,t+1}, y^{i,t+1})] . [IB(x^{i,t}, y^{i,t}, x^{i,t+1})]$$

Need to be noted that the first element indicates the output bias index and the second one shows the input bias index.

In their paper Lozano-Vivas and Humphrey (2002) noted that many of the studies in productivity growth in the banking industry have been overstated. The authors claimed that the problem is because of how the method is being utilized not for the technique being used. They mentioned that it is easy to see in the banking industry due the nature of the data which is at hand. Moreover, they claimed that the bias is not considerable when all outputs and inputs are taken inro the analysis, ensuring that the balance sheet restriction is met.

Ten Raa and Mohnen (2002) tried to estimate the total factor productivity growth without recourse to data on input prices. The authors defined the factor conductivities as Lagrange multipliers to the program that maximizes the level of domestic final demand.

Hwang and Chang (2003) in regards of the data envelopment analysis technique and the malmquist productivity index tried to assess the managerial performance of hotels.

Jimenez et al. (2003) in order to assess the system of community care, utilized the non-parametric malmquist index approach with which technical efficiency changes, scale effects and technological change can be acquired.

Krishnasamy (2003) considering non-parametric methodology data envelopment analysis technique and malmquist total factor productivity index for estimating efficiency scores and productivity changes for Malaysian Post Merger banks.

In his paper Chen (2003) instead of radial evaluations introduced the malmquist productivity index based on a non-radial evaluations. Also, the author tried to consider the decision maker's preference into the analysis. The author noted that the non-radial malmquist productivity index eliminates possible inefficiency represented by the non-zero slacks. Then, three Chinese major industries are taken into account to be applied in the presented method for measuring the productivity change.

Consider $\alpha_i, i = 1,...,m$ as the user-specific weights over inputs. Following model evaluates relative efficiency of the unit under assessment (DMU_o) at time t when technology is considered at time $t+1$.

$$\tilde{\theta}_o^{t+1}(x_o^t, y_o^t) = \frac{1}{\sum\limits_{i=1}^{m} \alpha_i} \min \ \sum\limits_{i=1}^{m} \alpha_i \theta_o^i$$

$$s.t. \quad \sum\limits_{j=1}^{n} \lambda_j x_{ij}^{t+1} \leq \theta_o^t x_{io}^t, \quad i = 1,...,m, \tag{2}$$

$$\sum\limits_{j=1}^{n} \lambda_j y_{rj}^{t+1} \geq y_{ro}^t, \quad r = 1,...,s,$$

$$\lambda_j \geq 0, \quad j = 1,...,n,$$

Considering times t and $t+1$ for both technology and the DMU under assessment, $\tilde{\theta}_o^t(x_o^t, y_o^t), \tilde{\theta}_o^{t+1}(x_o^{t+1}, y_o^{t+1})$ and $\tilde{\theta}_o^t(x_o^{t+1}, y_o^{t+1})$ can also be defined same as the following model. Thus input-oriented non-radial malmquist productivity index is defined as follows:

$$P\tilde{I}_o = \frac{\tilde{\theta}_o^t(x_o^t, y_o^t)}{\tilde{\theta}_o^{t+1}(x_o^{t+1}, y_o^{t+1})} [\frac{\tilde{\theta}_o^{t+1}(x_o^{t+1}, y_o^{t+1})}{\tilde{\theta}_o^t(x_o^{t+1}, y_o^{t+1})} \frac{\tilde{\theta}_o^{t+1}(x_o^t, y_o^t)}{\tilde{\theta}_o^t(x_o^t, y_o^t)}]^{(1/2)}$$

Galanopoulos et al. (2004) used the DEA-based malmquist productivity index in the agricultural sectors in the EU countries and tried for the evaluation of the comparative effectiveness of each firm.

Tsekouras et al. (2004) considered the data set with zero values and tried to provide a technique for the parametric estimation of the malmquist productivity index. They considered a dummy variable technique according to the work of Battese to extend a translog specification of the input distance function. Moreover, they investigated that the technical changes (TCs) are decomposed into neutral and biased components. Finally for demonstration of the presented method the provided method is applied to the Greek prefect ural training councils.

Briec Kerstens (2004) introduced a new Luenberger-Hicks-Moorsteen productivity indicator. They investigated that to some extend the logarithm of the Hicks-Moorsteen productivity index and the Luenberger-Hicks-Moorsteen productivity indicators are equal. Moreover, they provided conditions under which the Luenberger-Hicks-Moorsteen indicator equals the Luenberger indicator. The input- and output-oriented versions of this Luenberger productivity indicator based on input and output directional distance functions defines as follows:

The input Luenberger productivity indicator defines as follows:

$$L_i((x^t, y^t), (x^{t+1}, y^{t+1}); g_i^t, g_i^{t+1}))$$

$$= L((x^t, y^t), (x^{t+1}, y^{t+1}); (g_i^t, 0), (g_i^{t+1}, 0))$$

As well, the output Luenberger productivity indicator is as follows:

$$L_i((x^t, y^t), (x^{t+1}, y^{t+1}); g_i^t o, g_o^{t+1}))$$

$$= L((x^t, y^t), (x^{t+1}, y^{t+1}); (0, g_o^t), (0, g_o^{t+1}))$$

They noted that the Luenberger- Hicks-Moorsteen indicator which is defined as the difference between a Luenberger output quantity and a Luenberger input quantity indicators in period *t*, is as follows:

$$LHM_{T(t)}(x^{t+1}, y^{t+1}, x^t, y^t : g^t, g^{t+1})$$

$$= LO_{T(t)}(x^t, y^t, y^{t+1} : g_o^t, g_o^{t+1}) - LI_{T(t)}(x^t, x^{t+1}, y^t : g_i^t, g_i^{t+1}$$

Estache et al. (2004) took the malmquist index into account for measuring and decomposing the changes in productivity, in terms of Greek prefectural training council infrastructure, for Mexico's 11 main ports.

Barros and Alves (2004) evaluated total productivity change of a Portuguese retail store using data envelopment analysis technique and decomposed it into technically efficient change and technological change. Moreover, they ranked the stores according to their total productivity alterations.

Nowadays, measuring productivity gains an important attention among senior managersa and also researchers. Thus, in regrds of the known input prices and producers who are cost minimizers, Maniadakis and Thanassoulis [30] (2004) in their paper tries to provide an index for productivity assessment. They provided this indicator on the basis of malmquist productivity index. An important feature of the presented index is that the presented distance function considers input cost instead of input quantity. Moreover, the authors decomposed productivity change into two parts namely overall efficiency and cost technical change.

Also, the authors claimed that the overall efficiency change and cost technical change are, respectively, decomposed into technical and allocative efficiency change, and a part capturing shifts of input quantities and relative input prices. Further, for showing the applicability and clarity of the provide method the authors utilized the mentioned method in hospitals to show the applicability of the method.

Maniadakis and Thanassoulis (2004) mentioned the cost malmquist (CM) productivity index in time period of t and $t+1$ as follows:

$$CM = [\frac{w^t x^{t+1} / C^t(y^{t+1}, w^t)}{w^t x^t / C^t(y^t, w^t)} \times \frac{w^{t+1} x^{t+1} / C^{t+1}(y^{t+1}, w^{t+1})}{w^{t+1} x^t / C^{t+1}(y^t, w^{t+1})}]^{(1/2)}$$

Note that, $C^t(y^t, w^t) = min_{x^t}\{w^t x^t : x^t \in L^t(y^t), w^t > 0\}$. Also let $L^t(y^t)$ defines a boundary to the input requirement set. Also, the cost ratio $w^t x^t / C^t(y^t, w^t)$ shows the amount of reduction in the aggregate production cost, in time t, which can still secure the output vector y^t having the input price vector w^t. The authors investigated for the cost malmqiust index decomposition and introduced the *CM* factor as follows:

$$CM = \frac{w^{t+1} x^{t+1} / C^{t+1}(y^{t+1}, w^{t+1})}{w^t x^t / C^t(y^t, w^t)} \times [\frac{w^t x^{t+1} / C^t(y^{t+1}, w^t)}{w^{t+1} x^{t+1} / C^{t+1}(y^{t+1}, w^{t+1})} \times$$

$$w^t x^t / C^t(y^t, w^t) w^{t+1} x^t / C^{t+1}(y^{t+1}, w^{t+1})]^{(1/2)}$$

They introduced the first term as overall efficiency change (OEC) and the second one as the cost-technical change (CTC). Furthermore, OEC is itself decomposed into the following terms: technical efficiency change (TEC) and allocative efficiency change (AEC) as follows:

$$OEC = \frac{D_i^{t+1}(y^{t+1}, x^{t+1})}{D_i^t(y^t, x^t)} \times$$

$$\frac{w^{t+1}x^{t+1} \, / \, (C^{t+1}(y^{t+1}, w^{t+1})D_i^{t+1}(y^{t+1}, x^{t+1}))}{w^t x^t \, / \, (C^t(y^t, w^t)D_i^t(y^t, x^t))}$$

Note that, CTC is decomposed into the following terms named technical change (TC) and price effect (PE):

$$CTC = [\frac{D_i^t(y^{t+1}, x^{t+1})}{D_i^{t+1}(y^{t+1}, x^{t+1})} \frac{D_i^t(y^t, x^t)}{D_i^{t+1}(y^t, x^t)}]^{(1/2)} \times [\frac{w^t x^{t+1} \, / \, (C^t(y^{t+1}, w^t)D_i^t(y^{t+1}, x^{t+1}))}{w^{t+1}x^{t+1} \, / \, (C^{t+1}(y^{t+1}, w^{t+1})D_i^{t+1}(y^{t+1}, x^{t+1}))} \times$$

$$\frac{w^t x^t \, / \, (C^t(y^t, w^t)D_i^t(y^t, x^t))}{w^{t+1}x^t \, / \, (C^{t+1}(y^t, w^{t+1})D_i^{t+1}(y^t, x^t))}]^{(1/2)}$$

Asmild (2004) utilized data envelopment analysis as long as window analysis and reached the efficiency scores for the 20 year period 1981–2000. Moreover, for calculating productivity changes over time, malmquist indices are obtained from DEA scores.

Can (2004) considering a multi input-output production technology and survey data from Jinzhai County, China, tried to measure the production performance of rural households, efficiency, economy of scale, and productivity.

Zaim (2004) according to this fact that the air pollution is a byproduct of manufacturing activity, proposed a new definition of pollution intensity and a new method for assessing the aggregate pollution intensity. In doing so, Zaim presented a variant of malmquist quantity index which satisfies well-established axiomatic properties.

In their paper Chen and Iqbal Ali [34] (2004) noted that as the DEA-based malmquist productivity index is decomposed into the technical change and the frontier shift, thus they claimed that these components their selves can further be analyzed. They also provided a new approach to introduce patterns of productivity change while presents a new interpretation for the managerial implication of each malmquist component. Furthermore, they tried to distinguish the strategy shifts of individual firms according to the isoquant changes. Thus, they claimed that it is possible to know if such strategy shifts are desirable or not. They considered

$$\frac{D_o^t(x_o^{t+1}, y_o^{t+1})}{D_o^{t+1}(x_o^{t+1}, y_o^{t+1})}$$

and

$$\frac{D_o^t(x_o^t, y_o^t)}{D_o^{t+1}(x_o^t, y_o^t)}$$

while DMU_o is taken into account.

Then they illustrated the presented method with a set of Fortune Global 500 Computer and Office Equipment companies.

Pastor and Lovell (2005) proved that as the geometric mean malmquist productivity index is not circular, thus they proposed a global malmquist productivity index that is circular which results in a single measure of productivity change.

Pastor and Lovell considered a contemporaneous malmquist productivity index on T_C^s as follows:

$$M_C^s(x^t, y^t, x^{t+1}, y^{t+1}) = \frac{D_C^s(x^{t+1}, Y^{t+1})}{D_C^s(x^t, Y^t)}$$

where $D_C^s(x, Y) = min\{\phi > 0 \mid (x, Y / \phi) \in T_C^s\}$.

Note that the defined global malmquist productivity index on T_C^G is as follows:

$$M_C^G(x^t, y^t, x^{t+1}, y^{t+1}) = \frac{D_C^G(x^{t+1}, Y^{t+1})}{D_C^G(x^t, Y^t)}$$

Pastor and Lovell investigated that the proposed index can be decomposed as follows:

$$M_C^G(x^t, y^t, x^{t+1}, y^{t+1}) = EC_C \times \{\frac{BPG_C^{G,t+1}(x^{t+1}, x^{t+1})}{BPG_C^{G,t}(x^t, x^t)}\} = EC_C \times BPC_C$$

Where the authors called *EC* as efficiency change and *BPG* as best practice gap between T_C^G and T_C^S measure along rays (x^S, y^S), $s = t, t+1$. Also, *BPC* means change in BPG_c. $BPC_C \geq (\leq)1$ shows whether the benchmark technology is closer to or further from the global benchmark technology.

Ball et al. (2005) noted that as absence of price data for the social outputs limits measuring the productivity growth, thus an alternative productivity growth measure is constructed utilizing activity analysis.

The authors verified that the provided method can be easily used. Then for demonstration the applicability of the provided method they used it in an application to US agriculture.

Ball et al. assumed that the bad outputs are assumed to be byproducts of production of good outputs, thus defined;

$$(x, y, b) \in T \quad and \quad b = 0 \quad implies \quad y = 0$$

Consider the following equations with which Ball et al. means each bad output is produced by at least one activity each activity produces at least one bad output.

$$\sum_{k=1}^{K} b_{ki} > 0, \quad i = 1,...,I.$$

$$\sum_{i=1}^{I} b_{ki} > 0, \quad k = 1,...,K.$$

Note that good outputs are freely disposable thus:

$$(x, y, b) \in T \quad and \quad y' \leq y \quad imply \quad (x, y', b) \in T$$

Now consider the technology as follows:

$$T = \{(x, y, b) : \sum_{k=1}^{K} z_k x_{kn} \leq x_n, n = 1,..., N, \sum_{k=1}^{K} z_k y_{km} \geq y_m, m = 1,..., M,$$

$$\sum_{k=1}^{K} z_k b_{ki} = b_i, i = 1,..., I, z_k \geq 0, k = 1,..., K\}$$

Thus the authors defined the minimum cost mode as follows:

$$C(y, b, w) = min[wx : (x, y, b) \in T]$$

Finally consider the malmquist cost productivity (MCP) index as follows:

$$MCP_t^{t+1} = [\frac{c^t(y^{t+1}, b^{t+1}, w^{t+1}).c^{t+1}(y^{t+1}, b^{t+1}, w^{t+1})}{c^t(y^t, b^t, w^t).c^{t+1}(y^t, b^t, w^t)}]^{1/2} \frac{c^t}{c^{t+1}}$$

Hseu and Shang (2005) tried to assess the productivity of pulp and paper industry in OECD countries. They considered data envelopment analysis technique to acquire the malmquist productivity index. In the analysis, they also used the components of this index as technical change and efficiency change.

Mussard and Peypoch (2006) presented the multi decomposition of the aggregate malmquist productivity index. They defined the aggregate malmquist productivity index as follows:

$$AM = \frac{\sum_{k=1}^{K} D_{t+1}^k(z_{t+1}^k)}{\sum_{k=1}^{K} D_t^k(z_t^k)} [\frac{\sum_{k=1}^{K} D_t^k(z_t^k)}{\sum_{k=1}^{K} D_{t+1}^k(z_t^k)} \cdot \frac{\sum_{k=1}^{K} D_t^k(z_{t+1}^k)}{\sum_{k=1}^{K} D_{t+1}^k(z_{t+1}^k)}]^{1/2}$$

The authors noted that as usual this index is decomposed into the efficiency change (EC) and the technical change (TC).

Considering the work of Färe and Zelenyuk (2003), Zelenyuk (2006) tried to find new method for aggregation for the malmquist productivity index over individual decision making units into a group of malmquist productivity index. They, moreover, taken into account the aggregation of decomposed parts of the malmquist productivity index thus it is possible to decompose the malmquist productivity index for a particular group.

The authors expressed that, one way of defining the group technology is considering the additive structure of aggregation of the output sets as what has been defined by Fare and Zelenyuk (2006), in periods s and t .

$$\bar{p}_\tau(X) \equiv \sum_{k=1}^{n} p_\tau^k(X^k), \quad \tau = s, t.$$

According to what Zelenyuk (2006) has been done, the group revenue function is defined as follows:

$$\bar{R}_\tau(X,p) \equiv max_y\{py : y \in \bar{P}_\tau(X)\}, \quad \tau = s,t.$$

The group analog of revenue efficiency of an individual unit is defined as follows:

$$\bar{RE}_\tau(X,\bar{Y},p) \equiv \bar{R}_\tau(X,p) / p\bar{Y}, \quad \tau = s,t.$$

Considering periods s and t, the group or aggregate analog of the malmquist productivity index is defined as follows:

$$RM(p_s,p_t,\bar{Y}_s,\bar{Y}_t,X_s,X_t) \equiv [(\frac{\bar{RE}_s(X_t,\bar{Y}_t,p_t)}{\bar{RE}_s(X_s,\bar{Y}_s,p_s)} \times \frac{\bar{RE}_t(X_t,\bar{Y}_t,p_t)}{\bar{RE}_t(X_s,\bar{Y}_s,p_s)})^{-1}]^{1/2}$$

Odeck (2006) investigated for the target achievements of the operational units of the Norwegian Public Roads Administration (NPRA) charged with traffic safety services using data envelopment analysis method.

Specificly, Odeck used the BCC model with a unique constant input which can be equivalently interpreted as no input which is an important issue in applicational issue. Then, a DEA-based malmquist index is taken into account to measure productivity growth in target achievements. Moreover, for obtaining more factual results Odeck utilized a bootstrapping technique for obtaining the confidence intervals for efficiency scores and also testing hypotheses for productivity growth or regress.

Camanho and Dyson (2006) in accordance to the malmquist index provided new measures. An important feature of this new measure is that it helps the decision making units' inefficiencies to be distinguished from those associated with their group characteristics. The authors show the applicability of provided method in bank branches' performance.

Considering malmquist index the authors defined overall measure for the comparison of performance between two groups of decision making units, groups A and B, as following:

$$I^{AB} = [\frac{(\prod_{j=1}^{\delta_A}D^A(X_j^A,Y_j^A))^{1/\delta_A}}{(\prod_{j=1}^{\delta_B}D^A(X_j^B,Y_j^B))^{1/\delta_B}} \cdot \frac{(\prod_{j=1}^{\delta_A}D^B(X_j^A,Y_j^A))^{1/\delta_A}}{(\prod_{j=1}^{\delta_B}D^B(X_j^B,Y_j^B))^{1/\delta_B}}]^{1/2}$$

Note that (X_j^A, Y_j^A), $j = 1, ..., \delta_A$ is the input-output data of DMU_j belongs to group A, the same is true for the group B. Note that I^{AB} evaluates the distance of the DMUs to a single reference technology. Camanho and Dyson noted that the first term in this expression evaluates the average distance of DMUs in group A divided by the average distance of DMUs from group B. Also, they noted that the second ratio is a similar to the first one while considering group Bs frontier. Camanho and Dyson claimed that as there is no preference for the groups A or B thus the geometric mean of these two is taken into account. Considering the input-output data of DMU_j belongs to group A as (X_j^A, Y_j^A), $j = 1, ..., \delta_A$ the provided measure can be decomposed as follows:

$$I^{AB} = \frac{[\prod_{j=1}^{\delta_A} D^A(X_j^A, Y_j^A)]^{1/\delta_A}}{[\prod_{j=1}^{\delta_B} D^B(X_j^B, Y_j^B)]^{1/\delta_B}} \cdot \left[\frac{(\prod_{j=1}^{\delta_A} D^B(X_j^A, Y_j^A))^{1/\delta_A}}{(\prod_{j=1}^{\delta_A} D^A(X_j^A, Y_j^A))^{1/\delta_A}} \cdot \frac{(\prod_{j=1}^{\delta_B} D^B(X_j^B, Y_j^B))^{1/\delta_B}}{(\prod_{j=1}^{\delta_B} D^A(X_j^B, Y_j^B))^{1/\delta_B}} \right]^{1/2}$$

The authors noted that the first part compares within-group efficiency spreads. Also, the term inside square brackets assessed the productivity gap between the frontiers of the two groups. The authors verified that having less dispersion in the efficiency levels of the DMUs in one group compared to the other, the dominance of the best practice frontier are the reasons of better performance.

In their paper, Raab and Feroz, (2007) provided a generalized efficiency index for a much larger set of 57 national governments by employing four components of gross national product and five resource-availability indicators. They used a data envelopment analysis technique for maximizing the components of Gross National Product (GNP) while it is aimed to minimize specific resource-input measures.

Wang (2007) decomposed energy productivity change into several components namly as effects of the changes in the ratios of non-energy inputs to energy, energy supply composition, and output composition, technical efficiency change, technological change, using output distance function. Also, they used this method for demonstration the energy productivity change in OECD countries.

$$\frac{(Y_1^{t+i} + ... + Y_m^{t+i}) / (E_1^{t+i} + ... + E_n^{t+i})}{(Y_1^t + ... + Y_m^t) / (E_1^t + ... + E_n^t)} \times \frac{D_o^t(k^t, l^t, e^t, y^t)}{D_o^t(k^{t+i}, l^{t+i}, e^{t+i}, y^{t+i})} \times$$

$$\frac{D_o^{t+i}(k^{t+i}, l^{t+i}, e^{t+i}, y^{t+i})}{D_o^t(k^t, l^t, e^t, y^t)} \times \frac{D_o^t(k^{t+i}, l^{t+i}, e^{t+i}, y^{t+i})}{D_o^{t+i}(k^{t+i}, l^{t+i}, e^{t+i}, y^{t+i})}$$

$$= PEPCH^t \times EFFCH \times TECH(t+i)$$

PEPCH, EFFCH and TECH are respectively named after potential energy productivity change, technical efficiency change and technological change. Moreover, the authors investigated that $PEPCH^t$ can be decomposed into:

$$= KECHE^t \times LECHE^t \times ESCHE^t \times OSCHE^t$$

in which $KECHE^t, LECHE^t, ESCHE^t$ and $OSCHE^t$, respectively measure the effect of the change in capital– energy ratio; the effect of the change in labor–energy ratio; the effect of the change in energy supply composition; the effect of the change in output composition.

Telle and Larssonv (2007) used regression analysis of productivity growth on regulatory stringency using plant level data. They noted that to credit a plant for emission reductions, thus they included emissions as inputs when it is aimed to calculate an environmental malmquist productivity index.

Asmild and Tam (2007) provided a way of calculating global malmquist indices and global frontier shift indices with which a better estimation of the true frontier shift and furthermore is obtained.

They considered a technology index number (TI) as at time t as follows:

$$TI^t(\overline{X}, \overline{Y}) = (\prod_{k=1,\dots,K; \tau=1,\dots,T} D^t(x_k^\tau, y_k^\tau))^{1/(K \times T)}$$

Need to be noted that K represents the number of Ddecision making unts observed in T times periods. They considered the global frontier shift in times t and $t+1$ as follows:

$$TC^G(t, t+i; \overline{X}, \overline{Y}) = \frac{TI^{t+i}(\overline{X}, \overline{Y})}{TI^t(\overline{X}, \overline{Y})}$$

$$= (\frac{(\prod_{k=1,\dots,K; \tau=1,\dots,T} D^{t+i}(x_k^\tau, y_k^\tau)}{(\prod_{k=1,\dots,K; \tau=1,\dots,T} D^t(x_k^\tau, y_k^\tau)})^{1/(K \times T)}$$

They suggested to consider the global version of the adjacent productivity change index between times t and $t+1$ is as follows:

$$M^G(t, t+i; (\bar{X}, \bar{Y})) = TC^G(t, t+i; (X^t, Y^t)) \times EC^G(t, t+i; (X^t, Y^t), (X^{t+i}, Y^{t+i}))$$

$$= \prod_{k=1,...,K} [\frac{D^t(x_k^t, y_k^t)}{D^{t+i}(x_k^{t+i}, y_k^{t+i})}]^{1/k}$$

Kutana and Yigit (2007) provided a stochastic endogenous growth model for evaluating the impact of European Union (EU) integration on productivity growth. Kutana and Yigit utilized the structural break tests and data envelopment analysis for analyzing this issue.

Lin and Berg (2008) evaluated quality-incorporated firm performance and identified changes in efficiency, technology and service quality in Peru Water Sector. For evaluation performance analysis Lin and Berg considered the nonparametric data envelopment analysis model, a preference structure model, and the quality-incorporated malmquist productivity index.

Kortelainen (2008) proposed a new method for environmental performance analysis from a static to a dynamic setting in order to construct an environmental performance index (EPI) using frontier efficiency techniques and a malmquist index approach. The authors claimed that the provided model is belt upon the basis of the standard definition of eco efficiency compared to other dynamic environmental productivity and efficiency analysis approaches. Kortelainen demonstrated that alterations in overall environmental performance can be decomposed into changes in relative eco efficiency and shifts in environmental technology. They also applied the presented method at the macro level to dynamic environmental performance analysis of 20 member states of the European Union.

Kortelainen considered $EE_k(Z^s, V^s, t)$ to be the relative eco efficiency of DMU_k in time s when the frontier is in time t.

$$[EE_k((Z^s, V^s, t)]^{-1} = \min_w \quad \{w_1 \frac{Z_{k1}(s)}{V_k(s)} + w_2 \frac{Z_{k2}(s)}{V_k(s)} + ... + w_M \frac{Z_{kM}(s)}{V_k(s)}\}$$

$$s.t. \qquad w_1 \frac{Z_{n1}(s)}{V_n(s)} + w_2 \frac{Z_{n2}(s)}{V_n(s)} + ... + w_M \frac{Z_{nM}(s)}{V_n(s)} \geq 1, \quad n = 1,...,N,$$

$$w_m \geq 0, \quad m = 1,...,M.$$

Kortelainen considered:

$$EPI_k(t) = \frac{EE_k((Z^t, V^t, t))}{EE_k((Z^{t-1}, V^{t-1}, t))}$$

as the environmental performance index of unit DMU_k where t is the period of reference technology. Moreover, the frontier of period $t-1$ as a benchmark is considered as:

$$EPI_k(t-1) = \frac{EE_k((Z^t, V^t, t-1))}{EE_k((Z^{t-1}, V^{t-1}, t-1))}$$

Taking geometric average of the two measures consider environmental performance index (EPI) as follows:

$$EPI_k(t-1, t) = (\frac{EE_k((Z^t, V^t, t-1))}{EE_k((Z^{t-1}, V^{t-1}, t-1))} \times \frac{EE_k((Z^t, V^t, t))}{EE_k((Z^{t-1}, V^{t-1}, t))})^{(1/2)} \quad t = 2, ..., T$$

Kortelainen noted that this index can be decomposed into the relative eco efficiency change and environmental technical change as following:

$$EPI_k(t-1, t) = (\frac{EE_k((Z^t, V^t, t))}{EE_k(Z^{t-1}, V^{t-1}, t-1)}) \times$$

$$(\frac{EE_k((Z^{t-1}, V^{t-1}, t-1))}{EE_k(Z^{t-1}, V^{t-1}, t)} \times \frac{EE_k(Z^t, V^t, t-1)}{EE_k(Z^t, V^t, t)})^{(1/2)}$$

Tortosa-Ausina et al. (2008) explored productivity growth and productive efficiency for Spanish savings banks over the post-deregulation period taking data envelopment analysis into account and also bootstrapping techniques.

Liu and Wang (2008) considered the SBM model of data envelopment analysis technique in order to acquire the malmquist productivity index for performance assessment of different firms in Taiwan. They verified that the malmquist productivity has three components namely as measurement of technical change, the measurement of the frontier forward shift, and the measurement of the frontier backward shift of a company. Finally, Liu and Wang's research showed the strategy shifts of individual companies are based upon isoquant changes.

Silva-Portela and Thanassoulis (2006) claimed that there exists some bias in the analysis of total factor productivity change using distance functions. Therefore, for dimming this difference they provided a procedure measured total productivity index changes just with the observed values. They verified that the presented entire total productivity index changes are made up of efficiency change, technological change, and a residual effect.

Portela and Thanassoulis considered the geometric distance function as follows. Note that this index shows the ratio between a benchmark of the input and an observed input and also shows the ratio between a target and an observed output:

$$GDF = \frac{(\prod_i \theta_i)^{1/m}}{(\prod_r \beta_r)^{1/s}}$$

The authors mentioned that the GDE is a non-oriented measure that considerers both input decrease and output increase in comparison to the frontier.

Thus they defined the malmquist type index based on the GDF is as follows:

$$MGDM = (\frac{GDF^t(y_{t+1}, x_{t+1})}{GDF^t(y_t, x_t)} \times \frac{GDF^{t+1}(y_{t+1}, x_{t+1})}{GDF^{t+1}(y_t, x_t)})$$

Its decomposition consists of the following expressions.

$$MGDM = (\frac{GDF^{t+1}(y_{t+1}, x_{t+1})}{GDF^t(y_t, x_t)} \times [\frac{GDF^t(y_{t+1}, x_{t+1})}{GDF^{t+1}(y_{t+1}, x_{t+1})} \times \frac{GDF^t(y_t, x_t)}{GDF^{t+1}(y_t, x_t)}]^{1/2}$$

They showed that it can also be summarized into:

$$MGDF = EFCH \times THCH$$

Decomposing this factor into two terms, one is $MGDF$ and the other is residual, now total factor productivity can be written as follows:

$$TFP = MGDF \times (\frac{x_t^{*t} / x_{t+1}^{*t}}{y_t^{*t} / y_{t+1}^{*t}} \times \frac{x_t^{*t+1} / x_{t+1}^{*t+1}}{y_t^{*t+1} / y_{t+1}^{*t+1}})^{(1/2)}$$

Kim and Lee (2004) in their research tried to search for the relation between productivity changes and *R&D* in the presence of embodied and disembodied international spillovers of technology for total manufacturing industries in OECD countries. In order to do so they used the malmquist total factor productivity index.

Abbaspour et al.(2009) noted that as usually in most real world problems there exist indicators which are non-discretionary or semi-discretionary. In accordance to this fact they provided the DEA-based malmquist productivity index in order to contrast the group performance at the same period of time while there exist such factors. Abbaspour et al. illustrated the presented methods by the contrasting the environmental performance for the two groups of Iranian and International oil and gas general contractors.

Oliveira et al. (2009) explored the evolution of productivity of the artisanal dredge fleet operating in the south of Portugal. In their study they try to determine alterations in productivity over a time window of 10 years. Moreover, Oliveira et al. searched for distinguishing the performance of local and coastal vessels. They utilized malmquist index for assessing productivity change and explored the impact of changes in stock conditions.

Chang et al. (2009) in their paper utilized data envelopment analysis method for measuring the malmquist index of productivity and efficiency changes. They expressed this fact that malmquist index is used as it can distinguish between changes in technical efficiency and performance efficiencies for each decisionn making unit. The mentioned techniques are used to investigate changes in productive efficiency for 62 of the largest US public accounting firms.

Odeck (2009) combined data envelopment analysis method and a malmquist productivity index with a bootstrap technique for acquiring the statistical inferences which determines the performance of grain producers in Eastern Norway.

In their paper Guan and Chen (2009) provided a new methodological framework for effectively measuring the production frontier performance (PFP) of macro-scale research and develop activities. They used a non-radial model in data envelopment analysis technique as long as a non-radial malmquist index. Guan and Chen also applied this method for evaluation of *R&D* activities of Chinese provinces.

In their paper Chang et al. (2009) investigated the productivity growth, technical progress, and efficiency change considering a group of the largest CPA firms in the US. In doing so, a data envelopment analysis technique is used to calculate malmquist productivity index.

Kao (2010) aimed at calculating the global malmquist productivity index. In doing so, they proposed a common-weights data envelopment analysis model for time-series evaluations. Thus, for comparing the productivity changes of all decision making units have a common basis. Also, Kao claimed that the common-weights global malmquist productivity index produces reliable results.

Consider the following model which minimizes the total squared difference between the ideal efficiency of DMU_k at the time of q, E_q^k, and the efficiency calculated from the common weights of each DMU.

$$\min \quad \sum_{t=1}^{p}\sum_{j=1}^{n}(E_j^{(t)} - \sum_{r=1}^{s}u_r Y_{rj}^{(t)} / \sum_{i=1}^{m}v_i X_{ij}^{(t)})^2$$

$$s.t. \quad \sum_{r=1}^{s}u_r Y_{rj}^{(t)} - \sum_{i=1}^{m}v_i X_{ij}^{(t)} \qquad i = 1,...,m,$$

$$u_r \geq \varepsilon, v_i \geq \varepsilon, \qquad\qquad r = 1,...,s, i = 1,...,m.$$

In the above-mentioned model u^* and v^* are considered to be as the optimal solutions. Thus, they proposed the common weights global malmquist productivity index of DMU_k considering time t and $t+1$ as follows:

$$M_k^{CW} = \frac{\sum_{r=1}^{s}u_r^* Y_{rk}^{(t+1)} / \sum_{i=1}^{m}v_i^* X_{ik}^{(t+1)}}{\sum_{r=1}^{s}u_r^* Y_{rk}^{(t)} / \sum_{i=1}^{m}v_i^* X_{ik}^{(t)}}$$

They also utilized this index for performance evaluation of Taiwan forests and with the common-weights global malmquist productivity index approach they identified districts with unsatisfactory performance before the reorganization and those with unsatisfactory productivity improvement after the reorganization.

In their study, Sözen et al. (2010), tried to evaluate thermal power plants utilizing data envelopment analysis technique. They defined two efficiency indexes, operational and environmental performance.

Hosseinzadeh Lotfi et al. (2010) in their paper utilized the malamquist index in a powerhouse collection which had four units, for measuring the productivity.

Portela and Thanassoulis (2010) in their paper developed an indicator of productivity change considering negative data. In doing so, the range directional model (RDM) is considered in order to compute efficiency with negative data. They utilized *RDM* efficiency measures for the malmquist-type index, and also they used RDM inefficiency measures for Luenberger productivity indicator. Note that the indexes are developed according to a fixed meta technology and they are referred to as a meta malmquist index and meta Luenberger indicator. The provided method is then applied to a sample of bank branches where negative data were implicated.

Portela and Thanassoulis defined the meta-malmquist index as follows:

$$MM_j^{t,t+1} = \frac{\vec{R}DM^{mf}(x_j^{t+1}, y_j^{t+1}, 0, R_{y_j^{t+1}}^{mf})}{\vec{R}DM^{mf}(x_j^{t}, y_j^{t}, 0, R_{y_j^{t}}^{mf})}$$

$MM_j^{t,t+1} > 1$ shows productivity growth of unit j and the Productivity loss by $MM_j^{t,t+1} < 1$.

Note that superscript *mf* on *RDM* indicates the distance function is in relation to the meta-frontier, while the superscript *mf* on *R* indicates that the ideal point for computing the range R is a global ideal point defined over the meta-period. Also, RDM is referred to the optimal solution of the following model.

$$\vec{R}DM^t(x_k^t, y_k^t, 0, R_{y_k^t}) = \beta_k^*$$

$$
\begin{aligned}
\min \quad & \beta_k \\
s.t. \quad & \sum_{j=1}^{n} \lambda_j y_{rj}^t \geq y_{rk}^t + \beta_k R_{y_{rk}^t}, \quad && r = 1,\ldots,s, \\
& \sum_{j=1}^{n} \lambda_j x_{ij}^t \leq \theta x_{ik}^t, \quad && i = 1,\ldots,m, \\
& \sum_{j=1}^{n} \lambda_j = 1, \\
& \lambda_j \geq 0, \quad && j = 1,\ldots,n.
\end{aligned}
\tag{5}
$$

Fallahi et al. (2011) utilized data envelopment analysis technique for estimation of the relative technical efficiency and productivity change in power electric generation management companies. Moreover, a stability test is taken into analysis for verification of the model.

Using both optimistic and pessimistic data envelopment analysis (DEA) at the same time Wang and Lan (2011) tried to measuring malmquist productivity index and called it double frontiers data envelopment analysis (DFDEA). They noted that this method is then used to test with a numerical example which is applied to the productivity analysis of the industrial economy of China.

The optimistic DEA-based malmquist productivity index requires the solution of the following CCR model where the decision making unit which is under evaluation is in time t and the technology is in time $t+1$.

$$D_o^{t+1}(x_o^t, y_o^t) = \min \quad \theta$$

$$s.t. \qquad \sum_{j=1}^{n} \lambda_j x_{ij}^{t+1} \leq \theta^* x_{io}^t, \quad i = 1,...,m,$$

$$\sum_{j=1}^{n} \lambda_j y_{rj}^{t+1} \geq y_{ro}^t, \quad r = 1,...,s, \qquad (6)$$

$$\lambda_j \geq 0, \quad j = 1,...,n,$$

Considering times t and $t+1$, three other LP problems can also be considered like the mentioned model.

Then Wang and Lan considered the optimistic malmquist productivity index as follows:

$$MPI_o(optimistic) = \frac{D_o^{t+1}(x_o^{t+1}, y_o^{t+1})}{D_o^t(x_o^t, y_o^t)} \left[\frac{D_o^t(x_o^t, y_o^t)}{D_o^{t+1}(x_o^t, y_o^t)} \cdot \frac{D_o^t(x_o^{t+1}, y_o^{t+1})}{D_o^{t+1}(x_o^{t+1}, y_o^{t+1})} \right]^{(1/2)}$$

Wang and Lan obtained the pessimistic efficiency of DMU_o at time t where the technology is at time $t+1$, by solving the following pessimistic DEA model:

$$D_o^{t+1}(x_o^t, y_o^t) = \max \quad \phi$$

$$s.t. \qquad \sum_{j=1}^{n} \lambda_j x_{ij}^{t+1} \ geq \phi^* x_{io}^t, \quad i = 1,...,m,$$

$$\sum_{j=1}^{n} \lambda_j y_{rj}^{t+1} \leq y_{ro}^t, \quad r = 1,...,s, \qquad (7)$$

$$\lambda_j \geq 0, \qquad\qquad j = 1,...,n,$$

Considering times t and $t+1$, three other measures, like $D_o^{t+1}(x_o^{t+1}, y_o^{t+1})$, $D_o^t(x_o^t, y_o^t)$ and $D_o^t(x_o^{t+1}, y_o^{t+1})$, defined by the authors.

$$MPI_o(pessimistic) = \frac{D_o^{t+1}(x_o^{t+1}, y_o^{t+1})}{D_o^t(x_o^t, y_o^t)} \left[\frac{D_o^t(x_o^t, y_o^t)}{D_o^{t+1}(x_o^t, y_o^t)} \cdot \frac{D_o^t(x_o^{t+1}, y_o^{t+1})}{D_o^{t+1}(x_o^{t+1}, y_o^{t+1})} \right]^{(1/2)}$$

Finally, Wang and Lan considered the aggregation of malmquist productivity index is as follows:

$$MPI_o(DFDEA) = [MPI_o(optimistic).MPI_o(pessimistic)]^{(1/2)}$$

Zhang (2011) in their paper considered the malmquist–Luenberger (ML) productivity index for assessing China's growth in total factor productivity. An important feature of what Zhang has done is that undesirable outputs which exist in the analysis are taken into account. The malmquist–Luenberger productivity index and its components are derived from the directional distance function in which an increase is considered for the good outputs and a decrease for the undesirable outputs.

Zhang considered the solution of the following linear programming problem as the directional distance functions. They noted that four problems can also be considered in times t and $t+1$. Now, let DMU_k to be under evaluation and all observations are in time t. Zhang considered the directional distance function presented by .... as follows:

$$\vec{D}_o^t(x, y, b; g) = sup\{\beta : (y, b) + \beta \in P(x)\}$$

where $g = (v, -b)$ is the direction which helps good outputs to be increased and bad outputs decreased.

$$\vec{D}_o^t(x^{t,k'}, y^{t,k'}, b^{t,k'}; y^{t,k'}, -b^{t,k'}) = \max \quad \beta$$

s.t.
$$\sum_{k=1}^{K} z_k^t y_{mk}^t \geq (1+\beta)y_{mk'}^t, \quad m = 1, ..., M,$$

$$\sum_{k=1}^{K} z_k^t b_{mik}^t + (1-\beta)b_{ik'}^t, \quad i = 1, ..., L,$$

$$\sum_{k=1}^{K} z_k^t x_{nk}^t \leq x_{nk'}^t, \quad m = 1, ..., M,$$

$$z_k^t \geq 0, \quad k = 1, ..., K.$$

(8)

Taking into account the above mentioned model, thus the malmquist–Luenberger Productivity index defined as follows:

$$ML_t^{t+1} = [\frac{(1+\vec{D}_o^{t+1}(x^t,y^t,b^t;y^t,-b^t))}{(1+\vec{D}_o^{t+1}(x^{t+1},y^{t+1},b^{t+1};y^{t+1},-b^{t+1}))} \times \frac{(1+\vec{D}_o^t(x^t,y^t,b^t;y^t,-b^t))}{(1+\vec{D}_o^t(x^{t+1},y^{t+1},b^{t+1};y^{t+1},-b^{t+1}))}]^{(1/2)}$$

Macpherson et al. (2013) used malmquist index for assessment of the predicted environmental performance. They noted that the scenarios used in their study are such as project population, urban development, and environmental impacts. They considered data envelopment analysis for estimation of malmquist index.

Assaf and Barros (2011) uses the malmquist index with bias correction in order to measure the performance of hotel chains from the UAE, Saudi Arabia and Oman.

Gitto and Mancuso (2012) used data envelopment analysis to assess the operational performance of 28 Italian airports in a time period of 2000 through 2006. The non-parametric data envelopment analysis is bootstrapped in order to be used to correct total factor productivity estimates for bias.

The presented procedure by Gitto and Mancuso is as follows:

First, compute the malmquist productivity index, $\hat{M}_i^{t,t+1}$. Then, calculate the pseudo data set (x_{it}^*, y_{it}^*); $i = 1,...,n$; $t = 1,2$ for gaining the reference bootstrap technology. Next, Compute the bootstrap estimate of the malmquist index, $\hat{M}_{i,b}^{t,t+1}$. Repeat these the mentioned steps B times to obtain the bootstrap sample $\hat{M}_{i,1}^{t,t+1},...., \hat{M}_{i,B}^{t,t+1}$. Finally, in accordance to the bootstrap sample, one can compute bias-corrected estimates and confidence intervals for the malmquist index.

Finally, Gitto and Mancuso presented the bias-corrected which estimates the malmquist index, is as follows:

$$\hat{M}_i^{t,t+1} = \hat{M}_i^{t,t+1} - bias_i = 2\hat{M}_i^{t,t+1} - B^{-1}\sum_{b=1}^{B}\hat{M}_{i,B}^{t,t+1}, \quad i = 1,...,n$$

Emrouznejad et al. (2011) noted that for determining the profit malmquist productivity index (MPI), the observed values in real problems are often imprecise. They noted that these imprecise data can be suitably characterized with fuzzy methods. Therefore, the authors formulate the conventional profit malmquist productivity index problem as an imprecise data envelopment analysis problem, and introduced two other methods for calculating the overall profit malmquist productivity index considering the inputs, outputs, and price vectors as fuzzy data.

Considering times t and $t+1$, the constant returns to scale overall profit malmquist productivity index can be decomposed using four output distance functions. As an instance Emrouznejad et al. considered DMU_o at time t and technology at time $t+1$.

$$D_o^{t+1}(x_o^t, y_o^t) = \max \quad \phi - \theta$$

$$s.t. \qquad \phi[(r_j^{(t+1)})^T y_o^{t+1}] \leq (r_j^{(t)})^T Y^t \lambda, \quad \forall j,$$
$$\theta[(c_j^{(t+1)})^T x_o^{t+1}] \geq (c_j^{(t)})^T X^t \lambda, \quad \forall j, \qquad (9)$$
$$\lambda \geq 0.$$

Noted that the efficiency scores of the presented model computed as follows:

If $\phi - \theta \geq 0$ then $\rho = \dfrac{1}{1 + \phi - \theta}$.

If $\phi - \theta \leq 0$ then $\rho = 1 + \theta - \phi$.

Considering overall profit efficiency change and technology change at times t and $t+1$, the overall profit MPI for DMU_o is calculated as follows:

$$M_o = [\frac{\rho_o^t(X_o^{t+1}, y_o^{t+1})}{\rho_o^t(X_o^t, y_o^t)} \times \frac{\rho_o^{t+1}(X_o^{t+1}, y_o^{t+1})}{\rho_o^{t+1}(X_o^t, y_o^t)}]^{(1/2)}$$

Qazi and Zhao Yulin (2012) considered fifteen high technology industries over the period of ten years for evaluating productivity changes by data envelopment analysi based malmquist index.

Costa (2012) assessed the efficiency and productivity of Intellectual Capital (IC) using data envelopment analysis and malmquist productivity index. It describes the strategic importance of the organization intellectual capital as a source of achievement of competitive advantage. Costa assessed the efficiency and productivity analysis of Italian yachting companies in the 4 years period 2005–2008.

Chou et al. (2012) studied the IT value from an unconventional perspective: the production of IT capital goods. They evaluated the performance of IT industries for 19 Organization of Economic Cooperation and Development (OECD) countries utilizing the true fixed-effects model of translog stochastic production frontier. They examined the productivity growth of these IT industries according to the malmquist index and further analyzed these productivity patterns through technological change and efficiency change.

Pires and Fernandes (2012) in their paper assessed the financial efficiency of airlines from different countries. They evaluate the profitability of these firms. In doing so, they used malmquist index in order to show the capital structure changes in airlines.

Jahantighi et al. (2012) noted that when a decision making unit is not considered as a black box, various processes can be considered as sub processes frequently in series structural network. In order to performance evaluation of a unit with its sub processes and what it did in the past malmquist productivity index, can be taken into account. The authors developed MPI in order to be used for series structural DMUs, with two components, in which intermediate inputs and outputs exist.

In their paper, Chang et al. (2013) noted the results of an empirical study of corporate sustainability conducted at the industry level. Thus, they aimed at determining the change in corporate sustainability performance over time. They created a composite index of corporate sustainability performance while relative efficiency scores are obtained from data envelopment analysis technique, and the changes in efficiency were measured using the malmquist productivity index.

Egilmez and McAvoy (2012) used a model based on malmquist index developed by data envelopment analysis for evaluation of productivity and relative efficiency of U.S. states in reducing the number of fatal crashes.

In their paper Asche et al. (2013) assessed total factor productivity changes in the Norwegian salmon aquaculture sector from 1996 to 2008. In doing so, malmquist productivity index approach is used for evaluating the total factor productivity change using data envelopment analysis method for construction of the underlying production frontier. Moreover, Asche et al. considered a bootstrap approach for construction of the confidence intervals for the malmquist .

As mentioned in literature, the important weaknesses of the standard malmquist productivity index is its infeasibility. Aparicio et al. (2013) in their paper discussed about a disadvantage of the malmquist Luenberger index decomposition that questions its validity as an empirical tool for environmental productivity measurement that considers bad outputs. Thus, the authors demonstrated that considering numerical value the usual interpretation of the technical change component in terms of production frontier shifts can be inconsistent. Thus, it results in interpretation of this component with errors. Therefore, Aparicio et al. provided a solution for this inconsistency issue in accordance with the incorporation of a new postulate for the technology about producing bad outputs.

In their paper Sueyoshi and Goto (2013) studied a new use of data envelopment analysis technique for environmental assessment in a time horizon which is utilized data envelopment analysis and malmquist index to examine the degree of a frontier shift among multiple periods. They noted that the frontier shift shows a technology progress.

Hosseinzadeh Lotfi et al. (2013) reminded that the classic malmquist productivity index shows regress and progress of a decision making unit in different periods with efficiency and technology variations without considering the present value of money. The index developed by Hosseinzadeh Lotfi et al., is defined in terms of modified malmquist productivity index model, which can calculate progress and regress by using the factor of present time value of money.

If the efficiency-related information does not indicate an obvious status of the organization or in case it is inaccurate, it can lead to poor decision-making by managers. Thus Hosseinzadeh Lotfi et al. (2013) considered this shortcoming of data envelopment analysis method in efficiency assessment in successive periods and provided a combined model which is introduced consider this situation.

Utilized data envelopment analysis for finding the inefficiencies in the European countries', Menegaki (2013) demonstrated that considering a panel data set they have to utilize malmquist index for measuring total factor productivity.

Zhang and Choi (2013) tried to measure the dynamic changes in total-factor CO_2 emission performance proposed the meta frontier non-radial malmquist CO_2 emission performance index. This index took the incorporation of group heterogeneity and non-radial slack into the considerations.

Zhang and Choi defined the nonradial directional distance function (NDDF) as follows:

$$\overrightarrow{D}(K, L, F, E, C; g) = sup\{W^T\beta : (K, L, F, E, C) + g.diag(\beta) \in T\}$$

Note that the symbol "diag" is used to show diagonal matrices. In the above formula a normalized weight vector denotes the numbers of inputs and outputs as $w^T = (w_K, w_L, w_F, w_E, w_C)^T$. Also a directional vector denoted by $g = (-g_K, -g_L, -g_F, g_E, -g_C)$ and $\beta = (\beta_K, \beta_L, \beta_F, \beta_E, \beta_C)^T > 0$ shows a vector of scaling factors which shows individual inefficiency measures.

They noted that by solving the following data envelopment analysis model it is possible to calculate the nonradial directional distance function value for each if the n plants.

$$\vec{D}(K,L,F,E,C;g) = \max \quad W_k\beta_k + W_l\beta_l + W_f\beta_F + W_c\beta_c$$

$$s.t. \quad \sum_{n=1}^{N} z_n K_n \leq K_{n'} - \beta_K g_K,$$

$$\sum_{n=1}^{N} z_n L_n \leq L_{n'} - \beta_L g_L,$$

$$\sum_{n=1}^{N} z_n F_n \leq F_{n'} - \beta_F g_F,$$

$$\sum_{n=1}^{N} z_n E_n \geq E_{n'} + \beta_E g_E, \qquad (10)$$

$$\sum_{n=1}^{N} z_n C_n = C_{n'} - \beta_C g_C,$$

$$z_n \geq 0, \quad n = 1,...,N,$$

$$\beta_K, \beta_L, \beta_F, \beta_E, \beta_C \geq 0.$$

Three definitions of production technology sets are required for defining and decomposing the non-radial malmquist CO2 emission performance index. Thus, they considered three different production technologies as contemporaneous production technology, the intertemporal production technology, and the global production technology.

First, they defined the contemporaneous environmental production technology of group R_h at period t as:

$$T_{R_h}^C = \{(K^t, L^t, F^t, E^t, C^t) : (K^t, L^t, F^t) \quad can \quad produce \quad (E^t, C^t)\}, \quad t = 1,...,T$$

In continue, Zhang and Choi defined the intertemporal environmental production technology as: $T_{R_h}^I = T_{R_h}^1 \cup T_{R_h}^2 \cup ... \cup T_{R_h}^T$. Finally, they supposed that there exist H distinct intertemporal technologies thus the global environmental production technology defined as: $T^G = T_{R_1}^I \cup T_{R_2}^I \cup ... \cup T_{R_H}^I$. Which means the global environmental production technology includes all intertemporal environmental production technologies. In accordance to the definition of the nonradial directional distance function the global nonradial directional distance function is defined as follows:

$$\vec{D}^G(.) = sup\{W^T \beta^G : ((K,L,F,E,C) + g.diag(\beta^G)) \in T^G\}$$

The authors noted that according to what presented six different NDD functions can be defined each of which used a data envelopment analysis model, as following:

$$\overrightarrow{D}^{d}(K^{s}, L^{s}, F^{s}, E^{s}, C^{s}; g) = \max \quad W_{k}\beta_{k}^{s} + W_{l}\beta_{l}^{s} + W_{f}\beta_{F}^{s} + W_{c}\beta_{c}^{s}$$

$$s.t. \qquad \sum_{n=1}^{N} z_{n}^{s} K_{n}^{s} \leq K_{n'} - \beta_{K}^{s} g_{K},$$

$$\sum_{n=1}^{N} z_{n}^{s} L_{n}^{s} \leq L_{n'} - \beta_{L}^{s} g_{L},$$

$$\sum_{n=1}^{N} z_{n}^{s} F_{n}^{s} \leq F_{n'} - \beta_{F}^{s} g_{F}, \qquad (11)$$

$$\sum_{n=1}^{N} z_{n}^{s} E_{n}^{s} \geq E_{n'} + \beta_{E}^{s} g_{E},$$

$$\sum_{n=1}^{N} z_{n}^{s} C_{n}^{s} = C_{n'} - \beta_{c}^{s} g_{C},$$

$$z_{n}^{s} \geq 0, \quad n = 1, ..., N,$$

$$\beta_{K}^{s}, \beta_{L}^{s}, \beta_{F}^{s}, \beta_{E}^{s}, \beta_{C}^{s} \geq 0.$$

Need to be noted that $s = t, t+1$ and d can be contemporaneous, intertemporal, or global. Note that there can be considered six different total factor performance indexes with $s = t, t+1$ and d can be contemporaneous, intertemporal, or global as follows:

$$TCPI^{d}(K^{s}, L^{s}, F^{s}, E^{s}, C^{s}) = [\frac{(C - \beta_{C}^{d*}C) / (E + \beta_{E}^{d*}E)}{C / E}]^{s} = (\frac{1 - \beta_{C}^{d*}}{1 + \beta_{E}^{d*}})$$

Finally, the non-radial malmquist CO2 emission performance index based on the set T^{G} defined as follows:

$$MNMCPI(K^{s}, L^{s}, F^{s}, E^{s}, C^{s}) = \frac{TCPI^{G}(K^{t+1}, L^{t+1}, F^{t+1}, E^{t+1}, C^{t+1})}{TCPI^{G}(K^{t}, L^{t}, F^{t}, E^{t}, C^{t})}$$

The decomposition of this index can be considered as follows:

$$MNMCPI(K^s, L^s, F^s, E^s, C^s) = [\frac{TE^{t+1}}{TE^t}] * [\frac{BPR^{t+1}}{BPR^t}] * [\frac{TGR^{t+1}}{TGR^t}] = EC * BPC * TGR$$

Note that, *EC*, *BPC* and *TGR* respectively means *efficiency Change*, *Best Practicegap Change* and *Tecnological Change*. Note that $EC >$ (or $<$) 1 means efficiency gain (or loss), $BPC >$ (or $<$) 1 means the contemporaneous technology frontier shifts toward (or far away from) the intertemporal technology frontier and $TGR >$ (or $<$) 1 means a decrease (increase) in the technology gap between the intertemporal technology for a specific group and the global technology.

Nicola et al. (2013) analyzed the productivity of Italian airports management companies. In doing so, they used a data envelopment analysis malmquist index which is also contains a quality component. The demonstrated the methodology for the first time to the airport industry.

Consider x to be the inputs, y the desirable outputs, and a level of quality. Then, at time t, the production technology of each airport demonstrated as follows:

$$S^t = \{(y^t, a^t, x^t) \mid x^t \quad can \quad produce \quad y^t \quad at \quad the \quad levelof \quad a^t\}$$

They considered the Shepard's distance function, introduced by Shepard, [86], as follows in which the maximum decrease in x^t is desired considering the output set (y^t, a^t):

$$D_i^t(y^t, a^t, x^t) = sup\{\lambda : (x^t / \lambda, y^t, a^t) \in S^t\}$$

Finally, Nicola et al. introduced the input-based productivity index considering periods t and $t+1$ is as follows:

$$M = M_i^{t,t+1}(y^{t+1}, a^{t+1}, x^{t+1}, y^t, a^t, x^t) = \frac{D_i^t(y^{t+1}, a^{t+1}, x^{t+1})D_i^{t+1}(y^{t+1}, a^{t+1}, x^{t+1})}{D_i^t(y^t, a^t, x^{t1})D_i^{t+1}(y^t, a^t, x^t)}(1/2)$$

Alvarez and Blazquez (2014), in their paper, considering the road network on private regional activity, measured the economic effects of investment. They used panel data in the period of 27 years and by considering the nonparametric frontier techniques, Data Envelopment Analysis, tried to reach the malmquist productivity index. Therefore, they declared that in this way they are enabling to examine the evaluation of the productivity growth.

In their paper Ahn and Min (2014) tried to evaluate the comparative efficiencies of international airports for a multi-year period using data envelopment analysis intended for dynamic benchmarking and malmquist productivity index built on time-series analysis. In their study Ahn and Min showed that the productivity of an airport was influenced by exogenous factors such as shifts in government policies and technological advances rather than endogenous factors driven by improvements in managerial practices.

In their study, Essid et al. (2014), measured the productivity of a sample of 189 Tunisian high schools. They decomposed the malmquist productivity index into technical efficiency, scale efficiency and technological progress and this matter let them associate each component of the productivity variation to its source.

Essid et al. proposed the decomposition which includes the quasi-fixed inputs as follows:

$$M(X_{t_1}, Z_{t_1}, Y_{t_1}, X_{t_2}, Z_{t_2}, Y_{t_2}) =$$

$$[\frac{D^{t_2}(X_{t_2}, Z_{t_2}, Y_{t_2} \mid VRS)}{D^{t_1}(X_{t_1}, Z_{t_1}, Y_{t_1} \mid VRS)}] \times [\frac{D^{t_1}(X_{t_2}, Z_{t_2}, Y_{t_2} \mid VRS)}{D^{t_2}(X_{t_2}, Z_{t_2}, Y_{t_2} \mid VRS)} \times \frac{D^{t_1}(X_{t_1}, Z_{t_1}, Y_{t_1} \mid VRS)}{D^{t_2}(X_{t_1}, Z_{t_1}, Y_{t_1} \mid VRS)}]^{(1/2)} \times$$

$$\{[\frac{D^{t_1}(X_{t_2}, Z_{t_2}, Y_{t_2} \mid CRS) / D^{t_1}(X_{t_2}, Z_{t_2}, Y_{t_2} \mid VRS)}{D^{t_1}(X_{t_1}, Z_{t_1}, Y_{t_1} \mid CRS) / D^{t_1}(X_{t_1}, Z_{t_1}, Y_{t_1} \mid VRS)}] \times$$

$$[\frac{D^{t_2}(X_{t_2}, Z_{t_2}, Y_{t_2} \mid CRS) / D^{t_2}(X_{t_2}, Z_{t_2}, Y_{t_2} \mid VRS)}{D^{t_2}(X_{t_1}, Z_{t_1}, Y_{t_1} \mid CRS) / D^{t_2}(X_{t_1}, Z_{t_1}, Y_{t_1} \mid VRS)}]\}^{(1/2)}$$

They noted that the first term is "technical efficiency change ($TE\Delta$)", the second and the third are, respectively, "the geometric mean of technological change over the same period ($T\Delta$)" and "measures the contribution of the returns to scale to the productivity change ($SE\Delta$)".

The malmquist index is smaller than one, when productivity of a given unit increases between t_1 and t_2, it is equal to one when the productivity is constant and larger than one when productivity decreases.

Kao and Liu (2014) claimed that measuring the efficiency of a set of decision-making units while considering multiple periods may ignores the operations of individual periods and many inefficient units will be evaluated as efficient. Thus for better measuring efficiencies of units in this case, Kao and Liu proposed a method which uses a relational network model to consider the operations of individual periods. They used this method for measuring the efficiency change of 22 Taiwanese commercial banks.

Considering what proposed in literature by Kao for the multi-period system in which each period is viewed as a process of a network system, and then it resembles the structure of a parallel production system with q processes.

$$E_k^{KL} = \max \quad \sum_{r=1}^{s} u_r Y_{rk}$$

$$s.t. \quad \sum_{r=1}^{s} u_r Y_{rk} - \sum_{i=1}^{m} v_i X_{ik} \leq 0, \qquad j = 1,...,n,$$

$$\sum_{r=1}^{s} u_r Y_{rk}^{(P)} - \sum_{i=1}^{m} v_i X_{ik}^{(P)} \leq 0, \qquad p = 1,...,q, j = 1,...,n,$$

$$u_r \geq \varepsilon, v_i \geq \varepsilon, \qquad r = 1,...,s, i = 1,...,m.$$

$$(12)$$

Taking into account the third constraint, the optimal solution of this model will not exceed that obtained from CCR model. Calculating the optimal solution of this model, u^*, v^*, the overall efficiency and the period efficiency, respectively denoted as E_k^{KL} and $E_k^{(P)}$, can be obtained as follows:

$$E_k^{KL} = \frac{\sum_{r=1}^{s} u_r^* Y_{rk}}{\sum_{i=1}^{m} v_i^* X_{ik}} = \sum_{r=1}^{s} u_r^* Y_{rk}$$

$$E_k^{(P)} = \frac{\displaystyle\sum_{r=1}^{s} u_r^* Y_{rk}^{(P)}}{\displaystyle\sum_{i=1}^{m} v_i^* X_{ik}^{(P)}}, \quad p = 1,...,q$$

They noted that the set of selected weights by each unit is the most advantageous one to calculate the overall efficiency, and they may not be the same for all decision making units.

Kao and Liu considered $\hat{E}_k^{(t)}$ as the efficiency of DMU_k based of the global frontier in time t.

$$\hat{E}_k^{(t)} = \max \quad \sum_{r=1}^{s} u_r Y_{rk}^{(t)}$$

$$s.t. \qquad \sum_{i=1}^{m} v_i X_{ik}^{(t)} = 1,$$

$$\sum_{r=1}^{s} u_r Y_{rk}^{(P)} - \sum_{i=1}^{m} v_i X_{ik}^{(P)} \leq 0, \quad p = 1,...,q, j = 1,...,n,$$

$$u_r \geq \varepsilon, v_i \geq \varepsilon, \qquad\qquad r = 1,...,s, i = 1,...,m.$$

(13)

According to this fact that all of the observations are taken into consideration thus $\hat{E}_k^{(t)}$ is less than or equal one. Thus, they proposed the global MPI of DMU_k between periods t and $t+h$ is as follows:

$$MPI_k^{t,t+h} = \hat{E}_k^{(t+h)} / \hat{E}_k^{(t)}$$

It should be noted that if $MPI_k^{t,t+h} > 1$ thus the performance of DMU_k has improved over this period of time and $MPI_k^{t,t+h} < 1$ shows that this unit has made a regress.

Kao and Hwang (2014) noted that two stage data envelopment analysis models measure the overall performance while considering a specified period of time and ignoring the variations in different periods. They worked on developing a multi period two stage data envelopment analysis model while considering operations of individual periods in order to measure the overall and period efficiencies at the same time. An important issue is that they have proved that the overall efficiency of a decision making unit in the specified period of time can be decomposed into the process efficiency of each period. Thus, the obtained efficiencies used to calculate a common weight global malmquist productivity index between two periods. Kao and Hwang noted in that the overall malmquist productivity index then can be considered as the product of the two processes of malmquist productivity indexes.

Kao and Hwang proposed the following model for efficiency evaluation in time t as follows:

$$
\begin{aligned}
\tilde{E}_k^{s(t)} = \max \quad & \sum_{r=1}^{s} u_r Y_{rk}^{(t)} \\
s.t. \quad & \sum_{i=1}^{m} v_i X_{ik}^{(t)} = 1, \\
& \sum_{f=1}^{g} w_f Z_{fj}^{(P)} - \sum_{i=1}^{m} v_i X_{ij}^{(P)} \leq 0, \quad p = 1,...,q, j = 1,...,n, \\
& \sum_{r=1}^{s} u_r Y_{rj}^{(P)} - \sum_{f=1}^{g} w_f Z_{fj}^{(P)} \leq 0, \quad i = 1,...,m, f = 1,...,g, \\
& u_r \geq \varepsilon, v_i \geq \varepsilon, w_f \geq \varepsilon, \quad r = 1,...,s, i = 1,...,m., f = 1,...,g.
\end{aligned}
$$

(14)

Thus they defined the global malmquist productivity index as follows:

$$
MPI^{s(t,h)} = \frac{\tilde{E}_k^{s(h)}}{\tilde{E}_k^{s(t)}}
$$

The authors utilized this model in the non-life insurance industry in Taiwan and then explained why some companies performed unsatisfactorily in the specified period of time.

Chen et al. (2014) studied alterations in productivity of general insurance firms in Malaysia. Their main aim was to examine the impact of intellectual capital on changes in productivity. Chen et al. proposed a two stage data envelopment analysis method of productivity index in the first stage and then tried to bootstraps malmquist productivity index to evaluate changes in productivity. Secondly, they examined the impact of intellectual capital on changes in productivity.

Bassem (2014) considered an application and tried to investigate productivity changes of 33 Middle East and North Africa micro finance institutions using the malmquist productivity index method and a balanced panel data set.

Wang et al. (2014) in their paper assessed chemical industry companies with environmental expenditures to find the better financial performance. They use data envelopment analysis technique for efficiency evaluation of companies. They also utilized malmquist productivity index to evaluate productivity of these companies and then aimed to find statistically significance of these firms. Moreover, for demonstrating the provided method they analyzed the U.S. chemical industry.

CONCLUSION

As malmquist productivity index is an important indicator for managers used for better decision-making in the organizations under their authority. In this chapter it is tried to consider most of the subjects discussed malmquist productivity index, from the oldest ones to the newest, provided in literature of data envelopment analysis technique. The aim of the authors of this chapter is to gather different papers about malmquist productivity index to give a chance for the researchers to have information about variety aspects of this issue to better improve this index for applicational and theoretical issues. Some of the subjects gathered here are based upon introducing a new distance function for MPI, which can affect this index well in different applications and examples: Lozano-Vivas and Humphrey (2002), Krishnasamy (2003) and Tortosa-Ausina et al. (2008) explored productivity growth and productive efficiency for different banks, Chen (2003) considered Chinese major industries, Galanopoulos et al. (2004) research in agricultural sectors in the EU countries, Tsekouras et al. (2004) provided an application in Greek prefectural training councils, Estache et al. (2004) assessed Greek prefectural training councils infrastructure, Hwang and Chang (2003) used an example in various hotels, Barros and Alves (2004) considered Portuguese retail store, Maniadakis and Thanassoulis (2004) provided models for cost mamquist to be used in hospitals, Can (2004) taken into account rural households, Chang et al. [56] considered largest US public accounting firms as an example, Chang et al. (2009) investigates productivity growth of the largest CPA firms in the US, Sözen et al. (2010), tried to evaluate thermal power plants, Hosseinzadeh Lotfi et al. (2010) used the Malamquist index in a powerhouse collection, Fallahi et al. (2011) considered productivity change in power electric generation management companies, Macpherson et al. (2013) used malmquist indices for assessment of the predicted environmental performance, Gitto and Mancuso (2012) assessed the operational performance of 28 Italian airports, Qazi and Zhao Yulin (2012) considered fifteen hi-tech industries, Costa (2012) assessed the efficiency and productivity of Intellectual Capital, Chou et al. (2012) studied IT industries for 19 Organization of Economic Cooperation and Development, Chang et al. (2013) considered an empirical study of corporate sustainability conducted at the industry-level, Egilmez and McAvoy (2013) evaluated productivity and relative efficiency of U.S. states, Asche et al. (2013) assessed total factor productivity change in the

Norwegian salmon aquaculture sector, Ahn and Min (2014) assessed the comparative efficiencies of international airports, Essid et al. (2014) measured the productivity of a sample of 189 Tunisian high schools, Chen et al. (2014) studies productivity of general insurance firms in Malaysia, Bassem (2014) investigated productivity changes of 33 Middle East and North Africa micro finance institutions, Wang et al. (2014) evaluated chemical industry companies, Hseu and Shang (2005) assessed the productivity of pulp and paper industry in OECD countries. In some other paper it is tried to moot and make improvements for better considering and evaluating the situations, such as: Zaim (2004) taken into consideration air pollution which is a bad output presented the method, Ball et al. (2005) constructed an alternative productivity growth measure using activity analysis, Odeck (2006) considered a bootstap method for investigating the target achievements of the operational units of the Norwegian Public Roads Administration, Kutana and Yigit (2007) provided a stochastic endogenous growth model, Kortelainen (2008) proposed a new method for environmental performance analysis, Silva-Portela and Thanassoulis (2006) claimed that there exist some bias in the analysis of total factor productivity change using distance functions, Abbaspour et al. (2009) considered non-discretionary indicator into analysis, Odeck (2009) considered combination of DEA and a malmquist index with a bootstrap method, Guan and Chen (2009) provided a new methodological framework for effectively measuring the production frontier performance, Kao (2010) provided a method for calculating the global malmquist productivity index, Portela and Thanassoulis (2010) developed the indicator of productivity change with negative data, Wang and Lan (2011) tried to measuring malmquist index using both optimistic and pessimistic data envelopment analysis simoultaniously,Zhang (2011) considered the malmquist–Luenberger(ML) productivity index for assessing China's growth, Assaf and Barros (2011) used the malmquist index with bias correction, Emrouznejad et al. (2011) provided the profit malmquist productivity index, Jahantighi et al. (2012) taken into account MPI in DMU with series structural process, Aparicio et al. (2013) addressed a new drawback of the malmquist–Luenberger, Sueyoshi and Goto (2013) studied a new use of DEA for environmental assessment which examines the degree of a frontier shift among multiple periods, Hosseinzadeh Lotfi et al. (2013) invatigated for the regress and progress of a DMU in different periods considering the present value of money, Hosseinzadeh Lotfi et al. (2013) considered this shortcoming of data envelopment analysis in efficiency assessment in successive periods and provided a combined model for it, Menegaki (2013) consider malmquist index with a panel data set, Zhang and Choi (2013) investigated for measuring dynamic changes in total-factor CO_2 emission, Nicola et al. (2013) analyzed the productivity of Italian airports management companies considering a quality component, Kao and Liu (2014) taken into consideration measuring the efficiency of a set of decision making units in multiple periods, Kao and Hwang (2014) calculated a common-weight global malmquist productivity index between two periods. In terms of total considerations different introduced indexes try to better analyze variety aspects about what happened in real world problems.

REFERENCES

Abbaspour, M., Hosseinzadeh Lotfi, F., Karbassi, A. R., Roayaei, E., & Nikomaram, H. (2009). Development of the Group Malmquist Productivity Index on non-discretionary Factors. *International Journal of Environmental of Research, 3*, 109–116.

Ahn, Y., & Min, H. (2014). Evaluating the multi-period operating efficiency of international airports using data envelopment analysis and the Malmquist productivity index. *Journal of Air Transport Management, 39*, 12–22. doi:10.1016/j.jairtraman.2014.03.005

Althin, R. (2001). Measurement of Productivity Changes: Two Malmquist Index Approahes. *Journal of Productivity Analysis, 16*(2), 107–128. doi:10.1023/A:1011682625976

Alvarez, I. C., & Blazquez, R. (2014). The influence of the road network on private productivity measures using Data Envelopment Analysis: A case study from Spain. *Transportation Research Part A, Policy and Practice, 65*, 33–43. doi:10.1016/j.tra.2014.04.002

Aparicio, J., Pastor, J. T., & Zofio, J. L. (2013). On the inconsistency of the Malmquist. Luenberger index. *European Journal of Operational Research, 229*(3), 738–742. doi:10.1016/j.ejor.2013.03.031

Arcelus, F. J., & Arozena, P. (1999). Measuring sectoral productivity across time and across countries. *European Journal of Operational Research, 119*(2), 254–266. doi:10.1016/S0377-2217(99)00129-0

Asche, F., Guttormsen, A. G., & Nielsen, R. (2013). Future challenges for the maturing Norwegian salmon aquaculture industry: An analysis of total factor productivity change from 1996 to 2008. *Aquaculture (Amsterdam, Netherlands)*, 396–399.

Asmild, M., Paradi, J., Aggarwall, V., & Schhaffnit, C. (2004). Combining DEA Window Analysis with the Malmquist Index Approach in a Study of the Canadian Banking Industry. *Journal of Productivity Analysis, 21*(1), 67–89. doi:10.1023/B:PROD.0000012453.91326.ec

Asmild, M., & Tam, F. (2007). Estimating global frontier shifts and global Malmquist indices. *Journal of Productivity Analysis*, *27*(2), 137–148. doi:10.1007/s11123-006-0028-0

Assaf, A. G., & Barros, C. (2011). Performance analysis of the Gulf hotel industry: A Malmquist index with bias correction. *International Journal of Hospitality Management*, *30*(4), 819–826. doi:10.1016/j.ijhm.2011.01.002

Atkinson, S. E., & Cornwell, C. (1998). Estimating Radial Measures of Productivity Growth: Frontier vs Non-Frontier Approaches. *Journal of Productivity Analysis*, *10*(1), 35–46. doi:10.1023/A:1018394231538

Ball, E., Fare, R., Grosskopf, S., & Zaim, O. (2005). Accounting for externalities in the measurement of productivity growth: The Malmquist cost productivity measure. *Structural Change and Economic Dynamics*, *16*(3), 374–394. doi:10.1016/j.strueco.2004.04.008

Banker, R. D., Charnes, A., & Cooper, W. W. (1984). Some models for estimating technical and scale efficiencies in data envelopment analysis. *Management Science*, *30*(9), 1078–1092. doi:10.1287/mnsc.30.9.1078

Barros, C. P., & Alves, C. (2004). An empirical analysis of productivity growth in a Portuguese retail chain using Malmquist productivity index. *Journal of Retailing and Consumer Services*, *11*(5), 269–278. doi:10.1016/S0969-6989(03)00053-5

Bassem, B. S. (2014). Total factor productivity change of MENA microfinance institutions: A Malmquist productivity index approach. *Economic Modelling*, *39*, 182–189. doi:10.1016/j.econmod.2014.02.035

Briec, W., & Kerstens, K. (2004). A Luenberger-Hicks-Moorsteen productivity indicator: Its relation to the Hicks-Moorsteen productivity index and the Luenberger productivity indicator. *Economic Theory*, *23*(4), 925–939. doi:10.1007/s00199-003-0403-2

Camanho, A. S., & Dyson, R. G. (2006). Data envelopment analysis and Malmquist indices for measuring group performance. *Journal of Productivity Analysis*, *26*(1), 35–49. doi:10.1007/s11123-006-0004-8

Can, L. (2004). Measurement and Analysis of Production Performance of Rural Households in Jinzhai County. Anhui Province. *Forestry Studies in China*, *6*(3), 20–27. doi:10.1007/s11632-004-0036-y

Caves, D. W., Christensen, L. R., & Diewert, W. E. (1982). The economic theory of index numbers and the measurement of input, output and productivity. *Econometrica, 50*(6), 1393–1414. doi:10.2307/1913388

Chang, D., Kuo, L. R., & Chen, Y.-. (2013). Industrial changes in corporate sustainability performance e an empirical overview using data envelopment analysis. *Journal of Cleaner Production, 56*, 147–155. doi:10.1016/j.jclepro.2011.09.015

Chang, H., Choy, H. L., Cooper, W. W., Parker, B. R., & Ruefli, T. W. (2009). Measuring productivity growth, technical progress, and efficiency changes of CPA firms prior to, and following the Sarbanes–Oxley Act. *Socio-Economic Planning Sciences*, 1–8.

Chang, H., Choy, H. L., Cooper, W. W., & Ruefli, T. W. (2009). Using Malmquist Indexes to measure changes in the productivity and efficiency of US accounting firms before and after the Sarbanes-Oxley Act. *Omega, 37*(5), 951–960. doi:10.1016/j.omega.2008.08.004

Chang, P., Hwangt, S., & Cheng, W. (1995). Using Data Envelopment Analysis to Measure the Achievement and Change of Regional Development in Taiwan. *Journal of Environmental Management, 43*(1), 49–66. doi:10.1016/S0301-4797(95)90319-4

Charnes, A., Cooper, W.W., Rhodes, E. (1978). Measureing the efficiency of decision making units. *European Journal of Operational Research, 2*, 429-444.

Chen, F., Liu, Z., & Kwehc, Q. L. (2014). Intellectual capital and productivity of Malaysian general insurers. *Economic Modelling, 36*, 413–420. doi:10.1016/j.econmod.2013.10.008

Chen, Y. (2003). A non-radial Malmquist productivity index with an illustrative application to Chinese major industries. *International Journal of Production Economics, 83*(1), 27–35. doi:10.1016/S0925-5273(02)00267-0

Chen, Y., & Ali, A. I. (2004). DEA Malmquist productivity measure: New insights with an application to computer industry. *European Journal of Operational Research, 159*(1), 239–249. doi:10.1016/S0377-2217(03)00406-5

Chou, Y., Shao, B., & Lin, W. T. (2012). Performance evaluation of production of IT capital goods across OECD countries: A stochastic frontier approach to Malmquist index. *Decision Support Systems, 54*(1), 173–184. doi:10.1016/j.dss.2012.05.003

Costa, R. (2012). Assessing Intellectual Capital efficiency and productivity: An application to the Italian yacht manufacturing sector. *Expert Systems with Applications, 39*(8), 7255–7261. doi:10.1016/j.eswa.2012.01.099

De Nicola, A., Gitto, S., & Mancuso, P. (2013). Airport quality and productivity changes: A Malmquist index decomposition assessment. *Transportation Research Part E, Logistics and Transportation Review, 58*, 67–75. doi:10.1016/j.tre.2013.07.001

Egilmez, G., & McAvoy, D. (2013). Benchmarking road safety of U.S. states: A DEA-based Malmquist productivity index approach. *Accident; Analysis and Prevention, 53*, 55–64. doi:10.1016/j.aap.2012.12.038 PMID:23376545

Emrouznejad, A., Rostamy-Malkhalifeh, M., Hatami-Marbini, A., Tavana, M., & Aghayi, N. (2011). An overall profit Malmquist productivity index with fuzzy and interval data. *Mathematical and Computer Modelling, 54*(11-12), 2827–2838. doi:10.1016/j.mcm.2011.07.003

Essid, H., Ouellette, P., & Vigeant, S. (2014). Productivity, efficiency, and technical change of Tunisian schools: A bootstrapped Malmquist approach with quasi-fixed inputs. *Omega, 42*(1), 88–97. doi:10.1016/j.omega.2013.04.001

Estache, A., de la Fé, B. T., & Trujillo, L. (2004). Sources of efficiency gains in port reform: A DEA decomposition of a Malmquist TFP index for Mexico. *Utilities Policy, 12*(4), 221–230. doi:10.1016/j.jup.2004.04.013

Fallahi, A., Ebrahimi, R., & Ghaderi, S. F. (2011). Measuring efficiency and productivity change in power electric generation management companies by using data envelopment analysis: A case study. *Energy, 36*(11), 6398–6405. doi:10.1016/j.energy.2011.09.034

Fare, R., & Zelenyuk, V. (2003). On aggregate Farrell efficiency scores. *European Journal of Operational Research, 146*(3), 615–620. doi:10.1016/S0377-2217(02)00259-X

Farrell, M. J. (1957). The measurement of productive efficiency. *Journal of the Royal Statistical Society. Series A (General), 120*(3), 253–281. doi:10.2307/2343100

Fuentes, H. J., Grifell-Tatje, E., & Perelman, S. (2001). A Parametric Distance Function Approach for Malmquist Productivity Index Estimation. *Journal of Productivity Analysis, 15*(2), 79–94. doi:10.1023/A:1007852020847

Galanopoulos, K., Karagiannis, G., & Koutroumanidis, T. (2004). Malmquist Productivity Index Estimates for European Agriculture in the 1990s Operational Research. *International Journal (Toronto, Ont.), 4*, 73–91.

Gitto, S., & Mancuso, P. (2012). Bootstrapping the Malmquist indexes for Italian airports. *International Journal of Production Economics, 135*(1), 403–411. doi:10.1016/j.ijpe.2011.08.014

Giuffrida, A. (1999). Productivity and efficiency changes in primary care: A Malmquist index approach. *Health Care Management Science*, 2(1), 11–26. doi:10.1023/A:1019067223945 PMID:10916598

Grifell-Tatje, E., & Lovell, C. A. K. (1995). A note on the Malmquist productivity index. *Economics Letters*, 47(2), 169–175. doi:10.1016/0165-1765(94)00497-P

Grifell-Tatjé, E., & Lovell, C. A. K. (1997). A DEA-based analysis of productivity change and intertemporal managerial performa. *Annals of Operations Research*, 73, 177–189. doi:10.1023/A:1018925127385

Grifell-Tatjé, E., Lovell, C.A.K. (1999). A Generalized Malmquist productivity index. *Sociedad de Estadistica e Investigación Operativa Top*, 7, 81-101.

Grifell-Tatjé, E., Lovell, C. A. K., & Pastor, J. T. (1998). A Quasi-Malmquist Productivity Index. *Journal of Productivity Analysis*, 10(1), 7–20. doi:10.1023/A:1018329930629

Guan, J., & Chen, K. (2009). Modeling macro- $R \& D$ production frontier performance: An application to Chinese province-level .*Scientometrics*.

Hosseinzadeh Lotfi, F., Aryanezhad, M. B., Ebnrasoul, S. A., & Najafi, S. E. (2010). Evaluating Productivity in the Units of the Powerhouse Collection by Using Malmquist Index. *Journal of International Management*, 4, 29–42.

Hosseinzadeh Lotfi, F., Jahanshahloo, G. R., Vaez-Ghasemi, M., & Moghaddas, Z. (2013). Modified Malmquist Productivity Index Based on Present Time Value of Money.Journal of Applied Mathematics.

Hosseinzadeh Lotfi, F., Jahanshahloo, G.R., Vaez-Ghasemi, M., & Moghaddas, Z. (2013). Periodic efficiency measurement for achieving correct efficiency among several terms of evaluation. *Int. J. Operational Research*.

Hseu, J., & Shang, J. (2005). Productivity changes of pulp and paper industry in OECD countries, 1991–2000: A non-parametric Malmquist approach. *Forest Policy and Economics*, 7(3), 411–422. doi:10.1016/j.forpol.2003.07.002

Hwang, S., & Chang, T. (2003). Using data envelopment analysis to measure hotel managerial efficiency change in Taiwan. *Tourism Management*, 24(4), 357–369. doi:10.1016/S0261-5177(02)00112-7

Jahantighi, M. A., Moghaddas, Z., & Vaez Ghasemi, M. (2012). Two-stage Malmquist Productivity Index with Intermediate Products. *Int. J. Industrial Mathematics*, 4, 31–40.

Jimenez, J. S., Chaparro, F. P., & Smith, P. C. (2003). Evaluating the introduction of a quasi-market in community care. *Socio-Economic Planning Sciences*, *37*(1), 1–13. doi:10.1016/S0038-0121(02)00042-3

Kao, C. (2010). Malmquist productivity index based on common-weights DEA:The case of Taiwan forests after reorganization. *Omega*, *38*(6), 484–491. doi:10.1016/j.omega.2009.12.005

Kao, C., & Hwang, S. (2014). Multi-period efficiency and Malmquist productivity index in two-stage production systems. *European Journal of Operational Research*, *232*(3), 512–521. doi:10.1016/j.ejor.2013.07.030

Kao, C., & Liu, S. (2014). Multi-period efficiency measurement in data envelopment analysis: The case of Taiwanese commercial banks. *Omega*, *47*, 90–98. doi:10.1016/j.omega.2013.09.001

Kim, J. W., & Lee, H. K. (2004). Embodied and disembodied international spillovers of $R \& D$. *Technovation*, *24*(4), 359–368. doi:10.1016/S0166-4972(02)00096-2

Kortelainen, M. (2008). Dynamic environmental performance analysis: A Malmquist index approach. *Ecological Economics*, *64*(4), 701–715. doi:10.1016/j.ecolecon.2007.08.001

Krishnasamy, G., Hanuum Ridzwa, A., & Perumal, V. (2003). Banking and Finance, Malaysian Post Merger Banks' Productivity: Application of Malmquist Productivity Index. *Managerial Finance, 30*.

Kutana, A. M., & Yigit, T. M. (2007). productivity growth and real convergence. *European Economic Review*, *51*(6), 1370–1395. doi:10.1016/j.euroecorev.2006.11.001

Lin, C., & Berg, S. V. (2008). Incorporating Service Quality into Yardstick Regulation: An Application to the Peru Water Sector. *Review of Industrial Organization*, *32*(1), 53–75. doi:10.1007/s11151-008-9160-5

Liu, F., & Wang, P.-. (2008). DEA Malmquist productivity measure: Taiwanese semiconductor companies. *International Journal of Production Economics*, *1*(1), 367–379. doi:10.1016/j.ijpe.2007.03.015

Lozano-Vivas, A., & Humphrey, D. B. (2002). Bias in Malmquist index and cost function productivity measurement in banking. *International Journal of Production Economics*, *76*(2), 177–188. doi:10.1016/S0925-5273(01)00162-1

Macpherson, A. J., Principe, P. P., & Mehaffey, M. (2013). Using Malmquist Indices to evaluate environmental impacts of alternative land development scenarios. *Ecological Indicators*, *34*, 296–303. doi:10.1016/j.ecolind.2013.05.009

Maniadakis, N., & Thanassoulis, E. (2004). A cost Malmquist productivity index. *European Journal of Operational Research, 154*(2), 396–409. doi:10.1016/S0377-2217(03)00177-2

Menegaki, A. N. (2013). Growth and renewable energy in Europe: Benchmarking with data envelopment analysis. *Renewable Energy, 60*, 363–369. doi:10.1016/j.renene.2013.05.042

Mussard, S., & Peypoch, N. (2006). On multi-decomposition of the aggregate Malmquist productivity index. *Economics Letters, 91*(3), 436–443. doi:10.1016/j.econlet.2006.01.015

Odeck, J. (2000). Assessing the relative efficiency and productivity growth of vehicle inspection services: An application of DEA and Malmquist indices. *European Journal of Operational Research, 126*(3), 501–514. doi:10.1016/S0377-2217(99)00305-7

Odeck, J. (2006). Identifying traffic safety best practice: An application of DEA and Malmquist indices. *Omega, 34*(1), 28–40. doi:10.1016/j.omega.2004.07.017

Odeck, J. (2009). Statistical precision of DEA and Malmquist indices: A bootstrap application to Norwegian grain producers. *Omega, 37*(5), 1007–1017. doi:10.1016/j.omega.2008.11.003

Oliveira, M. M., Gaspar, M. B., Paixao, J. P., & Camanho, A. S. (2009). Productivity change of the artisanal fishing fleet in Portugal: A Malmquist index analysis. *Fisheries Research, 95*(2-3), 189–197. doi:10.1016/j.fishres.2008.08.020

Pastor, J. T., & Lovell, C. A. K. (2005). A global Malmquist productivity index. *Economics Letters, 88*(2), 266–271. doi:10.1016/j.econlet.2005.02.013

Pires, H. M., & Fernandes, E. (2012). Malmquist financial efficiency analysis for airlines. *Transportation Research Part E, Logistics and Transportation Review, 48*(5), 1049–1055. doi:10.1016/j.tre.2012.03.007

Portela, C. A. S., & Thanassoulis, E. (2010). Malmquist-type indices in the presence of negative data: An application to bank branches Maria. *Journal of Banking & Finance, 34*(7), 1472–1483. doi:10.1016/j.jbankfin.2010.01.004

Qazi, A. Q., & Yulin, Z. (2012). Productivity Measurement of Hi-tech Industry of China Malmquist Productivity Index DEA Approach. *Procedia Economics and Finance, 1*, 330–336. doi:10.1016/S2212-5671(12)00038-X

Raa, T. T., & Mohnen, P. (2002). Neoclassical Growth Accounting and Frontier Analysis: A Synthesis. *Journal of Productivity Analysis, 18*(2), 111–128. doi:10.1023/A:1016558816247

Raab, R. L., & Feroz, E. H. (2007). A productivity growth accounting approach to the ranking of developing and developed nations. *The International Journal of Accounting, 42*(4), 396–415. doi:10.1016/j.intacc.2007.09.004

Rebelo, J., Mendes, V. (2000). Malmquist Indices of Productivity Change in Portuguese Banking: The Deregulation Period. *IAER, 6.*

Shepard, R. W. (1970). *Theory of Cost and Production Functions.* Princeton, NJ: Princeton University Press.

Silva Portela, M. C. A. (2006). Emmanuel Thanassoulis, Malmquist indexes using a geometric distance function (GDF): Application to a sample of Portuguese bank branches. *Journal of Productivity Analysis, 25*(1-2), 25–41. doi:10.1007/s11123-006-7124-z

Sözen, A., Alp, I., & Özdemir, A. (2010). Assessment of operational and environmental performance of the thermal power plants in Turkey by using data envelopment analysis. *Energy Policy, 38*(10), 6194–6203. doi:10.1016/j.enpol.2010.06.005

Sueyoshi, T., & Goto, M. (2013). DEA environmental assessment in a time horizon: Malmquist index on fuel mix, electricity and CO. *Energy Economics, 40*, 370–382. doi:10.1016/j.eneco.2013.07.013

Telle, K., Larssonv, J. (2007). Do environmental regulations hamper productivity growth? How accounting for improvements of plants' environmental performance can change the conclusion. *Ecological Economics, 61*, 438–445.

Tortosa-Ausina, E., Grifell-Tatje, E., Armero, C., & Conesa, D. (2008). Sensitivity analysis of efficiency and Malmquist productivity indices: An application to Spanish savings banks. *European Journal of Operational Research, 184*(3), 1062–1084. doi:10.1016/j.ejor.2006.11.035

Tsekouras, K. D., Pantzios, C. J., & Karagiannis, G. (2004). Malmquist productivity index estimation with zero-value variables: The case of Greek prefectural training councils. *International Journal of Production Economics, 89*(1), 95–106. doi:10.1016/S0925-5273(03)00211-1

Uri, N. D. (2000). Measuring productivity change in telecommunications. *Telecommunications Policy, 24*(5), 439–452. doi:10.1016/S0308-5961(00)00030-6

Wang, C. (2007). Decomposing energy productivity change: A distance function approach. *Energy, 32*(8), 1326–1333. doi:10.1016/j.energy.2006.10.001

Wang, W., Lu, W., & Wang, S. (2014). The impact of environmental expenditures on performance in the U.S. chemical industry. *Journal of Cleaner Production, 64,* 447–456. doi:10.1016/j.jclepro.2013.10.022

Wang, Y., & Lan, Y. (2011). Measuring Malmquist productivity index: A new approach based on double frontiers data envelopment analysis. *Mathematical and Computer Modelling, 54*(11-12), 2760–2771. doi:10.1016/j.mcm.2011.06.064

Worthington, A. C. (1999). Malmquist indices of productivity change in Australian financial services. *Journal of International Financial Markets, Institutions and Money, 9*(3), 303–320. doi:10.1016/S1042-4431(99)00013-X

Zaim, O. (2004). Measuring environmental performance of state manufacturing through changes in pollution intensities: A DEA framework. *Ecological Economics, 48*(1), 37–47. doi:10.1016/j.ecolecon.2003.08.003

Zelenyuk, V. (2006). Aggregation of Malmquist productivity indexes. *European Journal of Operational Research, 174*(2), 1076–1086. doi:10.1016/j.ejor.2005.02.061

Zhang, C., Liu, H., Bressers, H. T. A., & Buchanan, K. S. (2011). Productivity growth and environmental regulations - accounting for undesirable outputs: Analysis of China's thirty provincial regions using the Malmquist–Luenberger index. *Ecological Economics, 70*(12), 2369–2379. doi:10.1016/j.ecolecon.2011.07.019

Zhang, N., & Choi, Y. (2013). Total-factor carbon emission performance of fossil fuel power plants in China: A metafrontier non-radial Malmquist index analysis. *Energy Economics, 40,* 549–559. doi:10.1016/j.eneco.2013.08.012

Chapter 7
Ranking Models in Data Envelopment Analysis Technique

Z. Moghaddas
Islamic Azad University, Qazvin Branch, Iran

M. Vaez-Ghasemi
Islamic Azad University, Rasht Branch, Iran

ABSTRACT

Data envelopment analysis as a mathematical technique formulated based on linear programming problems which enables decision makers to evaluate Decision-Making Units (DMUs) with multiple inputs and outputs. One of the important issue in DEA technique which is widely discussed by researchers is ranking efficient units. Since these units are not comparable among each other. Ranking DMUs is an important issue in theory and practice and many applications in this field are performed. Considering the ranking order senior managers try to better guiding the system. In literature there exist different ranking models each of which tries to make improvements in this subject. Many researchers try to make advances in theory of ranking units and overcome the difficulties exist in presented methods. Each of the existing ranking method has its own specialties and advantages. As each of the existing method can be viewed from different aspects, it is possible that somewhat these groups have overlapping with the others.

DOI: 10.4018/978-1-5225-0596-9.ch007

INTRODUCTION

Data envelopment analysis is a mathematical programming technique introduced by Charnes et al.(1978) and then developed Banker et al. (1984). With this technique managers can obtained the relative efficiency of a set of decision making units. This technique is based on evaluating units in optimistic viewpoint to acquire the weights of inputs and outputs. Data envelopment analysis as a mathematical tool was initiated by Charnes et al.(1978). They formulated a linear programming problem with which it is possible to evaluate decision-making units (DMUs) with multiple inputs and outputs. Note that in this technique it is not necessary to know the production function. Considering the optimal weights those units whoes weighted outputs to weighted inputs is equal to 1 are called best practice units. Since they used inputs and produced outputs efficiently. In accordance to the efficacy score obtained for each unit it is possible to rank them. But, efficient units are not ranked considering their efficiency scores. Thus, ranking efficient units gains an important attention in theory and application. Many researchers provided variety of ranking methods each of which rank efficient units from different aspects. Cross efficiency method is another important filed in ranking introduced by Sexton et al.(1986), Contreras (2012), Wu et al.(2012), Mustafa et al.(2013), Wu (2012), Rodder and Reucher (2011), Wang et al.(2011), Orkju and Bal (2011), Jafatri et al.(2011). Super efficiency is one of the important fields in ranking units as first introduced by Andersen and Petersen (1993), Mehrabian et al. (1999), Tone (2002), Jahanshahllo et al.(2004), Tohidi et al. (2004), chen et al.(2004), Amirteimoori et al.(2005), Pourkarimi et al.(2006), Li et al.(2007), Omrani et al.(2011), Gholam abri et. al (2011), Moazami Goudarzi et al.(2011), Fanati Rashidi et al.(2011), Ashrafi et al.(2011), Chen et a.(2011), Rezai Balf et al. (2012) and Chen et al.(2013). Considering Multi-criteria decision analysis (MCDA) is another significant fields in ranking, Hosseinzadeh Lotfi et al. (2013),Wang and Jiang (2012), Jablonsky (2011), Chen (2007), Strassert and Prato (2002) introduced different ranking methods. Benchmarking method is another important field in ranking units introduced by Torgersen et al. (1996), Jahanshahloo et al.(2007),Lu et al.(2009) and Deng et al. (2011). There exist other methods based on finding optimal weights in DEA analysis by Jahanshahloo et al.(2004), Hosseinzadeh Lotfi et al.(2005), Alirezaee and Afsharian (2007), Liu and Peng (2008), Wang et al.(2007),Wang et al (2011) and Reshadi et al. (2011). Considering the application of statistical tools for ranking units first suggested by Friedman and Sinuany-Stern (1997) and Mecit and Alp (2013). In addition to those papers discussed theatrical aspects of ranking efficient units, there exist different paper consider applicational issues such as, Martic and Savic (2001), Leeneer and Pastijn (2002), Estellita Lins et a.(2003), Paralikas and Lygeros (2005), Ali and Nakosteen (2005), Martin and Roman (2006), Raab and Feroz (2007), Wang et al.(2007), Williams and Van Dyke

(2007), Giokas and Pentzaropoulos (2008), Darvish et al.(2009), Lu and Lo (2009), Feroz et al.(2009), Sadjadi et al.(2011), Ramn et al.(2012) and Sitarz (2013). There exist some papers which review the ranking methods, as Adler et al. (2001), Adler et al.(2002), and Hosseinzade et al.(2013).

BACKGROUND

In order to performance evaluation of a set of decision making units, nowadays, data envelopment analysis technique is widely used. A brief introduction to this method is given in the following.

Consider a set of n decision making units is at hand each of which produces s outputs y_{rj} (r=1,..., s) using m inputs x_{ij} (i=1,..., m). Need to be noted that, $X_j \in R^m$ and $Y_j \in R^s$ are non-negative vectors. One of the popular definition of production possibility is $T = \{(X,Y) \mid X\ can produce\ Y\}$.

Considering variable and constant returns to scale form of technologies results $T = T_{BCC}$ and $T = T_{CCR}$ thus:

$$T_{BCC} = \{(x,y) \mid \quad x \geq \sum_{j=1}^{n}\lambda_j x_j, y \leq \sum_{j=1}^{n}\lambda_j y_j, \sum_{j=1}^{n}\lambda_j = 1, \lambda_j \geq 0, j = 1,...,n\}$$

$$T_{CCR} = \{(x,y) \mid \quad x \geq \sum_{j=1}^{n}\lambda_j x_j, y \leq \sum_{j=1}^{n}\lambda_j y_j, \lambda_j \geq 0, j = 1,...,n\}$$

Charnes et al. (1978), introduced CCR model as follows:

$$\min \quad \theta - \varepsilon(\sum_{i=1}^{m}s_i^- + \sum_{r=1}^{s}s_r^+)$$

$$s.t. \quad \sum_{j=1}^{n}\lambda_j x_{ij} + s_i^- = \theta x_{io}, \quad i = 1,...,m,$$

$$\sum_{j=1}^{n}\lambda_j y_{rj} - s_r^+ = y_{ro}, \quad r = 1,...,s, \tag{1}$$

$$\lambda_j \geq 0, \quad j = 1,...,n.$$

Banker et al. (1984), considered variable returns to scale form of technology and introduced BCC model as follows:

$$\min \quad \theta - \varepsilon\left(\sum_{i=1}^{m} s_i^- + \sum_{r=1}^{s} s_r^+\right)$$

$$\text{s.t.} \quad \sum_{j=1}^{n} \lambda_j x_{ij} + s_i^- = \theta x_{io}, \quad i = 1, \dots, m,$$

$$\sum_{j=1}^{n} \lambda_j y_{rj} - s_r^+ = y_{ro}, \quad r = 1, \dots, s, \qquad (2)$$

$$\sum_{j=1}^{n} \lambda_j = 1,$$

$$\lambda_j \geq 0, \quad j = 1, \dots, n.$$

Considering best practice or efficient units, those units with efficiency score equals one, an envelope is constructed over all the DMUs. Inefficient DMUs are those are not located onto this envelope which is also called efficient frontier.

Need to be noted that it is possible to project inefficient units onto the efficient via the following formulas.

$$\begin{cases} \hat{x}_{io} = \theta^* x_{io} - s_i^{-*} = \sum_{j=1}^{n} \lambda_j^* x_{ij}, \quad i = 1, \dots, m, \\[2em] \hat{y}_{ro} = y_{ro} + s_r^{+*} = \sum_{j=1}^{n} \lambda_j^* y_{rj}, \quad r = 1, \dots, s. \end{cases} \qquad (3)$$

Considering the dual theorem, it can be easily verified that the dual model is as follows:

$$\max \quad \sum_{r=1}^{s} u_r y_{ro}$$

$$\text{s.t.} \quad \sum_{i=1}^{m} v_i x_{io} = 1,$$

$$\sum_{r=1}^{s} u_r y_{rj} - \sum_{i=1}^{m} v_i x_{ij} \leq 0, \quad j = 1, \dots, n, \qquad (4)$$

$$U \geq 0, \quad V \geq 0.$$

Inefficient DMUs can be ranked (sorted) in accordance to the scores, but in the case of existing more than one efficient DMUs it is not possible to sort or rank these efficient units. Since all of them have the score equal to one. As a result of this, ranking efficient units are taken a great attention among researchers and also managers who what to make decision for the system under their control. Many researchers work on the issue of ranking efficiency DMUs from different aspect each of which has advantages or disadvantages. Many ranking models in context of data envelopment analysis are provided in the literature.

One of the important method of ranking units is cross-efficiency evaluation with which units are self and peer evaluated. Another method considers multiple-criteria decision methodologies as long as DEA technique. Another ranking method is based on the optimal weights obtained DEA model. The other technique is super efficiency method which is based on analyzing the changes of frontier while the unit under assessment is being excluded from the set of entire units. Another method ranks inefficient units considering proportional measures of inefficiency. The other method is based on the idea of being the benchmark for inefficient units. Another method is based upon the multivariate statistical techniques which is usually used after the DEA classification. In the following section some of the ranking models are reviewed.

MAIN FOCUS OF THE CHAPTER

Sexton et al. (1986) noted that as units can be self and peer evaluated thus it is possible to present a model for ranking efficient units based on this idea. Therefore, he suggested to first obtain the efficiency of each of the n DMUs, while considering the weights chosen by DMU_o. Thus, they proposed the following formula in which U_o^*, V_o^* are optimal weights acquired from model (5) when DMU_o is being evaluated.

$$\theta_{oj} = \frac{U_o^* Y_j}{V_o^* X_j}$$

$$\begin{aligned}
\min \quad & V^t X_o \\
s.t. \quad & U^t Y_o = 1, \\
& U^t Y_j - V^t X_j \leq 0, \quad j = 1, \dots, n, \\
& U \geq 0, \quad V \geq 0.
\end{aligned} \tag{5}$$

Sexton et al. proposed $\overline{\theta}_o = \sum_{j=1}^{n} \theta_{oj} / n$ which is the average cross efficiency score corresponds to and $DMU_o, o \in \{1, ..., n\}$.

Adler (2002) in a paper addressed Green et al. (1996). Doyle and Green (1994) who gave more details about the average cross efficiency introduced by Sexton et al.

Super efficiency models introduced in DEA technique are based upon the idea of one leave out and assess this unit trough the remanding units.

Andersen and Petersen (1993) while considering the idea of super efficiency measurement, provided a model for ranking efficient units which is as follows:

$$\text{min} \quad \theta$$

$$\begin{aligned}
\textit{s.t.} \quad & \sum_{\substack{j=1 \\ j \neq o}}^{n} \lambda_j x_{ij} \leq \theta x_{io}, \quad i = 1, ..., m, \\
& \sum_{\substack{j=1 \\ j \neq o}}^{n} \lambda_j y_{rj} \geq y_{ro}, \quad r = 1, ..., s, \\
& \lambda_j \geq 0, \quad j = 1, ..., n, j \neq o.
\end{aligned}$$

(6)

At its time, this method is unique and very useful. But, as time passed and more applications and examples run considering this method it has been noted that there exist some shortcomings. As Thrall (1996) noted that that super efficiency of CCR model may result in infeasibility. More completely, Zhu (1996a), Seiford and Zhu (1999) and Dula and Hickman (1997), mentioned the conditions under which infeasibility happens.

Considering the issue of ranking efficient units, Hashimoto (1997) presented a model. The author focused on the issue of one-leave-out and assurance region.

In (1998), Friedman et al. (1998) considering and as the inputs and outputs provided the ratio of linear combinations of these two using canonical correlation analysis as:

$$T_j = \frac{W_j}{Z_j}$$

They also verified that the scaling ratio T_j of the canonical correlation analysis/ DEA may be unbounded.

In order to rank efficient units, considering the linear discriminant analysis technique Sinuany-Stern et al. (1994) introduced the index of D_j as follows:

$$D_j = \sum_{r=1}^{s} u_r y_{rj} + \sum_{i=1}^{m} v_r(-x_{ij}).$$

DMU_j is said to be efficient if $D_j > D_c$. Need to be noted that as Morrison (1976) mentioned this index is a critical value based on the midpoint of the means of the discriminant function value of the two groups. DMU_j has a better rank order, while it is compared to other DMUs, if it has larger amount of D_j.

Friedman et al.(1998) noted that the canonical correlation analysis as well as the DEA analysis can be considered for ranking efficient units. Canonical correlation analysis, for each of the inputs and outputs of all DMUS, tries to search for a vector of common weights. As, Adler et al.(2002) noted canonical correlation analysis can also be considered as the extension of regression analysis.

Tatsuoka et al.(1998) presented the following model.

They mentioned that S_{xx}, S_{yy} and S_{xy} are, respectively, considered to be the matrices of the sums of squares and sums of products of the variables, Z_j, W_j are the composite input and output, and V', U' as corresponding weights.

$$\max \quad r_{z,w} = \frac{V'S_{xy}U}{(V'S_{xx}V)(U'S_{yy}U)^{(1/2)}}$$
$$s.t. \quad V'_{xx}V = 1, \tag{7}$$
$$U'_{yy}U = 1.$$

Each of the method of cross efficiency /DEA, canonical correlation analysis/DEA and discriminant analysis/ DEA, for ranking DMUs, has its own specialty. Thus, it is very natural that the obtained results may differ from one another. Considering these differences, Friedman et al. (1998) proposed a Combined ranking (CO/DEA) method. This method considered all the ranking orders from the above-mentioned methods. As Siegel and Castellan (1998) noted, statistical tests such as goodness of fit between DEA and a definite ranking method and also testing correlation between different ranking orders, can also be considered.

One of the shortcoming of super efficiency method presented in literature is that it can not rank all the units. For overcoming this difficulty, Mehrabian et al. (1999) presented a complete ranking method. As the authors verified, in this model the difficulties of the proposed model by Andersen and Petersen (1993) are removed.

$$\min \quad w_p + 1$$

$$s.t. \quad \sum_{j=1\,j\neq p}^{n} \lambda_j x_{ij} \leq x_{ip} + w_p 1, \quad i = 1,\ldots,m,$$

$$\sum_{j=1\,j\neq p}^{n} \lambda_j y_{rj} \geq y_{rp}, \quad r = 1,\ldots,s, \qquad (8)$$

$$\lambda_j \geq 0, \quad j \neq p.$$

Need to be noted that the disadvantages of the presented model is that it does not the ability of ranking non-extreme efficient units.

Ranking efficient units are one of the important issues in real world problems as many researches performed different ranking method on different case studies. Sueyoshi et al.(1999) presented a method which is a combination of DEA and OERA (Offensive Earned-Run Average) for baseball evaluation. With the contribution of this method it is possible to find the best unit as well as the ranking orders. For obtaining a complete ranking order and overcoming the problem of existing more than one efficient unit, Sueyoshi et al., used Slack-Adjusted DEA model.

A multiple-objective linear program (MOLP) is presented by Li and Reeves (1999) for making discrimination power of DEA improved. In doing so, they considered the the standard DEA objective function as well as minimax and minimum efficiencies.

For acquiring an overall order of options, Strassert and Prato (2002) presented a procedure consists of three steps for the balancing and Ranking. An outranking matrix, for all options, is obtained in the first step. Noted that considering this matrix the frequency of higher ranked options can be revealed. In the second step, from the outranking matrix an implicit pre-ordering or provisional ordering of options are obtained. The degree to which a complete overall order of options can be obtained is shown in the outranking matrix. In regards of the obtained information in the advantages– disadvantages table, the provisional ordering is subjected to different screening and balancing operations in the third step.

Tone (2002) introduced the super efficiency of SBM model. This model, as well as, the SBM model, benefits from the existence of the nonradial slcks which are considered in the analysis. Tone verified that this model is stable and feasible.

$$\min \quad \frac{\displaystyle\sum_{i=1}^{m} \overline{x}_i / x_{io}}{\displaystyle\sum_{r=1}^{s} \overline{y}_r / y_{ro}}$$

$$\text{s.t.} \quad \sum_{j=1 j \neq o}^{n} \lambda_j x_{ij} \leq \overline{x}_i, \qquad i = 1,...,m, \qquad\qquad (9)$$

$$\sum_{j=1 j \neq o}^{n} \lambda_j y_{rj} \geq \overline{y}_r, \qquad r = 1,...,s,$$

$$\overline{x}_i \geq x_{io}, 0 \leq \overline{y}_r \leq y_{ro}, \quad i = 1,...,m, r = 1,...,s,$$

$$\lambda_j \geq 0, \qquad\qquad\quad j \neq o.$$

The context-dependent DEA method is presented by Seiford and Joe Zhu (2003) for ranking efficient units. They considered n DMUs to be evaluated as $J^1 = \{DMU_j, j = 1,...,n\}$ and $E^l = \{DMU_k \in J^l \mid \phi^*(l,k) = 1\}$ where $\phi^*(l,k) = 1$ is obtained from the following model.

$$\max_{\lambda_j, \phi(l,k)} \quad \phi^*(l,k) = \phi(l,k)$$

$$\text{s.t.} \quad \sum_{j \in F(J^l)} \lambda_j y_j \geq \phi(l,k) y_k,$$

$$\sum_{j \in F(J^l)} \lambda_j x_j \leq \phi(l,k) x_k, \qquad\qquad (10)$$

$$\lambda_j \geq 0, \quad j \in F(J^l).$$

Consider $l = 1$ results in the CCR model presented by Charnes et al.(1986). Seiford and Joe Zhu (2003) noted that DMUs located in E^1 constructed the first level of efficient frontier. Eliminating the first level of efficient frontier, the second level of efficient frontier is obtained. For this case in the above model let $l = 2$. The authors, provided the following algorithm to find the efficient levels.

1. Evaluate each of the existing units (J^1)by CCR model (let $l = 1$). In doing so the first level of efficient units are identified, E^1.
2. Consider $J^{l+1} = J^l - E^l$. Note that if $J^{l+1} = \emptyset$ stop. Omit the efficient DMUs in the first level and runs the DEA model for the rest of them.
3. Distinguish J^{l+1} and E^{l+1}. In this step the new subset of inefficient DMUs as well as the new set of efficient DMUs obtained.
4. Let $l = l + 1$ and then do to 2. Note that if $J^{l+1} = \emptyset$ stop.

As regards of these steps, Seiford and Joe Zhu claimed that the DMUs in the first efficient frontier can be ranked in accordance to their attractiveness scores.

Jahanshahloo et al.(2004) presented a new model for ranking efficient DMUs as following. They noted that the presented model is the Andersen and Petersen model in multiplier form to which some ratio constraints are added.

$$
\begin{aligned}
\max \quad & \sum_{r=1}^{s} u_r y_{ro} \\
s.t. \quad & \sum_{i=1}^{m} v_r x_{io} = 1, \\
& \sum_{r=1}^{s} u_r y_{rj} - \sum_{i=1}^{m} v_r x_{ij} \leq 0, \quad j = 1,...,n, j \neq o, \\
& \tilde{t}^{pq} \leq \frac{v_p}{v_q} \leq \bar{t}^{pq}, p,q = 1,...,m, p < q, \\
& \hat{t}^{kw} \leq \frac{v_k}{v_w} \leq \breve{t}^{kw}, k,w = 1,...,s, k < w, \\
& U,V \geq \varepsilon.
\end{aligned}
\tag{10}
$$

Considering the above model if the optimal value is greater than or equal one then the unit under evaluation is called efficient.

Also, for ranking efficient units, Jahanshahllo et al (2004) provided a method with the concept of advantage in data envelopment analysis technique.

Considering the gradient line, Jahanshahloo et al.(2004) presented a method for ranking units. An important key feature of the presented method is stability and robustness. They introduced the following model

$$
\begin{aligned}
\max \quad & H_o = -V^T X_o + U^T Y_o \\
s.t. \quad & -V^T X_j + U^T Y_j \leq 0, \quad j = 1,...,n, j \neq o, \\
& V^T e + U^T e = 1, \\
& V,U \geq \varepsilon 1.
\end{aligned}
\tag{11}
$$

From which the optimal value, $(U^*, -V^*)$, is considered to be the gradient of supporting hyperplane on T_c'. Need to be noted that T_c' is the obtained production possibility set from T_c when the unit under evaluation is eliminated. The authors proved that a unit is efficient if and only if the optimal objective function of the following model is greater than zero. They introduced P_o and S_o as follows:

$$P0 = \{(X,Y) : X = \alpha X_o, Y = \beta Y_o\}$$

$$S0 = \{(X,Y) \in P_0 : X = \alpha X_o, Y = \beta Y_o, \alpha \geq 0, \beta \geq 0\}$$

Consider $(-V^{*T}X_o)\alpha + (U^{*T}Y_o)\beta = 0$ which is a half line obtained from the intersection of S_o and efficient surface of T_c'. For ranking units, they introduced the following formula with which, in (α, β) space, the length of connecting arc DMU_o with intersection point of line and previous ellipse.

$$\alpha^* = (\frac{K_\alpha^2 K_\beta^2}{K_\beta^2 + (V^{*T}X_o / U^{*T}Y_o)^2 K_\alpha^2})^{1/2}$$

$$\beta^* = (V^{*T}X_o / U^{*T}Y_o)\alpha^*.$$

Consider the (α, β) space, for computing the length of connecting arc DMU_o to the point corresponding to α^*, β^* they used: $I = \int_1^{\alpha^*} (1 + \beta)^{1/2} d\alpha$, where

$$K_\alpha = (\frac{\sum_{j=1}^{n} x_{io}^2 + \sum_{r=1}^{s} y_{io}^2}{\sum_{j=1}^{n} x_{io}^2})^{1/2}$$

$$K_\beta = (\frac{\sum_{j=1}^{n} x_{io}^2 + \sum_{r=1}^{s} y_{io}^2}{\sum_{r=1}^{s} y_{ro}^2})^{1/2}$$

Considering the idea of one leave out and L_1 norm Jahanshahloo et al. (2004) provided a method for ranking efficient. The advantages of the presented method is feasibility and stability.

$$\min \quad \sum_{i=1}^{m} x_i - \sum_{r=1}^{s} y_r + \alpha$$

$$\text{s.t.} \quad \sum_{j=1, j \neq o}^{s} \lambda_j x_{ij} \leq x_i, \quad i = 1, \dots, m,$$

$$\sum_{j=1, j \neq o}^{s} \lambda_j y_{rj} \geq y_r, \quad r = 1, \dots, s, \tag{12}$$

$$x_i \geq x_{io}, \quad i = 1, \dots, m,$$

$$0 \leq y_r \leq y_{ro}, \quad r = 1, \dots, s,$$

$$\lambda_j \geq 0, \quad j = 1, \dots n, j \neq o.$$

where $\alpha = \sum_{r=1}^{s} y_{ro} - \sum_{i=1}^{m} x_{io}$.

Non radial super efficiency is presented by Chen et al. (2004). As Chen et al. discussed in their papr this method has many advantages in comparison to the existing method till that time. As an example, considering the units of the data measured, they proved that this model is invariant to this factor. Consider $J^o = $ as $J / \{DMU_o\}$, they introduced the following steps.

Step 1: In order to find the extreme efficient units in J^o, first, sole the following model.

$$\min \quad \theta_k^{super}$$

$$\text{s.t.} \quad \sum_{j \neq o, k} \lambda_j x_{ij} \leq \theta_k^{super} x_{io}, \quad i = 1, \dots, m,$$

$$\sum_{j \neq o, k} \lambda_j y_{rj} \geq y_r, \quad r = 1, \dots, s, \tag{13}$$

$$\lambda_j \geq 0, \quad j = 1, \dots n, j \neq o, k.$$

They defined the of efficient units of J^o as E^o.

Step 2: Consider the following model.

$$\min \quad \theta_k^{super}$$

$$\begin{aligned} s.t. \quad & \sum_{j \in E^o} \lambda_j x_{ij} + s_i^{o-} = \theta x_{io}, \quad i = 1, \ldots, m, \\ & \sum_{j \in E^o} \lambda_j y_{rj} - s_r^{o+} = y_{ro}, \quad r = 1, \ldots, s, \\ & \lambda_j \geq 0, \quad j \in E^o. \end{aligned} \tag{14}$$

By solving this model, θ^* is obtained, which is the optimal solution of this model. Now, considering θ^* as the optimal solution of this model, it is used in the next model as follows. Consider $p \in \{1, \ldots, m\}$.

$$\max \quad s_p^{o-}$$

$$\begin{aligned} s.t. \quad & \sum_{j \in E^o} \lambda_j x_{pj} + s_p^{o-} = \theta^* x_{po}, \\ & \sum_{j \in E^o} \lambda_j x_{ij} + s_i^{o-} = \theta^* x_{io}, \quad i \neq p, \\ & \sum_{j \in E^o} \lambda_j y_{rj} - s_r^{o+} = y_{ro}, \quad r = 1, \ldots, s, \\ & \lambda_j \geq 0, \quad j \in E^o. \end{aligned} \tag{15}$$

By solving this model we have $x_{io}^{(1)} = \theta * x_{io}, s_i^{o-*}(0) = s_i^{o-*}$, and $\theta^*(0) = \theta^*$, $I(t) = \{i : s_i^{o-*}(t-1) \neq 0\}, i = 1, \ldots, m$.

Step 3: In the third step, solve the following model.

$$\min \quad \theta(t)$$

$$\begin{aligned} s.t. \quad & \sum_{j \in E^o} \lambda_j x_{ij} \leq \theta(t) x_{io}^{(t)}, \quad i \in I(t) \\ & \sum_{j \in E^o} \lambda_j x_{ij} = x_{io}^{(t)}, \quad i \ / \quad I(t), \\ & \sum_{j \in E^o} \lambda_j y_{rj} - s_r^{o+} = y_{ro}, \quad r = 1, \ldots, s, \\ & \lambda_j \geq 0, \quad j \in E^o. \end{aligned} \tag{16}$$

Having to the optimal solution of this model, for each $p \in I(t)$ solve the following model.

$$\min \quad s_p^{o-}(t)$$

$$\text{s.t.} \quad \sum_{j \in E^o} \lambda_j x_{ij} + s_p^{o-}(t) = \theta^*(t) x_{po}^{(t)}, \quad p \in I(t)$$

$$\sum_{j \in E^o} \lambda_j x_{ij} + s_p^{o-}(t) = \theta^*(t) x_{io}^{(t)}, \quad i \ne p \in I(t),$$

$$\sum_{j \in E^o} \lambda_j x_{ij} = x_{io}^{(t)}, \quad i \; / \quad I(t), \tag{17}$$

$$\sum_{j \in E^o} \lambda_j y_{rj} - s_r^{o+}(t) = y_{ro}, \quad r = 1, ..., s,$$

$$\lambda_j \ge 0, \quad j \in E^o.$$

Step 4: Let $x_{io}^{(t+1)} = \theta^*(t) x^{(t)}$ for $i \in I(t)$ and $x_{io}^{(t+1)} = x^{(t)}$ for $i \; / \quad I(t)$. If $I(t+1) = \emptyset$ then stop otherwise if $I(t+1) \ne \emptyset$ let $t = t+1$ and go to step 3

Finally, θ^o is defined as the average RNSE-DEA index.

$$\theta^o = \frac{\sum_{t=1}^{T} n_I(T) \theta_t^o + \tilde{n}_I(T) \theta_{t+1}^o}{\sum_{t=1}^{T} n_I(T) + \tilde{n}_I(T)}.$$

In regards of the Mont Carlo method Jahanshahloo et al.(2005) provided a method of ranking units. The presented methods contain the following steps.

Step 1: A sequence of $\{U_j\}_{j=1}^{2n}$ on $(0,1)$ which is uniformly distributed should be generated.

Step 2: Random numbers should be classified into N pairs like $(U_1, U_1'), ..., (U_N, U_N')$ in a way that each number used just one time.

Step 3: In this step, one should compute $X_i = a + U_i(b-a)$ and $f(X_i) > cU_i'$.

Step 4: The integral I is estimated where $\theta_I = c(b-a) \dfrac{N_H}{N}$.

Now consider DMU_o as an efficient unit. As for dome DMUs it would be un-bounded thus the authors, for each unit, bounded the region. Then, for DMU_o if $(-X_o, Y_o) \ge (-\bar{X}, \bar{Y})$ then $(-\bar{X}, \bar{Y})$ is in the RED of DMU_o. Now by using $V_p = V^* \dfrac{N_H}{N}$ the measure of RED for DMU_p cab is obtained.

Calculating the distance of the unit under evaluation to the full inefficient frontier, Jahanshahloo et al.(2006) presented a method for ranking units. They presented two models, one for radial and for nonradial evaluation.

$$\min \quad \phi$$

$$s.t. \quad \sum_{j=1}^{n} \lambda_j x_{ij} = \phi x_{io}, \quad i = 1, \ldots, m,$$

$$\sum_{j=1}^{n} \lambda_j y_{rj} = y_{ro}, \quad r = 1, \ldots, s, \tag{18}$$

$$\sum_{j=1}^{n} = 1,$$

$$\lambda_j \geq 0, \quad j = 1, \ldots, m.$$

$$\max \quad \sum_{i=1}^{m} s_i^- + \sum_{r=1}^{s} s_r^+$$

$$s.t. \quad \sum_{j \in J - \{b\}} \lambda_j x_{ij} - s_i^- = x_{io}, \quad i = 1, \ldots, m,$$

$$\sum_{j \in J - \{b\}} \lambda_j y_{rj} + s_r^+ = y_{ro}, \quad r = 1, \ldots, s, \tag{19}$$

$$\sum_{j=1}^{n} = 1,$$

$$s_i^- \geq 0, s_r^+ \geq 0, \quad i = 1, \ldots, m, \quad r = 1, \ldots, s,$$

$$\lambda_j \geq 0, \quad j = 1, \ldots, n.$$

For complete ranking using common set of weights, Jahanshahloo et al.(2005) provided a model and given a note and introduce only one problem with which it is possible to determine the common set of weighs.

$$\max \quad z$$

$$s.t. \quad \sum_{r=1}^{s} u_r y_{rj} + u_0 - z \sum_{i=1}^{m} v_i x_{ij} \geq 0, j \in A,$$

$$\sum_{r=1}^{s} u_r y_{rj} + u_0 - \sum_{i=1}^{m} v_i x_{ij} \leq 0, j = 1, \ldots, n, \quad j \ / \quad \in A, \tag{20}$$

$$U, V, \eta \geq \varepsilon, u_0 free.$$

Note that A is considered to be the set of efficient units of the following model:

$$\max \quad \left\{ \frac{\sum\limits_{r=1}^{s} u_r y_{r1} + u_0}{\sum\limits_{i=1}^{m} v_i x_{i1}} \cdots \frac{\sum\limits_{r=1}^{s} u_r y_{rn} + u_0}{\sum\limits_{i=1}^{m} v_i x_{in}} \right\}$$

$$s.t. \quad \frac{\sum\limits_{r=1}^{s} u_r y_{rj} + u_0}{\sum\limits_{i=1}^{m} v_i x_{ij}} \leq 1, j = 1,...,n, \tag{21}$$

$$U, V, \eta \geq \varepsilon, u_0 free.$$

Finally they ranked DMUs in accordance to the measure of efficiencies.

Amirteimoori et al.(2005) for ranking efficient units presented a distance based method. In this new method, the authors used L_2 norm in a distance function. As compared to the other methods, they claimed that the presented approach does suffer from those difficulties of other methods have.

$$\max \quad \beta^T Y_p - \alpha^T X_p$$
$$s.t. \quad \beta^T Y_j - \alpha^T X_j + s_j = 0, \quad j \in E, j \neq p,$$
$$\alpha^T 1_m + \beta^T 1_s = 1$$
$$s_j \leq (1 - \gamma_j)M, \quad j \in E, j \neq p, \tag{22}$$
$$\sum_{j \in E, j \neq p} \gamma_j \geq m + s + 1,$$
$$\alpha \geq \varepsilon.1_m, \beta \geq \varepsilon.1_s,$$
$$\alpha_j \in \{0,1\}, j \in E, j \neq p.$$

As noted by the authors, the presented method cannot be used for ranking non-extreme efficient units. Modified MAJ method is presented by Jahanshahloo et al.(2006) for better ranking efficiency units. Note that M_i is considered to be as $MAx\{x_{ij} \mid DMU_j is \quad efficient\}$. Need to be note that with this method it is not possible to rank non-extreme efficient units.

$$\min \quad w_p + 1$$

$$s.t. \quad \sum_{j=1 j \neq p}^{n} \lambda_j \frac{x_{ij}}{M_i} \leq \frac{x_{ip}}{M_i} + w_p 1, \quad i = 1, ..., m,$$

$$\sum_{j=1 j \neq p}^{n} \lambda_j y_{rj} \geq y_{rp}, \quad r = 1, ..., s, \tag{23}$$

$$\lambda_j \geq 0, \quad j \neq p.$$

Estimate the rank and the efficiency of association rules with multiple Criteria, Chen (2007) utilized DEA technique which is a non-parametric approach in following steps.

Step 1: Input data for association rule mining.

Step 2: Mine association rules by using the A priori algorithm with minimum support and minimum confidence.

Step 3: In this step one should determine subjective interestingness.

Step 4: In accordance to the Cook and Kress's (1990) DEA model, one should calculate the preference scores of association rules.

Step 5: Considering the Obata and Ishii's (2003) discriminate model the efficient association rules found in Step 3 should be discriminated.

Step 6: Select rules for implementation by considering the reference scores generated in Step 5 and domain related knowledge.

In regards of the idea of comparing units with the inefficient frontier Amirteimoori (2007) considered both efficient and anti-efficient frontiers for efficiency analysis and ranking units.

According to make changes in the reference set, Jahanshahloo et al.(2007) presented a new model for ranking units. They provided this method in regards of the fact that inefficient units imitate efficient units, as the their role model, to improve their performance.

$$\min \quad \partial_{a,b} = \theta - \varepsilon (\sum_{i=1}^{m} s_i^- + \sum_{r=1}^{s} s_r^+)$$

$$s.t. \quad \sum_{j \in J - \{b\}} \lambda_j x_{ij} + s_i^- - \theta x_{ia}, \quad i = 1, ..., m,$$

$$\sum_{j \in J - \{b\}} \lambda_j y_{rj} - s_r^+ = y_{ra}, \quad r = 1, ..., s, \tag{24}$$

$$\theta free, s_i^- \geq 0, s_r^+ \geq 0, \quad i = 1, ..., m, \quad r = 1, ..., s,$$

$$\lambda_j \geq 0, \quad j \in J - \{b\}.$$

Finally the rank of each efficient unit, b, obtain by:

$$\mho_b = \sum_{a \in J_n} \partial_{a,b} / \tilde{n}.$$

The authors noted that with this method it is not possible to rank non-extreme efficient units.

Wang et al.(2007) provided an aggregating preference ranking. They provided the use of ordered weighted averaging (OWA) operator for aggregating preference rankings. If w_j is set to be the relative importance weight for the jth ranking order and v_{ij} is assumed to be the vote which is received by the candidate i in the jth ranking place, the total score of each candidate is then considered as $z_i = \sum_{i=1}^{m} v_{ij} W_j, i = 1,...,m$.

Li et al.(2007) presented a new method for ranking units which is proved to be always feasible and stable.

$$\begin{aligned}
\min \quad & 1 + \frac{1}{m} \sum_{i=1}^{m} \frac{s_{i2}^+}{R_i^-} \\
s.t. \quad & \sum_{\substack{j=1 \\ j \neq p}}^{n} \lambda_j x_{ij} + s_{i1}^- - s_{i2}^+ = x_{ip}, \quad i = 1,...,m, \\
& \sum_{\substack{j=1 \\ j \neq p}}^{n} \lambda_j y_{rj} - s_r^+ = y_{rp}, \quad r = 1,...,s, \\
& s_{i2}^- \geq 0, s_{i1}^- \geq 0, s_r^+ \geq 0, \quad i = 1,...,m, \quad r = 1,...,s, \\
& \lambda_j \geq 0, \quad j \neq p.
\end{aligned} \quad (25)$$

As this method is based upon the idea of one leave out, thus it is not possible to rank extreme efficient units.

Alirezaee and Afsharian (2007) while considering the multiplier model, where shadow prices can be obtained, considered $\sum_{r=1}^{s} u_r y_{rj}$ and $\sum_{i=1}^{m} v_i x_{ij}$ as total revenue and cost of DMU_j in optimization problem. The authors noted that $\sum_{r=1}^{s} u_r y_{rj} - \sum_{i=1}^{m} v_i x_{ij} \leq 0, j = 1,...,n$ can be considered as the profit restriction for DMU_j. If $F(x,y) = 0$ be the efficient production function then

$$\sum_i \frac{\partial F}{\partial x_i} x_i + \sum_j \frac{\partial F}{\partial y_j} y_j = 0.$$

The authors introduced the balance index for each unit as the sum of quantities of profit restrictions of other units. Thus, they said the rank of DMU1 is better than that of DMU2, if DMU1 is efficient but, DMU2 is inefficient or both units have the same the same efficiency score and acquired more negative quantity in Balance index.

Khodabakhshi (2007) provided a method discussed super-efficiency on improved outputs. The idea of this method is the infeasibility of the model presented by Andersen and Petersen (1993) under variable returns to scale form of the technology. In accordance to the presented method it is possible to acquire a complete ranking order when getting an input combination for improving outputs is suitable.

For ranking efficient units Liu and Peng (2008) provided a method for determining the common set of weights. Liu and Peng provided the following model:

$$\Delta^* = \min \quad \sum_{j \in E} \Delta_j^o + \Delta_j^i$$

$$s.t. \quad \frac{\sum_{r=1}^{s} y_{rj} U_r + \Delta_j^o}{\sum_{i=1}^{m} x_{ij} V_i - \Delta_j^i} = 1, j \in E,$$

$$\Delta_j^o, \Delta_j^i \geq 0, |\ forall j \in E,$$

$$U_r \geq \varepsilon, r = 1, \dots, s,$$

$$V_i \geq \varepsilon, i = 1, \dots, m.$$

(26)

Considering data envelopment analysis Wang et al.(2009) proposed a method for ranking decision making units by imposing a minimum weight restriction. The authors mentioned that as using DEA technique it is not possible to discriminate among efficient units, thus it is desired to present a method for ranking units using imposing minimum weight restriction for the input-output data. They noted that decision makers should mention these weights restrictions.

Lu et al.(2009) presented a model based on the interactive benchmark for ranking efficient units. The idea of Lu et al. is that a fixed unit is considered as a benchmark and then other units, one by one, compared to this unit and the efficiency of units obtained. In this manner each of the units are considered to be as a target unit for each of the other units. Let DMU_o be a unit under evaluation and DMU_b a benchmark unit and consider

$$\bar{x}_i = x_{io}(1 + \phi_i), \bar{y}_r = y_{ro}(1 - \varphi_r).$$

$$\text{min} \quad \theta_o^{*b} = \frac{1 + \frac{1}{m}\sum_{i=1}^{m}\phi_i}{1 - \frac{1}{s}\sum_{r=1}^{s}\varphi_r}$$

$$s.t. \quad \lambda_b x_{ib} - x_{io}\phi_i \leq x_{io}, \quad i = 1,...,m,$$

$$\lambda_b y_{rb} - y_{ro}\varphi_r \geq y_{ro}, \quad r = 1,...,s,$$

$$\phi_i \geq o, \varphi_r \leq y_{ro}, \quad i = 1,...m, r = 1,...,s,$$

$$\lambda_j \geq 0, \quad j = 1,...,n.$$

(27)

The authors used $\frac{\sum_{b=1}^{n}\theta_o^{b*}}{n}, o = 1,...,n$ and obtain the efficiency of benchmark of DMU_o. They used the following index for ranking units. This index considers an increase in the efficiency of a unit by moving from peer appraisal to self-apprais-al.

This index indicates that the less the magnitude of this index is the better rank for corresponding unit will be.

$$TE_o^{IBM} = \frac{(TE_k^{BCC} - STD_k^{IBM})}{(STD_k^{IBM}}$$

Considering DMU_k, TE_k^{BCC} and STD_k^{IBM}, respectively, are efficiency in BCC model and normalization of TE^{IBM}.

In order to construct composite indicators for ranking units, Hatefi and Torabi (2010) proposed a common weight multi criteria decision analysis data envelopment analysis. As the authors mentioned with the help of the provided model it is possible to discriminate between efficient units. Hatefi and Torabi mentioned that the obtained common weights are distinct from those acquired from previous models. Also, robustness and discriminating power of the presented model is then verified by Spearman's rank correlation coefficient.

Kao (2010) mentioned that determining the weights of individual criteria in multiple criteria decision analysis in a way that all alternatives can be compared according to the aggregate performance of all criteria is one of the subjects that are under attention of researchers. As Kao noted this problem tries to find those alternatives with a shorter and longer distance, in other words it means the ideal and anti-ideal units. Kao proposed a measure considered the calculation of the relative position of an alternative between the ideal and anti-ideal for finding an appropriate ranking.

Considering the data envelopment analysis technique Chen et al. (2011) presented a model for ranking efficient and inefficient units. Their method is based on eliminating units from the reference set. At first solve the following model which measures the efficiency of DMU_a when DMU_b is eliminated from the reference set.

$$
\begin{aligned}
\min \quad & \rho_{a,b} = \theta_a^s - \varepsilon\left(\sum_{i=1}^{m} s_i^- + \sum_{r=1}^{s} s_r^+\right) \\
s.t. \quad & \sum_{j=1 j\neq b}^{n} \lambda_j x_{ij} + s_i^- = \theta_a^s x_{ia}, \quad i = 1,...,m, \\
& \sum_{j=1 j\neq b}^{n} \lambda_j y_{rj} - s_r^+ = y_{ra}, \quad r = 1,...,s, \\
& \sum_{j=1 j\neq b}^{n} = 1, \\
& \theta_a^s \geq 0, s_i^- \geq 0, s_r^+ \geq 0, \quad i = 1,...,m, \quad r = 1,...,s, \\
& \lambda_j \geq 0, \quad j \neq b.
\end{aligned}
\tag{28}
$$

Then, this model is solved in order to compute the efficiency score of each inefficient units when, one by one, each of efficient units are omitted form the reference set η_a^* and calculated the efficiency change.

$$
\tau_{a,b} = \rho_{a,b}^* - \eta_a^*.
$$

Finally, the index which is called "MCDE" is calculated for each efficient and inefficient unit.

$$
E_a = \sum_{b\in V_E} W_b^* \rho_{a,b}^*, \quad E_b = \sum_{b\in V_I} W_b^* \rho_{a,b}^*.
$$

Considering this index according to the magnitude of the index it is possible to rank units. Note that each unit has higher score have better ranking order.

On basis of multiple criteria decision Making techniques, goal programming and analytic hierarchy process Jablonsky (2011) provided two models, named super SBM and AHP, for ranking units. The author formulated Super SBM model as follows:

$$\min \quad \theta_q^G = 1 + t\gamma + (1-t)(\sum_{i=1}^{m} s_{1i}^{+} / x_{iq} + \sum_{i=1}^{m} s_{2k}^{-} / y_{kq})$$

$$s.t. \quad \sum_{j=1 j \neq q}^{n} \lambda_j x_{ij} + s_{1i}^{-} - s_{1i}^{+} = x_{iq}, \quad i = 1,...,m,$$

$$\sum_{j=1 j \neq q}^{n} \lambda_j y_{kj} + s_{2k}^{-} - s_{2k}^{+} = y_{kq}, \quad k = 1,...,r, \qquad (29)$$

$$s_{1i}^{+} \leq \gamma, \quad i = 1,...,m,$$

$$s_{2k}^{-} \leq \gamma, \quad k = 1,...,r,$$

$$t \in \{0,1\}, \lambda_j \geq 0, S_1^{+}, S_2^{+} \geq 0, S_1^{-}, S_2^{-} \geq 0, \quad j = 1,...,n.$$

Considering DEA technique for ranking efficient units, Ashrafi et al.(2011) introduced an enhanced Russell measure of super efficiency. The authors introduced the linear counter part of the proposed model as following:

$$\max \quad \frac{1}{m} \sum_{i=1}^{m} u_i$$

$$s.t. \quad \sum_{r=1}^{s} v_r = s,$$

$$\sum_{\substack{j=1 \\ j \neq o}}^{n} \alpha_j x_{ij} \leq u_i x_{io}, i = 1,...,m, \qquad (30)$$

$$\sum_{\substack{j=1 \\ j \neq o}}^{n} \alpha_j y_{rj} \leq v_i y_{ro}, r = 1,...,s,$$

$$\alpha_j \geq 0, u_i \geq \beta \quad j = 1,...,n, j \neq k, \quad i = 1,...,m,$$

$$o \leq \beta \leq 0, v_r \geq \beta \quad r = 1,...s.$$

They noted that this model has not the ability to rank non-extreme efficient units.

On basis of the simultaneous input-output projection Chen et al.(2011) provided a model named a modified super efficiency model for ranking units. As Chen et al. claimed this model overcomes the infeasibility problem.

$$p_1 = \min \quad \frac{\theta_o^{sr}}{\phi_o^{sr}}$$

$$\text{s.t.} \quad \sum_{\substack{j=1 \\ j \neq o}} \lambda_j x_{ij} \leq \theta_o^{sr} x_{io}, \quad i = 1, \ldots, m,$$

$$\sum_{\substack{j=1 \\ j \neq o}} \lambda_j y_{rj} \geq \phi_o^{sr} y_{ro}, \quad r = 1, \ldots, s,$$

$$\sum_{\substack{j=1 \\ j \neq o}} \lambda_j = 1,$$

$$0 < \theta_o^{sr} \leq 1, \quad \phi_o^{sr} \geq 1, \quad i = 1, \ldots, m, \quad r = 1, \ldots, s,$$

$$\lambda_j \geq 0, \quad j = 1, \ldots, n.$$

(31)

For ranking efficient units, Sadjadi et al.(2011) introduced a robust super efficiency DEA based model. The authors mentioned that usually exact data do not exist thus they tried to consider stochastic data and presented stochastic super efficiency model. Thy noted that model presented incorporates the robust counterpart of super efficiency DEA.

$$\min \quad \theta_o^{RS}$$

$$\text{s.t.} \quad \sum_{j=1 j \neq o}^{n} \lambda_j \overline{x}_{ij} - \theta_o^{RS} \overline{x}_{io} + \varepsilon \Omega (\sum_{\substack{j=1 \\ j \neq o, j \in J_i}}^{n} \lambda_j^2 \overline{x}_{ij}^2 + (\theta_o^{RS} \overline{x}_{io})^2)^{(1/2)} \leq 0, \quad i = 1, \ldots, m,$$

$$\sum_{\substack{j=1 \\ j \neq o}}^{n} \lambda_j \overline{y}_{rj} - \varepsilon \Omega (\overline{y}_{ro}^2 + \sum_{\substack{j=1 \\ j \neq o, j \in J_i}}^{n} \lambda_j^2 \overline{y}_{rj}^2)^{(1/2)} \geq \overline{y}_{ro}, \quad r = 1, \ldots, s,$$

$$\lambda_j \geq 0, \quad j = 1, \ldots, n.$$

(32)

In the above model, $\overline{X}, \overline{Y}$ are considered to be the input-output data. They mentioned that the presented model does not rank non-extreme efficient units and it may be unstable and infeasible.

For ranking efficient units Hosseinzadeh Lotfi et al. (2011) proposed a new method based on applying aggregate units. In doing so they considered artificial units and called them aggregate units. Thus they defined this unit as follows.

$$x_{i\overline{a}}^p = \sum_{k \in R_p} x_{ik}, y_{r\overline{a}}^p = \sum_{k \in R_p} y_{rk}, \quad i = 1, \ldots, m, r = 1, \ldots, s$$

Where $R_p = \{j \mid DMU_j \in E_p\}, E_p = E\{DMU_p\}$ and E is the set of efficient units. Need to be noted the above mentioned formula showed the aggregate unit corresponds to the $DMU_{\bar{a}}$.

They mentioned that, in first step, the efficiency score of the $DMU_{\bar{a}}$ is tried to be maximized and then the efficiency score of the $DMU_{\bar{a}}^p$. For overcoming the problem of alternative optimal solutions Hosseinzadeh Lotfi et al. presented an approach contains (m + s) simple linear problems to find the most appropriate optimal solutions while all alternative optimal solutions are computed.

Thus, they defined the RI-index with which it is possible to rank all the units. Considering the optimal solution of the multiplier model as $U_{\bar{a}}, V_p \tilde{a}$ and $U_{\bar{a}}^p, V_{\bar{a}}^p$ while $DMU_{\bar{a}}$ and $DMU_{\bar{a}}^p$ are being evaluated, the RI-index is as follows:

$$\eta_{\bar{a}} = \sum_{r=1}^{s} u_{r\bar{a}} - \sum_{i=1}^{m} v_{i\bar{a}}, \quad \eta_{\bar{a}}^p = \sum_{r=1}^{s} u_{r\bar{a}}^p - \sum_{i=1}^{m} v_{i\bar{a}}^p$$

Therefore

$$RI_p = \eta_{\bar{a}}^o - \eta_{\bar{a}}$$

In order to obtain common set of weights for ranking efficient units, Wang et al (2011) presented two nonlinear regression models as follows:

$$\min \quad z = \sum_{j=1}^{n} (\theta_j^* - \sum_{r=1}^{s} u_r y_{rj} / \sum_{i=1}^{m} v_i x_{ij})^2 \tag{33}$$
$$s.t. \quad U, V \geq 0.$$

$$\min \quad \sum_{j=1}^{n} (\sum_{r=1}^{s} u_r y_{rj} - \theta_j^* \sum_{i=1}^{m} v_i x_{ij})^2$$
$$s.t. \quad \sum_{r=1}^{s} u_r (\sum_{j=1}^{n} y_{rj}) + \sum_{i=1}^{m} v_i (\sum_{j=1}^{n} x_{ij}) = n, \tag{34}$$
$$U, V \geq 0.$$

Considering Representation theory, Gholam Abri et. al (2011) tried to rank efficient units. In doing so, they showed that it is possible to distinguish efficient units and represent the DMU under assessment as a convex combination of them. Gholam Abri et. Al mentioned that for each DMU which can be represented as the convex combination of efficient units it is desired that performance of the unit under evaluation, DMU_o, is similar to those efficient units in convex combinations. Therefore the authors provided the following equations:

$$(X_o, Y_o) = \sum_{j=1}^{s} \lambda_j (X_j, Y_j), \sum_{j=1}^{n} \lambda_j = 1, j = 1, ..., s.$$

They noted that in accordance to the representation theorem the defined system has m+s-1 constraints and s variables as introduced by $(\lambda_1, ..., \lambda_s)$. Note that in the case that the system under assessment has a unique solution it is possible to show that $\theta_o^* = \sum_{j=1}^{n} = 1, \lambda_j^* \theta_j$. Otherwise the authors provided the following models.

$$\min \sum_{j=1}^{s} \lambda_j \theta_j$$

$$s.t. \quad (X_o, Y_o) = \sum_{j=1}^{s} \lambda_j (X_j, Y_j),$$

$$\sum_{j=1}^{s} \lambda_j = 1,$$

$$\lambda_j \geq 0, \quad j = 1, ..., s. \tag{35}$$

$$\max \sum_{j=1}^{s} \lambda_j \theta_j$$

$$s.t. \quad (X_o, Y_o) = \sum_{j=1}^{s} \lambda_j (X_j, Y_j),$$

$$\sum_{j=1}^{s} \lambda_j = 1,$$

$$\lambda_j \geq 0, \quad j = 1, ..., s. \tag{36}$$

They mentioned that if θ_1 and θ_2 respectively be the optimal solution of the models presented. Thus, in the case that θ_1 equals θ_2 therefore this case is the same as what has been mentioned above and the models have unique solutions. In the case that $\theta_1 < \theta_2$, then an interval is constructed with which it is possible to rank units. Need to be noted that it is also possible to have the ranking score with a bounded interval $[\theta_1, \theta_2]$.

Rodder and Reucher (2011) for ranking units provided a consensual peer based model in regards of DEA technique. As the important characteristics of the presented model is that this method is somehow generalized from two different aspects. The first one is that an optimal efficiency improved considering input allocation. The second is that a peer-DMU should be chosen in a way that the corresponding price can be acceptable for the other units.

$$
\begin{aligned}
\max \quad & V_k^{*T} W_l \\
\text{s.t.} \quad & U_k^{*T} Y_l - V_k^{*T} W_l \le 0, \\
& W_l - \sum_j \mu_{lj} X_j \ge 0, \\
& \sum_j \mu_{lj} Y_j \ge Y_l, \\
& \mu_{lj} \ge 0, \quad \forall j.
\end{aligned}
\tag{37}
$$

Finally they noted that if the degree of input- variation is higher thus the chance of units to be efficient is more.

Considering the shortcoming of the cross efficiency model for ranking efficient units, Jahanshahloo et al.(2011) presented a model overcoming this difficulty.

In the provided method the authors tried to avoid the existence of alternative optimal weights in cross efficiency method.

The authors used TOPSIS technique and presented a new method for ranking units. They provided the following model:

$$
\theta_{ij} = \{ \frac{U^t Y_i}{V^t X_i} \mid \frac{U^t Y_l}{V^t X_l} \le 1, \frac{U^t Y_j}{V^t X_j} = \theta_{jj}, l = 1,...,n, l \ne i, U \ge 0, V \ge 0 \}
$$

In the above-mentioned equation θ_{jj} is considered as the efficiency scores of DMU_J using corresponding weights. Also θ_{ij} is considered to be the efficiency of DMU_i when optimal weights of DMU_j is being used.

In accordance to this fact that the more effective and useful units in society in comparison to others should have better ranking orders, Noura et al.(2011) provided a method for ranking efficient units. They provided the following steps.

Step 1: For each set of inputs and outputs choose the lower and upper bounds. Define E as the set of efficient units.

$$x_i^{*u} = Max_{j \in E} \mid x_{ij} \mid, \quad x_i^{*l} = Min_{j \in E} \mid x_{ij} \mid, i = 1, ..., m$$

$$y_r^{*u} = Max_{j \in E} \mid y_{rj} \mid, \quad y_r^{*l} = Min_{j \in E} \mid y_{rj} \mid, r = 1, ..., s$$

Step 2: Considering step 1, they introduced the utility inputs and outputs as follows:

$$\underline{x} = x_i^{*l}, \forall i (i \in D_i^-), \quad \overline{x} = x_i^{*u}, \forall i (i \in D_i^+)$$

$$\underline{y} = y_r^{*l}, \forall r (r \in D_o^-), \quad \overline{y} = y_r^{*u}, \forall r (r \in D_o^+)$$

Step 3: Considering each of the efficient units belongs to E, they introduced the dimensionless (d_i, d_r) as follows:

$$\forall i (i \in D_i^+) \quad dij = \frac{x_{ij}}{x_{ij} + \xi}, \quad \forall i (i \in D_i^-) \quad dij = \frac{\overline{x_i}}{x_i + \xi}$$

$$\forall r (r \in D_r^+) \quad drj = \frac{y_{rj}}{y_r + \xi}, \quad \forall r (r \in D_r^-) \quad drj = \frac{\overline{y_r}}{y_{rj} + \xi}$$

Note that ξ is considered to be a small and non-zero number in order to avoid dividing by zero. The authors define the following equation:

$$D_j = \sum_{i \in I} d_{ij} + \sum_{r \in R} d_{rj}$$

They noted that the larger value of the D_j shows that DMU_j is more successful. where $I = D_i^+ \cup D_i^-, \quad R = D_r^+ \cup D_r^-$.

Orkju and Bal (2011) provided a modified model considering a goal programming technique to be used in the second stage of the cross evaluation.

$$\min \quad a = \{\sum_{j=1}^{n} \eta_j, \sum_{j=1}^{n} \alpha_j\}$$

$$s.t. \quad \sum_{i=1}^{m} v_{ip} x_{ip} = 1,$$

$$\sum_{r=1}^{s} u_{rp} y_{rp} - \theta_{pp}^{*} \sum_{i=1}^{m} v_{ip} x_{ip} = 0, \tag{38}$$

$$\sum_{r=1}^{s} u_{rp} y_{rj} - \sum_{i=1}^{m} v_{ip} x_{ij} + \alpha_j = 0, \quad j = 1,...,n,$$

$$M - \alpha_j + \eta_j - p_j = 0, \quad j = 1,...,n,$$

$$u_{rp} \geq 0, v_{ip} \geq 0, r = 1,...,s, i = 1,...,m,$$

$$\alpha_j \geq 0, \eta_j \geq 0, p_j \geq 0, j = 1,...,n.$$

The authors noted that using this model there is still a difficulty of existing alternative optimal solutions.

Wu et al.(2011) described the main suffering of cross efficiency and used Shannon entropy for obtaining the weights utilized in the cross efficiency method.

Jahanshahloo et al.(2011) presented a model in order to obtain the symmetric weights to be used in cross efficacy method based on DEA technique.

The authors first compute the efficiency of DMUs.

Then, in accordance to the following model they choose the solutions as the secondary goal for each DMU:

$$\min \quad e^T Z_o e$$

$$s.t. \quad u_o y_o = 1,$$

$$\quad v_o X_o = \theta_o,$$

$$\quad u_o Y - v_o X \leq 0, \tag{39}$$

$$\quad u_{oi} y_{oi} - u_{oj} y_{oj} \leq z_{oij}, \forall i, j,$$

$$\quad u_{oj} y_{oj} - u_{oi} y_{oi} \leq z_{oij}, \forall i, j,$$

$$\quad u_o, v_o \geq d.$$

After that the cross-efficiency for any DMU_j is computed by the weights DMU_o from the above model. Finally, they introduced the following index:

$$\theta_{oj} = \frac{u_o^* Y_j}{v_o^* X_j}.$$

In regards of ideal and anti-ideal units Wang et al.(2011) presented a cross efficiency evaluation. The authors mentioned that a DMU should make its distance smaller to the ideal DMU and larger to the anti-ideal unit by choosing a unique set of weights.

Thus, they proposed the following steps for cross efficiency evaluation considering this idea.

Step 1: Minimization of the distance from ideal DMU.
Step 2: Maximization of the distance from anti ideal DMU.
Step 3: Maximization of the distance between ideal DMU and anti-ideal DMU.
Step 4: Maximization of the relative closeness.

The authors noted that if the relative closeness of a DMU is bigger than the performance of this DMU will be better.

Ramon et al. (2011) tried to avoid using unrealistic weighs thus they used the profiles of weights in cross-efficiency evaluation. While calculating the cross-efficiency scores, they authors ignored the profiles of the weights of those units that cannot choose non-zero weights from among the alternative optimal solutions. They also proposed the "peer-restricted" cross-efficiency evaluation in which the units assessed in a peer evaluation. By this method they meant that the profiles of weights of some inefficient units are not taken into account. Finally, the presented approach extended to derive a common set of weights.

On basis of DEA technique, Wang and Jiang (2012) presented an alternative mixed integer linear programming models to find the most efficient units. The advantage of the presented model is that it uses the input and output information completely and there is no need to specify any assurance regions for input and output weights to avoid zero weights.

$$
\begin{aligned}
\min \quad & \sum_{i=1}^{m} v_i \left(\sum_{j=1}^{n} x_{ij} \right) - \sum_{r=1}^{s} u_r \left(\sum_{j=1}^{n} y_{rj} \right) \\
s.t. \quad & \sum_{r=1}^{s} u_r y_{rj} - \sum_{i=1}^{m} v_i x_{ij} \leq I_j, \quad j = 1,...,n, \\
& \sum_{j=1}^{n} I_j = 1, \\
& I_j \in \{0,1\}, \quad j = 1,...,n, \\
& u_r \geq \frac{1}{(m+s)max_j\{y_{rj}\}}, \quad r = 1,...,s, \\
& v_i \geq \frac{1}{(m+s)max_j\{x_{ij}\}}, \quad i = 1,...,m.
\end{aligned}
\tag{40}
$$

Considering the DEA technique Khodabakhshi and Aryavash (2012) presented a method for completely ranking all units. In the first step, considering this assumption that the sum of efficiency values of all units should equal to 1, they computed the minimum and maximum efficiency values of each. Then, in regards of the combination of units' minimum and maximum efficiency values, they determined the rank of each.

Considering undesirable outputs and restrictions in DEA technique, Guo and Wu (2012) provided a complete ranking of units. The authors mentioned that an important aspect of the provided model is that this model provided a unique ranking of units considering "maximal balanced index" according to the obtained optimal shadow prices.

$$
\begin{aligned}
\max \quad & \sum_{i=1}^{m} v_i w_i + \sum_{t=1}^{k} \eta_t h_t - \sum_{r=1}^{s} u_r q_r \\
s.t. \quad & \sum_{r=1}^{s} u_r y_{rj} - \sum_{i=1}^{m} v_i x_{ij} - \sum_{t=1}^{k} \eta_t b_{tj} \leq 0, \quad j = 1, \dots, n, \\
& \sum_{i=1}^{m} v_i x_{ip} + \sum_{t=1}^{k} \eta_r b_{tp} = 1, \\
& \sum_{r=1}^{s} u_r y_{rp} = EEF_p, \\
& U, V, \eta \geq 0.
\end{aligned}
\tag{41}
$$

Note that by EEF_p is stand for the optimal objective function of multiplier model.

Ramon et al.(2012) tried to introduce a new insight for ranking units while considering a common set of weights. Their idea is based upon minimizing the deviations of the common weights from the nonzero weighs of DEA technique. Furthermore, they utilized several norms for measuring such differences.

Considering a system of voting, Zerafat Angiz et al.(2012) aggregated the opinions of experts in this system and tried to provide a method considers fuzzy concept which is computationally efficient and can fully rank alternatives. They described the presented method as follows:

First of all, number of votes given to a rank position grouped to construct fuzzy numbers and after that they introduced the artificial ideal alternative. Furthermore, considering DEA technique the efficiency measure of alternatives obtained while artificial ideal alternative is being compared by each of the alternative pair by pair and then at the final alternatives ranked in accordance to their efficiency scores. The authors noted that in the case that this method cannot completely rank alternatives weight restrictions based on fuzzy concept should be imposed into the analysis.

According to the idea of optimizing the rank position of units Contreras (2012) used cross evaluation for ranking units in DEA technique.

$$
\begin{aligned}
\min \quad & r_{kk} \\
s.t. \quad & \theta_{kk} = \theta_{kk}^{*}, \\
& \theta_{lk} - \theta_{jk} + \delta_{lj}^{k}\beta \geq 0, l \neq j, \\
& \theta_{lk} - \theta_{jk} + \gamma_{lj}^{k}\beta \geq \varepsilon, l \neq j, \\
& \delta_{lj}^{k} + \delta_{jl}^{k} \leq 1, l \neq j, \\
& \delta_{lj}^{k} + \gamma_{jl}^{k} = 1, l \neq j, \\
& r_{lk} = \sum_{\substack{j=1 \\ j \neq l}}^{n} \frac{\delta_{lj}^{k} + \gamma_{jl}^{k}}{2} + 1, \quad l = 1, \dots, n, \\
& \gamma_{lj}^{k}, \delta_{lj}^{k} \in \{0,1\}, l \neq j.
\end{aligned}
\tag{42}
$$

They introduced the following index and Considering this index they solved the following model.

$$
\theta_{jk} = \frac{U_{k}^{*} Y_{j}}{V_{k}^{*} X_{j}}
$$

$$
\begin{aligned}
\min \quad & r_{kk} \\
s.t. \quad & \theta_{kk}^{*} \cdot \sum_{h=1}^{m} v_{hk} x_{hj} - \sum_{r=1}^{s} u_{rk} y_{rj} + \delta_{kj}\beta \geq 0, j \neq k, \\
& -\theta_{kk}^{*} \cdot \sum_{h=1}^{m} v_{hk} x_{hj} + \sum_{r=1}^{s} u_{rk} y_{rj} + \delta_{jk}\beta \geq 0, j \neq k, \\
& \theta_{kk}^{*} \cdot \sum_{h=1}^{m} v_{hk} x_{hj} - \sum_{r=1}^{s} u_{rk} y_{rj} + \gamma_{kj}\beta \geq \varepsilon, j \neq k, \\
& -\theta_{kk}^{*} \cdot \sum_{h=1}^{m} v_{hk} x_{hj} + \sum_{r=1}^{s} u_{rk} y_{rj} + \gamma_{jk}\beta \geq \varepsilon, j \neq k, \\
& \delta_{lj}^{k} + \delta_{jl}^{k} \leq 1, l \neq j, \\
& \delta_{lj}^{k} + \gamma_{jl}^{k} = 1, l \neq j, \\
& r_{kk} = 1 + \frac{1}{2} \sum_{\substack{j=1 \\ j \neq k}}^{n} \delta_{kj} + \gamma_{kj}, \\
& \gamma_{kj}, \gamma_{jk}, \delta_{kj}, \delta_{jk} \in \{0,1\}, j \neq k.
\end{aligned}
\tag{43}
$$

They authors mentioned that non uniqueness of optimal weight may occur.

Considering Tchebycheff norm Rezai Balf et al. (2012) provide a model for ranking units. They proved that this model is always feasible and stable and claimed that it has advantages while comparing to other methods.

$$
\begin{aligned}
\max \quad & V_p \\
s.t. \quad & V_p \geq \sum_{\substack{j=1 \\ j \neq o}}^{n} \lambda_j x_{ij} - x_{ip}, \quad i = 1, \ldots, m, \\
& V_p \geq y_{rp} - \sum_{\substack{j=1 \\ j \neq o}}^{n} \lambda_j y_{rj}, \quad r = 1, \ldots, s, \\
& \lambda_j \geq 0, \quad j = 1, \ldots, n.
\end{aligned}
\tag{44}
$$

Note that

$$
V_p = Max\{ (\sum_{\substack{j=1 \\ j \neq o}}^{n} \lambda_j x_{ij} - x_{ip}) i = 1, \ldots, m, (y_{rp} - \sum_{\substack{j=1 \\ j \neq p}}^{n} \lambda_j y_{rj}) r = 1, \ldots, s \}.
$$

Wu et al.(2012) tried to provide a weight balanced DEA model for decreasing the differences in weights.

$$
\begin{aligned}
\min \quad & \sum_{r=1}^{s} | \alpha_r^d | + \sum_{i=1}^{m} | \beta_i^d | \\
s.t. \quad & \sum_{i=1}^{m} w_{id} x_{ij} - \sum_{r=1}^{s} \mu_{rd} y_{rj} \geq 0, \quad j = 1, \ldots, n, \\
& \sum_{i=1}^{m} w_{id} x_{id} = 1, \\
& \sum_{i=1}^{m} \mu_{rd} y_{rd} = E_{dd}, \\
& \mu_{rd} y_{rd} + \alpha_r^d = E_{dd} / s, r = 1, \ldots, s, \\
& w_{id} x_{id} + \beta_i^d = 1 / m, i = 1, \ldots, m, \\
& w \geq 0, \mu \geq 0, \beta^d, \alpha^d \, free.
\end{aligned}
\tag{45}
$$

They obtained the cross-efficiency score of DMU_j from the following formula:

$$E_j = \frac{1}{n}\sum_{d=1}^{n} E_{dj}, j = 1,...,n.$$

where

$$E_{dj} = \frac{\sum_{r=1}^{s} \mu_{rd}^{*} y_{rj}}{\sum_{i=1}^{m} w_{id}^{*} x_{ij}}.$$

Note that optimal weights may be uniqueness.

Hosseinzadeh Lotfi et al. (2013) in order to rank alternatives presented an improved three-stage method in multiple criteria decision analysis.

First, for each alternative they tried to get the rank position in accordance to the best and worst weights while considering the optimistic and pessimistic cases. As regards of the fact that the optimal weights are not unique they introduced a secondary goal. At the end, while considering the optimistic or pessimistic cases the ranks of the alternatives computed. The authors mentioned that in the third stage a multi-criteria decision making model is introduced and they solved it with the technique of mixed integer programming. For sake of simplicity in computation the authors provided a LP model as a counterpart of this model.

$$\min \quad 2nr_o^o + \sum_{i=1 i\neq o}^{n} (n+1-r_i^{i*})r_i^o$$

$$s.t. \quad \sum_{j=1}^{k} w_j^o v_{ij} - \sum_{j=1}^{k} w_j^o v_{hj} + \delta_{ih}^o M \geq 0, \quad i = 1,...,n, i \neq h,$$

$$\delta_{ih}^o + \delta_{hi}^o = 1, \quad i = 1,...,n, i \neq h,$$

$$\delta_{ih}^o + \delta_{hk}^o + \delta_{ki}^o \geq 1, \quad i = 1,...,n, i \neq h \neq k, \quad (46)$$

$$r_i^o = 1 + \sum_{h\neq i}^{n} \delta_{ih}^o, \quad i = 1,...,n,$$

$$w^o \in \phi,$$

$$\delta_{ih}^o \in \{0,1\}, i = 1,...,n, i \neq h.$$

Considering the ideal rank from the above model, the rank vector for each alternative is computed.

According to this fact that the ranking order is more important than efficiency score, Zerafat engiz et al.(2013) introduced a cross efficiency matrix. In doing so, they have provided the following procedure:

Step 1: Run the CCR model and calculate the efficiency score of all DMUs while considering the Z_{pp}^* as the efficiency score of DMU_p.

Step 2: Then construct the cross-efficiency diagonal matrix Z considering $(z_{jp}^*)_{n \times n}$ with the diagonal elements of Z_{pp}^*.

Step 3: The cross-efficiency matrix in this step should be converted into a cross-ranking matrix R that the elements are considered as $(r_{jp})_{n \times n}$. Note that in the matrix of R, r_{jp} is considered as the ranking order of z_{jp}^* which is replaced in the column p of matrix Z.

Step 4: Construct the preference matrix W with the element of $(w_{jk})_{n \times n}$. In doing so, Taking into account the matrix R in which w_{jk} is the number of time that DMU_j is placed in rank k.

Step 5: Construct matrix Ω as $(\hat{\theta}_{jp})_{n \times n}$ in which $\hat{\theta}_{jk}$ is calculated by summing the efficiency scores in matrix Z, corresponds to DMU_j, being placed in rank k.

Step 6: Obtain a common set of weights for final ranking of DMUs using the following modified Cook and Kress (1990) method:

$$\max \quad \beta = \frac{\sum_{k=1}^{n} \mu_k \hat{\theta}_{jk}}{\beta_j^*}$$

$$s.t. \quad \sum_{k=1}^{n} \mu_k \hat{\theta}_{jk} \leq 1, \quad j = 1, ..., n, \tag{47}$$

$$\mu_k - \mu_{k+1} \geq d(k, \varepsilon), \quad k = 1, ..., n-1,$$

$$\mu_n \geq d(n, \varepsilon).$$

Note that $\hat{\theta}_{jk}$ is obtained from step 5 and β_j^* is the optimal solution of model which is proposed by Cook and Kress (1990). Finally, the DMUs are ranked based on their $z_j^* = \sum_{k=1}^{n} \mu_k^* \hat{\theta}_{jk}$ values.

Washio and Yamada (2013) presented a model called rank-based measure (RBM) which tries to find the best ranking since in reality best ranking order is important than having the most advantage weight and maximizing the efficiency. Thus Washio and Yamada suggested a method for acquiring those weights resulted from the best ranking as long as calculating those weights that maximize the efficiency score. Finally they applied the presented model the cross efficiency assessment.

Chen et al.(2013) considered the problem of infeasibility that may happen in variable returns to scale form of the technology provided a super efficiency DEA model in regards of the directional distance function presented by Nerlove–Luenberger.

CONCLUSION

In this chapter some of the existing models discussed ranking methods based on DEA technique were reviewed. Each of these methods tries to investigate the problem of how to rank efficient units from different viewpoints. Cross efficiency, super efficiency, multi-criteria decision-making methodologies, benchmarking, optimal weights, and statistical are of important methods introduced for ranking units. Obviously, considering each method there exist advantages and disadvantages while comparing to the other methods. Knowing the ranking order of units can help senior manager in better decision making.

REFERENCES

Adler, N., Friedman, L., & Sinuany-Stern, Z. (2002). Review of ranking methods in the data envelopment analysis context. *European Journal of Operational Research*, *140*(2), 249–2652. doi:10.1016/S0377-2217(02)00068-1

Adler, N., & Golany, B. (2001). Evaluation of deregulated airline networks using data envelopment analysis combined with principal component analysis with an application to Western Europe. *European Journal of Operational Research*, *132*(2), 18–31. doi:10.1016/S0377-2217(00)00150-8

Ali, A. I., & Nakosteen, R. (2005). Ranking industry performance in the US. *Socio-Economic Planning Sciences*, *39*(1), 11–24. doi:10.1016/j.seps.2003.10.003

Alirezaee, M. R., & Afsharian, M. (2007). A complete ranking of DMUs using restrictions in DEA models. *Applied Mathematics and Computation*, *189*(2), 1550–1559. doi:10.1016/j.amc.2006.12.031

Amirteimoori, A. (2007). DEA efficiency analysis: Efficient and anti-efficient frontier. *Applied Mathematics and Computation*, *186*(1), 10–16. doi:10.1016/j.amc.2006.07.006

Amirteimoori, A., Jahanshahloo, G. R., & Kordrostami, S. (2005). Ranking of decision making units in data envelopment analysis: A distance-based approach. *Applied Mathematics and Computation*, *171*(1), 122–135. doi:10.1016/j.amc.2005.01.065

Andersen, P., & Petersen, N. C. (1993). A procedure for ranking efficient units in data envelopment analysis. *Management Science*, *39*(10), 1261–1294. doi:10.1287/mnsc.39.10.1261

Ashrafi, A., Jaafar, A. B., Lee, L. S., & Abu Bakar, M. R. (2011). An Enhanced Russell Measure of Super-Efficiency for Ranking Efficient Units in Data Envelopment Analysis. *American Journal of Applied Sciences*, *8*(1), 92–96. doi:10.3844/ajassp.2011.92.96

Banker, R. D., Charnes, A., & Cooper, W. W. (1984). Some models for estimating technical and scale inefficiencies in data envelopment analysis. *Management Science*, *30*(9), 1078–1092. doi:10.1287/mnsc.30.9.1078

Bardhan, L., Bowlin, W. B., Cooper, W. W., & Sueyoshi, T. (1996). Models for efficiency dominance in data envelopment analysis. Part I: Additive models and MED measures. *Journal of the Operations Research Society of Japan*, *39*, 322–332.

Belton, V., & Stewart, T. J. (1999). DEA and MCDA: Competing or complementary approaches? In N. Meskens & M. Roubens (Eds.), *Advances in Decision Analysis*. Norwell: Kluwer Academic Publishers. doi:10.1007/978-94-017-0647-6_6

Charnes, A., Clark, C. T., Cooper, W. W., & Golany, B. (1985a). A developmental study of data envelopment analysis in measuring the efficiency of maintenance units in the US air forces. *Annals of Operations Research*, *2*(1), 95–112. doi:10.1007/BF01874734

Charnes, A., Cooper, W. W., Golany, B., Seiford, L., & Stutz, J. (1985b). Foundations of data envelopment analysis for Pareto–Koopmans efficient empirical production functions. *Journal of Econometrics*, *30*(1-2), 91–107. doi:10.1016/0304-4076(85)90133-2

Charnes, A., Cooper, W. W., Huang, Z. M., & Sun, D. B. (1990). Polyhedral cone-ratio data envelopment analysis models with an illustrative application to large commercial banks. *Journal of Econometrics*, *46*, 73–91. doi:10.1016/0304-4076(90)90048-X

Charnes, A., Cooper, W. W., & Li, S. (1989). Using data envelopment analysis to evaluate the efficiency of economic performance by Chinese cities. *Socio-Economic Planning Sciences, 23*(6), 325–344. doi:10.1016/0038-0121(89)90001-3

Charnes, A., Cooper, W. W., & Rhodes, E. (1978). Measuring the efficiency of decision-making units. *European Journal of Operational Research, 2*(6), 429–444. doi:10.1016/0377-2217(78)90138-8

Charnes, A., Cooper, W. W., Seiford, L., & Stutz, L. (1982). A multiplicative model for efficiency analysis. *Socio-Economic Planning Sciences, 6*(5), 223–224. doi:10.1016/0038-0121(82)90029-5

Chen, J.-X. (2011). A modofied super-efficiency measure based on simoultanious input-output projection in data envelopment analysis. *Computers & Operations Research, 38*, 496–504. doi:10.1016/j.cor.2010.07.008

Chen, J.-X., & Deng, M. (2011). A cross-dependence based ranking system for efficient and inefficient units in DEA. *Expert Systems with Applications, 38*(8), 9648–9655. doi:10.1016/j.eswa.2011.01.165

Chen, M.-C. (2007). Ranking discovered rules from data mining with multiple criteria by data envelopment analysis. *Expert Systems with Applications, 33*(4), 1110–1116. doi:10.1016/j.eswa.2006.08.007

Chen, Y., Du, J., & Huo, J. (2013). Super-efficiency based on a modified directional distance function. *Omega, 41*(3), 621–625. doi:10.1016/j.omega.2012.06.006

Chena, Y., & Sherman, H. D. (2004). The benefits of non-radial vs. radial super-efficiency DEA: An application to burden-sharing amongst NATO member nations. *Socio-Economic Planning Sciences, 38*(4), 307–320. doi:10.1016/j.seps.2003.10.007

Contreras, I. (2012). Optimizing the rank position of the DMU as secondary goal in DEA cross-evaluation. *Applied Mathematical Modelling, 36*(6), 2642–2648. doi:10.1016/j.apm.2011.09.046

Cook, W. D., Doyle, J., Green, R., & Kress, M. (1996). Ranking players in multiple tournaments. *Computers & Operations Research, 23*(9), 869–880. doi:10.1016/0305-0548(95)00082-8

Cook, W. D., & Johnston, D. A. (1992). Evaluating suppliers of complex systems: A multiple criteria approach. *The Journal of the Operational Research Society, 43*(11), 1055–1061. doi:10.1057/jors.1992.163

Cook, W. D., & Kress, M. (1990a). A data envelopment model for aggregating preference rankings. *Management Science, 36*(11), 1302–1310. doi:10.1287/mnsc.36.11.1302

Cook, W. D., & Kress, M. (1990b). An mth generation model for weak ranking of players in a tournament. *The Journal of the Operational Research Society, 41*(12), 1111–1119.

Cook, W. D., & Kress, M. (1991). A multiple criteria decision model with ordinal preference data. *European Journal of Operational Research, 54*(2), 191–198. doi:10.1016/0377-2217(91)90297-9

Cook, W. D., & Kress, M. (1994). A multiple-criteria composite index model for quantitative and qualitative data. *European Journal of Operational Research, 78*(3), 367–379. doi:10.1016/0377-2217(94)90046-9

Cook, W. D., Kress, M., & Seiford, L. M. (1993). On the use of ordinal data in data envelopment analysis. *The Journal of the Operational Research Society, 44*(2), 133–140. doi:10.1057/jors.1993.25

Cook, W. D., Kress, M., & Seiford, L. M. (1996). Data envelopment analysis in the presence of both quantitative and qualitative factors. *The Journal of the Operational Research Society, 47*(7), 945–953. doi:10.1057/jors.1996.120

Cooper, W. W., Park, K. S., & Yu, G. (1999). IDEA and ARIDEA: Models for dealing with imprecise data in data envelopment analysis. *Management Science, 45*(4), 597–607. doi:10.1287/mnsc.45.4.597

Cooper, W. W., & Tone, K. (1997). Measures of inefficiency in data envelopment analysis and stochastic frontier estimation. *European Journal of Operational Research, 99*(1), 72–88. doi:10.1016/S0377-2217(96)00384-0

Darvish, M., Yasaei, M., & Saeedi, A. (2009). Application of the graph theory and matrix methods to contractor ranking. *International Journal of Project Management, 27*(6), 610–619. doi:10.1016/j.ijproman.2008.10.004

Doyle, J. R., & Green, R. (1994). Efficiency and cross-efficiency in data envelopment analysis: Derivatives, meanings and uses. *The Journal of the Operational Research Society, 45*(5), 567–578. doi:10.1057/jors.1994.84

Dula, J. H., & Hickman, B. L. (1997). Effects of excluding the column being scored from the DEA envelopment LP technology matrix. *The Journal of the Operational Research Society, 48*(10), 1001–1012. doi:10.1057/palgrave.jors.2600434

Dyson, R. G., & Thanassoulis, E. (1988). Reducing weight flexibility in data envelopment analysis. *The Journal of the Operational Research Society*, *39*(6), 563–576. doi:10.1057/jors.1988.96

Farrell, M. J. (1957). The measurement of productive efficiency. *Journal of the Royal Statistical Society A*, *120*(3), 253–281. doi:10.2307/2343100

Feroz, E. H., Raab, R. L., Ulleberg, G. T., & Alsharif, K. (2009). Kamal Alsharif. Global warming and environmental production efficiency ranking of the Kyoto Protocol nations. *Journal of Environmental Management*, *90*(2), 1178–1183. doi:10.1016/j.jenvman.2008.05.006

Friedman, L., & Sinuany-Stern, Z. (1997). Scaling units via the canonical correlation analysis and the data envelopment analysis. *European Journal of Operational Research*, *100*(3), 629–637. doi:10.1016/S0377-2217(97)84108-2

Friedman, L., & Sinuany-Stern, Z. (1998). Combining ranking scales and selecting variables in the data envelopment analysis context: The case of industrial branches. *Computers & Operations Research*, *25*(9), 781–791. doi:10.1016/S0305-0548(97)00102-0

Gholam Abri, A., Jahanshahloo, G. R., Hosseinzadeh Lotfi, F., Shoja, N., & Fallah Jelodar, M. (2011). A new method for ranking non-extreme efficient units in data envelopment analysis. *Optimization Letters*, *2011*. doi:10.1007/s11590-011-0420-1

Giokas, D. I., & Pentzaropoulos, G. C. (2008). Efficiency ranking of the OECD member states in the area of telecommunications: A composite AHP/DEA study. *Telecommunications Policy*, *32*(9-10), 672–685. doi:10.1016/j.telpol.2008.07.007

Golany, B. (1988). An interactive MOLP procedure for the extension of data envelopment analysis to effectiveness analysis. *The Journal of the Operational Research Society*, *39*(8), 725–734. doi:10.1057/jors.1988.127

Golany, B., & Roll, Y. A. (1994). Incorporating standards via data envelopment analysis. In A. Charnes, W. W. Cooper, A. Y. Lewin, & L. M. Seiford (Eds.), *Data Envelopment Analysis: Theory, Methodology and Applications*. Norwell: Kluwer Academic Publishers. doi:10.1007/978-94-011-0637-5_16

Green, R. H., & Doyle, J. R. (1995). On maximizing discrimination in multiple criteria decision making. *The Journal of the Operational Research Society*, *46*(2), 192–204. doi:10.1057/jors.1995.24

Green, R. H., Doyle, J. R., & Cook, W. D. (1996). Preference voting and project ranking using data envelopment analysis and cross-evaluation. *European Journal of Operational Research, 90*, 461–472. doi:10.1016/0377-2217(95)00039-9

Guo, D., & Wu, J. (2012). A complete ranking of DMUs with undesirable outputs using restrictions in DEA models. *Mathematical and Computer Modelling*.

Halme, M., Joro, T., Korhonen, P., Salo, S., & Wallenius, J. (1999). A value efficiency approach to incorporating preference information in data envelopment analysis. *Management Science, 45*(1), 103–115. doi:10.1287/mnsc.45.1.103

Hashimoto, A. (1997). A ranked voting system using a DEA/AR exclusion model: A note. *European Journal of Operational Research, 97*(3), 600–604. doi:10.1016/S0377-2217(96)00281-0

Hatefi, S. M., & Torabi, S. A. (2012). A common weight MCDA-DEA approach to construct composite indicators. *Ecological Economics, 70*(1), 114–120. doi:10.1016/j.ecolecon.2010.08.014

Hosseinzadeh Lotfi, F., Noora, A. A., Jahanshahloo, G. R., & Reshadi, M. (2011). One DEA ranking method based on applying aggregate units. *Expert Systems with Applications, 38*(10), 13468–13471. doi:10.1016/j.eswa.2011.02.145

Hosseinzadeh Lotfi, F., Rostamy-Malkhalifeh, M., Aghayi, N., Ghelej Beigi, Z., & Gholami, K. (2013). An improved method for ranking alternatives in multiple criteria decision analysis. *Applied Mathematical Modelling, 37*(1-2), 25–33. doi:10.1016/j.apm.2011.09.074

Hougaard, J. L. (1999). Fuzzy scores of technical efficiency. *European Journal of Operational Research, 115*(3), 529–541. doi:10.1016/S0377-2217(98)00165-9

Hwang, C. L., & Yoon, K. (1981). *Multiple Attribute Decision Making Methods and Applica- tions*. Berlin, Heidelberg: Springer. doi:10.1007/978-3-642-48318-9

Jablonsky, J. (2011). Multicriteria approaches for ranking of efficient units in DEA models. *Central European Journal of Operations Research*. doi:10.1007/s10100-011-0223-6

Jahanshahloo, G. R., & Afzalinejad, M. (2006). A ranking method based on a full-inefficient frontier. *Applied Mathematical Modelling, 30*(3), 248–260. doi:10.1016/j.apm.2005.03.023

Jahanshahloo, G. R., Hosseinzadeh Lotfi, F., Jafari, Y., & Maddahi, R. (2011). Selecting symmetric weights as a secondary goal in DEA cross-efficiency evaluation. *Applied Mathematical Modelling, 35*(1), 544–549. doi:10.1016/j.apm.2010.07.020

Jahanshahloo, G. R., Hosseinzadeh Lotfi, F., Shoja, N., Tohidi, G., & Razavian, S. (2004). Ranking using l1-norm in data envelopment analysis. *Applied Mathematics and Computation, 153*(1), 215–224. doi:10.1016/S0096-3003(03)00625-8

Jahanshahloo, G. R., Hosseinzadeh Lotfi, F., Zhiani Rezai, H., & Rezai Balf, F. (2005). Using Monte Carlo method for ranking efficient DMUs. *Applied Mathematics and Computation, 162*(1), 371–379. doi:10.1016/j.amc.2003.12.139

Jahanshahloo, G. R., Junior, H. V., Hosseinzadeh Lotfi, F., & Akbarian, D. (2007). A new DEA ranking system based on changing the reference set. *European Journal of Operational Research, 181*(1), 331–337. doi:10.1016/j.ejor.2006.06.012

Jahanshahloo, G. R., Khodabakhshi, M., Hosseinzadeh Lotfi, F., & Moazami Goudarzi, M. R. (2011). A cross-efficiency model based on super-efficiency for ranking units through the TOPSIS approach and its extension to the interval case. *Mathematical and Computer Modelling, 53*(9-10), 1946–1955. doi:10.1016/j.mcm.2011.01.025

Jahanshahloo, G. R., Memariani, A., Hosseinzadeh Lotfi, F., & Zhiani Rezai, H. (2005). A note on some of DEA models and finding efficiency and complete ranking using common set of weights. *Applied Mathematics and Computation, 166*(2), 265–281. doi:10.1016/j.amc.2004.04.088

Jahanshahloo, G. R., Pourkarimi, L., & Zarepisheh, M. (2006). Modified MAJ model for ranking decision making units in data envelopment analysis. *Applied Mathematics and Computation, 174*(2), 1054–1059. doi:10.1016/j.amc.2005.06.001

Jahanshahloo, G. R., Sanei, M., Hosseinzadeh Lotfi, F., & Shoja, N. (2004). Using the gradient line for ranking DMUs in DEA. *Applied Mathematics and Computation, 151*(1), 209–219. doi:10.1016/S0096-3003(03)00333-3

Jahanshahloo, G. R., Sanei, M., Hosseinzadeh Lotfi, F., & Shoja, N. (2004). Using the gradient line for ranking DMUs in DEA. *Applied Mathematics and Computation, 151*(1), 209–219. doi:10.1016/S0096-3003(03)00333-3

Jahanshahloo, G. R., Sanei, M., & Shoja, N. (2004). *Modified ranking models, using the concept of advantage in data envelopment analysis*. Working paper.

Joro, T., Korhonen, P., & Wallenius, J. (1998). Structural comparison of data envelopment analysis and multiple objective linear programming. *Management Science, 44*(7), 962–970. doi:10.1287/mnsc.44.7.962

Jürges, H., & Schneider, K. (2007). Fair ranking of teachers. *Empirical Economics, 32*(2-3), 411–431. doi:10.1007/s00181-006-0112-3

Kao, C. (2010). Weight determination for consistently ranking alternatives in multiple criteria decision analysis. *Applied Mathematical Modelling, 34*(7), 1779–1787. doi:10.1016/j.apm.2009.09.022

Karsak, E. E. (1998). A two-phase robot selection procedure. *Production Planning and Control, 9*(7), 675–684. doi:10.1080/095372898233678

Khodabakhshi, M. (2007). A super-efficiency model based on improved outputs in data envelopment analysis. *Applied Mathematics and Computation, 184*(2), 695–703. doi:10.1016/j.amc.2006.06.110

Kornbluth, J. S. H. (1991). Analyzing policy effectiveness using cone restricted data envelopment analysis. *The Journal of the Operational Research Society, 42*(12), 1097–1104. doi:10.1057/jors.1991.203

Leeneer, I. D. (2002). Selecting land mine detection strategies by means of outranking MCDM techniques. *European Journal of Operational Research, 139*(2), 327–338. doi:10.1016/S0377-2217(01)00372-1

Li, S. H., Jahanshahloo, G. R., & Khodabakhshi, M. (2007). A super-efficiency model for ranking efficient units in data envelopment analysis. *Applied Mathematics and Computation, 184*(2), 638–648. doi:10.1016/j.amc.2006.06.063

Li, X. B., & Reeves, G. R. (1999). A multiple criteria approach to data envelopment analysis. *European Journal of Operational Research, 115*(3), 507–517. doi:10.1016/S0377-2217(98)00130-1

Lins, M. P., Gomes, E. G., Soares de Mello, J. C. C. B., & Soares de Mello, A. J. R. (2003). Olympic ranking based on a zero sum gains DEA model. *European Journal of Operational Research, 148*(2), 312–322. doi:10.1016/S0377-2217(02)00687-2

Liu, F., & Hsuan Peng, H. (2008). Ranking of units on the DEA frontier with common weights. *Computers & Operations Research, 35*(5), 1624–1637. doi:10.1016/j.cor.2006.09.006

Liu, F. H. F., & Peng, H. H. (2008). Ranking of DMUs on the DEA frontier with common weights. *Computers & Operations Research, 35*(5), 1624–1637. doi:10.1016/j.cor.2006.09.006

Lu, W.-M., & Lo, S.-F. (2009). An interactive benchmark model ranking performers - Application to financial holding companies. *Mathematical and Computer Modelling, 49*(1-2), 172–179. doi:10.1016/j.mcm.2008.06.008

Lu, W.-M., & Lo, S.-F. (2009). An interactive benchmark model ranking performers Application to financial holding companies. *Mathematical and Computer Modelling, 49*(1-2), 172–179. doi:10.1016/j.mcm.2008.06.008

Martic, M., & Savic, G. (2001). An application of DEA for comparison analysis and ranking of region in Serbia with regards to Social economic development. *European Journal of Operational Research, 132*, 343-356.

Martin, J. C., & Roman, C. (2006). A Benchmarking Analysis of Spanish Commercial Airports. A Comparison Between SMOP and DEA Ranking Methods. *Networks and Spatial Economics, 6*(2), 111–134. doi:10.1007/s11067-006-7696-1

Mecit, E. D., & Alp, I. (2013). A new proposed model of restricted data envelopment analysis by correlation coefficients. *Applied Mathematical Modelling, 3*(5), 3407–3425. doi:10.1016/j.apm.2012.07.010

Mehrabian, S., Alirezaee, M. R., & Jahanshahloo, G. R. (1999). A complete efficiency ranking of decision making units in data envelopment analysis. *Computational Optimization and Applications, 14*(2), 261–266. doi:10.1023/A:1008703501682

Morrison, D. F. (1976). *Multivariate Statistical Methods*. New York: McGraw-Hill.

Noura, A. A., Hosseinzadeh Lotfi, F., Jahanshahloo, G. R., & Fanati Rashidi, S. (2001). Super-efficiency in DEA by effectiveness of each unit in society. *Applied Mathematics Letters, 24*(5), 623–626. doi:10.1016/j.aml.2010.11.025

Obata, T., & Ishii, H. (2003). A method for discriminating efficient candidates with ranked voting data. *European Journal of Operational Research, 151*(1), 233–237. doi:10.1016/S0377-2217(02)00597-0

Oral, M., Kettani, O., & Lang, P. (1991). A methodology for collective evaluation and selection of industrial R. *Management Science, 7*(37), 871–883. doi:10.1287/mnsc.37.7.871

Orkcu, H. H., & Bal, H. (2011). Goal programming approaches for data envelopment analysis cross efficiency evaluation. *Applied Mathematics and Computation, 218*(2), 346–356. doi:10.1016/j.amc.2011.05.070

Paralikas, N., & Lygeros, A. I. (2005). A multi-criteria and fuzzy logic based methodology for the lerative ranking of the fire hazard of chemical substances and installations. *Process Safety and Environmental Protection, 83*(2B2), 122–134. doi:10.1205/psep.04236

Raab, R. L., & Feroz, E. H. (2007). A productivity growth accounting approach to the ranking of developing and developed nations. *The International Journal of Accounting, 42*(4), 396–415. doi:10.1016/j.intacc.2007.09.004

Ramón, N., Ruiz, J. L., & Sirvent, I. (2011). Reducing differences between profiles of weights: A "peer-restricted" cross-efficiency evaluation. *Omega, 39*(6), 634–6411. doi:10.1016/j.omega.2011.01.004

Ramón, N., Ruiz, J. L., & Sirvent, I. (2012). Common sets of weights as summaries of DEA profiles of weights: With an application to the ranking of professional tennis players. *Expert Systems with Applications, 39*(5), 4882–4889. doi:10.1016/j.eswa.2011.10.004

Rezai Balf, F., Zhiani Rezai, H., Jahanshahloo, G. R., & Hosseinzadeh Lotfi, F. (2012). Ranking efficient DMUs using the Tchebycheff norm. *Applied Mathematical Modelling, 1*(1), 46–56. doi:10.1016/j.apm.2010.11.077

Rödder, W., & Reucher, E. (2011). A consensual peer-based DEA-model with optimized cross-efficiencies – Input allocation instead of radial reduction. *European Journal of Operational Research, 212*(1), 148–154. doi:10.1016/j.ejor.2011.01.035

Sadjadi, S.J., Mrani, H. O, Abdollahzadeh, S., Alinaghian, M., & Mohammadi, H. (2011). A robust super-efficiency data envelopment analysis model for ranking of provincial gas companies in Iran. *Expert Systems with Applications, 38*.

Seiford, L. M. (1996). Data envelopment analysis: The evolution of the state of the art (1978–1995). *Journal of Productivity Analysis, 7*(2–3), 99–137. doi:10.1007/BF00157037

Seiford, L. M., & Thrall, R. M. (1990). Recent developments in data envelopment analysis: The mathematical programming approach to frontier analysis. *Journal of Econometrics, 46*, 7–38. doi:10.1016/0304-4076(90)90045-U

Seiford, L. M., & Zhu, J. (1999). Infeasibility of super-efficiency data envelopment analysis models. *INFOR, 37*(2), 174–187.

Seiford, L. M., & Zhu, J. (2003). Context-dependent data envelopment analysis Measuring attractiveness and progress. *Omega, 31*(5), 397–408. doi:10.1016/S0305-0483(03)00080-X

Sexton, T. R., Silkman, R. H., & Hogan, A. J. (1986). Data envelopment analysis: Critique and extensions. In R. H. Silkman (Ed.), *Measuring Efficiency: An Assessment of Data Envelopment Analysis* (pp. 73–105). San Francisco, CA: Jossey-Bass.

Siegel, S., & Castellan, N. J. (1998). *Nonparametric statistics for the behavioral sciences*. New York: McGraw-Hill BOOK CO.

Sinuany-Stern, Z., & Friedman, L. (1998). Data envelopment analysis and the discriminant analysis of ratios for ranking units. *European Journal of Operational Research, 111*, 470–478. doi:10.1016/S0377-2217(97)00313-5

Sinuany-Stern, Z., Mehrez, A., & Barboy, A. (1994). Academic departments efficiency via data envelopment analysis. *Computers & Operations Research, 21*(5), 543–556. doi:10.1016/0305-0548(94)90103-1

Sinuany-Stern, Z., Mehrez, A., & Hadad, Y. (2000). An AHP/DEA methodology for ranking decision making units. *International Transactions in Operational Research, 7*(2), 109–124. doi:10.1111/j.1475-3995.2000.tb00189.x

Sitarz, S. (2013). The medal points' incenter for rankings in sport. *Applied Mathematics Letters, 26*(4), 408–412. doi:10.1016/j.aml.2012.10.014

Soltanifar, M., & Hosseinzadeh Lotfi, F. (2011). The voting analytic hierarchy process method for discriminating among efficient decision making units in data envelopment analysis. *Computers & Industrial Engineering, 60*(4), 585–592. doi:10.1016/j.cie.2010.12.016

Strassert, G., & Prato, T. (2002). Selecting Farming Systems Using a New Multiple Criteria Decision Model: The Balancing and Ranking Method. *Ecological Economics, 40*(2), 269–277. doi:10.1016/S0921-8009(02)00002-2

Sueyoshi, T. (1999). Data envelopment analysis non-parametric ranking test and index measurement: Slack-adjusted DEA and an application to Japanese agriculture cooperatives. *Omega International Journal of Management Science, 27*, 315–326. doi:10.1016/S0305-0483(98)00057-7

Tatsuoka, M. M., & Lohnes, P. R. (1988). *Multivariant analysis: Techniques for educational and psycologial research* (2nd ed.). New York: Macmillan Publishing Company.

Thanassoulis, E., & Dyson, R. G. (1992). Estimating preferred target input–output levels using data envelopment analysis. *European Journal of Operational Research, 56*(1), 80–97. doi:10.1016/0377-2217(92)90294-J

Thompson, R. G., Langemeier, L. N., Lee, C. T., & Thrall, R. M. (1990). The role of multiplier bounds in efficiency analysis with application to Kansas farming. *Journal of Econometrics, 46*(1-2), 93–108. doi:10.1016/0304-4076(90)90049-Y

Thompson, R. G., Lee, E., & Thrall, R. M. (1992). DEA/AR efficiency of U.S. independent oil/gas producers over time. *Computers & Operations Research*, *19*(5), 377–391. doi:10.1016/0305-0548(92)90068-G

Thompson, R. G., Singleton, F. D. Jr, Thrall, R. M., & Smith, B. A. (1986). Comparative site evaluations for locating a highenergy physics lab in Texas. *Interfaces*, *16*(6), 35–49. doi:10.1287/inte.16.6.35

Thrall, R. (1996). Duality, classification and slacks in data envelopment analysis. *Annals of Operations Research*, *66*, 109–138. doi:10.1007/BF02187297

Tone, K. (2002). A slack-based measure of super-efficiency in data envelopment analysis. *European Journal of Operational Research*, *143*(1), 32–41. doi:10.1016/S0377-2217(01)00324-1

Torgersen, A. M., Forsund, F. R., & Kittelsen, S. A. C. (1996). Slack-adjusted efficiency measures and ranking of efficient units. *Journal of Productivity Analysis*, *7*, 379–398. doi:10.1007/BF00162048

Troutt, M. D. (1995). A maximum decisional efficiency estimation principle. *Management Science*, *41*(1), 76–82. doi:10.1287/mnsc.41.1.76

Wang, Y.-M., Chin, K.-S., & Luo, Y. (2011). Cross-efficiency evaluation based on ideal and anti-ideal decision making units. *Expert Systems with Applications*, *38*(8), 10312–10319. doi:10.1016/j.eswa.2011.02.116

Wang, Y.-M., & Jiang, P. (2012). Alternative mixed integer linear programming models for identifying the most efficient decision making unit in data envelopment analysis. *Computers & Industrial Engineering*, *62*(2), 546–553. doi:10.1016/j.cie.2011.11.003

Wang, Y.-M., Luo, Y., & Hua, Z. (2007). Aggregating preference rankings using OWA operator weights. *Information Sciences*, *177*(16), 3356–3363. doi:10.1016/j.ins.2007.01.008

Wang, Y.-M., Luo, Y., & Lan, Y.-X. (2011). Common weights for fully ranking decision making units by regression analysis. *Expert Systems with Applications*, *38*(8), 9122–9128. doi:10.1016/j.eswa.2011.01.004

Wang, Y.-M., Luo, Y., & Liang, L. (2009). Ranking decision making units by imposing a minimum weight restriction in the data envelopment analysis. *Original Research Article Journal of Computational and Applied Mathematics*, *223*(1), 469–484. doi:10.1016/j.cam.2008.01.022

Washio, S., & Yamada, S. (2013). Evaluation method based on ranking in data envelopment analysis. *Expert Systems with Applications*, *40*(1), 257–262. doi:10.1016/j. eswa.2012.07.015

Williams, R., & Van Dyke, N. (2007). Measuring the international standing of universities with an application to Australian universities. *Higher Education*, *53*(6), 819–841. doi:10.1007/s10734-005-7516-4

Wong, Y.-H. B., & Beasley, J. E. (1990). Restricting weight flexibility in data envelopment analysis. *The Journal of the Operational Research Society*, *41*(9), 829–835. doi:10.1057/jors.1990.120

Wu, J., Sun, J., & Liang, L. (2012). Cross efficiency evaluation method based on weight-balanced data envelopment analysis model. *Computers & Industrial Engineering*, *63*(2), 513–519. doi:10.1016/j.cie.2012.04.017

Wu, J., Sun, J., Liang, L., & Zha, Y. (2011). Determination of weights for ultimate cross efficiency using Shannon entropy. *Expert Systems with Applications*, *38*(5), 5162–5165. doi:10.1016/j.eswa.2010.10.046

Young, F. W., & Hamer, R. M. (1987). *Multidimensional Scaling, History, Theory and Applications*. London: Lawrence Erlbaum.

Zerafat Angiz, M., Mustafa, A., & Kamali, M. J. (2013). Cross-ranking of Decision Making Units in Data Envelopment Analysis. *Applied Mathematical Modelling*, *37*(1-2), 398–405. doi:10.1016/j.apm.2012.02.038

Zerafat Angiz, M., Tajaddini, A., Mustafa, A., & Jalal Kamali, M. (2012). Ranking alternatives in a preferential voting system using fuzzy concepts and data envelopment analysis. *Computers & Industrial Engineering*, *63*(4), 784–790. doi:10.1016/j. cie.2012.04.019

Zhu, J. (1996a). Robustness of the efficient decision-making units in data envelopment analysis. *European Journal of Operational Research*, *90*(3), 451–460. doi:10.1016/0377-2217(95)00054-2

Zhu, J. (1996b). Data envelopment analysis with preference structure,(1996b). *The Journal of the Operational Research Society*, *47*(1), 136–150. doi:10.1057/ jors.1996.12

Chapter 8
Performance Evaluation of Suppliers with Undesirable Outputs Using DEA

Alireza Shayan Arani
Islamic Azad University, Iran

Hamed Nozari
Islamic Azad University, Iran

Meisam Jafari-Eskandari
Payam Noor University of Shemiranat, Iran

ABSTRACT

Performance evaluation and selection and ranking of suppliers is very important due to the competitiveness of companies in the present age. The nature of this kind of decision is usually complex and lacks clear structure and many qualitative and quantitative performance criteria such as quality, price, flexibility, and delivery times must be considered to determine the most suitable supplier. Given that in the supplier evaluation may offer undesirable outputs and random limitations, providing a model for evaluating the performance of suppliers is of utmost importance. With regard to the issue of multi-criteria selection of suppliers, one of the most efficient models to choose suppliers is DEA.in this paper to measure the strong performance and development of undesirable output and random limitations concept the SBM model is used.

DOI: 10.4018/978-1-5225-0596-9.ch008

INTRODUCTION

Today, the performance measurement of organizational units and Evaluate the effectiveness has particular importance as an important part of the organizational process. The importance of this as far as many large organizations planning their own activities on this basis. Supply chain management evaluated supplier performance potential by multiple criteria instead of cost factors. In this context, methods and models been suggested to choose and evaluate. DEA traditional models such as: CCR and BCC measure the only weak radial performance and are not able to measure strong performance. To resolve this deficiency and strong performance measurements SBM model was used in this article. Also in this article with concept of random limitations SBM model developed for the consideration of undesirable outputs. This method (DEA) which use multiple input and output to select the best single decision, first time was used In 1976, Carnegie university and in 1978 in an article entitled "Measuring the efficiency of decision making units" were presented.

The Concept of DEA

Data envelopment analysis shows a concept of calculating the levels of efficiency within an organization that the performance of each unit is calculated in comparison with the highest performance. Data envelopment analysis is a mathematical model to the observed data that provide the new method for estimating the efficiency frontier Such as the production function that is basis of modern economic (Charnes, 1978).

DEA is a mathematical programming method to evaluate the decision making units. The purpose of the DMU is an organizational unit or a separate organization that managed by a person called director or chief on the condition that the organization or organizational unit has a systematic process. The system consists of production systems and services or the profit and nonprofit or governmental and non-governmental (Cooper, 2004).

SBM Model

Since the introduction of the DEA in 1978 by Charnes and others, application and study about it quickly spread and by 1996 more than 1000 article about it was published. CCR model uses fractional Planning model that are multiple input and output ratio in others DMUs in order to calculate the relative efficiency of decision making units. A decision-making unit in CCR model is effective when the optimum value of the objective function has value one. In 2001 Tone, in order to solve the problems of the CCR, and robust performance measurement, SBM model to be introduced below.

In this episode, the development of models of collective is goal that first provides a scalar as efficiency to each unit and secondly, the objective function is sustainable compared to unit change.

In this section, we introduce a measure for collective models and it called SBM that has the following properties:

1. The present size, Compared to unit change are sustainable both the inputs and the outputs.
2. Compared to Input and output are strictly monotonic.

The Mathematical Definition of SBM Model

N Decision Making Unit with input and output matrix is as follows:

$$X = (x_{ij}) \in R^{m \times n} \tag{1}$$

$$Y = (y_{ij}) \in R^{s \times n} \tag{2}$$

We assume that the data are positive:

$$x \geq 0$$

$$y \geq 0$$

Production ability set is defined as follows:

$$P = \left[(x, y) \middle| x \geq X\lambda, y \leq Y\lambda, \lambda \geq 0 \right] \tag{3}$$

Where λ is a non-negative vector in R.
To define the decision making unit (x_0, y_0) expression considered to be:

$$x_0 = X\lambda + s^- \tag{4}$$

$$y_0 = Y\lambda - s^+ \tag{5}$$

$$S^- \geq 0, S^+ \geq 0, \lambda \geq 0$$

These vectors are as follows:

$$s^+ \in R^m, s^- \in R^m \tag{6}$$

$X \geq 0$ and $\lambda \geq 0$ condition that makes it always: $x_0 \geq s^-$

Using the s^+ and s^-, ρ index is defined as follows:

$$\rho^* = min \frac{1 - \frac{1}{m} \sum_{i=1}^m \frac{s_i^-}{x_{i0}}}{1 + \frac{1}{s} \left(\sum_{r=1}^s \frac{s_r^+}{y_{r0}} \right)} \tag{7}$$

Where ρ is approximately between zero and one. In order to estimate the efficiency of a DMU, fractional program is formulated as follows:

$$min\rho^* = \frac{1 - \frac{1}{m} \sum_{i=1}^m \frac{s_i^-}{x_{i0}}}{1 + \frac{1}{s} \left(\sum_{r=1}^s \frac{s_r^+}{y_{r0}} \right)} \tag{8}$$

s.t.

$$x_0 = X\lambda + s^-$$

$$y_0 = Y\lambda - s^+$$

$$S^- \geq 0, S^+ \geq 0, \lambda \geq 0$$

SBM now with the introduction of a positive scalar variable t be converted to the following program:

$$\min \tau = t - \frac{1}{m} \sum_{i=1}^{m} \frac{t_{si}^{-}}{x_{i0}}$$

s.t.

$$1 = t + \frac{1}{s} \sum_{r=1}^{s} \frac{t_{sr}^{+}}{y_{r0}} \qquad (9)$$

$$\mathbf{x}_0 = \mathbf{X}\boldsymbol{\lambda} + \mathbf{s}^{-}$$

$$\mathbf{y}_0 = \mathbf{Y}\boldsymbol{\lambda} - \mathbf{s}^{+}$$

$$\mathbf{S}^{-} \geq 0 \,, \mathbf{S}^{+} \geq 0 \,, \boldsymbol{\lambda} \geq 0 \,, \mathbf{t} > 0$$

Now we define:
SBM becomes the following linear program:

$$\min \tau = t - \frac{1}{m} \sum_{i=1}^{m} \frac{S_{i}^{-}}{x_{i0}}$$

s.t.

$$1 = t + \frac{1}{s} \sum_{r=1}^{s} \frac{S_{r}^{+}}{y_{r0}} \qquad (10)$$

$$t\mathbf{x}_0 = \mathbf{X}\boldsymbol{\Lambda} + \mathbf{S}^{-}$$

$$\mathbf{y}_0 = \mathbf{Y}\boldsymbol{\Lambda} - \mathbf{S}^{+}$$

$$\mathbf{S}^{-} \geq 0, \mathbf{S}^{+} \geq 0, \boldsymbol{\lambda} \geq 0, \mathbf{t} > 0$$

A DMU (x, y) is efficient if and only if $\rho* = 1$ that this condition is equivalent to:

$$s_i^{-*} = 0, s_r^{+*} = 0$$

Models with Undesirable Inputs and Outputs

The general attitude in evaluating the performance of the unit is to reduce the amount of input and Increase the amount of output that improves the performance and the best performance.

CCR and BCC models are based on the grounds. But in practice, it should be noted that organizations are not always looking for maximum output and minimum input, because the outputs and inputs can be Acceptable (good) or inappropriate (bad).

DEA's usually assumed that a greater amount of output bring greater efficiency, But it should be noted there are outputs such as pollution, dangerous withdrawals, downtime which said to be undesirable outputs, DMU efficiency is reduced by their increasing.

The Proposed Model for Choosing Suppliers with Undesirable Outputs

Our aim in this section, is Present a model so evaluation and selection of suitable suppliers in conditions of uncertainty or potentially.

Primary model SBM that we want to develop as follows:

$$\rho^* = min \ \frac{1 - \frac{1}{m} \sum_{i=1}^{m} \frac{s_i^-}{x_{i0}}}{1 + \frac{1}{s_1 + s_2} \left(\sum_{r=1}^{s_1} \frac{s_r^g}{y_{r0}^g} + \sum_{r=1}^{s_2} \frac{s_r^b}{y_{r0}^b} \right)}$$

s.t.   (11)

$$x_0 = X\lambda + s^-$$

$$y_0^g = Y^g\lambda - s^g$$

$$y_0^b = Y^b\lambda + s^b$$

$$S^- \geq 0, S^g \geq 0, S^b \geq 0, \lambda \geq 0$$

According to the given input and output as random variables and α as a risk or probability of satisfying the equation, for the first constraint (input) are:

$$x_0 = \sum_{j=1}^{n} x_j \lambda_j + s_i^- \rightarrow p \left\{ \sum_{j=1}^{n} \tilde{x}_j \lambda_j \leq \tilde{x}_0 \right\} \geq 1 - \alpha \tag{12}$$

We suppose ζ_r is auxiliary external amount for r th output. So we can choose the auxiliary external amount that applies in following equation:

$$p \left\{ \sum_{j=1}^{n} \tilde{x}_j \lambda_j - \tilde{x}_0 \leq 0 \right\} = 1 - \alpha + \xi \tag{13}$$

There is $s_i^+ > 0$ s so that:

$$p \left\{ \sum_{j=1}^{n} \tilde{x}_j \lambda_j + s_i^- \leq \tilde{x}_0 \right\} = 1 - \alpha \Rightarrow \quad \alpha = p \left\{ \sum_{j=1}^{n} \tilde{x}_j \lambda_j + s_i^- \geq \tilde{x}_0 \right\} \tag{14}$$

Can be easily realized that $\zeta_r = 0$, if and only if $s_i^- = 0$.
We had above expression in terms of α:

$$\alpha = p \left\{ \sum_{j=1}^{n} \tilde{x}_j \lambda_j - \tilde{x}_0 \geq -s_i^- \right\} \tag{15}$$

Then we write the probability of above expression by the standard normal distribution function. Z is standard normal (with 0 mean and 1 variance).

$$\alpha = p \left\{ z \geq \frac{-s_i^- - \left(\sum_{j=1}^{n} \tilde{x}_j \lambda_j - \tilde{x}_{i0} \right)}{\sigma_i^I (\lambda)} \right\} \tag{16}$$

To convert random equations to certain equations, we write following equation In terms of Φ that is the standard normal distribution function.

$$\alpha = 1 - p \left\{ z \leq \frac{-s_i^- - \left(\sum_{j=1}^{n} \tilde{x}_j \lambda_j - \tilde{x}_{i0} \right)}{\sigma_i^I(\lambda)} \right\}$$

$$\alpha = 1 - \Phi \left[\frac{-s_i^- - \left(\sum_{j=1}^{n} \tilde{x}_j \lambda_j - \tilde{x}_{i0} \right)}{\sigma_i^I(\lambda)} \right]$$

$$1 - \alpha = \Phi \left[\frac{-s_i^- - \left(\sum_{j=1}^{n} \tilde{x}_j \lambda_j - \tilde{x}_{i0} \right)}{\sigma_i^I(\lambda)} \right] \Rightarrow \Phi_{(1-\alpha)}^{-1} \left[\frac{-s_i^- - \left(\sum_{j=1}^{n} \tilde{x}_j \lambda_j - \tilde{x}_{i0} \right)}{\sigma_i^I(\lambda)} \right]$$

The first constraint in certain modes is as follows:

$$\sum_{j=1}^{n} x_j \lambda_j + s_i^- + \Phi_{(1-\alpha)}^{-1} \sigma_i^I(\lambda) = x_0 \tag{17}$$

Variance formula in stochastic model is as follows:

$$\left(\sigma_i^I(\lambda) \right)^2 = \sum_{j \neq 0} \sum_{k \neq 0} \lambda_j \lambda_k \mathrm{cov}\left(\tilde{x}_{ij}, \tilde{x}_{ik} \right) + 2 \left(\lambda_0 - 1 \right) \sum_{j \neq 0} \lambda_j \mathrm{cov}\left(\tilde{x}_{ij}, \tilde{x}_{i0} \right) \tag{18}$$

$$+ \left(\lambda_0 - 1^2 \right) \mathrm{var}\left(\tilde{x}_{i0} \right)$$

Similarly for second constraint (desired output):

$$y_0^g = \sum_{j=1}^{n} y_j^g \lambda_j - s_r^g \xrightarrow{p} \quad p \left\{ \sum_{j=1}^{n} \tilde{y}_j \lambda_j \geq \tilde{y}_0^g \right\} \geq 1 - \alpha$$

319

$$p\left\{\sum_{j=1}^{n}\tilde{y}_j\lambda_j - \tilde{y}_0^g \geq 0\right\} = 1 - \alpha + \xi$$

$$p\left\{\sum_{j=1}^{n}\tilde{y}_j\lambda_j - \tilde{y}_0^g \geq s_r^{g+}\right\} = 1 - \alpha \Rightarrow \alpha = p\left\{\sum_{j=1}^{n}\tilde{y}_j\lambda_j - \tilde{y}_0^g \leq s_r^{g+}\right\}$$

$$\alpha = p\left\{z \leq \frac{s_r^{g+} - \left(\sum_{j=1}^{n}\tilde{y}_j^g\lambda_j - \tilde{y}_0^g\right)}{\tilde{A}_r^0(\lambda)}\right\}$$

$$\alpha = \Phi\left\{\frac{s_r^{g+} - \left(\sum_{j=1}^{n}\tilde{y}_j^g\lambda_j - \tilde{y}_0^g\right)}{\sigma_r^0(\lambda)}\right\}$$

$$\Phi_{(\alpha)}^{-1}\left\{\frac{s_r^{g+} - \left(\sum_{j=1}^{n}\tilde{y}_j^g\lambda_j - \tilde{y}_0^g\right)}{\tilde{A}_r^0(\lambda)}\right\}$$

The second constraint for desired output in the case of deterministic equations is as follows:

$$\sum_{j=1}^{n}y_j^g\lambda_j - s_r^{g+} + \Phi_{(\alpha)}^{-1}\sigma_r^0(\lambda) = y_0^g \tag{19}$$

$$\left(\sigma_r^0(\lambda)\right)^2 = \sum_{i\neq 0}\sum_{j\neq 0}\lambda_i\lambda_j\mathrm{cov}\left(\tilde{y}_{ri},\tilde{y}_{rj}\right) + 2\left(\lambda_0 - 1\right)\sum_{i\neq 0}\lambda_i\mathrm{cov}\left(\tilde{y}_{ri},\tilde{y}_{r0}\right) + \tag{20}$$

$$\left(\lambda_0 - 1^2\right)\mathrm{var}\left(\tilde{y}_{r0}\right)$$

For the third constraint (undesirable output) are:

$$y_0^b = \sum_{j=1}^{n} y_j^b \lambda_j + s_r^b \xrightarrow{p} \quad p\left\{\sum_{j=1}^{n} \tilde{y}_j \lambda_j \leq \tilde{y}_0^b\right\} \geq 1 - \alpha$$

$$p\left\{\sum_{j=1}^{n} \tilde{y}_j \lambda_j - \tilde{y}_0^b \leq 0\right\} = 1 - \alpha + \xi$$

$$p\left\{\sum_{j=1}^{n} \tilde{y}_j^b \lambda_j + s_r^b \leq \tilde{y}_0^b\right\} = 1 - \alpha \Rightarrow \quad \alpha = \quad p\left\{\sum_{j=1}^{n} \tilde{y}_j^b \lambda_j + s_r^{b+} \geq \tilde{y}_0^b\right\}$$

$$\alpha = p\left\{z \geq \frac{-s_r^b - \left(\sum_{j=1}^{n} \tilde{y}_j^b \lambda_j - \tilde{y}_0^b\right)}{\sigma_r^0(\lambda)}\right\}$$

$$\alpha = 1 - p\left\{z \leq \frac{-s_r^b - \left(\sum_{j=1}^{n} \tilde{y}_j^b \lambda_j - \tilde{y}_0^b\right)}{\sigma_r^0(\lambda)}\right\}$$

$$1 - \alpha = \Phi\left\{\frac{-s_r^b - \left(\sum_{j=1}^{n} \tilde{y}_j^b \lambda_j - \tilde{y}_0^b\right)}{\sigma_r^0(\lambda)}\right\}$$

$$\Phi_{(1-\alpha)}^{-1}\left\{\frac{-s_r^b - \left(\sum_{j=1}^{n} \tilde{y}_j^b \lambda_j - \tilde{y}_0^b\right)}{\sigma_r^0(\lambda)}\right\}$$

The third constraint for undesirable outputs in the case of deterministic equations is as follows:

$$\sum_{j=1}^{n} y_j^b \lambda_j + s_r^b + \Phi_{(1-\alpha)}^{-1} \sigma_r^0 (\lambda) = y_0^b \tag{21}$$

Variance formula for undesirable output in stochastic model is as follows:

$$\left(\sigma_r^0 (\lambda)\right)^2 = \sum_{i \neq 0} \sum_{j \neq 0} \lambda_i \lambda_j \text{cov} \left(\tilde{y}_{ri}, \tilde{y}_{rj}\right) + 2\left(\lambda_0 - 1\right) \sum_{i \neq 0} \lambda_i \text{cov} \left(\tilde{y}_{ri}, \tilde{y}_{r0}\right) \tag{22}$$

$$+ \left(\lambda_0 - 1^2\right) \text{var} \left(\tilde{y}_{r0}\right)$$

As a result, deterministic model is as follows:

$$\rho^* = \min \frac{1 - \dfrac{1}{m} \sum_{i=1}^{m} \dfrac{s_i^-}{x_{i0}}}{1 + \dfrac{1}{s_1 + s_2} \left(\sum_{r=1}^{s_1} \dfrac{s^g}{y_{r0}^g} + \sum_{r=1}^{s_2} \dfrac{s_r^b}{y_{r0}^b}\right)}$$

s.t. $\tag{23}$

$$\sum_{j=1}^{n} x_j \lambda_j + s_i^- + \Phi_{(1-\alpha)}^{-1} \sigma_i^I (\lambda) = x_0 \qquad\qquad i = 1, \ldots\ldots\ldots m$$

$$\sum_{j=1}^{n} y_j^g \lambda_j - s_r^g + \Phi_{(\alpha)}^{-1} \sigma_r^0 (\lambda) = y_0^g \qquad\qquad r = 1, \ldots\ldots\ldots s^g$$

$$\sum_{j=1}^{n} y_j^b \lambda_j + s_r^b + \Phi_{(1-\alpha)}^{-1} \sigma_r^0 (\lambda) = y_0^b \qquad\qquad r = 1, \ldots\ldots\ldots s^b$$

$$S^- \geq 0, \quad S^g \geq 0, \quad S^b \geq 0, \quad \lambda \geq 0$$

Index and Input and Output Variables

In selection of suppliers indices and variables have been studied that examples are as follows:

Timely delivery, price (cost), quality, flexibility, service, responsiveness, technology, credit, management, organization, geographic location, production facilities and capacity, rate of interest, collaboration, and performance history ....

A software company as one of the largest producers of software systems was considered as case study in this paper. It should be noted in this case study, 20 companies have been considered.

To evaluate customers the different indicators has been used that have been collected by experts over the past few years.

Some of these indicators are shown in Table 1.

Among the indicators candidate we chose four indicators for model, which of these indicators were considered two inputs and two outputs.

These indicators include:

- Profit margin
- Expert
- Customer Satisfaction
- The average service time

Table 1. Indicators of assessment

The average number of personnel	Per capita customer to personnel
The number of customers	Percent of receipt
Sales performance	Sale budget
sales budget percent	Percent of sign
Remained of the annual demands	System per capita to expert
Profit margin	Sales Per capita to expert
Number of instantaneous service	The average certificate to support staff
Customer Satisfaction	Contact time to fulfill the customer needs
Ratio of referring to the service	Expert
The ratio of Services to members	The number of duplicate services per customer per day
The mean time of signature and receipt	Sales of new systems

There were different ways of dealing with undesirable variables. So in this article we will compare the results of different methods. Here, only the results of the paper mentioned and compared.

As you can see performance results are almost equal to each other by a small margin And only the results of the first method in DMU 15 and 17 has a wide margin with undesirable SBM and second method that the reason is eliminating undesirable variables in the first method.

So it seems the first method does not consider the efficiency of DMU 15 and 17 by eliminating undesirable variables and show inefficient these DMUs (table 2, figures 1 and 2).

Thus, according to the Comparisons, undesirable SBM and switching position methods Have almost identical results and reverse and transfer methods, too.

Table 2. Results of efficient and inefficient different ways in dealing with undesirable variable

Removal procedure to undesirable output	Method for switching position	Transfer method	Reversal method	Undesirable SBM method	Names of suppliers
0.52	0.60	**1.00**	**1.00**	0.46	D1
0.30	0.34	0.73	0.61	0.23	D2
0.17	0.14	0.20	0.16	0.12	D3
0.38	0.30	0.32	0.22	0.26	D4
0.45	0.34	0.18	0.18	0.31	D5
1.00	**1.00**	**1.00**	0.87	**1.00**	D6
0.12	0.12	0.16	0.14	0.08	D7
0.33	0.37	0.20	0.10	0.26	D8
0.48	0.41	0.23	0.14	0.35	D9
0.46	0.37	0.14	0.14	0.33	D10
0.11	0.09	0.06	0.10	0.08	D11
0.07	0.06	0.12	0.10	0.05	D12
0.23	0.18	0.32	0.27	0.16	D13
0.32	0.34	0.38	0.31	0.25	D14
0.67	**1.00**	0.56	**1.00**	**1.00**	D15
0.49	0.66	0.45	0.58	0.64	D16
0.67	**1.00**	0.56	0.99	**1.00**	D17
0.67	0.61	0.69	0.55	0.53	D18
0.06	0.05	0.08	0.08	0.04	D19
0.36	0.41	**1.00**	**1.00**	0.29	D20

Figure 1. compare the efficacy and inefficiency --- 1 and 2 methodologies and undesirable SBM

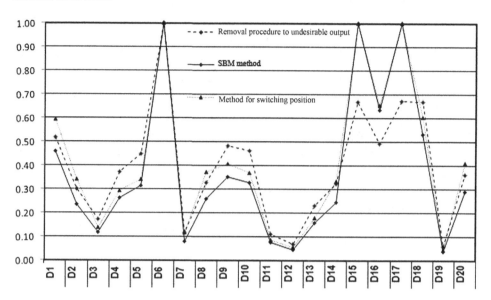

Figure 2. compare the efficacy and inefficiency --- 3 and 4 methodologies and undesirable SBM

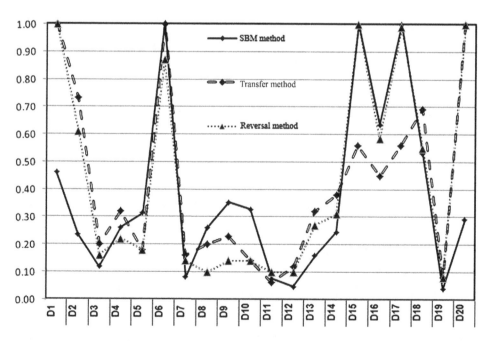

CONCLUSION

With the changes that have occurred in recent years, the supply of goods and services has increased than the demand in many manufacturing sectors and increasing production and capital on the one hand and the subject of globalization on the other hand, has led to The competition to survive and thrive in the business market. Given the importance of choosing suppliers, many methods have been proposed for this purpose and it continues. One of the best methods selecting and evaluating suppliers in the supply chain model is DEA. According to the DEA method to calculate the weight of their decision variables are used without any changes, this is of utmost importance. Given that in supplier evaluation there will also be random constraints and undesirable outputs, Therefore, we must be careful in choosing the appropriate method. The results show that methods such as reverse, transfer... have not similar result for efficiency. Therefore, an effective model for evaluating the performance of suppliers appears to be necessary.

REFERENCES

Agpak, K., & Gokcen, H. (2007). A chance-constrained approach to stochastic line balancing problem. *European Journal of Operational Research, 180*(3), 1098–1115.

Banker, R. D., & Thrall, R. M. (1992). Estimation of returns to scale using Data Envelopment Analysis. *European Journal of Operational Research, 62*(1), 74–84. doi:10.1016/0377-2217(92)90178-C

Barla, S. B. (2003). A case study of supplier selection for lean supply by using a mathematical model. *Logistics Information Management, 16*(6), 451–459. doi:10.1108/09576050310503420

Bayazit, O. (2006). Use of analytic network process in vendor selection decisions. Benchmarking. *International Journal (Toronto, Ont.), 13*(5), 566–579.

Bevilacqua, M., Ciarapica, F. E., & Giacchetta, G. (2006). A fuzzy-QFD approach to supplier selection. *Journal of Purchasing and Supply Management, 12*(1), 14–27. doi:10.1016/j.pursup.2006.02.001

Bhattacharya, U. K. (2009). A chance-constrained goal programming model for the dvertising planning problem. *European Journal of Operational Research, 192*(2), 382–395. doi:10.1016/j.ejor.2007.09.039

Boer, D., Labro, E., & Moralacchi, P. (2001). A review of methods supporting supplier selection. *European Journal of Purchasing and Supply Management, 7*(2), 75-89.

Bottani, E., & Rizzi, A. (2008). An adapted multi-criteria approach to suppliers and products selection An application oriented to lead-time reduction. *International Journal of Production Economics, 111*(2), 763–781. doi:10.1016/j.ijpe.2007.03.012

Braglia, M., & Petroni, A. (2000). A quality assurance-oriented methodology for handling trade-offs in supplier selection. *International Journal of Physical Distribution & Logistics Management, 30*(2), 96–111. doi:10.1108/09600030010318829

Çebi, F., & Bayraktar, D. (2003). An integrated approach for supplier selection. *Logistics Information Management, 16*(6), 395–400. doi:10.1108/09576050310503376

Chan, F. T. S. (2003). Interactive selection model for supplier selection process: An analytical hierarchy process approach. *International Journal of Production Research, 41*(15), 3549–3579. doi:10.1080/00207540310001383358

Chan, F.T.S., & Kumar, N. (2007). Global supplier development considering risk factors using fuzzy extended AHP-based approach. *OMEGA – International Journal of Management Science, 35*(4), 417–431.

Charnes, A., & Cooper, W. W. (1957). Chance Constrained Programming. *Management Science, 6*(1), 73–79. doi:10.1287/mnsc.6.1.73

Charnes, A., Cooper, W. W., & Rhodes, E. (1978). Measuring the efficiency of decision making units. *European Journal of Operational Research, 2*(6), 429–444. doi:10.1016/0377-2217(78)90138-8

Chen, C. T., Lin, C. T., & Huang, S. F. (2006). A fuzzy approach for supplier evaluation and selection in supply chain management. *International Journal of Production Economics, 102*(2), 289–301. doi:10.1016/j.ijpe.2005.03.009

Compilation of References

Abbaspour, M., Hosseinzadeh Lotfi, F., Karbassi, A. R., Roayaei, E., & Nikomaram, H. (2009). Development of the Group Malmquist Productivity Index on non-discretionary Factors. *International Journal of Environmental of Research, 3*, 109–116.

Abbott, M. (2006). The productivity and efficiency of the Australian electricity supply industry. *Energy Economics, 28*(4), 444–454. doi:10.1016/j.eneco.2005.10.007

Adler, N., Friedman, L., & Sinuany-Stern, Z. (2002). Review of Ranking Methods in the DEA Context. *European Journal of Operational Research, 140*, 249–265. doi:10.1016/S0377-2217(02)00068-1

Adler, N., & Golany, B. (2001). Evaluation of deregulated airline networks using data envelopment analysis combined with principal component analysis with an application to Western Europe. *European Journal of Operational Research, 132*(2), 18–31. doi:10.1016/S0377-2217(00)00150-8

Aghdam, R. F. (2011). Dynamics of productivity change in the Australian electricity industry: Assessing the impacts of electricity reform. *Energy Policy, 39*(6), 3281–3295. doi:10.1016/j.enpol.2011.03.019

Agpak, K., & Gokcen, H. (2007). A chance-constrained approach to stochastic line balancing problem. *European Journal of Operational Research, 180*(3), 1098–1115.

Ahn, D., & Seiford, L.M. (1993). Determining of impact differentiation output on the ranking, in public and private universities. *Socio Economic Journal, 7*(8).

Ahn, T., Arnold, V., Charnes, A., & Cooper, W. W. (1989). DEA and ratio efficiency analyses for public institutions of higher learning in Texas. *Research in Governmental and Nonprofit Accounting, 5*, 165–185.

Ahn, Y., & Min, H. (2014). Evaluating the multi-period operating efficiency of international airports using data envelopment analysis and the Malmquist productivity index. *Journal of Air Transport Management, 39*, 12–22. doi:10.1016/j.jairtraman.2014.03.005

Alem, S. M., Azadeh, A., Shirkouhi, S. N., & Rezaie, K. (2009). A decision making methodology for vendor selection problem based on DEA, FDEA and CCDEA models.*Third Asia International Conference on Modeling & Simulation.* doi:10.1109/AMS.2009.69

Compilation of References

Ali, A. I., & Nakosteen, R. (2005). Ranking industry performance in the US. *Socio-Economic Planning Sciences*, *39*(1), 11–24. doi:10.1016/j.seps.2003.10.003

Ali, A. I., & Seiford, L. M. (1990). Translation invariance in data envelopment analysis. *Operations Research Letters*, *9*(6), 403–405. doi:10.1016/0167-6377(90)90061-9

Alirezaee, M. R., & Afsharian, M. (2007). A complete ranking of DMUs using restrictions in DEA models. *Applied Mathematics and Computation*, *189*(2), 1550–1559. doi:10.1016/j.amc.2006.12.031

Althin, R. (2001). Measurement of Productivity Changes: Two Malmquist Index Approahes. *Journal of Productivity Analysis*, *16*(2), 107–128. doi:10.1023/A:1011682625976

Alvarez, I. C., & Blazquez, R. (2014). The influence of the road network on private productivity measures using Data Envelopment Analysis: A case study from Spain. *Transportation Research Part A, Policy and Practice*, *65*, 33–43. doi:10.1016/j.tra.2014.04.002

Amin, G. R., & Sadeghi, H. (2010). Application of prioritized aggregation operators in preference voting. *International Journal of Intelligent Systems*, *25*(10), 1027–1034. doi:10.1002/int.20437

Amin, G. R., & Toloo, M. (2007). Finding the most efficient DMUs in DEA: An improved integrated model. *Computers & Industrial Engineering*, *52*(1), 71–77. doi:10.1016/j.cie.2006.10.003

Amirteimoori, A. and Kordrostami, S. An alternative clustering approach: a DEA-based procedure, Optimization: A Journal of Mathematical Programming and Operations Research 62 (2), 227-240, 2013.

Amirteimoori, A. and Kordrostami, S.A Euclidean distance-based measure of efficiency in data envelopment analysis, Optimization: A Journal of Mathematical Programming and Operations Research 59 (7), 985-996, 2010.

Amirteimoori, A. (2007). DEA efficiency analysis: Efficient and anti-efficient frontier. *Applied Mathematics and Computation*, *186*(1), 10–16. doi:10.1016/j.amc.2006.07.006

Amirteimoori, A., Jahanshahloo, G. R., & Kordrostami, S. (2005). Ranking of decision making units in data envelopment analysis: A distance-based approach. *Applied Mathematics and Computation*, *171*(1), 122–135. doi:10.1016/j.amc.2005.01.065

Andersen, P., & Petersen, N. C. (1993). A procedure for ranking efficient units in data envelopment analysis. *Management Science*, *39*(10), 1261–1264. doi:10.1287/mnsc.39.10.1261

Antonio, A., & Santos, M. (2008). *Students and Teachers: A DEA Approach to the Relative Efficiency of Portuguese Public Universitie*. Academic Press.

Aparicio, J., Pastor, J. T., & Zofio, J. L. (2013). On the inconsistency of the Malmquist.Luenberger index. *European Journal of Operational Research*, *229*(3), 738–742. doi:10.1016/j.ejor.2013.03.031

Arabi, B., Munisamy, S., & Emrouznejad, A. (2015). A new slacks-based measure of Malmquist–Luenberger index in the presence of undesirable outputs. *Omega, 51,* 29–37. doi:10.1016/j.omega.2014.08.006

Arcelus, F. J., & Arozena, P. (1999). Measuring sectoral productivity across time and across countries. *European Journal of Operational Research, 119*(2), 254–266. doi:10.1016/S0377-2217(99)00129-0

Asche, F., Guttormsen, A. G., & Nielsen, R. (2013). Future challenges for the maturing Norwegian salmon aquaculture industry: An analysis of total factor productivity change from 1996 to 2008. *Aquaculture (Amsterdam, Netherlands),* 396–399.

Ashrafi, A., Jaafar, A. B., Lee, L. S., & Abu Bakar, M. R. (2011). An Enhanced Russell Measure of Super-Efficiency for Ranking Efficient Units in Data Envelopment Analysis. *American Journal of Applied Sciences, 8*(1), 92–96. doi:10.3844/ajassp.2011.92.96

Asmild, M., Paradi, J., Aggarwall, V., & Schhaffnit, C. (2004). Combining DEA Window Analysis with the Malmquist Index Approach in a Study of the Canadian Banking Industry. *Journal of Productivity Analysis, 21*(1), 67–89. doi:10.1023/B:PROD.0000012453.91326.ec

Asmild, M., & Tam, F. (2007). Estimating global frontier shifts and global Malmquist indices. *Journal of Productivity Analysis, 27*(2), 137–148. doi:10.1007/s11123-006-0028-0

Assaf, A. G., & Barros, C. (2011). Performance analysis of the Gulf hotel industry: A Malmquist index with bias correction. *International Journal of Hospitality Management, 30*(4), 819–826. doi:10.1016/j.ijhm.2011.01.002

Athanassopoulos, A., & Shale, E. (1997). Assessing the Comparative Efficiency of Higher Education in the U.K by Means of DEA. *Education Economics, 5*(2), 117–134. doi:10.1080/09645299700000011

Atkinson, S. E., & Cornwell, C. (1998). Estimating Radial Measures of Productivity Growth: Frontier vs Non-Frontier Approaches. *Journal of Productivity Analysis, 10*(1), 35–46. doi:10.1023/A:1018394231538

Avkiran, N. (2001). Investigating technical and scale efficiencies of Australian Universities through data envelopment analysis. *Socio-Economic Planning Sciences, 35*(1), 57–80. doi:10.1016/S0038-0121(00)00010-0

Babalos, V., Caporale, G. M., & Philippas, N. (2012). Efficiency evaluation of Greek equity funds. *Research in International Business and Finance, 26*(2), 317–333. doi:10.1016/j.ribaf.2012.01.003

Bal, H., Orkcu, H. H., & Celebioglu, S. (2010). Improving the discrimination power and weights dispersion in the data envelopment analysis. *Computers & Operations Research, 37*(1), 99–107. doi:10.1016/j.cor.2009.03.028

Ball, E., Fare, R., Grosskopf, S., & Zaim, O. (2005). Accounting for externalities in the measurement of productivity growth: The Malmquist cost productivity measure. *Structural Change and Economic Dynamics, 16*(3), 374–394. doi:10.1016/j.strueco.2004.04.008

Compilation of References

Banker, R. D., & Morey, R. C. (1986). Efficiency analysis for exogenously fixed inputs and outputs. Operations Research Society of America.

Banker, R. D. (1993). Maximum-Likelihood, Consistency and Data Envelopment Analysis - a Statistical Foundation. *Management Science, 39*(10), 1265–1273. doi:10.1287/mnsc.39.10.1265

Banker, R. D., Charnes, A., & Cooper, W. W. (1984). Some models for estimating technical and scale inefficiency in data envelopment analysis. *Management Science, 30*(9), 1078–1092. doi:10.1287/mnsc.30.9.1078

Banker, R. D., Janakiramang, S., & Natarajan, R. (2003). (Article in Press). Analysis of trends in technical and allocative efficiency: An application to Texas public school districts. *European Journal of Operational Research.*

Banker, R. D., & Thrall, R. M. (1992). Estimation of Returns to Scale Using Data Envelopment Analysis. *European Journal of Operational Research, 62*(1), 74–84. doi:10.1016/0377-2217(92)90178-C

Bardhan, L., Bowlin, W. B., Cooper, W. W., & Sueyoshi, T. (1996). Models for efficiency dominance in data envelopment analysis. Part I: Additive models and MED measures. *Journal of the Operations Research Society of Japan, 39*, 322–332.

Barla, S. B. (2003). A case study of supplier selection for lean supply by using a mathematical model. *Logistics Information Management, 16*(6), 451–459. doi:10.1108/09576050310503420

Barros, C. P., & Alves, C. (2004). An empirical analysis of productivity growth in a Portuguese retail chain using Malmquist productivity index. *Journal of Retailing and Consumer Services, 11*(5), 269–278. doi:10.1016/S0969-6989(03)00053-5

Bassem, B. S. (2014). Total factor productivity change of MENA microfinance institutions: A Malmquist productivity index approach. *Economic Modelling, 39*, 182–189. doi:10.1016/j.econmod.2014.02.035

Bayazit, O. (2006). Use of analytic network process in vendor selection decisions. Benchmarking. *International Journal (Toronto, Ont.), 13*(5), 566–579.

Beasley, J. E. (1990). Comparing university departments. *Omega-International Journal, 18*(2), 171-183.

Beasley, J. E. (1995). Determining Teaching and Research Efficiencies. *The Journal of the Operational Research Society, 46*(4), 441–452. doi:10.1057/jors.1995.63

Belton, V., & Stewart, T. J. (1999). DEA and MCDA: Competing or complementary approaches? In N. Meskens & M. Roubens (Eds.), *Advances in Decision Analysis*. Norwell: Kluwer Academic Publishers. doi:10.1007/978-94-017-0647-6_6

Belton, V., & Vickers, S. P. (1993). Demystifyin DEA-A visual interactive approach based on Multiple Criteria Analysis. *The Journal of the Operational Research Society, 44*, 883–896.

Benayoun, R., Montgolfier, J., Tergny, J., & Laritchev, O. (1971). Linear programming with multiple objective functions: Step method (STEM). *Mathematical Programming, 1*(1), 366–375. doi:10.1007/BF01584098

Bessent, A. M., & Bessent, E. W. (1980). Determining the comparative efficiency of schools through data envelopment analysis. *Educational Administration Quarterly, 16*(2), 57–75. doi:10.1177/0013161X8001600207

Bevilacqua, M., Ciarapica, F. E., & Giacchetta, G. (2006). A fuzzy-QFD approach to supplier selection. *Journal of Purchasing and Supply Management, 12*(1), 14–27. doi:10.1016/j.pursup.2006.02.001

Bhattacharya, U. K. (2009). A chance-constrained goal programming model for the dvertising planning problem. *European Journal of Operational Research, 192*(2), 382–395. doi:10.1016/j.ejor.2007.09.039

Bobe, B. (2009). Evaluating the efficiencies of university faculities: Adjusted data envelopment analysis. Paper for Accounting and Finance Association of Australia and New Zealand (AFAANZ) 2009 Conference, Adelaide, Australia.

Boer, D., Labro, E., & Moralacchi, P. (2001). A review of methods supporting supplier selection. *European Journal of Purchasing and Supply Management, 7*(2), 75-89.

Bottani, E., & Rizzi, A. (2008). An adapted multi-criteria approach to suppliers and products selection An application oriented to lead-time reduction. *International Journal of Production Economics, 111*(2), 763–781. doi:10.1016/j.ijpe.2007.03.012

Bowen, W. M. (1990). Subjective judgements and data envelopment analysis in site selection. *Computers, Environment and Urban Systems, 14*(2), 133–144. doi:10.1016/0198-9715(90)90018-O

Braglia, M., & Petroni, A. (2000). A quality assurance-oriented methodology for handling trade-offs in supplier selection. *International Journal of Physical Distribution & Logistics Management, 30*(2), 96–111. doi:10.1108/09600030010318829

Brams, S. J., & Fishburn, P. C. (2002). Voting procedures. In K. J. Arrow, A. K. Sen, & K. Suzumura (Eds.), *Handbook of Social, Choice and Welfare* (Vol. 1, pp. 173–236). Amsterdam: Elsevier. doi:10.1016/S1574-0110(02)80008-X

Breu, T. M., & Raab, R. L. (1994). Efficiency and perceived quality of the nation's "top 25" national universities and national liberal arts colleges: An application of data envelopment analysis to higher education. *Socio-Economic Planning Sciences, 28*(1), 33–45. doi:10.1016/0038-0121(94)90023-X

Briec, W., & Kerstens, K. (2004). A Luenberger-Hicks-Moorsteen productivity indicator: Its relation to the Hicks-Moorsteen productivity index and the Luenberger productivity indicator. *Economic Theory, 23*(4), 925–939. doi:10.1007/s00199-003-0403-2

Cai, Y., & Wu, W. (2001). Synthetic financial evaluation by a method of combining DEA with AHP. *International Transactions in Operational Research, 8*.

Compilation of References

Camanho, A. S., & Dyson, R. (2005). Cost efficiency measurement: DEA application to bank branch assessment. *European Journal of Operational Research, 161*, 432–446. doi:10.1016/j. ejor.2003.07.018

Camanho, A. S., & Dyson, R. G. (2006). Data envelopment analysis and Malmquist indices for measuring group performance. *Journal of Productivity Analysis, 26*(1), 35–49. doi:10.1007/s11123-006-0004-8

Can, L. (2004). Measurement and Analysis of Production Performance of Rural Households in Jinzhai County. Anhui Province. *Forestry Studies in China, 6*(3), 20–27. doi:10.1007/s11632-004-0036-y

Caves, D. W., Christensen, L. R., & Diewert, W. E. (1982). The economic theory of index numbers and the measurement of input, output and productivity. *Econometrica, 50*(6), 1393–1414. doi:10.2307/1913388

Çebi, F., & Bayraktar, D. (2003). An integrated approach for supplier selection. *Logistics Information Management, 16*(6), 395–400. doi:10.1108/09576050310503376

Chambers, R. G., Chung, Y., & Fare, R. (1998). Profit, directional distance functions, and nerlovian efficency. *Journal of Optimization Theory and Applications, 98*(2), 1078–1092. doi:10.1023/A:1022637501082

Chan, F.T.S., & Kumar, N. (2007). Global supplier development considering risk factors using fuzzy extended AHP-based approach. *OMEGA – International Journal of Management Science, 35*(4), 417–431.

Chan, F. T. S. (2003). Interactive selection model for supplier selection process: An analytical hierarchy process approach. *International Journal of Production Research, 41*(15), 3549–3579. doi:10.1080/0020754031000138358

Chang, D. S., Chun Kuo, Y., & Chen, T. Y. (2008). Productivity measurement of the manufacturing process for outsourcing decisions: The case of a Taiwanese printed circuit board manufacturer. *International Journal of Production Research, 46*(24), 6981–6995. doi:10.1080/00207540701429934

Chang, D., Kuo, L. R., & Chen, Y.-. (2013). Industrial changes in corporate sustainability performance e an empirical overview using data envelopment analysis. *Journal of Cleaner Production, 56*, 147–155. doi:10.1016/j.jclepro.2011.09.015

Chang, H., Choy, H. L., Cooper, W. W., Parker, B. R., & Ruefli, T. W. (2009). "Measuring Productivity Growth, Technical Progress, and Efficiency Changes of CPA Firms Prior to, and Following the Sarbanes-Oxley Act." Socio-Economic Planning Sciences. *The International Journal of Public Sector Decision-Making., 43*(4), 221–228.

Chang, H., Choy, H. L., Cooper, W. W., Parker, B. R., & Ruefli, T. W. (2009). Measuring productivity growth, technical progress, and efficiency changes of CPA firms prior to, and following the Sarbanes–Oxley Act. *Socio-Economic Planning Sciences*, 1–8.

Chang, H., Choy, H. L., Cooper, W. W., & Ruefli, T. W. (2009). Using Malmquist Indexes to measure changes in the productivity and efficiency of US accounting firms before and after the Sarbanes Oxley Act. *Omega, 37*(5), 951–960. doi:10.1016/j.omega.2008.08.004

Chang, P., Hwangt, S., & Cheng, W. (1995). Using Data Envelopment Analysis to Measure the Achievement and Change of Regional Development in Taiwan. *Journal of Environmental Management, 43*(1), 49–66. doi:10.1016/S0301-4797(95)90319-4

Charens, A., Cooper, W. W., Wei, Q. L., & Huang, Z. M. (1989). Cone ratio data envelopment analysis and multi objective programming. *International Journal of Systems Science, 20*(7), 1099–1118. doi:10.1080/00207728908910197

Charnes, A., Cooper, W.W., Rhodes, E. (1978). Measureing the efficiency of decision making units. *European Journal of Operational Research, 2*, 429-444.

Charnes, A., Clark, C. T., Cooper, W. W., & Golany, B. (1985a). A developmental study of data envelopment analysis in measuring the efficiency of maintenance units in the US air forces. *Annals of Operations Research, 2*(1), 95–112. doi:10.1007/BF01874734

Charnes, A., & Cooper, W. W. (1957). Chance Constrained Programming. *Management Science, 6*(1), 73–79. doi:10.1287/mnsc.6.1.73

Charnes, A., & Cooper, W. W. (1985). Preference to topics in data envelopment analysis. *Annals of Operations Research, 2*(1), 59–94. doi:10.1007/BF01874733

Charnes, A., Cooper, W. W., Golany, B., Seiford, L., & Stutz, J. (1985). Foundation of data envelopment analysis for Pareto-Koopmans efficient empirical production function. *Journal of Econometrics, 30*(1-2), 91–107. doi:10.1016/0304-4076(85)90133-2

Charnes, A., Cooper, W. W., Huang, Z. M., & Sun, D. B. (1990). Polyhedral cone-ratio data envelopment analysis models with an illustrative application to large commercial banks. *Journal of Econometrics, 46*, 73–91. doi:10.1016/0304-4076(90)90048-X

Charnes, A., Cooper, W. W., Lewin, A. Y., & Seiford, L. M. (1994). *Data envelopment analysis: theory, methodology, and applications* (pp. 253–272). Boston: Kluwer Academic Publishers. doi:10.1007/978-94-011-0637-5

Charnes, A., Cooper, W. W., & Li, S. (1989). Using data envelopment analysis to evaluate the efficiency of economic performance by Chinese cities. *Socio-Economic Planning Sciences, 23*(6), 325–344. doi:10.1016/0038-0121(89)90001-3

Charnes, A., Cooper, W. W., & Rhodes, E. (1978). Measuring the efficiency of decision making unit. *European Journal of Operational Research, 2*(6), 429–444. doi:10.1016/0377-2217(78)90138-8

Charnes, A., Cooper, W. W., & Rhodes, E. (1979). Short Communication Measuring the efficiency of decision making unit. *European Journal of Operational Research, 3*, 339. doi:10.1016/0377-2217(79)90229-7

Compilation of References

Charnes, A., Cooper, W. W., Seiford, L., & Stutz, L. (1982). A multiplicative model for efficiency analysis. *Socio-Economic Planning Sciences*, *6*(5), 223–224. doi:10.1016/0038-0121(82)90029-5

Chena, Y., & Sherman, H. D. (2004). The benefits of non-radial vs. radial super-efficiency DEA: An application to burden-sharing amongst NATO member nations. *Socio-Economic Planning Sciences*, *38*(4), 307–320. doi:10.1016/j.seps.2003.10.007

Chen, C. T., Lin, C. T., & Huang, S. F. (2006). A fuzzy approach for supplier evaluation and selection in supply chain management. *International Journal of Production Economics*, *102*(2), 289–301. doi:10.1016/j.ijpe.2005.03.009

Chen, F., Liu, Z., & Kwehc, Q. L. (2014). Intellectual capital and productivity of Malaysian general insurers. *Economic Modelling*, *36*, 413–420. doi:10.1016/j.econmod.2013.10.008

Chen, J.-X. (2011). A modofied super-efficiency measure based on simoultanious input-output projection in data envelopment analysis. *Computers & Operations Research*, *38*, 496–504. doi:10.1016/j.cor.2010.07.008

Chen, J.-X., & Deng, M. (2011). A cross-dependence based ranking system for efficient and inefficient units in DEA. *Expert Systems with Applications*, *38*(8), 9648–9655. doi:10.1016/j.eswa.2011.01.165

Chen, M.-C. (2007). Ranking discovered rules from data mining with multiple criteria by data envelopment analysis. *Expert Systems with Applications*, *33*(4), 1110–1116. doi:10.1016/j.eswa.2006.08.007

Chen, Y. (2003). A non-radial Malmquist productivity index with an illustrative application to Chinese major industries. *International Journal of Production Economics*, *83*(1), 27–35. doi:10.1016/S0925-5273(02)00267-0

Chen, Y., & Ali, A. I. (2004). DEA Malmquist productivity measure: New insights with an application to computer industry. *European Journal of Operational Research*, *159*(1), 239–249. doi:10.1016/S0377-2217(03)00406-5

Chen, Y., Du, J., & Huo, J. (2013). Super-efficiency based on a modified directional distance function. *Omega*, *41*(3), 621–625. doi:10.1016/j.omega.2012.06.006

Chiang, C. I., & Tzeng, G. H. (2000). A new efficiency measure for DEA: Efficiency achievement measure established on fuzzy multiple objectives programming.[in Chinese]. *Journal of Management*, *17*, 369–388.

Chou, Y., Shao, B., & Lin, W. T. (2012). Performance evaluation of production of IT capital goods across OECD countries: A stochastic frontier approach to Malmquist index. *Decision Support Systems*, *54*(1), 173–184. doi:10.1016/j.dss.2012.05.003

Chowdhurya, H., Zelenyukb, V., Laportec, A., & Walter, P. (2014). Analysis of productivity, efficiency and technological changes in hospital services in Ontario: How does case-mix matter? *International Journal of Production Economics*, *150*, 74–82. doi:10.1016/j.ijpe.2013.12.003

Coelli, T. (1996). *Assessing the performance of Australian universities using data envelopment analysis. internal report.* Center for Efficiency and Productivity Analysis, University of New England.

Colbert, A., Levary, R., & Shaner, C. (1999). Determining the relative efficiency of MBA programs using DEA. *European Journal of Operation Research.*

Contreras, I. (2012). Optimizing the rank position of the DMU as secondary goal in DEA cross-evaluation. *Applied Mathematical Modelling, 36*(6), 2642–2648. doi:10.1016/j.apm.2011.09.046

Cook, W. D., Doyle, J., Green, R., & Kress, M. (1996). Ranking players in multiple tournaments. *Computers & Operations Research, 23*(9), 869–880. doi:10.1016/0305-0548(95)00082-8

Cook, W. D., & Johnston, D. A. (1992). Evaluating suppliers of complex systems: A multiple criteria approach. *The Journal of the Operational Research Society, 43*(11), 1055–1061. doi:10.1057/jors.1992.163

Cook, W. D., & Kress, M. (1990). A data envelopment model for aggregating preference rankings. *Management Science, 36*(11), 1302–1310. doi:10.1287/mnsc.36.11.1302

Cook, W. D., & Kress, M. (1990b). An mth generation model for weak ranking of players in a tournament. *The Journal of the Operational Research Society, 41*(12), 1111–1119.

Cook, W. D., & Kress, M. (1991). A multiple criteria decision model with ordinal preference data. *European Journal of Operational Research, 54*(2), 191–198. doi:10.1016/0377-2217(91)90297-9

Cook, W. D., & Kress, M. (1994). A multiple-criteria composite index model for quantitative and qualitative data. *European Journal of Operational Research, 78*(3), 367–379. doi:10.1016/0377-2217(94)90046-9

Cook, W. D., Kress, M., & Seiford, L. M. (1993). On the use of ordinal data in data envelopment analysis. *The Journal of the Operational Research Society, 44*(2), 133–140. doi:10.1057/jors.1993.25

Cook, W. D., Kress, M., & Seiford, L. M. (1996). Data envelopment analysis in the presence of both quantitative and qualitative factors. *The Journal of the Operational Research Society, 47*(7), 945–953. doi:10.1057/jors.1996.120

Cooper, W. W. (2005). Origins, Uses of, and Relations Between Goal Programming and Data Envelopment Analysis. *Journal of Multi-Criteria Decision Analysis., 13*(1), 3–11. doi:10.1002/mcda.370

Cooper, W. W., Park, K. S., & Yu, G. (1999). IDEA and ARIDEA: Models for dealing with imprecise data in data envelopment analysis. *Management Science, 45*(4), 597–607. doi:10.1287/mnsc.45.4.597

Cooper, W. W., Seiford, L. M., & Tone, K. (2007). *Introduction to Data Envelopment Analysis and Its Uses with DEA-Solver Software and References* (2nd ed.). Springer.

Compilation of References

Cooper, W. W., & Tone, K. (1997). Measures of inefficiency in data envelopment analysis and stochastic frontier estimation. *European Journal of Operational Research*, *99*(1), 72–88. doi:10.1016/S0377-2217(96)00384-0

Costa, R. (2012). Assessing Intellectual Capital efficiency and productivity: An application to the Italian yacht manufacturing sector. *Expert Systems with Applications*, *39*(8), 7255–7261. doi:10.1016/j.eswa.2012.01.099

Daneshvar Royendegh, B., & Erol, S. (2010). A DEA – ANP hybrid Algorithm Approach to Evaluate a University's Performance. *International Journal of Basic & Applied Sciences IJBAS*, *9*(10).

Darvish, M., Yasaei, M., & Saeedi, A. (2009). Application of the graph theory and matrix methods to contractor ranking. *International Journal of Project Management*, *27*(6), 610–619. doi:10.1016/j.ijproman.2008.10.004

Davoodi, A., & Zhiani Rezai, H. (2012). Common set of weights in data envelopment analysis: A linear programming problem. *Central European Journal of Operations Research*, *20*(2), 355–365. doi:10.1007/s10100-011-0195-6

De Nicola, A., Gitto, S., & Mancuso, P. (2013). Airport quality and productivity changes: A Malmquist index decomposition assessment. *Transportation Research Part E, Logistics and Transportation Review*, *58*, 67–75. doi:10.1016/j.tre.2013.07.001

Dickson, G. (1966). An Analysis of Vendor Selection Systems and Decisions. *Journal of Purchasing*, (2), 28-41.

Dimitrov, S., & Sutton, W. (2010). Promoting symmetric weight selection in data envelopment analysis: A penalty function approach. *European Journal of Operational Research*, *200*(1), 281–288. doi:10.1016/j.ejor.2008.11.043

Doyle, J., & Green, R. (1994). Efficiency and cross-efficiency in DEA: Derivations, meanings and uses. *The Journal of the Operational Research Society*, *45*(5), 567–578. doi:10.1057/jors.1994.84

Dula, J. H., & Hickman, B. L. (1997). Effects of excluding the column being scored from the DEA envelopment LP technology matrix. *The Journal of the Operational Research Society*, *48*(10), 1001–1012. doi:10.1057/palgrave.jors.2600434

DurgaPrasad, K. G., VenkataSubbaiah, K., VenuGopalaRao, C., & NarayanaRao, K. (2012). Supplier evaluation through Data Envelopment Analysis. *Journal of Supply Chain Management Systems*, *1*(2), 1–11.

Dyson, R. G., & Thanassoulis, E. (1988). Reducing weight flexibility in data envelopment analysis. *The Journal of the Operational Research Society*, *39*(6), 563–576. doi:10.1057/jors.1988.96

Dyson, R. G., & Thanassoulis, E. (1998). Reducing weight flexiblity in data envelopment analysis. *J. Opl Res. Q.*, *41*, 829–835.

Ebrahimnejad, A. (2012). A new approach for ranking of candidates in voting systems. *OPSEARCH*, *49*(2), 103–115. doi:10.1007/s12597-012-0070-9

Ebrahimnejad, A. (2015). A novel approach for discriminating efficient candidates by classifying voters in the preferential voting framework. *Japan Journal of Industrial and Applied Mathematics*, *32*(2), 513–527. doi:10.1007/s13160-015-0172-x

Ebrahimnejad, A., & Bagherzadeh, M. A. (2016). Data envelopment analysis approach for discriminating efficient candidates in voting systems by considering the priority of voters. *Hacettepe Journal of Mathematics and Statistics*, *45*(1), 165–180.

Ebrahimnejad, A., Tavana, M., & Santos-Arteaga, F. J. (2016). An integrated data envelopment analysis and simulation method for group consensus ranking. *Mathematics and Computers in Simulation*, *119*, 1–17. doi:10.1016/j.matcom.2015.08.022

Egilmez, G., & McAvoy, D. (2013). Benchmarking road safety of U.S. states: A DEA-based Malmquist productivity index approach. *Accident; Analysis and Prevention*, *53*, 55–64. doi:10.1016/j.aap.2012.12.038 PMID:23376545

Emrouznejad, A., Rostamy-Malkhalifeh, M., Hatami-Marbini, A., Tavana, M., & Aghayi, N. (2011). An overall profit Malmquist productivity index with fuzzy and interval data. *Mathematical and Computer Modelling*, *54*(11-12), 2827–2838. doi:10.1016/j.mcm.2011.07.003

Ertugrul, K. E., & Mehtap, D. (2013). An Integrated QFD-DEA Framework with Imprecise Data for Supplier Selection. *Proceedings of the World Congress on Engineering*. WCE.

Essid, H., Ouellette, P., & Vigeant, S. (2014). Productivity,efficiency,and technical change of Tunisian schools: A bootstrapped Malmquist approach with quasi-fixed inputs. *Omega*, *42*(1), 88–97. doi:10.1016/j.omega.2013.04.001

Estache, A., de la Fé, B. T., & Trujillo, L. (2004). Sources of efficiency gains in port reform: A DEA decomposition of a Malmquist TFP index for Mexico. *Utilities Policy*, *12*(4), 221–230. doi:10.1016/j.jup.2004.04.013

Estellita Lins, M. P., Angulo-Meza, L., & Moreila da Silva, A. C. (2004). A multi-objective approach to determine alternative targets in data envelopment analysis. *The Journal of the Operational Research Society*, *55*(10), 1090–1101. doi:10.1057/palgrave.jors.2601788

Fallahi, A., Ebrahimi, R., & Ghaderi, S. F. (2011). Measuring efficiency and productivity change in power electric generation management companies by using data envelopment analysis: A case study. *Energy*, *36*(11), 6398–6405. doi:10.1016/j.energy.2011.09.034

Fare, R., Grosskof, S., Lindgren, B., & Roos, P. (1992). *Productivity Developments in Swedish Hospital: A Malmquist Output Index Approach. In Data Envelopment Analysis*. Boston: Kluwer Academic Publishers.

Fare, R., Grosskof, S., Lindgren, B., & Ross, P. (1994). *Productivity Developments in Swendish Hospital: A Malmquist Output Index Approach* (pp. 253–272). Boston: Kluwer.

Fare, R., Grosskof, S., Norris, M., & Zhang, Z. (1994). Productivity growth, Technical progress and Efficiency Changes in Industrialized Countries. *The American Economic Review*, *1*, 66–83.

Compilation of References

Fare, R., & Zelenyuk, V. (2003). On aggregate Farrell efficiency scores. *European Journal of Operational Research, 146*(3), 615–620. doi:10.1016/S0377-2217(02)00259-X

Farrell, M. J. (1957). The measurement of productive efficiency. *Journal of the Royal Statistical Society, Series A, 120*(3), 253-281.

Farrell, M. J. (1957). The measurement of productive efficiency. *Journal of the Royal Statistical Society. Series A (General), 120*(3), 253–281. doi:10.2307/2343100

Farzipoor, S. R. (2010). Developing a new data envelopment analysis methodology for supplier selection in the presence of both undesirable outputs and imprecise data. *International Journal of Advanced Manufacturing Technology, 51*(9-12), 1243–1250. doi:10.1007/s00170-010-2694-3

Feroz, E. H., Raab, R. L., Ulleberg, G. T., & Alsharif, K. (2009). Kamal Alsharif. Global warming and environmental production efficiency ranking of the Kyoto Protocol nations. *Journal of Environmental Management, 90*(2), 1178–1183. doi:10.1016/j.jenvman.2008.05.006

Forker, L. B., & Mendez, D. (2001). An analytical method for benchmarking best peer suppliers. *International Journal of Operations & Production Management, 21*(1–2), 195–209. doi:10.1108/01443570110358530

Foroughi, A. A., & Aouni, B. (2012). New approaches for determining a common set of weights for a voting system. *International Transactions in Operational Research, 19*(4), 521–530. doi:10.1111/j.1475-3995.2011.00832.x

Foroughi, A. A., Jones, D. F., & Tamiz, M. (2005). A selection method for a preferential election. *Applied Mathematics and Computation, 163*(1), 107–116. doi:10.1016/j.amc.2003.10.055

Foroughi, A. A., & Tamiz, M. (2005). An effective total ranking model for a ranked voting system. *Omega, 33*(6), 491–496. doi:10.1016/j.omega.2004.07.013

Freed, N., & Glover, F. (1986). Evaluating alternative linear programming models to solve the two-group discriminant problem. *Decision Sciences, 17*(2), 151–162. doi:10.1111/j.1540-5915.1986.tb00218.x

Friedman, L., & Sinuany-Sterm, Z. (1998). DEA and the discriminate analysis of ratio for ranking units. *Journal of Operational Research, 111*, 470-478.

Friedman, L., & Sinuany-Stern, Z. (1997). Scaling units via the canonical correlation analysis and the data envelopment analysis. *European Journal of Operational Research, 100*(3), 629–637. doi:10.1016/S0377-2217(97)84108-2

Friedman, L., & Sinuany-Stern, Z. (1998). Combining ranking scales and selecting variables in the data envelopment analysis context: The case of industrial branches. *Computers & Operations Research, 25*(9), 781–791. doi:10.1016/S0305-0548(97)00102-0

Fuentes, H. J., Grifell-Tatje, E., & Perelman, S. (2001). A Parametric Distance Function Approach for Malmquist Productivity Index Estimation. *Journal of Productivity Analysis, 15*(2), 79–94. doi:10.1023/A:1007852020847

Fuentes, R., & Lillo-Banuls, A. (2015). Smoothed bootstrap Malmquist index based on DEA model to compute productivity of tax offices. *Expert Systems with Applications, 42*(5), 2442–2450. doi:10.1016/j.eswa.2014.11.002

Galanopoulos, K., Karagiannis, G., & Koutroumanidis, T. (2004). Malmquist Productivity Index Estimates for European Agriculture in the 1990s Operational Research. *International Journal (Toronto, Ont.), 4*, 73–91.

Geoffrion, A. M., Dyer, J. S., & Feinberg, A. (1972). An interactive approach for multi-criterion optimization with an application to the operation of an academic department. Part I. *Management Science, 19*(4-part-1), 357–368. doi:10.1287/mnsc.19.4.357

Gholam Abri, A., Jahanshahloo, G. R., Hosseinzadeh Lotfi, F., Shoja, N., & Fallah Jelodar, M. (2013). A new method for ranking non-extreme efficient units in data envelopment analysis. *Optimization Letters, 7*(2), 309–324. doi:10.1007/s11590-011-0420-1

Giokas, D. I., & Pentzaropoulos, G. C. (2008). Efficiency ranking of the OECD member states in the area of telecommunications: A composite AHP/DEA study. *Telecommunications Policy, 32*(9-10), 672–685. doi:10.1016/j.telpol.2008.07.007

Gitto, S., & Mancuso, P. (2012). Bootstrapping the Malmquist indexes for Italian airports. *International Journal of Production Economics, 135*(1), 403–411. doi:10.1016/j.ijpe.2011.08.014

Giuffrida, A. (1999). Productivity and efficiency changes in primary care: A Malmquist index approach. *Health Care Management Science, 2*(1), 11–26. doi:10.1023/A:1019067223945 PMID:10916598

Golany, B. (1988). An Interactive MOLP Procedure for the Extension of DEA to Effectiveness Analysis. *The Journal of the Operational Research Society, 39*(8), 725–734. doi:10.1057/jors.1988.127

Golany, B., & Roll, Y. A. (1994). Incorporating standards via data envelopment analysis. In A. Charnes, W. W. Cooper, A. Y. Lewin, & L. M. Seiford (Eds.), *Data Envelopment Analysis: Theory, Methodology and Applications*. Norwell: Kluwer Academic Publishers. doi:10.1007/978-94-011-0637-5_16

Green, R. H., & Doyle, J. R. (1995). On maximizing discrimination in multiple criteria decision making. *The Journal of the Operational Research Society, 46*(2), 192–204. doi:10.1057/jors.1995.24

Green, R. H., Doyle, J. R., & Cook, W. D. (1996). Preference voting and project ranking using DEA and cross-evaluation. *European Journal of Operational Research, 90*(3), 461–472. doi:10.1016/0377-2217(95)00039-9

Grifell-Tatjé, E., Lovell, C.A.K. (1999). A Generalized Malmquist productivity index. *Sociedad de Estadistica e Investigación Operativa Top, 7*, 81-101.

Grifell-Tatje, E., & Lovell, C. A. K. (1995). A note on the Malmquist productivity index. *Economics Letters, 47*(2), 169–175. doi:10.1016/0165-1765(94)00497-P

Compilation of References

Grifell-Tatjé, E., & Lovell, C. A. K. (1997). A DEA-based analysis of productivity change and intertemporal managerial performa. *Annals of Operations Research*, *73*, 177–189. doi:10.1023/A:1018925127385

Grifell-Tatjé, E., Lovell, C. A. K., & Pastor, J. T. (1998). A Quasi-Malmquist Productivity Index. *Journal of Productivity Analysis*, *10*(1), 7–20. doi:10.1023/A:1018329930629

Guan, J., & Chen, K. (2009). Modeling macro- $R \& D$ production frontier performance: An application to Chinese province-level .*Scientometrics*.

Guo, D., & Wu, J. (2012). A complete ranking of DMUs with undesirable outputs using restrictions in DEA models. *Mathematical and Computer Modelling*.

Hadi-Vencheh, A. (2014). Two effective total ranking models for preference voting and aggregation. *Mathematical Sciences*, *8*(115), 1–4.

Hadi-Vencheh, A., & Mokhtarian, M. N. (2009). Three new models for preference voting and aggregation: A note. *The Journal of the Operational Research Society*, *60*(7), 1036–1037. doi:10.1057/jors.2008.153

Halme, M., Joro, T., Korhonen, P., Salo, S., & Wallenius, J. (1999). A value efficiency approach to incorporating performance information in Data Envelopment Analysis. *Management Science*, *45*(1), 103–115. doi:10.1287/mnsc.45.1.103

Halme, M., & Korhonen, P. (2000). Restricting weights in value efficiency analysis. *European Journal of Operational Research*, *126*(1), 175–188. doi:10.1016/S0377-2217(99)00290-8

Hashimoto, A. (1997). A ranked voting system using a DEA/AR exclusion model: A note. *European Journal of Operational Research*, *97*(3), 600–604. doi:10.1016/S0377-2217(96)00281-0

Hatefi, S. M., & Torabi, S. A. (2012). A common weight MCDA-DEA approach to construct composite indicators. *Ecological Economics*, *70*(1), 114–120. doi:10.1016/j.ecolecon.2010.08.014

Hermans, E., Brijs, T., Wets, G., & Vanhoof, K. (2009). Benchmarking road safety: Lessons to learn from a data envelopment analysis, Transportation Research Institute, Hasselt University. *Accident; Analysis and Prevention*, *41*(1), 174–182. doi:10.1016/j.aap.2008.10.010 PMID:19114152

Hosseinzadeh Lotfi, F., Jahanshahloo, G. R., Vaez-Ghasemi, M., & Moghaddas, Z. (2013). Modified Malmquist Productivity Index Based on Present Time Value of Money.Journal of Applied Mathematics.

Hosseinzadeh Lotfi, F., Jahanshahloo, G.R., Vaez-Ghasemi, M., & Moghaddas, Z. (2013). Periodic efficiency measurement for achieving correct efficiency among several terms of evaluation. *Int. J. Operational Research*.

Hosseinzadeh Lotfi, F., Aryanezhad, M. B., Ebnrasoul, S. A., & Najafi, S. E. (2010). Evaluating Productivity in the Units of the Powerhouse Collection by Using Malmquist Index. *Journal of International Management*, *4*, 29–42.

Hosseinzadeh Lotfi, F., & Fallahnejad, R. (2011). A note on A solution method to the problem proposed by Wang in voting systems. *Applied Mathematical Sciences*, *5*, 3051–3055.

Hosseinzadeh Lotfi, F., Hatami-Marbini, A., Agrell, P. J., Aghayi, N., & Gholami, K. (2013). Allocating fixed resources and setting targets using a common-weights DEA approach. *Computers & Industrial Engineering*, *64*(2), 631–640. doi:10.1016/j.cie.2012.12.006

Hosseinzadeh Lotfi, F., Jahanshahloo, G. R., Ebrahimnejad, A., Soltanifar, M., & Mansourzadeh, S. M. (2010). Target setting in the general combined-oriented CCR model using an interactive MOLP method. *Journal of Computational and Applied Mathematics*, *234*(1), 1–9. doi:10.1016/j.cam.2009.11.045

Hosseinzadeh Lotfi, F., Jahanshahloo, G. R., & Memariani, A. (2000). A Method for Finding Common Set of Weights by Multiple Objective Programming in Data Envelopment Analysis. *Southwest Journal of Pure and Applied Mathematics.*, *1*, 44–54.

Hosseinzadeh Lotfi, F., Jahanshahloo, G. R., Mozzaffari, M. R., & Gerami, J. (2011). Finding DEA-efficient hyperplanes using MOLP efficient faces. *Journal of Computational and Applied Mathematics*, *235*(5), 1227–1231. doi:10.1016/j.cam.2010.08.007

Hosseinzadeh Lotfi, F., Noora, A. A., Jahanshahloo, G. R., Jablonsky, J., Mozaffari, M. R., & Gerami, J. (2009). An MOLP based procedure for finding efficient units in DEA models. *Central European Journal of Operations Research*, *17*(1), 1–11. doi:10.1007/s10100-008-0071-1

Hosseinzadeh Lotfi, F., Noora, A. A., Jahanshahloo, G. R., & Reshadi, M. (2011). One DEA ranking method based on applying aggregate units. *Expert Systems with Applications*, *38*(10), 13468–13471. doi:10.1016/j.eswa.2011.02.145

Hosseinzadeh Lotfi, F., Rostamy-Malkhalifeh, M., Aghayi, N., Ghelej Beigi, Z., & Gholami, K. (2013). An improved method for ranking alternatives in multiple criteria decision analysis. *Applied Mathematical Modelling*, *37*(1-2), 25–33. doi:10.1016/j.apm.2011.09.074

Hougaard, J. L. (1999). Fuzzy scores of technical efficiency. *European Journal of Operational Research*, *115*(3), 529–541. doi:10.1016/S0377-2217(98)00165-9

Hseu, J., & Shang, J. (2005). Productivity changes of pulp and paper industry in OECD countries, 1991–2000: A non-parametric Malmquist approach. *Forest Policy and Economics*, *7*(3), 411–422. doi:10.1016/j.forpol.2003.07.002

Hwang, C. L., & Masud, A. S. M. d. (1979). *Multiple objective Decision Making: Methods and Applications*. Springer-Verlag. doi:10.1007/978-3-642-45511-7

Hwang, C. L., & Yoon, K. (1981). *Multiple Attribute Decision Making Methods and Applications*. Berlin, Heidelberg: Springer. doi:10.1007/978-3-642-48318-9

Hwang, S., & Chang, T. (2003). Using data envelopment analysis to measure hotel managerial efficiency change in Taiwan. *Tourism Management*, *24*(4), 357–369. doi:10.1016/S0261-5177(02)00112-7

Compilation of References

Jablonsky, J. (2011). Multicriteria approaches for ranking of efficient units in DEA models. *Central European Journal of Operations Research*. doi:10.1007/s10100-011-0223-6

Jafarinan-Moghaddam, A. R., & Ghoseiri, K. (2011). Fuzzy dynamic multi-objective Data Envelopment Analysis model. *Expert Systems with Applications*, *38*(1), 850–855. doi:10.1016/j. eswa.2010.07.045

Jahanshahloo, G. R., Sanei, M., & Shoja, N. (2004). *Modified ranking models, using the concept of advantage in data envelopment analysis.* Working paper.

Jahanshahloo, G. R., & Afzalinejad, M. (2006). A ranking method based on a full-inefficient frontier. *Applied Mathematical Modelling*, *30*(3), 248–260. doi:10.1016/j.apm.2005.03.023

Jahanshahloo, G. R., Hosseinzadeh Lotfi, F., Jafari, Y., & Maddahi, R. (2011). Selecting symmetric weights as a secondary goal in DEA cross-efficiency evaluation. *Applied Mathematical Modelling*, *35*(1), 544–549. doi:10.1016/j.apm.2010.07.020

Jahanshahloo, G. R., Hosseinzadeh Lotfi, F., Khanmohammadi, M., & Kazemimanesh, M. (2012). A method for discriminating efficient candidates with ranked voting data by common weights. *Mathematical and Computational Applications*, *17*(3), 1–8. doi:10.3390/mca17010001

Jahanshahloo, G. R., Hosseinzadeh Lotfi, F., Khanmohammadi, M., Kazemimanesh, M., & Rezaie, V. (2010). Ranking of units by positive ideal DMU with common weights. *Expert Systems with Applications*, *37*(12), 7483–7488. doi:10.1016/j.eswa.2010.04.011

Jahanshahloo, G. R., Hosseinzadeh Lotfi, F., Shoja, N., Tohidi, G., & Razavian, S. (2004). Ranking using l1-norm in data envelopment analysis. *Applied Mathematics and Computation*, *153*(1), 215–224. doi:10.1016/S0096-3003(03)00625-8

Jahanshahloo, G. R., Hosseinzadeh Lotfi, F., Zhiani Rezai, H., & Rezai Balf, F. (2005). Using Monte Carlo method for ranking efficient DMUs. *Applied Mathematics and Computation*, *162*(1), 371–379. doi:10.1016/j.amc.2003.12.139

Jahanshahloo, G. R., Junior, H. V., Hosseinzadeh Lotfi, F., & Akbarian, D. (2007). A new DEA ranking system based on changing the reference set. *European Journal of Operational Research*, *181*(1), 331–337. doi:10.1016/j.ejor.2006.06.012

Jahanshahloo, G. R., Khodabakhshi, M., Hosseinzadeh Lotfi, F., & Moazami Goudarzi, M. R. (2011). A cross-efficiency model based on super-efficiency for ranking units through the TOPSIS approach and its extension to the interval case. *Mathematical and Computer Modelling*, *53*(9-10), 1946–1955. doi:10.1016/j.mcm.2011.01.025

Jahanshahloo, G. R., Memariani, A., Hosseinzadeh Lotfi, F., & Rezai, H. Z. (2005). A note on some of DEA models and finding efficiency and complete ranking using common set of weights. *Applied Mathematics and Computation*, *166*(2), 265–281. doi:10.1016/j.amc.2004.04.088

Jahanshahloo, G. R., Pourkarimi, L., & Zarepisheh, M. (2006). Modified MAJ model for ranking decision making units in data envelopment analysis. *Applied Mathematics and Computation*, *174*(2), 1054–1059. doi:10.1016/j.amc.2005.06.001

Jahanshahloo, G. R., Sanei, M., Hosseinzadeh Lotfi, F., & Shoja, N. (2004). Using the gradient line for ranking DMUs in DEA. *Applied Mathematics and Computation, 151*(1), 209–219. doi:10.1016/S0096-3003(03)00333-3

Jahanshahloo, G. R., Zohrehbandian, M., Alinezhad, A., Abbasian Naghneh, S., Abbasian, H., & Kiani Mavi, R. (2011). Finding common weights based on the DM's preference information. *The Journal of the Operational Research Society, 62*(10), 1796–1800. doi:10.1057/jors.2010.156

Jahantighi, M. A., Moghaddas, Z., & Vaez Ghasemi, M. (2012). Two-stage Malmquist Productivity Index with Intermediate Products. *Int. J. Industrial Mathematics, 4*, 31–40.

Jian, B., Wei, C., Hua, Z., & Weifeng, P. (2013). Supplier's Efficiency and Performance Evaluation using DEA-SVM Approach. *Journal of Software, 8*(1), 25–30. doi:10.4304/jsw.8.1.25-30

Jimenez, J. S., Chaparro, F. P., & Smith, P. C. (2003). Evaluating the introduction of a quasi-market in community care. *Socio-Economic Planning Sciences, 37*(1), 1–13. doi:10.1016/S0038-0121(02)00042-3

Jiuping, X., Bin, L., & Desheng, W. (2009). Rough Data Envelopment Analysis and its Application to Supply Chain Performance Evaluation. *International Journal of Production Economics, 122*(2), 628–638. doi:10.1016/j.ijpe.2009.06.026

Joro, T., Korhonen, P., & Wallenius, J. (1998). Structural Comparison of Data Envelopment Analysis and Multiple Objective Linear Programming. *Management Science, 44*(7), 962–970. doi:10.1287/mnsc.44.7.962

Joumady, O., & Ris, C. (2005). Performance in European Higher Education: A Non-Parametric Production Frontier Approach. *Education Economics, 13*(2), 189–205. doi:10.1080/09645290500031215

Juhantila, O. P., & Virolainen, V. M. (2003). Buyers Expectation from their Suppliers. *19th IMP Conference.*

Jürges, H., & Schneider, K. (2007). Fair ranking of teachers. *Empirical Economics, 32*(2-3), 411–431. doi:10.1007/s00181-006-0112-3

Kannan, V. R., & Tan, K. C. (2002). Supplier Selection and Assessment: Their Impact on Business Performance. *The Journal of Supply Chain Management, 38*(3), 11–21. doi:10.1111/j.1745-493X.2002.tb00139.x

Kao, C., & Hung, H.T. (2008). Efficiency analysis of university departments: An empirical study. *Omega, 36*(4), 653-664.

Kao, C. (2010). Malmquist productivity index based on common-weights DEA: The case of Taiwan forests after reorganization. *Omega, 38*(6), 484–491. doi:10.1016/j.omega.2009.12.005

Kao, C. (2010). Weight determination for consistently ranking alternatives in multiple criteria decision analysis. *Applied Mathematical Modelling, 34*(7), 1779–1787. doi:10.1016/j.apm.2009.09.022

Compilation of References

Kao, C., & Hung, H. T. (2005). Data envelopment analysis with common weights: The compromise solution approach. *The Journal of the Operational Research Society, 56*(10), 1196–1203. doi:10.1057/palgrave.jors.2601924

Kao, C., & Hwang, S. (2014). Multi-period efficiency and Malmquist productivity index in two-stage production systems. *European Journal of Operational Research, 232*(3), 512–521. doi:10.1016/j.ejor.2013.07.030

Kao, C., & Liu, S. (2014). Multi-period efficiency measurement in data envelopment analysis: The case of Taiwanese commercial banks. *Omega, 47*, 90–98. doi:10.1016/j.omega.2013.09.001

Karsak, E. E. (1998). A two-phase robot selection procedure. *Production Planning and Control, 9*(7), 675–684. doi:10.1080/095372898233678

Karsak, E. E., & Ahishka, S. S. (2005). Practical common weight multi-criteria decision-making approach with an improved discriminating power for technology selection. *International Journal of Production Research, 43*(8), 1437–1554. doi:10.1080/13528160412331326478

Khodabakhshi, M. (2007). A super-efficiency model based on improved outputs in data envelopment analysis. *Applied Mathematics and Computation, 184*(2), 695–703. doi:10.1016/j.amc.2006.06.110

Kim, J. W., & Lee, H. K. (2004). Embodied and disembodied international spillovers of $R \& D$. *Technovation, 24*(4), 359–368. doi:10.1016/S0166-4972(02)00096-2

Kordrostami, S., & Bakhoda Bijarkani, Z. (2013). A new method to measure efficiency in parallel production systems with shared sourced in natural life. *International Journal of Biomathematics, 6*(6), 1–18. doi:10.1142/S1793524513500459

Korenbluth, J. S. H. (1991). Analysing policy effectiveness using cone Restricted DEA. *European Journal of Operational Research, 42*, 1097–1104. doi:10.1057/jors.1991.203

Korhonen, P., Tainio, R., & Wallenius, J. (2001). Value efficiency analysis academic research. *European Journal of Operational Research, 130*(1), 121–132. doi:10.1016/S0377-2217(00)00050-3

Kortelainen, M. (2008). Dynamic environmental performance analysis: A Malmquist index approach. *Ecological Economics, 64*(4), 701–715. doi:10.1016/j.ecolecon.2007.08.001

Krishnasamy, G., Hanuum Ridzwa, A., & Perumal, V. (2003). Banking and Finance, Malaysian Post Merger Banks' Productivity: Application of Malmquist Productivity Index. *Managerial Finance, 30.*

Krishnasamy, G., Hanuum Ridzwa, A., & Perumal, V. (2003). Malaysian post-merger banks' productivity: Application of Malmquist productivity index. *Managerial Finance, 30*(4), 63–74. doi:10.1108/03074350410769038

Kutana, A. M., & Yigit, T. M. (2007). productivity growth and real convergence. *European Economic Review, 51*(6), 1370–1395. doi:10.1016/j.euroecorev.2006.11.001

Lambert, D. M., & Pohlen, T. L. (2001). Supply chain metrics. *International Journal of Logistics Management, 12*(1), 1–19. doi:10.1108/09574090110806190

Lee, J. (2013). Directions for the Sustainable Development of Korean Small and Medium Sized Shipyards. *The Asian Journal of Shipping and Logistics, 29*(3), 335–60.

Leeneer, I. D. (2002). Selecting land mine detection strategies by means of outranking MCDM techniques. *European Journal of Operational Research, 139*(2), 327–338. doi:10.1016/S0377-2217(01)00372-1

Liang, L., Wu, J., Cook, W. D., & Zhu, J. (2008). Alternative secondary goals in DEA crossefficiency evaluation. *International Journal of Production Economics, 113*(2), 1025–1030. doi:10.1016/j.ijpe.2007.12.006

Lin, C., & Berg, S. V. (2008). Incorporating Service Quality into Yardstick Regulation: An Application to the Peru Water Sector. *Review of Industrial Organization, 32*(1), 53–75. doi:10.1007/s11151-008-9160-5

Lins, M. P., Gomes, E. G., Soares de Mello, J. C. C. B., & Soares de Mello, A. J. R. (2003). Olympic ranking based on a zero sum gains DEA model. *European Journal of Operational Research, 148*(2), 312–322. doi:10.1016/S0377-2217(02)00687-2

Li, S. H., Jahanshahloo, G. R., & Khodabakhshi, M. (2007). A super-efficiency model for ranking efficient units in data envelopment analysis. *Applied Mathematics and Computation, 184*(2), 638–648. doi:10.1016/j.amc.2006.06.063

Liu, F. H. F., & Peng, H. H. (2008). Ranking of units on the DEA frontier with common weight. *Computers & Operations Research, 35*(5), 1624–1637. doi:10.1016/j.cor.2006.09.006

Liu, F. H. F., & Wang, P. H. (2008). DEA Malmquist productivity measure: Taiwanese semiconductor companies. *International Journal of Production Economics, 112*(1), 367–379. doi:10.1016/j.ijpe.2007.03.015

Li, X. B., & Reeves, G. R. (1999). A multiple criteria approach to data envelopment analysis. *European Journal of Operational Research, 115*(3), 507–517. doi:10.1016/S0377-2217(98)00130-1

Llamazares, B., & Pena, T. (2009). Preference aggregation and DEA: An analysis of the methods proposed to discriminate efficient candidates. *European Journal of Operational Research, 197*(2), 714–721. doi:10.1016/j.ejor.2008.06.031

Llamazares, B., & Pena, T. (2013). Aggregating preferences rankings with variable weights. *European Journal of Operational Research, 230*(2), 348–355. doi:10.1016/j.ejor.2013.04.013

Lozano-Vivas, A., & Humphrey, D. B. (2002). Bias in Malmquist index and cost function productivity measurement in banking. *International Journal of Production Economics, 76*(2), 177–188. doi:10.1016/S0925-5273(01)00162-1

Compilation of References

Lu, W.-M., & Lo, S.-F. (2009). An interactive benchmark model ranking performers - Application to financial holding companies. *Mathematical and Computer Modelling, 49*(1-2), 172–179. doi:10.1016/j.mcm.2008.06.008

Macpherson, A. J., Principe, P. P., & Mehaffey, M. (2013). Using Malmquist Indices to evaluate environmental impacts of alternative land development scenarios. *Ecological Indicators, 34*, 296–303. doi:10.1016/j.ecolind.2013.05.009

Ma, J. L., Evans, D. G., Fuller, R. J., & Stewart, D. F. (2002). Technical efficiency and productivity change of China's iron and steel industry. *International Journal of Production Economics, 76*(3), 293–312. doi:10.1016/S0925-5273(01)00195-5

Malmquist, S. (1953). Index numbers and indifference surfaces. *Trabajos de Estatistica, 4*(2), 209–242. doi:10.1007/BF03006863

Maniadakis, N., & Thanassoulis, E. (2004). A cost Malmquist productivity index. *European Journal of Operational Research, 154*(2), 396–409. doi:10.1016/S0377-2217(03)00177-2

Manjari, S., Prince, A., Vaibhav, M., Monark, B., & Vrijendra, S. (2014). Supplier Selection through Application of DEA. *International Journal Engineering and Manufacturing, 1*, 1–9. doi:10.5815/ijem.2014.01.01

Martic, M., & Savic, G. (2001). An application of DEA for comparison analysis and ranking of region in Serbia with regards to Social economic development. *European Journal of Operational Research, 132*, 343-356.

Martin, E. (2003). *An Application of the Data Envelopment Analysis Methodology in the Performance Assessment of Zaragoza University Departments.* Available: www.google.com

Martin, J. C., & Roman, C. (2006). A Benchmarking Analysis of Spanish Commercial Airports. A Comparison Between SMOP and DEA Ranking Methods. *Networks and Spatial Economics, 6*(2), 111–134. doi:10.1007/s11067-006-7696-1

Mecit, E. D., & Alp, I. (2013). A new proposed model of restricted data envelopment analysis by correlation coefficients. *Applied Mathematical Modelling, 3*(5), 3407–3425. doi:10.1016/j.apm.2012.07.010

Mehrabian, S., Alirezaee, M. R., & Jahanshahloo, G. R. (1999). A complete efficiency ranking of decision making units in data envelopment analysis. *Computational Optimization and Applications, 14*(2), 261–266. doi:10.1023/A:1008703501682

Menegaki, A. N. (2013). Growth and renewable energy in Europe: Benchmarking with data envelopment analysis. *Renewable Energy, 60*, 363–369. doi:10.1016/j.renene.2013.05.042

Monczka, R. M., Kenneth, J. P., Robert, B. H., & Gary, L. R. (1998). Success Factors in Strategic Supplier Alliances: The Buying Company Perspective. *Decision Sciences, 29*(3), 553–577. doi:10.1111/j.1540-5915.1998.tb01354.x

Morrison, D. F. (1976). *Multivariate Statistical Methods.* New York: McGraw- Hill.

Mussard, S., & Peypoch, N. (2006). On multi-decomposition of the aggregate Malmquist productivity index. *Economics Letters*, *91*(3), 436–443. doi:10.1016/j.econlet.2006.01.015

Narasimhan, R., Srinivas, T., & Mendez, D. (2001). Supplier Evaluation and Rationalization via Data Envelopment Analysis: An empirical examination. *The Journal of Supply Chain Management*, *37*(3), 28–37. doi:10.1111/j.1745-493X.2001.tb00103.x

Ning-Sheng, W., Rong-Hua, Y., & Wei, W. (2008). Evaluating the performances of decision-making units based on interval efficiencies. *Journal of Computational and Applied Mathematics*, *216*(2), 328–343. doi:10.1016/j.cam.2007.05.012

Noguchi, H., Ogawa, M., & Ishii, H. (2002). The appropriate total ranking method using DEA for multiple categorized purposes. *Journal of Computational and Applied Mathematics*, *146*(1), 155–166. doi:10.1016/S0377-0427(02)00425-9

Noura, A. A., Hosseinzadeh Lotfi, F., Jahanshahloo, G. R., & Fanati Rashidi, S. (2001). Super-efficiency in DEA by effectiveness of each unit in society. *Applied Mathematics Letters*, *24*(5), 623–626. doi:10.1016/j.aml.2010.11.025

Nykowski, I., & Zolkiewski, Z. (1985). A compromise produce for the multiple objective linear fractional programming problem. *European Journal of Operational Research*, *19*(1), 91–97. doi:10.1016/0377-2217(85)90312-1

Obata, T., & Ishii, H. (2003). A method for discriminating efficient candidates with ranked voting data. *European Journal of Operational Research*, *151*(1), 233–237. doi:10.1016/S0377-2217(02)00597-0

Odeck, J. (2000). Assessing the relative efficiency and productivity growth of vehicle inspection services: An application of DEA and Malmquist indices. *European Journal of Operational Research*, *126*(3), 501–514. doi:10.1016/S0377-2217(99)00305-7

Odeck, J. (2006). Identifying traffic safety best practice: An application of DEA and Malmquist indices. *Omega*, *34*(1), 28–40. doi:10.1016/j.omega.2004.07.017

Odeck, J. (2009). Statistical precision ofDEAand Malmquist indices:Abootstrap application to Norwegian grain producers. *Omega*, *37*(5), 1007–1017. doi:10.1016/j.omega.2008.11.003

Oliveira, M. M., Gaspar, M. B., Paixao, J. P., & Camanho, A. S. (2009). Productivity change of the artisanal fishing fleet in Portugal: A Malmquist index analysis. *Fisheries Research*, *95*(2-3), 189–197. doi:10.1016/j.fishres.2008.08.020

Oral, M., Kettani, O., & Lang, P. (1991). A methodology for collective evaluation and selection of industrial R. *Management Science*, *7*(37), 871–883. doi:10.1287/mnsc.37.7.871

Orkcu, H. H., & Bal, H. (2011). Goal programming approaches for data envelopment analysis cross efficiency evaluation. *Applied Mathematics and Computation*, *218*(2), 346–356. doi:10.1016/j.amc.2011.05.070

Compilation of References

Ouellette, P., & Vierstraete, V. (2005). An evaluation of the efficiency of Quebec's school boards using the data envelopment analysis method. *Applied Economics*, *37*(14), 1643–1653. doi:10.1080/00036840500173247

Paradi, J. C., & Yang, X. (2014). Data Envelopment Analysis of Corporate Failure for Non-Manufacturing Firms Using a Slacks-Based Measure. *Journal of Service Science and Management*, *7*(04), 277–290. doi:10.4236/jssm.2014.74025

Paralikas, N., & Lygeros, A. I. (2005). A multi-criteria and fuzzy logic based methodology for the lerative ranking of the fire hazard of chemical substances and installations. *Process Safety and Environmental Protection*, *83*(2B2), 122–134. doi:10.1205/psep.04236

Pastor, J. T., & Lovell, C. A. K. (2005). A global Malmquist productivity index. *Economics Letters*, *88*(2), 266–271. doi:10.1016/j.econlet.2005.02.013

Pastor, J. T., Ruiz, J. L., & Sirvent, I. (1999). An enhanced DEA Russell graph efficiency measure. *The Journal of the Operational Research Society*, *115*(3), 596–607. doi:10.1016/S0377-2217(98)00098-8

Pilyavsky, A., & Staat, M. (2008). The Analysis of Technical Efficiency for Small Dairy Farms in Southern Chile: A Stochastic Frontier. *Journal of Productivity Analysis*, *29*(2), 143–154. doi:10.1007/s11123-007-0070-6

Pires, H. M., & Fernandes, E. (2012). Malmquist financial efficiency analysis for airlines. *Transportation Research Part E, Logistics and Transportation Review*, *48*(5), 1049–1055. doi:10.1016/j.tre.2012.03.007

Portela, M. C. A. S., & Thanassoulis, E. (2010). Malmquist-type indices in the presence of negative data:an application to bank branches. *Journal of Banking & Finance*, *34*(7), 1472–1483. doi:10.1016/j.jbankfin.2010.01.004

Protela, A.S., Thanassoulis, E. (2001). Decomposing school and school-type efficiency. *European of Operational Research, 132*.

Qazi, A. Q., & Yulin, Z. (2012). Productivity Measurement of Hi-tech Industry of China Malmquist Productivity Index DEA Approach. *Procedia Economics and Finance*, *1*, 330–336. doi:10.1016/S2212-5671(12)00038-X

Raab, R. L., & Feroz, E. H. (2007). A productivity growth accounting approach to the ranking of developing and developed nations. *The International Journal of Accounting*, *42*(4), 396–415. doi:10.1016/j.intacc.2007.09.004

Raa, T. T., & Mohnen, P. (2002). Neoclassical Growth Accounting and Frontier Analysis: A Synthesis. *Journal of Productivity Analysis*, *18*(2), 111–128. doi:10.1023/A:1016558816247

Ramanathan, R. (2006). Data Envelopment Analysis for Weight Derivation and Aggregation in the Analytic Hierarchy Process. *Journal of Computer and Operation Research*, *33*(5), 1289–1307. doi:10.1016/j.cor.2004.09.020

Ramazani-Tarkhorani, S., Khodabakhshi, M., Mehrabian, S., & Nuri-Bahmani, F. (2014). Ranking decision making units with Common Weights in DEA. *Applied Mathematical Modelling*, *38*(15-16), 3890–3896. doi:10.1016/j.apm.2013.08.029

Ramón, N., Ruiz, J. L., & Sirvent, I. (2011). Reducing differences between profiles of weights: A "peer-restricted" cross-efficiency evaluation. *Omega*, *39*(6), 634–6411. doi:10.1016/j.omega.2011.01.004

Ramón, N., Ruiz, J. L., & Sirvent, I. (2012). Common sets of weights as summaries of DEA profiles of weights: With an application to the ranking of professional tennis players. *Expert Systems with Applications*, *39*(5), 4882–4889. doi:10.1016/j.eswa.2011.10.004

Rebelo, J., Mendes, V. (2000). Malmquist Indices of Productivity Change in Portuguese Banking: The Deregulation Period. *IAER, 6*.

Retzlaff-Roberts, D. L. (1996). Relating discriminant analysis and data envelopment analysis to one another. *Computers & Operations Research*, *23*(4), 311–322. doi:10.1016/0305-0548(95)00041-0

Rezai Balf, F., Zhiani Rezai, H., Jahanshahloo, G. R., & Hosseinzadeh Lotfi, F. (2012). Ranking efficient DMUs using the Tchebycheff norm. *Applied Mathematical Modelling*, *1*(1), 46–56. doi:10.1016/j.apm.2010.11.077

Rödder, W., & Reucher, E. (2011). A consensual peer-based DEA-model with optimized cross-efficiencies – Input allocation instead of radial reduction. *European Journal of Operational Research*, *212*(1), 148–154. doi:10.1016/j.ejor.2011.01.035

Roll, Y., Cook, W. D., & Golany, Y. (1991). Controlling factor weights in data envelopment analysis. *IIE, 23*, 1–9.

Roll, Y., & Golany, B. (1993). Alternative methods of treating factor weights in DEA. *Omega*, *21*(1), 99–103. doi:10.1016/0305-0483(93)90042-J

Saati, S., Hatami-Marbini, A., Agrell, P. J., & Tavana, M. (2012). A common set of weight approach using an ideal decision making unit in data envelopment analysis. *Journal of Industrial and Management Optimization*, *8*(3), 623–637. doi:10.3934/jimo.2012.8.623

Saaty, T. L. (1996). *The analytic network process-decision making with dependence and feedback.* Pittsburgh, PA: RWS.

Sadjadi, S.J., Mrani, H. O, Abdollahzadeh, S., Alinaghian, M., & Mohammadi, H. (2011). A robust super-efficiency data envelopment analysis model for ranking of provincial gas companies in Iran. *Expert Systems with Applications, 38*.

Saen, R. F., Memariani, A., & Lot, F. H. (2005). Determining Relative Efficiency of Slightly Non-Homogeneous Decision-Making Units by Data Envelopment Analysis: A Case Study in IROST. Journal of Applied Mathematics and. *Computation*, *165*(2), 313–328.

Seiford, L. M. (1996). Data envelopment analysis: The evolution of the state of the art (1978–1995). *Journal of Productivity Analysis*, *7*(2–3), 99–137. doi:10.1007/BF00157037

Compilation of References

Seiford, L. M., & Thrall, R. M. (1990). Recent developments in data envelopment analysis: The mathematical programming approach to frontier analysis. *Journal of Econometrics*, *46*, 7–38. doi:10.1016/0304-4076(90)90045-U

Seiford, L. M., & Zhu, J. (1999). Infeasibility of super-efficiency data envelopment analysis models. *INFOR*, *37*(2), 174–187.

Seiford, L. M., & Zhu, J. (2003). Context-dependent data envelopment analysis Measuring attractiveness and progress. *Omega*, *31*(5), 397–408. doi:10.1016/S0305-0483(03)00080-X

Sexton, T. R., Silkman, R. H., & Hogan, A. J. (1986). Data Envelopment Analysis: Critique and Extensions. In Measuring Efficiency: An Assessment of Data Envelopment Analysis. Jossey-Bass.

Sexton, T. R., Silkman, R. H., & Hogan, A. J. Data envelopment Analysis: Critique and extensions, In: Silkman R H (1986) (Ed.), Measuring Efficiency: An Assessment of Data Envelopment Analysis, Jossey-bass, San Francisco, pp 73-105, 1986.

Sexton, T. R., Silkman, R. H., & Hogan, A. J. (1986). Data envelopment analysis: Critique and extensions. In R. H. Silkman (Ed.), *Measuring Efficiency: An Assessment of Data Envelopment Analysis* (pp. 73–105). San Francisco, CA: Jossey-Bass.

Sexton, T. R., Silkman, R. H., & Hogan, R. (1986). Data envelopment analysis: critique and extension. In R. H. Silkman (Ed.), *Measuring Efficiency: An Assessment of Data Envelopment Analysis Jossey-Bass* (pp. 73–105).

Seydel, J. (2006). Data envelopment analysis for decision support. *Industrial Management & Data Systems*, *106*(1), 81–95. doi:10.1108/02635570610641004

Shang, J., & Sueyoshi, T. (1995). A United Framework for the Selection of a Flexible Manufacturing System. *European Journal of Operational Research*, *85*(2), 297–31. doi:10.1016/0377-2217(94)00041-A

Shepard, R. W. (1970). *Theory of Cost and Production Functions*. Princeton, NJ: Princeton University Press.

Shimchi-Levi, D., Kaminsky, P., & Shimchi-Levi, E. (2000). *Designing and Managing the Supply chain: Concepts, Strategies and Case studies* (International Edition). Singapore: McGraw Hill.

Shirouyehzad, H., Hosseinzadeh, L. F., Mir, B. A., & Dabestani, R. (2011). Efficiency and Ranking Measurement of Vendors by Data Envelopment Analysis. *International Business Research*, *4*(2), 137–146.

Shokouhi, A. H., Hatami-Marbini, A., Tavana, M., & Saati, S. (2010). A robust optimization approach for imprecise data envelopment analysis. *Computers & Industrial Engineering*, *59*(3), 387–397. doi:10.1016/j.cie.2010.05.011

Siegel, S., & Castellan, N. J. (1998). *Nonparametric statistics for the behavioral sciences*. New York: McGraw-Hill BOOK CO.

Silva Portela, M. C. A. (2006). Emmanuel Thanassoulis, Malmquist indexes using a geometric distance function (GDF): Application to a sample of Portuguese bank branches. *Journal of Productivity Analysis*, 25(1-2), 25–41. doi:10.1007/s11123-006-7124-z

Sinuany-Stern, Z., & Friedman, L. (1998). Data envelopment analysis and the discriminant analysis of ratios for ranking units. *European Journal of Operational Research*, 111, 470–478. doi:10.1016/S0377-2217(97)00313-5

Sinuany-Stern, Z., Mehrez, A., & Barboy, A. (1994). Academic Departments Efficiency Via DEA. *Computers & Operations Research*, 21(5), 543–556. doi:10.1016/0305-0548(94)90103-1

Sinuany-Stern, Z., Mehrez, A., & Hadad, Y. (2000). An AHP/DEA methodology for ranking decision making units. *International Transactions in Operational Research*, 7(2), 109–124. doi:10.1111/j.1475-3995.2000.tb00189.x

Sitarz, S. (2013). The medal points' incenter for rankings in sport. *Applied Mathematics Letters*, 26(4), 408–412. doi:10.1016/j.aml.2012.10.014

Soltanifar, M., Ebrahimnejad, A., & Farrokhi, M. M. (2010). Ranking of different ranking models using a voting model and its application in determining efficient candidates. *International Journal of Society Systems Science.*, 2(4), 375–389. doi:10.1504/IJSSS.2010.035570

Soltanifar, M., & Hosseinzadeh Lotfi, F. (2011). The voting analytic hierarchy process method for discriminating among efficient decision making units in data envelopment analysis. *Computers & Industrial Engineering*, 60(4), 585–592. doi:10.1016/j.cie.2010.12.016

Sözen, A., Alp, I., & Özdemir, A. (2010). Assessment of operational and environmental performance of the thermal power plants in Turkey by using data envelopment analysis. *Energy Policy*, 38(10), 6194–6203. doi:10.1016/j.enpol.2010.06.005

Srinivas, T., & Narasimhan, R. (2004). A methodology for strategic sourcing. *European Journal of Operational Research*, 154(1), 236–250. doi:10.1016/S0377-2217(02)00649-5

Stein, W. E., Mizzi, P. J., & Pfaffenberger, R. C. (1994). A stochastic dominance analysis of ranked voting systems with scoring. *European Journal of Operational Research*, 74(1), 78–85. doi:10.1016/0377-2217(94)90205-4

Steuer, R.E. (1977). An interactive multiple objective linear programming procedure. *TIMS Studies in Management Science, 6*.

Steuer, R. E., & Choo, E. U. (1983). An interactive weighted Tchebycheff procedure for multiple objective programming. *Mathematical Programming*, 26(3), 326–344. doi:10.1007/BF02591870

Stewart, T. J. (1996). Relationships between Data Envelopment Analysis and Multi Criteria Decision Analysis. *The Journal of the Operational Research Society*, 47(5), 654–665. doi:10.1057/jors.1996.77

Compilation of References

Strassert, G., & Prato, T. (2002). Selecting Farming Systems Using a New Multiple Criteria Decision Model: The Balancing and Ranking Method. *Ecological Economics, 40*(2), 269–277. doi:10.1016/S0921-8009(02)00002-2

Stuere, R. E. (1986). *Multiple criteria optimization: theory, computation, and application*. New York: Wiley.

Sueyoshi, T. (1999). Data envelopment analysis non-parametric ranking test and index measurement: Slack-adjusted DEA and an application to Japanese agriculture cooperatives. *Omega International Journal of Management Science, 27*, 315–326. doi:10.1016/S0305-0483(98)00057-7

Sueyoshi, T. (1999). DEA-discriminant analysis in the view of goal programming. *European Journal of Operational Research, 115*(3), 564–582. doi:10.1016/S0377-2217(98)00014-9

Sueyoshi, T., & Goto, M. (2013). DEA environmental assessment in a time horizon: Malmquist index on fuel mix, electricity and CO_2 of industrial nations. *Energy Economics, 40*, 370–382. doi:10.1016/j.eneco.2013.07.013

Sueyoshi, T., & Kirihara, Y. (1998). Efficiency measurement and strategic classification of Japanese banking institutions. *International Journal of Systems Science, 29*(11), 1249–1263. doi:10.1080/00207729808929613

Sun, J., Wu, J., & Guo, D. (2013). Performance ranking of units considering ideal and anti-ideal DMU with common weights. *Applied Mathematical Modelling, 37*(9), 6301–6310. doi:10.1016/j.apm.2013.01.010

Talluri, S., & Baker, R. C. (2002). A multi-phase mathematical programming approach for effective supply chain design. *European Journal of Operational Research, 141*(3), 544–558. doi:10.1016/S0377-2217(01)00277-6

Talluri, S., & Sarkis, J. (2002). A model for performance monitoring of suppliers. *International Journal of Production Research, 40*(16), 4257–4269. doi:10.1080/00207540210152894

Tanase, L., & Tidor, A. (2012). Efficiency Progress and Productivity Change in Romania Machinery Industry 2001–2010. *Procedia Economics and Finance, 3*, 1055–1062. doi:10.1016/S2212-5671(12)00273-0

Tan, K. C. (2001). A framework of supply chain management literature. *European Journal of Purchasing & Supply Management, 7*(2), 39–48. doi:10.1016/S0969-7012(00)00020-4

Tatsuoka, M. M., & Lohnes, P. R. (1988). *Multivariant analysis: Techniques for educational and psycologial research* (2nd ed.). New York: Macmillan Publishing Company.

Tavana, M., & Hatami-Marbini, A. (2011). A group AHP-TOPSIS framework for human space flight mission planning at NASA. *Expert Systems with Applications, 38*, 13588–13603.

Tavana, M., Khalili-Damaghani, K., & Sadi-Nezhad, S. (2013). A fuzzy group data envelopment analysis model for high-technology project selection: A case study at NASA. *Computers & Industrial Engineering, 66*(1), 10–23. doi:10.1016/j.cie.2013.06.002

Tavana, M., Mirzagholtabar, H., Mirhedayatian, S. M., Farzipoor Saen, R., & Azadi, M. (2013). A new network epsilon-based DEA model for supply chain performance evaluation. *Computers & Industrial Engineering*, *66*(2), 501–513. doi:10.1016/j.cie.2013.07.016

Telle, K., Larssonv, J. (2007). Do environmental regulations hamper productivity growth? How accounting for improvements of plants' environmental performance can change the conclusion. *Ecological Economics, 61*, 438–445.

Thanassoulis, E., & Dyson, R. G. (1992). Estimating preferred target input-output levels using data envelopment analysis. *European Journal of Operational Research*, *56*(1), 80–97. doi:10.1016/0377-2217(92)90294-J

Thompson, R. G., Langemeier, L. N., Lee, C. T., & Thrall, R. M. (1990). The role of multiplier bounds in efficiency analysis with application to Kansas farming. *Journal of Econometrics*, *46*(1-2), 93–108. doi:10.1016/0304-4076(90)90049-Y

Thompson, R. G., Lee, E., & Thrall, R. M. (1992). DEA/AR efficiency of U.S. independent oil/gas producers over time. *Computers & Operations Research*, *19*(5), 377–391. doi:10.1016/0305-0548(92)90068-G

Thompson, R. G., Singleton, F. D. Jr, Thrall, R. M., & Smith, B. A. (1986). Comparative site evaluations for locating a highenergy physics lab in Texas. *Interfaces*, *16*(6), 35–49. doi:10.1287/inte.16.6.35

Thrall, R. (1996). Duality, classification and slacks in data envelopment analysis. *Annals of Operations Research*, *66*, 109–138. doi:10.1007/BF02187297

Thursby, G., & Kemp, S. (2002). Growth and productive efficiency of university intellectual property licensing. *Research Policy*, *31*.

Timmerman, E. (1986). An approach to vendor performance evaluation. *International Journal of Purchasing and Materials Management*, *22*(4), 2–8.

Toloo, M., & Ertay, T. (2014). The most cost efficient automotive vendor with price uncertainty: A new DEA approach. *Measurement.*, *52*, 135–144. doi:10.1016/j.measurement.2014.03.002

Tone, K. (2002). A slack-based measure of super-efficiency in data envelopment analysis. *European Journal of Operational Research*, *143*(1), 32–41. doi:10.1016/S0377-2217(01)00324-1

Torgersen, A. M., Forsund, F. R., & Kittelsen, S. A. C. (1996). Slack-adjusted efficiency measures and ranking of efficient units. *Journal of Productivity Analysis*, *7*, 379–398. doi:10.1007/BF00162048

Tortosa-Ausina, E., Grifell-Tatje, E., Armero, C., & Conesa, D. (2008). Sensitivity analysis of efficiency and Malmquist productivity indices: An application to Spanish savings banks. *European Journal of Operational Research*, *184*(3), 1062–1084. doi:10.1016/j.ejor.2006.11.035

Tracey, M., & Vonderembse, M. A. (2000). Building Supply Chains: A Key to Enhancing Manufacturing Performance. *American Journal of Business*, *15*(2), 11–20. doi:10.1108/19355181200000007

Compilation of References

Troutt, M. D. (1995). A maximum decisional efficiency estimation principle. *Management Science, 41*(1), 76–82. doi:10.1287/mnsc.41.1.76

Tsekouras, K. D., Pantzios, C. J., & Karagiannis, G. (2004). Malmquist productivity index estimation with zero-value variables: The case of Greek prefectural training councils. *International Journal of Production Economics, 89*(1), 95–106. doi:10.1016/S0925-5273(03)00211-1

Uri, N. D. (2000). Measuring productivity change in telecommunications. *Telecommunications Policy, 24*(5), 439–452. doi:10.1016/S0308-5961(00)00030-6

Vargass. (2000). Combining DEA and factor analysis to improve evaluation of academic departments given uncertaing about the output constructs. Departments of industrial Eng. University of Iowa.

Wang, Y.M., Liu, J., & Elhag, T.M.S. (2007). An integrated AHP-DEA methodology for bridge risk assessment. *Journal of Computer and Industrial Engineering*, 1-13.

Wang, C. (2007). Decomposing energy productivity change: A distance function approach. *Energy, 32*(8), 1326–1333. doi:10.1016/j.energy.2006.10.001

Wang, N., Yi, R., & Liu, D. (2008). A solution method to the problem proposed by Wang in voting systems. *Journal of Computational and Applied Mathematics, 221*(1), 106–113. doi:10.1016/j.cam.2007.10.006

Wang, W. K., Lu, W. M., & Liu, P. Y. (2014). A fuzzy multi-objective two-stage DEA model for evaluating the performance of US bank holding companies. *Expert Systems with Applications, 41*(9), 4290–4297. doi:10.1016/j.eswa.2014.01.004

Wang, W., Lu, W., & Wang, S. (2014). The impact of environmental expenditures on performance in the U.S. chemical industry. *Journal of Cleaner Production, 64*, 447–456. doi:10.1016/j.jclepro.2013.10.022

Wang, Y. M., & Chin, K. S. (2007). Discriminating DEA efficient candidates by considering their least relative total scores. *Journal of Computational and Applied Mathematics, 206*(1), 209–215. doi:10.1016/j.cam.2006.06.012

Wang, Y. M., & Chin, K. S. (2010). A neutral DEA model for cross-efficiency evaluation and its extension. *Expert Systems with Applications, 37*(5), 3666–3675. doi:10.1016/j.eswa.2009.10.024

Wang, Y. M., Chin, K. S., & Yang, J. B. (2007). Three new models for preference voting and aggregation. *The Journal of the Operational Research Society, 58*(10), 1389–1393. doi:10.1057/palgrave.jors.2602295

Wang, Y. M., Chin, K. S., & Yang, J. B. (2009). Improved linear programming models for preference voting and aggregation: Reply to Hadi-Vencheh and Mokhtarian. *The Journal of the Operational Research Society, 58*(7), 1037–1038. doi:10.1057/jors.2008.156

Wang, Y. M., & Luo, Y. (2006). DEA efficiency assessment using ideal and anti-ideal decision making units. *Applied Mathematics and Computation, 173*(2), 902–915. doi:10.1016/j.amc.2005.04.023

Wang, Y., & Lan, Y. (2011). Measuring Malmquist productivity index: A new approach based on double frontiers data envelopment analysis. *Mathematical and Computer Modelling, 54*(11-12), 2760–2771. doi:10.1016/j.mcm.2011.06.064

Wang, Y.-M., Chin, K.-S., & Luo, Y. (2011). Cross-efficiency evaluation based on ideal and anti-ideal decision making units. *Expert Systems with Applications, 38*(8), 10312–10319. doi:10.1016/j.eswa.2011.02.116

Wang, Y.-M., & Jiang, P. (2012). Alternative mixed integer linear programming models for identifying the most efficient decision making unit in data envelopment analysis. *Computers & Industrial Engineering, 62*(2), 546–553. doi:10.1016/j.cie.2011.11.003

Wang, Y.-M., Luo, Y., & Hua, Z. (2007). Aggregating preference rankings using OWA operator weights. *Information Sciences, 177*(16), 3356–3363. doi:10.1016/j.ins.2007.01.008

Wang, Y.-M., Luo, Y., & Lan, Y.-X. (2011). Common weights for fully ranking decision making units by regression analysis. *Expert Systems with Applications, 38*(8), 9122–9128. doi:10.1016/j.eswa.2011.01.004

Wang, Y.-M., Luo, Y., & Liang, L. (2009). Ranking decision making units by imposing a minimum weight restriction in the data envelopment analysis. *Original Research Article Journal of Computational and Applied Mathematics, 223*(1), 469–484. doi:10.1016/j.cam.2008.01.022

Washio, S., & Yamada, S. (2013). Evaluation method based on ranking in data envelopment analysis. *Expert Systems with Applications, 40*(1), 257–262. doi:10.1016/j.eswa.2012.07.015

Weber, C. A., & Desai, A. (1996). Determination of paths to vendor market Efficiency using parallel co-ordinates representation: A negotiation tool for buyers. *European Journal of Operational Research, 90*(1), 142–155. doi:10.1016/0377-2217(94)00336-X

Wei, Q. L., & Yu, G. (1993). *Analyzing the properties of K-cone in a generalized Data Envelopment Analysis model. CCS Research Report 700.* The University of Texas at Austin.

Wei, Q. L., Yu, G., & Lu, J. S. (1993). *Necessary and sufficient conditions for return-to-scale properties in generalized Data Envelopment Analysis models. CCS Research Report 708.* The University of Texas at Austin.

Wei, Q. L., Zhang, J., & Zhang, X. (2000). An inverse DEA model for inputs/outputs estimate. *European Journal of Operational Research, 121*(1), 151–163. doi:10.1016/S0377-2217(99)00007-7

Wierzbicki, A. (1980). The use of reference objectives in multiobjective optimization. In G. Fandel & T. Gal (Eds.), *Multiple Objective Decision Making. Theory and Application.* New York: Springer-Verlag. doi:10.1007/978-3-642-48782-8_32

Williams, R., & Van Dyke, N. (2007). Measuring the international standing of universities with an application to Australian universities. *Higher Education, 53*(6), 819–841. doi:10.1007/s10734-005-7516-4

Compilation of References

Wong, B. Y. H., Luquec, M., & Yang, J. B. (2009). Using interactive multiobjective methods to solve DEA problems with value judgements. *Computers & Operations Research*, *36*(2), 623–636. doi:10.1016/j.cor.2007.10.020

Wong, Y.-H. B., & Beasley, J. E. (1990). Restricting weight flexibility in data envelopment analysis. *The Journal of the Operational Research Society*, *41*(9), 829–835. doi:10.1057/jors.1990.120

Worthington, A. (1999). Malmquist Indices of Productivity Change in Australian Financial Services. *Journal of International Financial Markets, Institutions and Money*, *9*(3), 303–320. doi:10.1016/S1042-4431(99)00013-X

Wu, D. (2006). A note on DEA efficiency assessment using ideal point: An improvement of Wang and Luo's model. *Applied Mathematics and Computation*, *183*(2), 819–830. doi:10.1016/j.amc.2006.06.030

Wu, J., Liang, L., & Zha, Y. (2009). Preference voting and ranking using DEA game cross efficiency model. *Journal of the Operations Research Society of Japan*, *52*, 105–111.

Wu, J., Liang, L., Zha, Y., & Yang, F. (2009). Determination of cross-efficiency under the principle of rank priority in cross evaluation. *Expert Systems with Applications*, *36*(3), 4826–4829. doi:10.1016/j.eswa.2008.05.042

Wu, J., Sun, J., & Liang, L. (2012). Cross efficiency evaluation method based on weight-balanced data envelopment analysis model. *Computers & Industrial Engineering*, *63*(2), 513–519. doi:10.1016/j.cie.2012.04.017

Wu, J., Sun, J., Liang, L., & Zha, Y. (2011). Determination of weights for ultimate cross efficiency using Shannon entropy. *Expert Systems with Applications*, *38*(5), 5162–5165. doi:10.1016/j.eswa.2010.10.046

Yang, J. B. (1999). Gradient projection and local region search for multi-objective optimisation. *European Journal of Operational Research*, *112*(2), 432–459. doi:10.1016/S0377-2217(97)00451-7

Yang, J. B., & Li, D. (2002). Normal vector identification and interactive tradeoff analysis using minimax formulation in multi-objective optimization. *IEEE Transactions on Systems, Man, and Cybernetics. Part A, Systems and Humans*, *32*(3), 305–319. doi:10.1109/TSMCA.2002.802806

Yang, J. B., & Sen, P. (1996). Preference modelling by estimating local utility functions for multi-objective optimization. *European Journal of Operational Research*, *95*(1), 115–138. doi:10.1016/0377-2217(96)00300-1

Yang, J. B., Wong, B. Y. H., Xu, D. L., & Stewart, T. J. (2009). Integrating DEA-oriented performance assessment and target setting using interactive MOLP methods. *European Journal of Operational Research*, *195*(1), 205–222. doi:10.1016/j.ejor.2008.01.013

Yang, J., & Zeng, W. (2014). The trade-offs between efficiency and quality in the hospital production: Some evidence from Shenzhen, China. *China Economic Review*, *31*(C), 166–184. doi:10.1016/j.chieco.2014.09.005

Yang, T., & Kuo, C. (2003). A Hierarchical AHP/DEA Methodology for the Facilities Layout Design Problem. *European Journal of Operational Research*, *147*(1), 128–136. doi:10.1016/S0377-2217(02)00251-5

Young, F. W., & Hamer, R. M. (1987). *Multidimensional Scaling, History, Theory and Applications*. London: Lawrence Erlbaum.

Yu, G., Wei, Q. L., & Brockett, P. (1996). A Generalized Data Envelopment Analysis model: A unification and extension of existing methods for efficiency analysis of decision making units. *Annals of Operations Research*, 66.

Zaim, O. (2004). Measuring environmental performance of state manufacturing through changes in pollution intensities: A DEA framework. *Ecological Economics*, *48*(1), 37–47. doi:10.1016/j.ecolecon.2003.08.003

Zamani, P., & Hosseinzadeh Lotfi, F. (2013). Using MOLP based procedures to solve DEA problems.International Journal of Data Envelopment Analysis, 1.

Zelenyuk, V. (2006). Aggregation of Malmquist productivity indexes. *European Journal of Operational Research*, *174*(2), 1076–1086. doi:10.1016/j.ejor.2005.02.061

Zerafat Angiz, M., Mustafa, A., & Kamali, M. J. (2013). Cross-ranking of Decision Making Units in Data Envelopment Analysis. *Applied Mathematical Modelling*, *37*(1-2), 398–405. doi:10.1016/j.apm.2012.02.038

Zerafat Angiz, M., Tajaddini, A., Mustafa, A., & Jalal Kamali, M. (2012). Ranking alternatives in a preferential voting system using fuzzy concepts and data envelopment analysis. *Computers & Industrial Engineering*, *63*(4), 784–790. doi:10.1016/j.cie.2012.04.019

Zhang, X., & Cui, J. (1996). A project evaluation system in the state economic information system of China. Presented at IFORS'96 Conference, Vancouver, Canada.

Zhang, C., Liu, H., Bressers, H. T. A., & Buchanan, K. S. (2011). Productivity growth and environmental regulations - accounting for undesirable outputs: Analysis of China's thirty provincial regions using the Malmquist–Luenberger index. *Ecological Economics*, *70*(12), 2369–2379. doi:10.1016/j.ecolecon.2011.07.019

Zhang, N., & Choi, Y. (2013). Total-factor carbon emission performance of fossil fuel power plants in China: A metafrontier non-radial Malmquist index analysis. *Energy Economics*, *40*, 549–559. doi:10.1016/j.eneco.2013.08.012

Zhang, X. S., & Cui, J. C. (1999). A Project Evaluation System in the State Economic Information System of China: An Operations Research Practice in Public Sectors. *International Transactions in Operational Research*, *6*(5), 441–452. doi:10.1111/j.1475-3995.1999.tb00166.x

Zhou, P., Ang, B. W., & Han, J. Y. (2010). Total factor carbon emission performance: A Malmquist index analysis. *Energy Economics*, *32*(1), 194–201. doi:10.1016/j.eneco.2009.10.003

Compilation of References

Zhu, J. (1996). Data envelopment analysis with preference structure. *The Journal of the Operational Research Society*, *47*(1), 136–150. doi:10.1057/jors.1996.12

Zhu, J. (1996a). Robustness of the efficient decision-making units in data envelopment analysis. *European Journal of Operational Research*, *90*(3), 451–460. doi:10.1016/0377-2217(95)00054-2

Zimmerman, H. J. (1991). *Fuzzy set theory and its applications* (2nd ed.). Boston: Kluwer Academic Publishers. doi:10.1007/978-94-015-7949-0

Zimmermann, H. (1978). Fuzzy programming and linear programming with several objective function. *Fuzzy Sets and Systems*, *1*(1), 45–55. doi:10.1016/0165-0114(78)90031-3

Zionts, S., & Wallenius, J. (1976). An interactive programming method for solving the multiple criteria problem. *Management Science*, *22*(6), 625–663. doi:10.1287/mnsc.22.6.652

Zohrebandian, M. (2011). Using Ziants-Wallenius method to improve estimate of value efficiency in DEA. *Applied Mathematical Modelling*, *35*(8), 3769–3776. doi:10.1016/j.apm.2011.02.027

About the Contributors

Farhad Hosseinzadeh Lotfi is currently a full professor in Mathematics at the Science and Research Branch, Islamic Azad University (IAU), Tehran, Iran. In 1991, he received his undergraduate degree in Mathematics at Yazd University, Yazd, Iran. He received his MSc in Operations Research at IAU, Lahijan, Iran in 1995 and PhD in Applied Mathematics (O.R.) at IAU, Science and Research Branch, Tehran, Iran in 1999. His major research interests are operations research and data envelopment analysis. He has been Advisor and Co-advisor of 46 and 31 Ph.D. dissertations, respectively. He has published more than 300 scientific and technical papers in leading scientific journals, including European Journal of Operational Research, Computers and Industrial Engineering, Journal of the Operational Research Society, Applied Mathematics and Computation, Applied Mathematical Modelling, Mathematical and Computer Modelling, and Journal of the Operational Research Society of Japan, among others. He is Editor-in-Chief and member of editorial board of Journal of Data Envelopment Analysis and Decision Science. He is also manager and member of editorial board of International Journal of Industrial mathematics.

Esmail Najafi is an Assistant Professor of Industrial Engineering Department at the Islamic Azad University, Science and Research Branch in Tehran, Iran. He received his B.A. in Power and Water University of Technology (PWUT), his M.S. in Islamic Azad University. and his Ph.D. in Industrial Engineering from Science and Research Branch in Tehran, Iran. His research interests decision making, Data Envelopment Analysis, Engineering management and strategic maagment . His published research articles appear in journal or intelligent and fuzzy system, Mathematical Problems in Engineering, international journal of data envelopment analysis.

Hamed Nozari was born in Iran, in 1984. He received the BS. Degree in Mechanical engineering (fluid mechanic) in 2009, and continued his educations in Industrial Engineering (production planning and Socioeconomics engineering) in MSc and PhD levels. He has taught various courses in the field of Industrial Engineering and has published many books and papers as well. Now he is a researcher in the field of operations research and metaheuristic algorithms.

* * *

Amineh Ghazi is a PhD student in Islamic Azad University, Tehran Central Branch. Her interests are Operations Research (OR), Data Envelopment Analysis (DEA) and Multiple Criteria Decision Making (MCDM). Her current research focuses on relationships between DEA and MCDM methodologies.

Meisam Jafari-Eskandari is an assistant professor in Industrial Engineering, Payamnoor University.

Z. Moghaddas is an assistant professor at the Department of Mathematics, Qazvin Branch, Islamic Azad University. Her research interests include operation research and data envelopment analysis.

Chandra Sekhar Patro is currently pursuing his Ph.D in Commerce and Management Studies from Andhra University. He has post-graduate degree in Master of Commerce (M.Com.) from Andhra University, Master in Financial Management (MFM) from Pondicherry University, and also MBA (HR & Finance) from JNT University. Mr. Patro has over 8 years of teaching experience in higher education. Mr. Patro has gained very good knowledge in Human Resource Management and Accountancy/Finance subjects. He has published number of research papers in reputed National and International Journals and also presented papers in National and International Conferences.

Elahe Shariatmadari Serkani is a PhD student at Islamic Azad University, Sciences & Research Branch.

M. Vaez-Ghasemi is an assistant professor at the Department of Mathematics, Rasht branch, Islamic Azad University. He is also a Master of Industrial Engineering and his research interests include operation research, data envelopment analysis, and meta-heuristic Methods.

Index

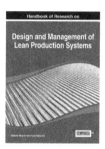
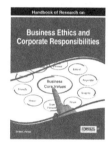

Printed in the United States
By Bookmasters